Democracy and Schooling in California

HISTORICAL STUDIES IN EDUCATION

Edited by William J. Reese and John L. Rury

William J. Reese, Carl F. Kaestle WARF Professor of Educational Policy Studies and History, the University of Wisconsin-Madison

John L. Rury, Professor of Education and (by courtesy) History, the University of Kansas.

This series features new scholarship on the historical development of education, defined broadly, in the United States and elsewhere. Interdisciplinary in orientation and comprehensive in scope, it spans methodological boundaries and interpretive traditions. Imaginative and thoughtful history can contribute to the global conversation about educational change. Inspired history lends itself to continued hope for reform, and to realizing the potential for progress in all educational experiences.

Published by Palgrave Macmillan:

Democracy and Schooling in California: The Legacy of Helen Heffernan and Corinne Seeds
By Kathleen Weiler

DEMOCRACY AND SCHOOLING IN CALIFORNIA

The Legacy of Helen Heffernan and Corinne Seeds

Kathleen Weiler

DEMOCRACY AND SCHOOLING IN CALIFORNIA
Copyright © Kathleen Weiler, 2011.
Softcover reprint of the hardcover 1st edition 2011 978-0-230-33824-1
All rights reserved.

First published in 2011 by
PALGRAVE MACMILLAN®
in the United States—a division of St. Martin's Press LLC,
175 Fifth Avenue, New York, NY 10010.

Where this book is distributed in the UK, Europe and the rest of the world, this is by Palgrave Macmillan, a division of Macmillan Publishers Limited, registered in England, company number 785998, of Houndmills, Basingstoke, Hampshire RG21 6XS.

Palgrave Macmillan is the global academic imprint of the above companies and has companies and representatives throughout the world.

Palgrave® and Macmillan® are registered trademarks in the United States, the United Kingdom, Europe and other countries.

ISBN 978-1-349-34126-9   ISBN 978-1-137-01591-4 (eBook)
DOI 10.1057/9781137015914

Library of Congress Cataloging-in-Publication Data
Weiler, Kathleen.
　Democracy and schooling in California : the legacy of Helen Heffernan and Corinne Seeds / Kathleen Weiler.
　　p. cm.—(Historical studies in education)
　　1. Education—California—History. 2. Progressive education—California—History. 3. Democracy and education—California. 4. Heffernan, Helen, 1896– 5. Seeds, Corinne A. (Corinne Aldine), 1889–1969. I. Title.
LA243.W45 2012
370.11'5—dc23   2011024116

A catalogue record of the book is available from the British Library.

Design by Newgen Imaging Systems (P) Ltd., Chennai, India.

First edition: December 2011

Contents

Foreword — vii
Acknowledgments — ix
Introduction — xi

1. Working Girls of the Golden West — 1
2. The Child and the Curriculum — 19
3. Dare the School Build a New Social Order? — 37
4. Was Progressive Education Progressive? — 59
5. Love and War — 79
6. Prejudice — 99
7. The Battle of Westwood Hills — 119
8. Exporting Democracy/Defending Democracy — 137
9. "Progressive" Education Is Subverting America — 157
10. How to Teach the California Child — 179

Epilogue: The Long Retreat from Democratic Education — 201

List of Abbreviations — 205
Notes — 207
Bibliography — 249
Index — 273

Foreword

Over the last century, American historians embraced a variety of intellectual, political, and ideological frameworks as they reconstructed the past. Over a century ago, several prominent "progressive historians" argued that history was a story of progress, as citizens challenged corporate power and advanced age-old demands for democracy and representative government. After World War II, several "consensus historians" rejected this view and claimed that Americans, even those who fought each other in the Civil War, shared basic assumptions about the nature of American society yet disagreed about the best way to realize their most cherished ideals. By the 1960s, a younger generation of scholars, shaped by the civil rights and antiwar movements, revived the idea that conflict was the engine of history but rejected most of the other assumptions of the progressive school. Since then, various approaches to historical writing—social history, psychohistory, the new "cultural" history, gay and lesbian studies, postmodernism in many expressions—have further broadened our perspectives on the past. Most importantly, feminist scholarship helped transform the liberal arts and humanistic disciplines.

Biography is one of the oldest genres of historical writing. It retains its resilience and appeal because it has a unique capacity to make the past palpable. It moves us past abstractions and generalizations; it allows us to live vicariously through the flesh-and-blood struggles of women and men who, like all of us, find themselves in historical situations not of their making. Biographies show that despite all the forces that shaped the past and present and place limits on freedom, individuals make choices, large and small, that frame their lives and those of their contemporaries.

Kathleen Weiler's *Democracy and Schooling in California* demonstrates the enduring value of biography in her remarkable, critical study of two fascinating women—Helen Heffernan and Corinne Seeds. She embeds their lives in the wider contexts of their times, deepening our appreciation of their world, their passions, and their professional and personal ties, which intertwined and were often inseparable. Advancing the cause of child-centered education, Heffernan and Seeds helped make California an incubator of progressive ideals, ever evolving after the 1920s, as they confronted male privilege and reactionary enemies.

Weiler's history addresses some of the most vexing questions that have bedeviled scholars studying the history of progressive education. Exactly how did child-centered ideals shape state-level policy and teacher training?

How did child-centered ideals change over time? What obstacles stood in the way of their implementation in schools?

Theoretically sophisticated and based on impressive archival sources, Weiler's *Democracy and Schooling in California* demonstrates the great power of biography and case studies in reorienting our understanding of the past. It charts a new course in the historiography of progressivism.

WILLIAM J. REESE AND JOHN L. RURY

Acknowledgments

This book would never have been written without the support and encouragement of numerous colleagues, friends, and family. The research was supported by a grant from the Spencer Foundation and by the Tufts University Faculty Research Fund. Material from this study was presented at various conferences; I greatly benefited from respondents' and colleagues' comments and suggestions over the years. Michele Clark, Wendy Luttrell, and Peter Weiler offered perceptive critical readings of the manuscript. Historical research of this kind cannot be done without the help of librarians and archivists. I want to thank the very helpful librarians and archivists at the Nevada Historical Society in Reno; Cubberley Library and the Hoover Institution Archives at Stanford University, the Bancroft Library at the University of California at Berkeley, University Library at California State University at Sacramento, Special Collections and University Archives at the Charles Young Research Library at UCLA, and Special Collections and Archives at the Tomas Rivera Library at the University of California at Riverside.

A project such as this one could never have been completed without the love and support of family and friends. I especially want to thank Jane and Richard Such, M'K Veloz, and Dan and Louise Weiler for providing me friendship, not to mention lodging and good meals, on my frequent research trips to California. My family has been my greatest support and inspiration. This book is dedicated to them: Sarah Weiler, Emma Weiler, Corey Steinman, Anna Steinman, Justin Weiler, Abby Steinman, and Helen Steinman, and most of all to my husband and partner, Peter, who has stood by me, provided intellectual companionship, critical insight, and love throughout these years.

INTRODUCTION

California schools now rank toward the bottom of educational achievement as measured by standardized tests, graduation rates, and spending per pupil. But California schools were not always in crisis. In the 1930s and 1940s they were considered among the nation's best and provided a model for school systems across the nation. California education in those years was led by two exceptional women, Helen Heffernan, chief of Rural and Elementary Education for the state between 1926 and 1965, and Corinne Seeds, the director of the University Elementary School at UCLA between 1925 and 1957. Heffernan and Seeds were at the center of a wide network of women educators in California for almost forty years and were key figures in what was probably the most concerted attempt to put the ideals of Deweyan progressive education into practice in a state-wide system of public education in the United States.

Helen Heffernan and Corinne Seeds championed a child-centered pedagogy and were committed to a conception of education for democratic citizenship. They held summer institutes for teachers, spoke frequently at conferences and local meetings, and encouraged teachers to envision themselves and their work as both challenging and socially meaningful. Their careers in the 1930s, 1940s, and 1950s encompassed dramatic and key events in the history of U. S. education. Although their close friends were primarily women and they had been early supporters of women's right to suffrage, they did not publicly define themselves in terms of women's issues, but rather in terms of broader conceptions of citizenship and equal rights. They never deviated from their conviction that their vision of progressive education was essential to a strong democracy in the United States.

This book is organized around their intertwined lives. But my intent here is not to document every action or thought of these two individual women or to present them as isolated and autonomous agents shaping events. Rather, I have attempted to follow C. Wright Mill's call "to grasp history and biography and the relations between the two within society."[1] It has become commonplace to assert that histories are constructed, not uncovered, and that historians employ both analysis and narrative techniques in their labors. Analysis is based on the categories the historian (sometimes self-consciously, sometimes not) has chosen to employ to interpret the jumble of archival evidence. Historical biographies, like novels, are written as narratives with beginnings, causes, effects, and endings; thus, the "story" in history. There are always multiple story lines around which biographical narratives can be organized.

I have addressed several overlapping historical questions in my telling of the lives and times of Helen Heffernan and Corinne Seeds. Perhaps most prominent is the feminist perspective that takes gender as central. Framing the lives of two women progressive educators around the fact that they were women and highlighting male power in the world in which they moved challenge conventional histories of the progressive education movement in which gender has largely been ignored as a category of analysis. A second goal of this narrative is to tie the personal to the political by making the relationship between Seeds and Heffernan central to their politics. Heffernan and Seeds, like a number of other single women educators in the first half of the twentieth century, had an intense romantic relationship and moved within a network of other women educators in same-sex partnerships. This women's world before the years of gay liberation is only now being explored by historians. Jacqueline Hall has asked: "How does the need for love, relatedness, erotic pleasure—which often leaves so little trace in the historical record—color and reflect ideas and political commitments? How do romantic, spiritual, and political quests entwine? And what do the answers to these questions tell us about where our stories of identity should begin and end?"[2] In the lives of Heffernan and Seeds, the relational and the political were deeply intertwined.

Another concern here is around race, focusing on the shifts in Heffernan's and Seeds's understanding of racial issues, their blindness to the privileges they enjoyed because of their whiteness, the fatal weaknesses in their claims of building democracy when they failed to engage racism, and their gradual coming to consciousness of racial injustice. Like other white liberal educators of their generation, Heffernan and Seeds had ignored racism in their early careers. It was only with the rise of Nazism in the 1930s, the awareness of American racism in the politics of the Second World War, and the growth of the African American civil rights movement that they began to address race and racism in the schools.

Finally, this study contributes to the history of progressive education in the United States, both by detailing the development of education in California in these years and by looking at the underlying political struggles that shaped the rise and fall of progressive education nationally. The history of education in California before the 1960s is not well known, but it provides a window into broader political developments—the struggle between liberals and conservatives; the continuing power of race and racism; the role of women as school and community leaders; the impact of the demographic and economic changes of the Depression, Second World War, and Cold War; and the ways different groups mobilized around both calls for democracy and claims of patriotism to attempt to shape educational policy. The story of Heffernan and Seeds illuminates the rise of the Right and the contest over ideas of citizenship, knowledge, and control of the public schools. In California, progressive education came to be opposed by a shifting conservative coalition that included traditionalists seeking to transmit what they saw as the valuable heritage of the past, those who sought clearer lines of authority in schools, with a set curriculum and stricter classroom discipline, as well as anti-Communist groups who were suspicious of what they saw as socialistic or Communistic tendencies in public education. In a Gramscian sense, this history documents the struggles among different groups to construct and assert hegemony and to define whose interests education should serve.

Feminist History

Helen Heffernan and Corinne Seeds were part of that generation of women educators whose political ideas were shaped by the progressive movements of the years before 1920. Historians have analyzed the role of white, native-born women in a number of progressive reform arenas—in the settlement house movement, the women's club movement, government agencies such as the Children's Bureau, and, of course, the suffrage movement. Women reformers of this period tended to focus on the needs of women and children, thus in some sense remaining safely within the domestic sphere even when they were publicly working for social change. In her study of women and social reform, Robyn Muncy calls this a "female dominion" of child welfare policy and reform.[3] Until recently, however, women's leadership in education has been comparatively overlooked. But women were active in the development of the progressive education movement as leaders of private schools and held significant positions as principals and superintendents in public school systems in the first half of the twentieth century. In the West, in particular, education offered opportunities for women.

Corinne Seeds and Helen Heffernan made the journey from their working-class families to powerful positions in California education. Both class and gender are central to understanding their histories. Unlike the better-known women social reformers, Seeds and Heffernan did not come from privileged upper-class backgrounds, nor were they connected to Eastern elites. Heffernan and Seeds grew up in the West, in a relatively fluid social world for young women. Their own identities were shaped by the representations of strong women in their childhood and youth. As successful and influential educators, they are representative of the politically committed single professional woman in the period between the first and second waves of the women's movement, years in which the possibilities and representations of strong independent women were being eroded. Although they came of age during the most militant period of the women's suffrage movement and showed an acute sensitivity to male privilege in their private correspondence, like many other professional women of their generation, they presented their public selves and their educational ideas without using the language or critique of feminism, even though they lived primarily in a woman-defined world. There was a sharp division between their professional and personal lives, which were powerfully shaped by their gender, and the educational philosophy and methods they expounded, in which gender was largely absent.

Neither Corinne Seeds nor Helen Heffernan married, and their friendship became a romantic relationship in the years between 1939 and 1947. Although Heffernan subsequently took a new partner, Afton Nance, with whom she later shared a household, the friendship and professional partnership between Heffernan and Seeds lasted until Seeds's death in 1969. The significant number of women educators and social reformers from the late 19th century through the 1940s whose primary relationships were with other women has been documented in numerous histories.[4] Teaching in particular provided a protected space for the development of lesbian relationships and identities because of the legacy of the married women teachers' bar. Until the Second World War, women teachers were not only expected to be single, in many places they would lose their positions if they married. Moreover, even though teachers' salaries were low, teaching did provide an income that allowed single women to support themselves outside of heterosexual marriage.

The romantic relationship between Seeds and Heffernan created a strong political alliance that furthered their common educational goals. Individually and in their collaborative work Seeds and Heffernan tied classroom methods and the content of the curriculum to wider political issues. Following Dewey, they saw a challenging and critical education available to all children as central to democracy in an advanced industrial society. As their personal relationship deepened, Heffernan and Seeds supported each other in their continuing successes, but they also faced criticism and opposition, both individually and collectively. As powerful, older, unmarried women, they raised the suspicions of more conservative men, and, in a time of officially sanctioned homophobia, their personal relationship was hidden from the outside world.

The national leaders of the progressive education movement were all men who concerned themselves with broad questions of politics and the economy. Although the male leaders of the movement called for the transformation of teaching, they had few interactions with actual classroom teachers, the great majority of whom were women. Instead, they saw themselves as the intellectual vanguard of an educational revolution. Progressive women educators and school leaders, who tended to be identified with early childhood and elementary education, were excluded from leadership positions. This split along gender lines was not remarked upon at the time, and later historians have tended to accept this division, focusing on the male leaders and ignoring the work of women progressives or seeing their work as a continuation of the depoliticized child-centered educators of the 1920s. But Helen Heffernan and Corinne Seeds do not fit this pattern. While they each continued to work with elementary education, they were hardly uninterested in politics. Neither of them framed their work in the discourse of nurturance or maternalism, but consistently presented their educational goals in the language of Deweyan democracy. And they both were well aware of the political nature of education and the need to form alliances and mobilize support for their programs.

The Rise and Fall of Progressive Education

The careers of Helen Heffernan and Corinne Seeds offer a case study of progressive education at the local level. Heffernan and Seeds proclaimed themselves progressive educators seeking to put into practice the ideas of John Dewey and William Heard Kilpatrick—in Seeds's case in a single demonstration school, in Heffernan's, in the elementary schools of an entire state. It is generally agreed that the progressive education movement in the United States was at its height in the period between the two world wars. What exactly is meant by progressive education and how to evaluate it, however, has been a point of dispute from the founding of the Progressive Education Association in 1919. Dewey himself acknowledged that there was no single entity called "progressive education."[5]

The most influential study of progressive education is Lawrence Cremin's *The Transformation of the School*, still the standard history of the movement. Cremin proposed that although there was no single definition of progressive education, he saw three strands as encompassing the movement: the administrative progressives, influenced by the psychological behaviorism of Edward Thorndike, who argued for institutional and bureaucratic reform; the child-centered progressives, influenced by the work of G. Stanley Hall and the child study movement, who emphasized the importance of the development of the individual child but who, according to Cremin, lacked a clear social or political vision; and the democratic progressives associated with Dewey and in the 1930s the more politically radical social reconstructionists, who demanded that the schools build a new social order.[6] By the 1940s, "progressive education" had come to imply both a pedagogical approach centering on the interests of the child and a political stance associated with liberalism.

The collapse of the progressive education movement in the 1950s has been presented in most historical accounts as the result of internal weaknesses. In *The Transformation of the School*, for example, Cremin claimed that progressive education collapsed because "it failed to keep pace with the continuing transformation of American society."[7] Other historians have pointed to the disjuncture between the collective vision of progressive educators and the individualism and competitive nature of a capitalist society. In his analysis of the collapse of the progressive education movement, Arthur Zilversmit has pointed out that "the ideals of progressive education were anomalous in a society that stressed competition more than cooperation and that placed an inordinate value on economic success, valuing it as an honorable reward for effort."[8] And then there was the tension between the goal of social transformation held by progressive or liberal teachers and the resistance to change on the part of conservative communities and school boards as well as corporate and political elites.

While the weaknesses of the life adjustment movement of the 1940s and the lack of structure of the more extreme "open" private schools have been well documented, an emphasis solely on these issues ignores the political nature of the fall of progressive education. What is left out of these analyses is the impact of the concerted ideological and political attack on the schools by the anti-Communist Right. Although Cremin included a brief discussion of the postwar right-wing attacks on the schools in *The Transformation of the School*, he failed to identify these attacks as one of the major causes of the collapse of the progressive education movement. Studies of progressive education following Cremin have tended to overlook the significance of the role of organized right-wing groups and conservative elected officials in undermining confidence in the schools. But in the 1940s, politicians, working in concert with organizations such as the American Legion and the Sons of the American Revolution, brought the weight of the government itself against progressive education and used the machinery of the state—in particular investigating committees—to shape common-sense understandings of what was going on in the schools. This was certainly the case in California, where both the Tenney Committee and the Dilworth Committee on Education tied progressive education to subversion. When viewed in the light of recent studies of the rise of conservative and radical-right social movements in post–World War II society, the struggles over education of the 1940s and 1950s appear as part of a wider contest over political power and meaning. From this perspective, the Right appears as much more active and significant in swaying public opinion and mobilizing popular discontent with progressive education than has been recognized.

The impact of the Cold War on the progressive education movement is only now being examined in any detail. Historians have explored the social anxieties that underlay the fear of "un-American" ideas, the embracing of the individual and rejection of the social, and the nostalgia for imagined traditional ways and values. In this sense the attack on progressive education can be seen as the expression of the anxieties created by the rapid social transformations of the postwar period. These desires were clearly present in the calls for traditional or fundamental education that marked Cold War criticisms of the schools. But there is no doubt that the struggles over the schools were deeply political. As Helen Heffernan wrote in 1951, as the anti-Communist campaign against the public schools gained momentum: "So long as the school remains a place where children and youth are taught to accept their own subordination, where they are not taught to analyze the conditions of life about them, where they are not taught how to think, education constitutes no threat to those who fear social mobility or resist social change."[9] It was statements like this that drew the wrath of traditionalists and conservatives. Heffernan and Seeds never wavered from their belief that a critical education for all children was vital for a democratic society.

A Roadmap

This book is organized chronologically and thematically. It provides the details of the lives of these two powerful women in the context of broader social and political developments, in education and in the broader society.

The first chapter examines the experiences of their families in the American West and the origins of their later politics in turn-of-the-century progressive and labor movements. Their generation of women born between 1880 and 1900 lived through rapid social and cultural changes that created a kind of discursive dissonance, as the imagined woman of the feminist and suffrage movement—independent, capable, deserving of citizenship—coexisted with the patriarchal representations of the domestic and maternal woman and later the sexualized housewife of the mid-twentieth century. Throughout their lives, Helen Heffernan and Corinne Seeds saw themselves as new women, an identity shaped by the legacy of progressive social reform and the militant labor movement of their formative years. In the second chapter, their educational paths are outlined as typical of the careers of talented young working-class women who went into teaching in the first two decades of the twentieth century. Their educational ideas are placed in the context of the development of child-centered progressive schools and theorists of the 1920s. In these years Heffernan and Seeds were converted to the educational vision of John Dewey and William Kilpatrick, both of whom taught at Teachers College, Columbia University, and who were considered to be at the center of the progressive education movement.

Chapters 3 and 4 turn to Heffernan and Seeds's activities and ideas in the 1930s. Chapter 3 explores the impact of the Depression on California and the growth of the network of educators, most of them women, who became followers of Heffernan and Seeds. The 1930s also saw the development of a much more radical stance among progressive educators centered on the group called the social reconstructionists at Teachers College. Although this group of men made few alliances with classroom teachers and showed little concern with the gendered structure of schools, both Heffernan and Seeds were influenced by their call that the schools should "build a new social order." Chapter 4 examines Heffernan and Seeds's pedagogical and political ideas in this period. Like other progressive educators of the time, both of them claimed the language of democracy, but their conception of democratic schools needs to be examined closely to consider which students they imagined as the democratic-minded citizens of the future and who they saw as the educators and experts who would guide these students. Heffernan and Seeds embraced diagnostic testing, extensive observation and record keeping on all children, and centralized state power at the same time that they championed a critical education as the foundation for democracy. This chapter considers the tension between the goals of equality and democracy on the one hand and the disciplining power of the school as an institution on the other.

Chapters five and six explore the dynamics of gender and race. In chapter 5, Heffernan and Seeds's intimate relationship is illuminated through a reading of Seeds's letters to Heffernan. They were both political allies and romantic partners, part of a network of women educators in intense same-sex relationships. As was true of other middle-class women in same-sex relationships, Heffernan and Seeds did not identify themselves privately as lesbians. Nor was there a public political movement with which they could identify as women who loved women. Chapter 6 moves to chronicle the impact of the Second World War on California education and, in particular, changing understandings of race and racism in response to Nazi claims of racial superiority, the Japanese internment, the Zoot Suit riots, and the heightened awareness of American racism that the war called forth. Seeds and Heffernan had failed to engage the issue of racism until the late 1930s. It was only with the war that they became concerned with prejudice and discrimination against minority ethnic groups, although they still did not build alliances with communities of color. Nor did they question the cultural content of the curriculum or their own right to advise parents about what was proper for their children.

In chapters 7 and 8 the story of Heffernan and Seeds becomes intertwined with the rise of the Right in the postwar world. The fight to save Corinne Seeds's school, Heffernan's year in Japan on MacArthur's staff trying to introduce democratic practices in Japanese elementary schools, and the beginnings of the attack on "subversive" textbooks and teachers in California schools all took place in the years between 1945 and 1949. Chapters 9 and 10, the last two chapters, follow the growth of the Right and the continued assault on progressive schools, most dramatically in the investigations of the Tenney and Dilworth Committees of the California legislature. The Dilworth Committee in particular made Heffernan one of its major targets. After Seeds retired in 1957, Heffernan continued to defend the ideals she had held from the beginning in the face of an ongoing campaign against her. The concerted attack on Heffernan and the ideas of progressive education culminated in the election of the conservative Max Rafferty as State Superintendent of Public Instruction in 1962. Heffernan retired in 1965, her network of supporters in disarray, her programs disbanded. But the three years between Rafferty's election and Heffernan's retirement saw the passage of the Civil Rights and Voting Rights Acts and the Free Speech movement at the University of California, Berkeley, harbingers of the social movements of the 1960s, and the rise of a new generation seeking education for democracy and social justice.

CHAPTER 1

Working Girls of the Golden West

Corinne Seeds and Helen Heffernan were born seven years apart—Seeds in 1889 and Heffernan in 1896. Both were born into families in which women were expected to work, and both spent their formative years in the American West. Corinne Seeds was born and lived until she was sixteen in Colorado Springs, Colorado; her father, Sherman, was a carpenter and her mother, Mary, had been a teacher. Helen Heffernan was born in the industrial city of Lawrence, Massachusetts, the youngest of the seven living children of Michael and Margaret Heffernan. Her father, a brick mason, died when she was a child of six. In 1906, when she was ten, she moved with her widowed mother, older brothers, and sister across the continent to the mining town of Goldfield, Nevada, where she attended high school. Both Corinne Seeds and Helen Heffernan grew up in western towns at a time when ideas of the frontier were being challenged by rapid social and technological change.[1] Colorado Springs and Goldfield were in some sense defined by older imaginings of the western frontier, but they were in fact intimately tied to developments in global capitalism and were sites of two of the most radical labor movements in the mining West. Colorado Springs, Colorado, in the 1890s was well known as a health resort that attracted wealthy visitors from the East and from Europe, but it was also the financial center for the nearby mining district of Cripple Creek, the site of one of the richest gold strikes and the most violent labor struggles in the history of the United States. Like Cripple Creek, Goldfield, Nevada, came into existence because of a rich gold strike and saw a dramatic labor conflict between radical miners and mine owners. Helen Heffernan and Corinne Seeds thus came of age in communities still influenced by an ideology of the individualistic and heroic frontier, but they also were firsthand observers of stark class conflicts.

As young girls, Corinne Seeds and Helen Heffernan must also have been influenced by both contemporary images of womanhood and the lives of the actual women they knew and observed. By the turn of the twentieth century, when Seeds and Heffernan were girls, the dominant Victorian image of nurturing and domestic "true women" was being challenged by a number of alternative identities for women—"new women," suffragists, and college graduates, as well as striking factory girls in eastern industrial cities, and in the West hardworking farm and ranch women and the dangerous but glamorous figures of prostitutes and dance hall girls. Although earlier accounts of the American West tended to present women on the frontier as either genteel civilizers or heroic drudges, more recently historians have argued that a much greater range of possibilities existed for western women. Historians have emphasized the intersection of race and class with gender and the dissonance between dominant ideas of womanhood and the realities of life in the rapidly changing West.[2] What possibilities did young girls like Helen Heffernan and Corinne Seeds see in the colorful and conflicted social world of the turn-of-the-century West? As children and teenagers, they lived in a world of violent strikes and ostentatious wealth. They would have seen the first automobiles, displaced Indians living on the edges of towns, Chinese laundrymen, strikers and goons, suffragists, respectable matrons, glamorous prostitutes, and their own families, struggling for respectability and security.

Goldfield

Helen Heffernan moved to Nevada in 1906, at the impressionable age of ten. But she had been born and had spent her early life in Lawrence, Massachusetts, a highly politicized community that Ardis Cameron has described as "a hot bed of grass roots agitation."[3] In 1906, the widowed Margaret Heffernan and several of her children—her grown children James, Edward, and Margaret; her sixteen-year-old son Arthur; and her ten-year-old daughter Helen—left Lawrence for the booming mining town of Goldfield, Nevada. Heffernan often told the story of being with her mother on a ferry boat in San Francisco Bay during the 1906 earthquake. Margaret Heffernan and her children must have been on their way to Goldfield on that day in San Francisco in April 1906. It is not clear what led the family to Nevada, but earlier that year Will Heffernan, a thirty-five-year-old California insurance adjuster, arrived in Goldfield, where he established a clothing business. Whatever the exact relationship between the Heffernans, it seems likely that some kind of connection was in place to bring Margaret Heffernan and her children across the continent to the rough boom town of Goldfield.

When Margaret Heffernan and her children arrived in Goldfield, they entered a complex social world, one promising freedom and riches. Compared to earlier boom camps, Goldfield, like neighboring Tonopah, rapidly developed the amenities of a settled community. The first school in Goldfield was opened in 1904. By 1909, Goldfield paid the highest teachers' salaries in the state. By 1907, there were public libraries in both Tonopah and Goldfield, while theaters brought in well-known entertainers and major productions. The first Goldfield baseball team was organized in 1904 and soon there were tennis courts, horse racing, automobile races on Dry Lake, and boxing matches to provide entertainment, in addition to the numerous saloons and gambling houses. Despite its prosperity, Goldfield in many ways replicated the conflicts between capital and labor that defined the world that the Heffernans had left behind in Lawrence.

The year the Heffernans arrived in Goldfield, 1906, marked the beginning of the intense struggle between the mine owners and two unions—the Western Federation of Miners (WFM) and the recently formed International Workers of the World (IWW). In early 1907, the IWW organized a parade and mass meeting commemorating "Bloody Sunday," the starting point of the 1905 revolution in Russia. Speakers denounced the United States Supreme Court as a "tool of corporate greed" and a motion was passed to send a message of support from the Goldfield miners to the workers of Russia, Poland, and Finland.[4] In response to the union's militancy, the owners organized the Goldfield Business Men's and Mine Operators' Association and immediately resolved that members would not hire any known member of the IWW. It then instituted a lockout, closing the mines until a more acceptable union was formed. When on March 10, 1907, John Silva, the owner of the Nevada Restaurant, died after a street fight with Morrie Preston and Joseph Smith, young IWW supporters, tensions rose even higher. By April 1907, Goldfield was described as an armed camp.

Eventually, the mine owners convinced John Sparks, the governor of Nevada, to call for federal troops. On April 3, 1908, the miners voted to end the strike, and soon the mines were back in operation, firmly in the control of the owners. Nonetheless, the vision of an alternative mode of organizing production, wealth, and labor that had been briefly put forth in Goldfield provided a sharp contrast to politics as usual in the United States. As was true of many other rural and working-class communities throughout the United States in the early years of the twentieth century, various forms of socialism were seen as possible alternatives to the abuses of unfettered capitalism. In the 1906 Nevada election socialists won 10 percent of the vote; in 1912 they won 6 percent in the national presidential election. Whether groups such as the WFM or the IWW were truly revolutionary may be a matter of interpretation, but there is no question that the everyday rhetoric of union leaders and participants was filled with terms and assumptions that would be seen as profoundly radical today.

Young Helen Heffernan came of age when such views were openly debated. And she may have been introduced to these ideas in her own family. The trial of Joseph Smith and Morrie Preston, the IWW supporters accused of murdering John Silver in 1907, provides unexpected evidence of the political ideas of the Heffernan family. The transcript of the Preston/Smith trial gives voice not only to their accusers, but their defenders as well. Among the witnesses for the defense of Preston and Smith was a waitress, Margaret Heffernan, who must have been Helen's older sister. Margaret Heffernan, who stated that she came to Goldfield in April 1906, which is consistent with stories Helen Heffernan told of her childhood, testified that she had been a member of the IWW as well as of the WFM.[5] Thus Helen Heffernan grew up with at least one strong prolabor voice in her family, in this case a politically active and articulate woman.

As a girl growing up in a working-class family where radical views may well have been discussed, Helen Heffernan must have encountered possibilities of adult womanhood quite different from respectable middle-class ideas of subordinate domesticity. In general, Goldfield and Tonopah provided a wider range of opportunities and identities for women than existed in more settled parts of the country. Contemporary accounts mention miners' wives and daughters, but also bar girls, laundresses, servants, shopkeepers, teachers, clerical workers, and even women miners. Women owned dance halls, restaurants, and hotels. There were even two women lawyers, two or three doctors, and a dentist.[6] It has also been estimated that at one point 500 prostitutes worked in the Goldfield red-light district. What is striking in accounts of Goldfield was the proximity of all these "good," "bad," and undefined women.[7] In preparation for her own future, Helen Heffernan took advantage of the well-supported high school at Goldfield to gain an education.

Although Goldfield was beginning its decline in the years between 1908 and 1912, when Helen Heffernan attended Goldfield High School, there was still enough tax money to support a well-paid staff and well-equipped school. Across the nation, the proliferating high schools were a source of opportunity for young women in these years. In 1890 there were just over 200,000 students in 2,526 public high schools in the United States. Ten years later, that number had more than doubled, to over 500,000 students in some 6,000 public high schools. And the majority of these students were young women.[8] Although it was still the case that only a minority of the school-age population attended high school and that the schools tended to serve the children of the white, English-speaking middle class, as free public institutions high schools were open to others, including the daughters of the respectable working class.

Goldfield High School was very small. Only eleven seniors graduated with Heffernan in 1912. At the high-school commencement she read an essay entitled "Nevada," which had earlier won the state declamation contest at Reno.[9] Her class prophecy in the school annual *The Joshua Palm* is instructive. Writing from 1925, thirteen years into the future, the class prophet wrote: "I had just returned from Washington after being sent there with an invitation to President Helen Heffernan to visit our World's Fair in Goldfield." Despite the prophecy that she was soon be elected president of the United States, Helen was not even elected class president of Goldfield High School; that honor went to a boy. And instead of preparing her for a career in politics or the law, high school led Helen Heffernan, like Corinne Seeds and so many other working-class and rural young women, to enter normal school, in her case the Nevada Normal School, where she could train to become a teacher.

Educating Teachers in the Sagebrush State

As for other young women in the late-nineteenth and early-twentieth century, education allowed Helen Heffernan and Corinne Seeds the opportunity to create autonomous lives. In these years the cultural expectation that women teachers would be docile and acquiescent was being challenged by the growth of an active suffrage movement and the disruptive figure of the "new woman." Activist educators like Ella Flagg Young and Margaret Haley in Chicago were arguing for the importance and value of the work of women teachers.[10] For working-class young women like Heffernan and Seeds, teaching was by far the easiest avenue to respectable waged work, and by the early-twentieth century a two-year normal school course was the most common way to gain teaching certification.[11]

Young normal-school students like Seeds and Heffernan could build upon the accomplishments of an earlier generation of activist women in imagining their own lives. However, these claims of women's rights and equality with men were not uncontested. Ideas about women's nature continued to be heatedly debated in the years of their adolescence and youth and played themselves out in the normal schools in which they were educated. Viewed as the sphere of women, normal schools were denigrated at the time by male academics in the rapidly expanding universities as providing only a limited and inferior education for the predominantly female students who attended them. Recent work has questioned that judgment; historians have argued that normal schools were much like other institutions in this period—contested spaces in which competing visions of womanhood circulated.[12] Normal schools were controlled by men, but at the same time offered opportunities to working-class women that they would otherwise not have—preparation for relatively good work as a teacher and the possibility of understanding themselves and the world in new ways.

Helen Heffernan entered the newly named College of Education at the University of Nevada in the fall of 1912. Fewer than 200 students attended the University of Nevada in 1912, and only twenty-three the College of Education.[13] By this time, entrance requirements for the College of Education were the same as for the University of Nevada as a whole—a diploma from an accredited high school. As was true for other state universities in these years, there was no tuition, but students had to provide their own books, room, and board. Students seeking elementary teaching certification had to complete a two-year course of study, but beginning in 1900, students in the two-year teaching course could easily move to the College of Arts and Sciences to complete their BA in four years if they met university requirements in foreign language, history and social science, and mathematics. Heffernan stayed on at the University of Nevada for a third year after completing the two-year elementary teaching course, graduating in the spring of 1915. Like other college students, she must have learned as much from the social world she inhabited as from the formal curriculum. Virtually all the students in the elementary teaching course were women, who, although they were formally considered a part of the university, took the great majority of their courses in the normal school. As women, as frequently the daughters of working-class or poorer families, as future teachers, they were thus both a part of the university and outside it.

In some respects, the University of Nevada was an egalitarian institution for women students. Classes were coeducational, and the gold medal for outstanding academic achievement was won by both men and women. But there are other indications of the institutional marking of gender. As was true nationwide, the rise of intercollegiate football served to glorify male athletic prowess. Although women's basketball was very popular in the years between 1900 and 1920, it soon lost out to football as the symbol of university identity. Women students were identified in other ways. Each year at graduation, for example, the women students performed a pageant of folk dances for the whole university community. Such pageants were common at colleges and universities in the first two decades of the twentieth century and marked women's culture just as football defined ideas of masculinity. Such public celebrations of "womanhood" valued gender differences but also served to exaggerate and even create them.

If the rituals of university life reinforced conventional ideas of womanhood, the University of Nevada, like other colleges and universities of the time, also provided alternatives and challenges to these ideas. Helen Heffernan came to Reno during the three-year campaign for women's suffrage in Nevada. This campaign, led by Anne Martin, spread ideas of women's rights throughout Nevada. The Nevada Equal Franchise Society, which had its headquarters in Reno, was founded in 1911, and in 1912, the year Heffernan arrived at the university, a campus suffrage club was established.[14] The club met with ridicule and hostility in the campus yearbook, *The Artemesia,* which doubtless reflected fears of social change and possible loss of male privilege. Despite the condescension or ridicule it elicited, the suffrage club provided an alternative vision for students like the young Helen Heffernan. And the achievement of women's right to vote in 1914 in Nevada must have given young women a sense of women's power and their own possibilities. Heffernan, like other young women at the University of Nevada, had to balance traditional views of women as future mothers and subordinate wives with other messages—the activities of the Suffrage Club, the ideas of the new woman, her youth in Goldfield, and her own family, held together by her widowed mother from the time she was a small child. For Helen Heffernan, the University of Nevada must have introduced a new world. It offered her the opportunity to prepare herself for waged work, her only option other than marriage, and it brought her into contact with middle-class culture. But it also offered contradictory and competing visions of what it might mean to be a teacher and a woman.

An Independent Schoolmarm

In the fall of 1915, nineteen-year-old Helen Heffernan returned from the University of Nevada to Goldfield, where she was hired as a second-grade teacher.[15] The Goldfield schools had an enrollment of just over 500 students that year, but attendance was declining. The Goldfield boom was over. The population of the town, which had been estimated at 15,000 in

1907, declined to 4,838 in 1910, and by the 1920 census sank to 1,558, one-tenth its size at the height of the boom thirteen years earlier. Heffernan left no written record of these years, but her friends later recalled stories of these early teaching experiences. One friend described the care and compassion Heffernan showed for the children she taught at Goldfield. There was Louie, a first grader, who fell asleep in class every morning. When Heffernan investigated, she learned that the family lived above the Last Chance saloon. Louie was not eating breakfast but was "drinking all the leftovers from the glasses and coming to school with a hangover." The friend continued, "After that, Helen gave him his breakfast, but let him sleep."[16] Another friend described how Heffernan "spent most of her first month's salary to buy more than two hundred daffodil bulbs which she planted in window boxes at her school. She carried water a long distance for them, and when they bloomed, people came from miles around to see them."[17] Heffernan later planted a plot of bright green alfalfa, watering it from a polluted well. Although these accounts of events many years before must be recognized as stories, doubtless embellished and elaborated as they were retold over the years, nonetheless they are consistent with and emphasize the later themes in Heffernan's life—her love of natural beauty, her attention to and care for a needy child, her self-reliance and energy. Years later, her garden in Sacramento was one of her passions.

In the spring of 1917, Heffernan resigned her position as second-grade teacher in Goldfield and that fall moved with her mother to Reno where she took up took a position at the McKinley Park Elementary School. But she only remained with her mother in Reno for one year. By the fall of 1918, she had found a new job teaching in Tremonten, Utah. She then moved to Jerome, Idaho. The 1920 census found her, then a twenty-four-year-old teacher, living in Jerome with her older brother Edward, who was listed as a concrete mason. It is not clear whether she moved first and Edward followed, or the reverse, but it is instructive (and unusual) that Helen is listed as head of this household in the census notation, since men were almost always cited as heads of household in the census. After three years in Jerome, she left again, this time for Lodi, California, where she took a position as a junior high school teacher. In the summer of 1921, before beginning the 1921–22 school year at Lodi, Heffernan attended the summer session of the University of California at Berkeley. In the fall of 1922, she transferred her credits from the University of Nevada and matriculated at the University of California.

The University of California

Helen Heffernan entered the University of California at Berkeley as a young woman who had independently supported herself as a teacher for seven years. In many ways the University of California at Berkeley in the 1920s was typical of large state universities throughout the United States. Although formally coeducational, the university was dominated by male faculty and students. Feminist historians of education have suggested that women in coeducational universities like the University of California were given the message that they were outsiders.[18] Knowledge was controlled by powerful male professors, and women students were made aware that they were inferior to male students—that they were only allowed to attend the university on sufferance. Although women students made up 46 percent of the student body by 1900, they were excluded from formal leadership roles or participation in campus politics. When organizations and activities for women were introduced, it was made clear that they were founded in response to women's different (domestic) natures and needs. As President Benjamin Wheeler commented in a speech to the Women's Associated Student Government in 1904: "Women need different organizations from the men, and they ought to have them.... You are not here with the ambition to be school teachers or old maids, but you are here for the preparation of marriage and motherhood. This education should tend to make you more serviceable as wives and mothers."[19]

A few women were on the faculty of the University of California in the early years of the twentieth century. In 1904 Jessica Peixotto became the first woman appointed to a full-time faculty position, teaching courses on political economy, socialism, poverty, children and the state, crime, and household economics. But Peixotto remained an exception. In 1906 Lucy Sprague Mitchell, the first dean of women at Berkeley, remembered her first impression when she arrived on the campus: "It came as a shock when I realized that most of the faculty thought of women frankly as inferior beings. The older men were solidly opposed to having any women on the faculty. Any woman who, intellectually, could hold such a position, must be a freak and 'unwomanly.'"[20] Not all women at the university accepted these messages. In 1908, as the campaign for women's suffrage in California gained momentum, the College Equal Suffrage League at the University of California was founded, and after women gained the vote in California in 1911, women at the university continued to work for the federal woman suffrage amendment until it was passed in 1920. But by the early 1920s, when Heffernan was a student, the university began to reflect the wider changes in perceptions of women that were occurring in the culture as a whole. Once known as "pelicans," a demeaning image of scrawny and unattractive spinsters, Berkeley women came to be known as "chickens," sexually desirable and willing modern flappers. As was true elsewhere, the introduction of greater social freedom and an acceptance of women's heterosexual desires led to weakening of feminist demands for equal political rights.[21]

We have no evidence of Heffernan's reaction to the cultural and social world she encountered at the University of California. Given her normal school education and experience as a teacher, she might have been expected to major in education, but instead she matriculated as a student in political science. She completed her undergraduate degree by taking five political science courses in the fall semester of 1922.

Corinne Seeds: From Colorado to Los Angeles Normal School

Corinne Seeds was born in Colorado Springs, Colorado, in 1889. Although Seeds's mother, Mary, had been a teacher, there is no evidence that her mother taught during Corinne's childhood in Colorado Springs. Her father Sherman was listed in the Colorado Springs city directories first as a carpenter, and then, in 1903 and 1904, as a contractor. Colorado Springs was an unusual western town in the 1890s and early years of the twentieth century. Founded as a health resort because of its hot springs and pure mountain climate, it was one of the earliest resort towns in the United States. But Colorado Springs was not inhabited solely by the wealthy. Fortune hunters, invalids, tradesmen, workers, and servants also lived there.[22] With the discovery of gold at nearby Cripple Creek in the early 1890s, Colorado Springs experienced rapid growth. In 1902, gold production from the Cripple Creek mines led the world. By 1900 the population of Colorado Springs reached 35,000 as the city became the center for finance and supplies for the goldfields. Sherman Seeds was one of the skilled workers who built and maintained the prosperous city.

In her accounts of her childhood and her family, Corinne Seeds always spoke of her father as a strong supporter of labor. We can assume that he almost certainly was a member of the carpenters' union in Colorado Springs. Although the members of Local 515 seem to have held a range of political positions, they, like organized carpenters throughout Colorado, tended to support progressive causes.[23] The Colorado Springs carpenters were doubtless influenced by the Cripple Creek miners, who for almost ten years had been led by the radical WFM, which was also central in the miners' struggles in Goldfield, Nevada. In 1903, the WFM led a strike of Cripple Creek miners; the mine owners, claiming that lives were in danger, demanded state protection; the governor sent in the militia. A series of violent incidents—bombings, arbitrary arrests, intimidation, and mob violence—led to the deaths of scores of miners. The next year the mine owners and the state brutally broke the strike. It was a profound defeat for the WFM.[24]

Although Corinne Seeds never referred to the bloody strikes at nearby Cripple Creek, she did make clear that her own family was working class and that her sympathies for ordinary people were grounded in her own class background. Speaking of her early experiences teaching in the poorer neighborhoods of Los Angeles in her oral history, for example, she said, "There were also some of the finest people I ever met, you know, working people, lovely people—I mean, like my folks."[25] We can speculate about the kind of political ideas the young Corinne Seeds would have encountered in a prounion household in Colorado Springs. Ideas of the collective ownership of production, the dignity of labor, and the need for a more equitable society were proudly held by union members and their supporters throughout the West in these years. As one Colorado Springs carpenter said: "Land should never be made private property. Coal land should always be owned and worked by the state. Pensions ought to be granted to aged persons without means."[26]

As the only child of a carpenter who was a strong labor man and a former school teacher, Seeds grew up on the cusp between working and middle class. But she also came of age at a time when possibilities for women to gain an independent living were rapidly expanding. Like Helen Heffernan, Corinne Seeds took advantage of the opportunities provided by the local coeducational public high school. But she did not graduate from Colorado Springs High School. In 1905, one year after the brutal repression of the WFM at Cripple Creek, Sherman and Mary Seeds left Colorado Springs for California. By the fall of 1906, Corinne Seeds was living with her parents in Pasadena, California, attending Pasadena High School.

Pasadena

The reasons for the Seeds family's move to Southern California are unclear. Both Pasadena and Colorado Springs were known for their healthful climates and attracted invalids and those with breathing problems. Perhaps Sherman or Mary Seeds had concerns about their health that led them to settle in these cities. Perhaps Sherman Seeds was disgusted by the violent suppression of the Cripple Creek strike and the antilabor climate that followed it. Whatever their reasons, when Sherman and Mary Seeds arrived in Pasadena in Southern California in 1905, they found a region in the midst of an economic boom, a place of warm sunshine, an extensive electric train system, cheap and available housing, and, doubtless, plentiful work for a carpenter/contractor like Sherman Seeds. Like Colorado Springs, Pasadena was well known as the home to a social elite with strong ties to eastern wealth.[27] At the turn of the twentieth century, Pasadena shared not only the optimism that marked all of Southern California, but a deep suspicion of organized labor as well.[28]

Unlike eastern cities, which were filled with European immigrants, at the turn of the twentieth century Los Angeles tended to attract native-born white Americans from the East and Midwest. As white English speakers sharing the dominant culture, these newcomers had a much easier time than immigrants from non-English-speaking countries, while racism gave them obvious privileges in terms of opportunities for jobs and housing. Robert Fogelson has pointed out that these new residents held a vision of the good life "epitomized by the residential suburb—spacious, affluent, clean, decent, permanent, predictable, and homogeneous—and violated by the great city—congested, impoverished, filthy, immoral, transient, uncertain and heterogeneous."[29] This idea of the good society with its self-congratulatory individualism stands in sharp contrast to the collective vision of the radical organizers of the WFM or the members of the carpenters' union of Colorado Springs.

Corinne Seeds's introduction to the social world of Pasadena came at Pasadena High School, which she entered as a junior. The well-to-do residents of Pasadena routinely sent their children, particularly their daughters, to the public high school. Of the sixty graduates in 1908, the year Corinne Seeds graduated, forty-two were young women.[30] Corinne Seeds then entered Los Angeles Normal School. In her oral history, she described this choice in terms of class: "I really wanted to go to Stanford and become a journalist. All my friends went off to college, because they were wealthy, but I wasn't."[31] Pasadena school records support her memory. Although the Pasadena school reports stopped listing the future plans of graduates in 1908, the year Seeds graduated, student choices were still listed in the previous year. In 1907, of fifty-eight graduates listed, eleven entered Stanford, ten entered other four-year colleges, and four went on to the Los Angeles Normal School. There was no tuition at Los Angeles Normal and it was possible to live at home in Pasadena and take the electric train in to Los Angeles Normal every day.

THE LOS ANGELES NORMAL SCHOOL

For Corinne Seeds, as for Helen Heffernan, normal school must have been the only realistic option for higher education given her family's limited resources. The world Seeds found at the Los Angeles Normal School was in some ways similar to the University of Nevada, but in other ways it was quite different. Heffernan was one of twenty-three students in the College of Education in 1912, and there were fewer than 200 students in the entire University of Nevada. In 1908, when Corinne Seeds entered, the Los Angeles Normal School was the largest normal school in the state, enrolling around 1,500 students annually, and was located in the heart of Los Angeles, a rapidly expanding city of over 750,000 people. The normal school accepted graduates of accredited high schools for a two-year course of study leading to certification as an elementary school teacher. There was no tuition charged, but there were other costs. Board, "including room with light and heat, which two persons share, in private families," cost from $18.00 to $25.00 per month.[32] But Corinne Seeds lived at home in Pasadena, commuting to school each day on the electric railway.

As was true at the University of Nevada, students received contradictory messages about women's proper role in the world at the Los Angeles Normal School. Women students were encouraged to think of themselves as capable and engaged professionals, but their personal lives were closely monitored, and prestige and power remained in men's hands. The gender ratio at LA Normal replicated the national pattern in the years between 1885 and 1910. In 1884–85, 12.5 percent of the student body were men; in 1900, 10.7 percent; and by 1906, only 2.1 percent of students were men.[33] But the faculty and administration were a different story. Although the faculty consisted of nine men and fourteen women, men with doctorates from eastern universities held the prestigious faculty positions, particularly in the new science of psychology.[34] Women faculty members taught the elementary school curriculum, and six of the fourteen women taught only part time. Although the publications of the Los Angeles Normal School expressed pride in the intellectual caliber of the student body, the structure of the curriculum and the regulations that governed students' lives spoke to a different set of values—of the need to oversee, discipline, and protect.[35]

Corinne Seeds graduated from the Los Angeles Normal School at the end of the fall term in 1909. Although the June 1910 class graduated about 200 students, there were only forty-one students in Corinne Seeds's fall graduating class—forty women and one man, Vierling Kersey, who later became of one of Seeds and Heffernan's most powerful adversaries. The president of the class was a woman, Myrtle McIntyre, and Corinne Seeds was vice president. Kersey held the ambiguous position of "chaperone." The relationship of Kersey to the women of his class is obscure. The class president wrote in the annual publication *The Exponent*: "During our second term we thought we had found a mascot in Mr. Kersey, but he turned out to be our father and often when we stood at his knee and begged him for a story he would say,

> A wise old owl lived in an oak
> The more he saw, the less he spoke;
> The less he spoke, the more he heard.
> Children, learn to be like this bird.
> —and we did.[36]

Corinne Seeds later called her normal school education "marvelous." But if that education prepared her for waged work as a teacher and gave her the foundation for her later career as an educator, the Los Angles Normal School also taught her lessons about male privilege and the exercise of power, lessons she would learn again and again in her professional life. Whatever the women of her normal school class thought of Vierling Kersey, the only man in their class, and whatever "chaperone" or "mascot" implied, it was Kersey, and not one of them, who was later elected California state superintendent of public instruction.

The Avenue 21 School

While Helen Heffernan spent her first years teaching in small towns in Nevada, Utah, and Idaho, Corinne Seeds began her teaching career in 1911 at the Mira Monte School, a Los Angeles County school south of Watts, just outside the Los Angeles city limits. After two years at Mira Monte, Seeds moved to the Avenue 21 School, a city school on the east bank of the Los Angeles River, "two blocks from the railroad yard," where she taught fifth and sixth grade and became the principal of an adult night school.[37] Mira Monte and the Avenue 21 School were typical of schools in central and south Los Angeles. They served the children of immigrants, African Americans, and "Mexicans" (a term that encompassed both those of Mexican descent born in the United States and immigrants from Mexico), as well as a smaller number of the children of wealthier white Protestants.

In her second year at the Avenue 21 School, when she was twenty-four-years old, Seeds was made principal of the adult night school. Adult night schools in Los Angeles had been established in the years before the First World War as part of the progressive reform effort and in response to the moral panic over immigration. Los Angeles had experienced explosive growth at the turn of the twentieth century. Between 1890 and 1909, its population increased from 50,000 to 319,000; by 1909 it trailed only San Francisco as a western manufacturing center, surpassing Seattle, Portland, and Denver.[38] Although Los Angeles did not experience as dramatic an influx of immigrants as did New York, Chicago, or even San Francisco, nonetheless concerns over "foreigners" were as widespread in Los Angeles as anywhere else in the country in this period. And, as was true across the nation, immigrants from Asia and Mexico were racialized and discriminated against, as were native-born African Americans.[39] As the principal of the Avenue 21 adult night school, Seeds was responsible for overseeing a wide range of activities, including the formal curriculum of Americanization, literacy classes, the work of home teachers, and recreational programs and social activities for the entire community.[40]

Unlike Helen Heffernan, who left no first-person account of her early career, Seeds discussed her early years teaching in the Los Angeles public schools in an oral history conducted after she retired. While her grasp of chronology and names was somewhat shaky, the oral history provides a window into her perceptions of herself as a teacher and her understanding of the people she met.[41] Seeds's account of her years teaching at the Avenue 21 School reflected many of the contradictions inherent in Americanization programs. One of the major purposes of schools like the Avenue 21 adult night school was to transform foreigners into Americans. Such schools were envisioned as protecting society as a whole from the danger of the political subversion, violence, and low morals associated in the popular mind with "foreignness."[42] Americanization pamphlets warned of the dangers of anarchism and social unrest. But there was virtually no acknowledgement of the possible reasons for dissatisfaction—exploitative and dangerous working conditions, the denial of citizenship or membership in the imagined American community to over 10 percent of the native-born U.S. population because of their race and to over half because of their gender. Nor was there any reference to the major social causes of the time—the antilynching campaign, the suffrage movement, trade unions—or the electoral support for Eugene Debs and the Socialists.

Americanization programs also reflected ironies around gender. The women teachers in these schools were almost always white, while those they were "Americanizing" were seen as non-white, or, in the case of Jewish and southern European immigrants, as slightly less than white. But white women's power was around race, not gender. As John McClymer has pointed out, Americanization primers and other materials used in literacy and citizenship classes "were invariant in their portrayal of the public domain of American life as an all-male preserve."[43] The native-born women like Seeds who instructed these immigrant men in the duties of citizenship were not only absent from the depictions of public life in the materials they taught, but were also themselves denied full rights of citizenship until 1920, when national women's suffrage was achieved. When Americanizers turned to the education of immigrant women, they emphasized their importance as mothers, who could teach the values of patriotism and loyalty.[44]

In her stories of contact with immigrant, Mexican American, and African American students, Seeds presented herself as the benevolent and powerful teacher, who held and dispensed cultural knowledge. She described the classroom of the adult evening school: "We had lovely blackboards and lots of chalk and I used to take their hands in mine and help to train them."[45] In this image, she physically guided the students to literacy. But she also respected her students and their families as hardworking people. In one passage, Seeds described the exploitation of the working people she taught: "That's what we were doing in those days—importing those poor people and exploiting them.... I would sit on the steps with an Italian woman, maybe help her to know a few words, and try to keep them out of the hands of the people that exploited them. I even begged the canning factory man to let me teach some English to the men, but he worked them ten hours and often kept them afterward."[46] This sense of solidarity with working people doubtless was grounded in her love and admiration for her father, the carpenter with a strong labor consciousness.

At the same time that Seeds expressed her sympathy for her students, she also assumed her superiority, particularly around race. Seeds's attitude toward students of color was a mix of compassion, physical unease, objectification, and cultural stereotyping. Consider this description of the sixty-five-year-old washerwoman, Mattie Lafayette, who, Seeds said, "lived in a house which was entirely out of...wooden boxes, with tin cans that she had cut and made into a roof." Mattie Lafayette did "the most beautiful washing and ironing I have ever seen in my life.... She was born a slave and had the best-blooded stock in her. She was a queen."[47] Seeds's rhetorical calling forth of the noble black granny who "was born a slave" with the bearing of a "queen" recalls Hortense Spillers's comment that black woman are seen through "markers so loaded with mythical prepossession that there is no easy way for the agents buried beneath them to come clean."[48]

Seeds's racial unease is striking in her description of conducting a literacy class in a black home. This story reveals Seeds's racial attitudes, but it is also fascinating in documenting the desire for education and literacy on the part of adults in the African American community. An African American woman, whom Seeds described as the "leader of the Negroes," asked Seeds to conduct literacy classes in the woman's home rather than the school. Seeds recalled that she was uneasy about going to the woman's house: "I didn't like it very much; I didn't really know what was going to happen, but when I got there, there were about fifty Negroes packed in a very small house. They all wanted to know how to read and write." Rather than remembering this incident as striking evidence of the desire for literacy, Seeds saw it as entry into a strange and frightening world. "I must admit I went home and took a bath afterwards, because it is something for one person to be surrounded in the beginning like that. I don't know whether it's instinct or what it is."[49] After the meeting at the house, Seeds continued to hold literacy classes, but only at the school.

In another passage, Seeds described a Japanese home she visited at the request of a home teacher, Miss Hasagawa, whom Seeds described as a "high born Japanese." Again she described a crowded house: "That place was simply jammed. The babies, the children, had flies crawling over their eyelids, and their eyes didn't blink." And once again, Seeds recalled, she "went home and bathed."[50] Seeds was later highly critical of the Japanese internment during the Second World War; she taught and supported Japanese and Japanese American students at UCLA. But she did not frame this memory in terms of her sympathy for Japanese Americans; here the crowded room, the flies mark poverty, but also foreignness and difference. Seeds's failure to challenge her own reactions in her oral history narrative reveals the ongoing assumption of privilege that undercut the democratic goals she embraced.

Although Seeds presented her work as benevolent, teaching in Americanization programs was not necessarily a selfless activity. For her, as for many other women teachers, it was a means of employment and a source of some public power. Although teachers lacked the status of the middle-class women reformers who led the Americanization movement, they shared some of the same motivation as these more powerful women. As Gayle Gullett has commented, the actions of middle-class women Americanizers were "at least partially self-serving," since by claiming a right to instruct immigrant women, "organized women thus created a political role for themselves as managers of other women's homes."[51] Seeds clearly enjoyed her role as principal of the Avenue 21 School for just these reasons. But the progressive reform impetus—the desire to help those seen as less fortunate, the desire to extend what were seen as the benefits of "being American" to newcomers, to educate the illiterate—also emerged in Seeds's account.[52] This tension, between her sense of power and belief in her own racial and cultural superiority, and her genuine sympathy for hardworking people like her parents and a desire to build a more equitable world, would characterize Seeds's views throughout her career.

Teachers College, Columbia University

In the summer of 1919, Corinne Seeds traveled across the continent to New York to attend summer school at Teachers College, Columbia, in order to strengthen her work as principal of the Avenue 21 School.[53] She doubtless also knew of Teachers College's national and international reputation. It was by then the largest school of education in the world. Students came to Teachers College from across the United States and abroad, and its faculty included such influential figures as Edward Thorndike, the founder of educational psychology and a powerful advocate of the idea that learning can be scientifically measured; the popular William Heard Kilpatrick; and John Dewey, the most distinguished scholar on the faculty, whose appointment was in the Philosophy Department at Columbia but who also taught at Teachers College.[54] As Seeds said later, it "was a galaxy of stars."[55] Seeds must have been impressed with her experiences that summer session. After returning to Los Angeles for the 1919–20 school year, she decided to go back to New York in 1920, to study full time for her BA degree.

When Seeds entered Teachers College in 1920, she entered an institution that was the center of innovative educational thinking. There was a sense of excitement and energy, as professors theorized about the "new education" that could meet the needs of the new age. But the faculty was hardly homogeneous in its views. Probably the sharpest and historically the most significant division was between Thorndike and his followers, who emphasized quantification and testing, and Dewey and those influenced by his thinking, who argued for a flexible curriculum that could meet the needs of individual children and emphasized the essential role of schools in a democracy. Although she did not immediately reject the ideas of Thorndike and his followers, it was the child-centered and democratic educators who captured Seeds's imagination.

Seeds attended lectures given by John Dewey in her first summer session at Teachers College in 1919, but she never took a formal course from him.[56] Dewey's early writings on education had been published while he was professor at the University of Chicago between 1896 and 1905. It was there, with the assistance of his wife, Alice, that he founded the famous University of Chicago Laboratory School. The methods developed at the Laboratory School became the focus of two of his most influential and popular writings on education, *School and Society* (1900) and "The Child and the Curriculum" (1902). In these works, Dewey set out the major themes that would characterize all of his educational writings: the need to focus instruction on the needs and understandings of the individual child, the need to make the learning experience authentic and engaging, and the school as a small community based on respect for students. Dewey explored the political implications of his theories in much greater depth in *Democracy and Education,* published in 1916, but his basic ideas about education had already been set out by the time he arrived in New York in 1905. Although Dewey was famous for his obscure and somewhat incoherent style of lecturing, he had a profound influence on other members of the Teachers College faculty.

Doubtless the best-known and most important popularizer of Dewey's ideas at Teachers College was William Heard Kilpatrick, and it was Kilpatrick who had the most lasting impact on Seeds. Kilpatrick had been Dewey's graduate student at Teachers College and had joined the faculty of Teachers College as professor of philosophy of education in 1911.[57] A charismatic teacher, Kilpatrick lectured to classes of over 600 and was estimated to have taught over 35,000 students in his career. Influenced by both Thorndike and Dewey, Kilpatrick tried to reconcile Dewey's commitment to education for democracy and his demand that schools abandon the rote memorization of facts with Thorndike's claim that learning could be scientifically measured and controlled. Kilpatrick's attempt to reconcile these different approaches culminated in the publication of his essay, "The Project Method," in *Teachers College Record* in 1918.[58] "The Project Method" made Kilpatrick famous. Lawrence Cremin later estimated that over 60,000 reprints of the article were printed in the twenty-five years after its initial publication.[59]

Reading "The Project Method" today, it is difficult to understand why the article had such an impact. It is a relatively brief and abstract essay, the central point of which is that children (and adults as well) learn best when they are interested in a topic and have some control over how they proceed in learning. Kilpatrick himself cautioned the reader that the idea of "the project" was another way of stating ideas that were already common. As he wrote: "Not a few readers will be disappointed that after all so little new is presented."[60] Kilpatrick argued that he had found the "unifying idea" that would reconcile "the laws of learning" (for which he cited Thorndike's *Educational Psychology*) and "the ethical quality of conduct" (a reference to Dewey). This idea was what he called "the purposeful act." As John Beineke has pointed out, Kilpatrick's debt to Dewey can be seen by comparing "The Project Method" with passages from Dewey's *Democracy and Education*, published two years earlier, in 1916. In *Democracy and Education*, Dewey described what he called "the essentials of method." First, a student had to have "a genuine situation of experience—that there be a continuous activity in which he is interested for its own sake." A problem would arrive from this activity and the student would have "the information and make observations needed to deal with it." Finally, he would "have opportunity and occasion to test his ideas by application, to make their meaning clear and to discover for himself their validity."[61] Kilpatrick's "purposeful act," the central concept of the project method, was essentially a restatement of Dewey's "essentials of method." However vague and general Kilpatrick's essay might have been, it captured in relatively simple form the essence of Dewey's pedagogy. For Corinne Seeds, Kilpatrick's project method became the touchstone of her lifework.

Conclusion

Helen Heffernan and Corinne Seeds were shaped by the historical world into which they were born and the possibilities it offered them. They were children of the American West, but that West was not the romantic frontier of rugged men spreading civilization over a savage land. Seeds and Heffernan grew up in a contested society defined by racism, class conflict, and rapidly shifting and competing expectations of women. As the daughters of working-class families with strong labor sympathies, they came of age during a time of social violence and political struggle. They observed the various ways women negotiated a world of nineteenth-century expectations and twentieth-century realities. Their own mothers were hardworking women who struggled to make their way and to support their children. But Corinne and Helen must also have seen other possibilities for a woman's life: suffragists, wealthy and middle-class women supported by their husbands, glamorous prostitutes, and independent school teachers. We cannot know their thoughts or feelings as young girls. We can only gather evidence of the worlds they inhabited as children—the crowded industrial city of Lawrence, the wealthy towns of Colorado Springs and Pasadena, the politically charged mining town of Goldfield. As daughters of working-class families, Helen and Corinne were fortunate to have come of age at the moment when high schools were being established in towns throughout the United States and when a high school education was encouraged for talented young women. For them, as for thousands of other working-class girls, the next step after high school was normal school, and then school teaching.

For young women like Corinne Seeds and Helen Heffernan, normal school was a formative experience. It prepared them for work as classroom teachers and introduced them to other capable and ambitious young women. Women normal-school students have not been looked at as intellectuals, because they were preparing to be teachers, because they were women, and because they frequently came from working-class and lower-middle-class families. The daughters of highly educated, professional, or wealthy families in this period attended elite women's colleges or coeducational universities. But as feminist historians have argued, normal schools need to be considered as sites in which young women were prepared for meaningful work and came to envision themselves as actors in the world. Late adolescence and early adulthood are periods in which people explore the possibilities of mature adulthood. In this process we come to see ourselves as men and women—defined by our sexual preference, race, and class—aspects of our identity that also mark hierarchies of power and privilege. Relatively equal participation of men and women in both formal classrooms and student organizations gave normal-school students the formal message that both men and women can learn, think, and speak. But while the College of Education at the University of Nevada and the Los Angeles Normal School were formally coeducational, virtually all the students were women while the leading administrators and most powerful professors were men. And when Heffernan and Seeds moved on to Teachers College and the University of California to study for their BA degrees, they entered institutions in which male privilege was unquestioned. We cannot know how Corinne Seeds and Helen Heffernan negotiated the contradictions of normal school and university, but their educations gave them the credentials to find relatively well-paid employment as teachers and provided the grounding for their future careers.

When they took positions as teachers in the public schools, they were entering a field relatively open to the advancement of talented women.[62] Although the social expectation was that they would remain in the classroom for only a few years until they married, as the educational state expanded, women found comparatively well-paid work as principals, supervisors, and even county superintendents, although men continued to dominate in the newly founded schools of education. Like many other women, Corinne Seeds and Helen Heffernan used teaching as only the first step in their exploration of the world.

CHAPTER 2

The Child and the Curriculum

In the 1920s, as Corinne Seeds and Helen Heffernan began their rise to prominence, California was a prosperous and rapidly growing state with a tradition of progressive politics and strong support for public education. The state shared the racist attitudes and institutions of the nation as a whole, but the racial categories in California were not simply a black and white binary. Instead, they encompassed a complex mix of those deemed white, Mexican, African American, and Asian. In the mid-1920s, Californians, like other Americans, were caught up in the consumerism and cultural changes of the decade. Although farmers in California as elsewhere were beginning to experience the economic crisis that presaged the Great Depression, the urban centers of San Francisco, Oakland, and Los Angeles continued to grow and prosper. The first talking moving picture was produced in 1926, and the movie industry, already flourishing, became an even stronger and more defining presence in Los Angles. And while the progressive era seemed to have ended in national politics, in California the situation was more complex. Progressives had taken control of the state in 1910 with the election of Governor Hiram Johnson, and even in the 1920s their influence continued to be strong.[1] Clement Young, the Republican governor elected in 1926, was closely connected to Johnson and the California progressives and was a strong supporter of education.

THE NATURAL CHILD

Nationally, historians have pointed to a sharp break in American politics around 1920, with the conclusion of the First World War, the failure of United States to join the League of Nations, the Red Scare, and the election of Warren Harding as president. Harding's election ushered in a decade of conservative dominance. It was an era that celebrated private consumption, business values, and ideas of efficiency and technology. In this climate, the progressives committed to the regulation of corporations, an activist state committed to social welfare, and the belief that social institutions like public schools should build democracy rather than serve the interests of elites were relegated to a minority. Public education was dominated by business-oriented school administrators and school boards who embraced the newly established testing movement as a way to identify and sort students in the public schools. But while faith in the efficacy of testing and measurement and the belief that school bureaucracy should be modeled on corporations increasingly defined public education, in these same years child-centered conceptions of progressive education flourished in private schools and among liberal intellectuals.

In the early 1920s the progressive education movement began to take on a more sharply defined identity. After the founding of the Progressive Education Association (PEA) in 1919, ideas of "the new education," as it was called, became increasingly attractive to the educated middle class. The PEA continued to grow, and its journal, *Progressive Education*, spread its ideas to a wider audience. The ideas of the progressive educators at Teachers College were taken up by educators in other universities and professional associations and by some teachers and administrators in public schools. The spread of ideas of progressive education among middle-class liberals needs to be understood in the broader political context of the 1920s. For liberals, the new education was seen as a way to contest the mechanistic and rigid practices of social efficiency that dominated the schools by offering the possibility of liberating what they saw as the natural child.

The progressive education movement in many ways mirrored postwar artists' and intellectuals' broader political alienation from and disillusionment with conservative politics and consumer society. In his classic work *The Transformation of the School,* Lawrence Cremin tied the appeal of progressive education to the individualistic, ironic, artistic world of the 1920s. The 1920s saw the increased dominance of corporate capitalism, which, despite the claims of free market ideology, meant the growth of bureaucracies of all kinds. In this world, the figure of "the individual" was highly charged. The freedom of the individual was a primary demand of conservatives, but in a world increasingly dominated by large corporations and in a bureaucratic public school system that viewed children as a mass to be measured and controlled through testing, what did "the individual" signify? It can certainly be argued that the figure of the child, standing for innocence and potentiality, becomes highly charged for parents in times when their own lives are increasingly shaped by large forces outside their control. The natural child seems both fragile and vulnerable but also a possible source of salvation and regeneration. Through the new education, the freed child could grow up to build a new society.[2]

The ideas of the new education were spread in numerous books and articles on progressive education published in the 1920s. They were taken up by liberal magazines, particularly by the *Nation* and the *New Republic*, and celebrated in a number of popular books claiming the emergence of a new form of education that would liberate the child and provide the foundation for a sounder democracy.[3] With around 30,000 subscribers each in the 1920s, the *Nation* and the *New Republic* were the most widely read and influential left-wing magazines published in the interwar period. In the 1920s, both magazines published articles on education, including Walter Lippman's series of articles in the *New Republic* in 1922, attacking the new movement of standardized intelligence testing and a number of articles on education by John Dewey.

Kilpatrick is often seen as the popularizer of progressive ideas, but in the 1920s John Dewey also wrote for a popular—if limited—audience in both the *New Republic* and the *Nation*. In these articles, Dewey built upon his analysis in *Democracy and Education* to argue that schools needed to offer a challenging and critical education to all students in order to build a strong democracy. Dewey's articles in the *New Republic* were particularly sharp in their criticism of existing classroom pedagogies and their commitment to the need for a politically critical curriculum. In a stinging 1922 article, for example, Dewey wrote that if most students were "walled off from all ideas and information about social affairs save those acquired in school, they would enter upon the responsibilities of social membership in complete ignorance that there are any social problems, any political evils, any industrial defects."[4] In contrast to traditional schools that encouraged this kind of social blindness, he argued, progressive schools should make themselves "dangerous outposts of a humane civilization" and "supremely interesting places."[5]

Although Dewey presented a sharp criticism of traditional public schools and called for a new conception of progressive schools as "dangerous outposts" of both humane values and political critique, most advocates of progressive education in the 1920s celebrated an apolitical depiction of schools as places in which the "natural child" could develop and grow. Such popular books as Edward Yeoman's *Shackled Youth* (1921), Agnes de Lima's *Our Enemy the Child* (1925), Stanwood Cobb's *The New Leaven* (1928), and Harold Rugg and Ann Shumaker's *The Child Centered School* (1928) condemned the dull and deadening world of the traditional public school and described the new education in an almost messianic tone. Central to the vision of the new educators was the claim that creativity and originality exist within each child and will emerge if only the shackles of routine, standardized texts, and rigid classroom practices are lifted. Rugg and Shumaker called the traditional school "the listening school," where "the chief weapons of education are chalk-talk on a dismal blackboard, a few intensely dull required texts, and a teacher's tired voice in continual strident pursuit of elusive young attention."[6] Agnes De Lima described the open structured progressive schools as "natural and intimate," places where children "are given an opportunity to gain experience at first hand, freely and naturally."[7] Reading these popular accounts makes clear the extent to which Corinne Seeds and Helen Heffernan were part of a much broader movement. They were not original thinkers but charismatic leaders who inspired others with their passionate commitment to the new ideas.

A New Movement in Education

Corinne Seeds was converted to the ideas of John Dewey and William Heard Kilpatrick in her time at Teachers College. But she did not immediately put these ideas into practice, even though she returned to Los Angeles "hell bent to see the children have purpose," as she said later.[8] According to her somewhat confusing account of this time in her oral history, she was unable to return to the Avenue 21 School because the principal, Grace Turner, told administrators in the central office that Seeds "wasn't efficient and that [her] father was a member of a labor union."[9] The Grace Turner story was similar to numerous other examples in Seeds's oral history of untrustworthy, powerful women who were "mean" or "jealous" and attempted to thwart Seeds. She told a similar story about Susan Dorsey, the Los Angeles superintendent of schools, who, Seeds said, sabotaged her attempt to become a principal in the Los Angeles schools because her father was a supporter of labor.[10] The themes of these stories of Seeds's early career were repeated over and over again in her narrative of her later life: her commitment to liberal causes because of the influence of her father, the labor man; the opposition of conservatives and businessmen; the jealousy and betrayal of women rivals; and Seeds's eventual triumph.

Whatever the reasons, Seeds did not pass the principals' examination and she did not return to the Avenue 21 School. Instead, she took a position teaching at the Roosevelt Elementary School in Los Angeles. But she did not stay at the Roosevelt School long enough to try out her new ideas. When a fourth grade teacher at the Training School of the Southern Branch of the University of California (formerly the Los Angeles Normal School) unexpectedly resigned, Seeds was offered the position. She left Roosevelt and began teaching fourth grade at the Training School in the fall of 1921. Her appointment marked the beginning of her career at the University of California at Los Angeles.

When Seeds began teaching in the Training School, it was part of the Southern Branch of the University of California, which would later become UCLA. The institutional structure of the Training School was always complex. It was a public school funded by the city of Los Angeles and accountable to the Los Angeles School Board, but it also functioned as a training site for students preparing to become teachers and was accountable to the college administration and ultimately to the regents of the University of California. The principal and teachers were employees of the university.[11] The Training School was strongly supported by Ernest Moore, who had been appointed president of the Normal School in 1917, and by Charles Waddell, who had been named director of teacher training that same year. Both Waddell and Moore considered themselves progressives. Waddell had studied with G. Stanley Hall, while Moore had studied under John Dewey at the University of Chicago and had been active at Hull House.[12] As director of the training school, Waddell encouraged what he saw as progressive innovations, but when Seeds arrived in the fall of 1921, she felt the Training School was still following a traditional approach. Seeds was unimpressed.

At first, according to Seeds's account, she did not really achieve the kind of teaching she hoped for.[13] In a Roman pageant that her class performed, Seeds saw the way forward. The pageant, she recounted, was a mixed success. For one thing, it was cold that day, and Caesar's mother insisted that he wear long underwear under his tunic, which ruined the effect. And when little girls playing Roman maidens scattered rose petals all over the lawn, the head gardener complained to the president, and the children had to return and pick up all the petals. Nonetheless, Seeds remembered the pageant as containing the germ of her future method. In Kilpatrick's terms, the pageant had captured the children's interests and so was a project based on their purposeful acts. But Seeds was still dissatisfied: "They did everything, but the ideas still were not coming strictly from them."[14]

While Seeds was beginning to experiment with progressive pedagogy, Charles Waddell was introducing new practices more characteristic of the "scientific" progressivism of Edward Thorndike. In the 1922–23 school year, he initiated a systematic testing program using an early version of the Stanford-Binet intelligence test.[15] But Waddell was also attracted to the child-centered approach. In the winter of 1923, influenced by Stanwood Cobb's *Atlantic Monthly* article, "A New Movement in Education," Waddell embarked on a one-month trip East to visit progressive schools. On his trip, Waddell visited over twenty schools that were self-consciously experimenting with the new approach, almost all either private schools or university laboratory schools.[16] When Waddell returned to Los Angeles, he encouraged his talented fourth grade teacher, Corinne Seeds, to return to New York to study for her master's degree at Teachers College, Columbia.

In 1924, Seeds returned to Teachers College. Her year in New York only strengthened her passionate commitment to the tenets of the new education. She took Kilpatrick's course on philosophy of education and audited a course given by Dewey. Seeds had had some hearing loss since her childhood, and she recounted later that she didn't trust herself with Dewey "because my ears were too risky."[17] In Kilpatrick's course, she was put in the front of the room, "among the Chinese," so she could hear. She also took a course from Bagley, "the traditionalist whom Dean Russell kept to offset Dewey and Kilpatrick in their staff meetings." Seeds herself always believed in a certain amount of conventional teaching, particularly of mathematics, spelling, and penmanship, but it was Dewey and particularly Kilpatrick who continued to inspire her.

Although Kilpatrick and his ideas have been criticized as derivative and banal, Seeds never seems to have wavered in her admiration for him. And he certainly looked upon her as a disciple. In an interview conducted in the mid-1950s, Kilpatrick was asked if there were still examples of schools using his approach. Kilpatrick replied, "Go to Los Angeles and see the University Elementary School, run by an outstanding Progressivist, Corinne A. Seeds."[18]

In the fall of 1925, when Seeds returned to the Training School with her master's degree, Charles Waddell, who had served as both director of teacher training and director of the Training School, felt he could no longer could manage both jobs. He decided to hire Seeds to replace him. In the fall of 1925, Seeds became principal of the Training School. Waddell later commented: "I thought to myself, here's a good time for me to get some help and let Miss Seeds take over. I regard this decision as one of my greatest contributions to education."[19] Seeds was now in a position to put the ideas of Dewey and Kilpatrick into practice. Waddell had seen the school as a laboratory to demonstrate new methods.[20] But his innovations did not really capture the new methods that were being developed in the schools of the newly formed PEA or that Corinne Seeds had heard described by Kilpatrick at Teachers College. By taking the burden of administrative and bureaucratic work on himself, Waddell left Seeds free to develop and spread her methods through her teaching, writing, speeches, and the summer Demonstration School.

The Move to Westwood

In 1927, the Southern Branch was renamed the University of California at Los Angeles and ground was broken for a new campus in Westwood in West Los Angeles. But when the university moved to Westwood in 1929, no provision had been made for the Training School. Finally the school's supporters convinced the Los Angeles School Board to allow the school to use a site owned by the city on Warner Avenue.[21] The temporary bungalows the school had been housed in at the downtown campus were moved to the Warren Avenue site and both site and bungalows were leased to the university for $1 a year.[22] According to Charles Waddell, there was some opposition to the new location, and "when the day came for the opening of school not a bungalow was on the site. In spite of this we set up a table under the doubtful shade of a young poplar tree and enrolled 225 children."[23] Despite this inauspicious beginning, the school flourished in the new site. It was at this time that the name of the school was changed from the Training School to the University Elementary School (UES).

The move to West Los Angeles had important consequences for Seeds and the approach to progressive education she was developing. The previous site of the Southern Branch had been on Vermont Avenue on the edge of downtown Los Angeles, then a dense cityscape similar to those of eastern cities. But by the mid-1920s Los Angeles was becoming a new kind of city, dependent on the automobile and seemingly limitless suburban development. The population of Los Angeles doubled between 1920 and 1930, from 577,000 to 1.24 million, making it the nation's fifth largest city.[24] There many different centers within the vast geographical area of Los Angeles. Westwood, the new site of the university, was in the then rural area of West Los Angeles, the home of the movie industry, an essential part of the Southern California economy. In 1930, there were fifty-two studios in Los Angeles, employing some 15,000 people.[25] But of course the movies were more than an employer. They defined cultural norms and fed the new culture of media celebrity. What happened to movie stars was news, and what happened in Hollywood and West Los Angeles had an impact that similar events in other areas of the country did not have. West Los Angeles included Hollywood and the suburban and wealthy areas of Beverly Hills and Bel Air, soon to be the home of writers, actors, producers, and émigré Europeans as well as more conventional wealthy professionals and business people. Many of the professionals and intellectuals who moved to the prosperous communities of West Los Angeles were politically liberal. They were fascinated by new movements such as psychoanalysis and sympathetic to progressive and radical political causes; as readers of liberal magazines like the *Nation* and the *New Republic* they would have been well acquainted with the ideas of the new education.

But Los Angeles was also home to deeply conservative groups. The largest open shop city in the nation, Los Angeles was notable for the power of business and the weakness of organized labor. In 1920 Los Angeles had the largest percentage of white, native-born residents of any large U.S. city. Although in the 1930s the population was becoming much more diverse through the internal migration of African Americans from the South and the northward immigration of Mexicans, the idea of Southern California as a "white man's haven" remained strong. In the 1920s, Los Angeles was home to one of the country's largest eugenics movements, a powerful local chapter of the Ku Klux Klan, and newly founded groups such as the Better America Foundation, which worked tirelessly to oppose organized labor and to further conservative business interests.[26] Thus West Los Angeles in 1929 was home to both liberal intellectuals and to conservative and wealthy businessmen who were deeply suspicious of liberal ideas. These were the families, both liberal and conservative, who would send their children to the increasingly prestigious University Elementary School.

By the time of the Training School's move to Westwood, Seeds had developed a clear rationale for the new education. An undated and only partially completed typescript addressed to the residents of Westwood, almost certainly written by Seeds, described the advantages of the new school. The school, which she called "one of the more progressive schools of California," was inspired by "the greatest educational philosophers of the present age, John Dewey and William Kilpatrick of the 'child-centered' or progressive (not extreme progressive) movement."[27] The typescript went on to set out the familiar dichotomy between the traditional and child-centered school, with the traditional school seeking to prepare the child for the future through the acquisition of skills and the memorization of facts, while the child-centered school prepared the child to "live richly here and now and always at each state of life."[28] While the traditional school prepared for autocracy UES as a child-centered school supported the aims of democracy.[29] It is not clear whether this manuscript was ever completed and sent out to prospective Westwood parents, but it is striking both for the clarity of its vision of the curriculum and methods of the school (from which Seeds never deviated) and for its claims for the political consequences of traditional vs. progressive education.

By 1929, when the school changed its name from the Training School to the University Elementary School and moved from Vermont Avenue to the

Warner Avenue site in Westwood, Seeds had clarified her goals for the school and established her leadership. At times UES was spoken of as a laboratory school, but the term is really inappropriate. The school did not explore different philosophies of education or approaches to pedagogy; instead, it came to exemplify one model—Seeds's interpretation of Kilpatrick's project method based on Dewey's philosophy. These methods were spread through the sale of mimeographed papers made available to the public beginning in the late 1920s.[30] UES in essence became a demonstration school, providing students at UCLA the opportunity to see Seeds's version of progressive education in action. As well as serving as principal of the Training School, Seeds was appointed assistant professor in 1928. That same year she began teaching a course in educational methods that came to be required of all students in elementary education.

Objective Measurement of Educational Progress

Like Corinne Seeds, Helen Heffernan moved from classroom teaching to greater responsibilities by the mid-1920s. And, like Seeds, Heffernan first pursued an advanced degree. The semester after she completed her BA at the University of California at Berkeley, she enrolled in a master's degree program—not in political science, her undergraduate major, but in the School of Education. Heffernan's decision to give up political science for education may have reflected both her class and gender position. She had earned her own living as a teacher since she was eighteen and had no family to help support her graduate work. Her experience at the university would hardly have suggested the possibility that she could become a university professor. But as an ambitious and talented young woman with teaching experience, Heffernan could look to a better-paid position in public school administration with a master's degree in education. In the fall of 1923, she took a position as a rural school supervisor in Kings County, continuing to take courses at Berkeley in the summer. She completed her master's degree in December 1924, writing her thesis on the rural schools of Kings County.

In certain ways Heffernan's experiences at the University of California paralleled those of Seeds at Teachers College, particularly around issues of gender. The School of Education at the University of California had been established in 1913, with a gender composition typical of the wider university. From the beginning the faculty was almost exclusively made up of men, while the great majority of the students were women. The most important difference in the graduate experiences of Seeds and Heffernan was the philosophical and political approach they encountered. When Heffernan entered the School of Education, the faculty was overwhelmingly made up of graduates of Teachers College, Columbia University.[31] But these men were not disciples of John Dewey and William Kilpatrick, who so influenced Corinne Seeds. Rather, they were students of Edward Thorndike, head of the Teachers College Department of Educational

Psychology and a leading advocate of scientific measurement and testing. Although John Dewey is doubtless better known today, Thorndike had enormous influence in establishing the legitimacy of educational testing, advocating for the addition of educational psychologists to school staffs, and training disciples who took up positions in schools of education across the United States.

Heffernan's master's thesis, "Objective Measurement of Educational Progress in Country Schools," a study of the rural schools of Kings County where she was employed as a rural school supervisor, not surprisingly reflected the approach she was introduced to in her classes at the University of California.[32] Absent from her bibliography was any work by John Dewey, but also missing was any reference to the work of Mabel Carney, a progressive rural school reformer who later became a friend of Heffernan's and whose influential book, *Country Life and the Country School,* had been published in 1912. By the late 1920s, Carney and Heffernan would become leaders of the progressive rural school reform movement, a movement deeply influenced by Deweyan ideas of democratic education, but if Heffernan was aware of Carney's work in 1924, when her thesis was written, she gave no indication of it.

In "Objective Measurement of Educational Progress in Country Schools," Heffernan sought to establish a scientific basis for the evaluation of teaching. In order to measure this progress, Heffernan tested students in the country schools of Kings County "in the fundamental subjects." She was very concerned to emphasize the objective nature of her study and to explain why standardized testing was needed to measure the effectiveness of rural school supervision.[33] Heffernan's master's thesis is interesting in a number of ways. First, it was very clearly written and well organized; it presaged her later concise and effective memoranda and speeches. Second, and typical of her later work, was her concern to move from research to practice. Last, of course, was her acceptance of the dominant view that learning and teaching could be accurately measured and that greater knowledge on the part of the state would lead to progress. Heffernan's embrace of ideas of scientific method and the need for knowledge and control of students and teachers underlay her recommendations at the end of her thesis. She suggested that a "detailed, scientific study of pupil classification be made by teachers" and that the results of tests be used to make teaching "more economical and effective."[34] What is interesting here is not only the trust in the scientific method and the benevolence of school officials, but also the very terminology that Heffernan used. In using the adjectives "scientific," "economical," "effective," she was speaking through the discourse she had mastered at the School of Education at the University of California, a discourse typical of what David Tyack has called the administrative tradition of progressive school reform.[35] Although Heffernan later embraced a Deweyan vision of education for democracy, she never lost her belief in the value of careful record keeping of children's academic and emotional progress or the state's right to monitor students.

KINGS COUNTY 1922–25

The year Helen Heffernan was hired as a rural school supervisor, 1923, was the first year that Kings County had employed a rural supervisor for general subjects. The position of rural school supervisor had only come into being in California three years earlier.[36] The call for greater supervision of rural teachers was part of the wider nationwide social concern with what was called "the rural school problem." As was true elsewhere, concerns over California rural schools were tied to anxieties about the seeming decline of white Protestant rural culture, the impact of urbanization and immigration, and a general sense of unease about rapid technological and social change. Although rural school supervision may have been initially conceived as a way for the state to gain greater knowledge of what was happening in isolated rural schools and a way to bring modern techniques to what were seen as young and poorly trained teachers, in practice, as is frequently the case with educational reform movements, it had unexpected consequences. One was to create a new professional position—that of rural school supervisor. Although this position had been envisioned as being filled by university-trained men, these jobs tended to be filled by women teachers with experience teaching in rural schools. Rural school supervisors made good salaries— double that of most classroom teachers.

When Helen Heffernan took her job as a rural school supervisor in Kings County, she was moving into a new, better-paid, more autonomous, and more prestigious position. Immediately after she was hired and moved to Hanford, the county seat, Heffernan bought a car, a 1923 Chevrolet, paying it off in monthly installments of $44.80. She clearly need the car in order to visit schools as a rural school supervisor, but for her, as for other women in the 1920s, the car surely also would have strengthened her sense of independence and competence.[37] Heffernan was hired by the Kings County superintendent of schools, Miss Lee Richmond, who herself embodied both traditional small-town values and a commitment to modern, progressive ideas of rural school reform.

Lee Richmond became a life-long friend. Throughout her life, Helen Heffernan's emotional world revolved around intense relationships with women. The only account we have of her relationship with Lee Richmond is a note from Richmond included in Heffernan's personal papers. Richmond wrote to "Dear Miss Heffernan": "I was very much surprised and not a little disappointed at your sudden departure. However, it is perhaps just as well. You have not really had any vacation, and every one needs some holiday time.... I am sure that you and Mrs. Archer had a lovely trip back. I am sorry not to have seen more of Mrs. Archer. She seemed very interesting." The note was signed, "Very sincerely and cordially yours, M. L. Richmond."[38] This brief note raises a number of questions. First of all, there is the question of why Helen Heffernan kept it all those years. The note is found in a box containing other letters and notes from close women friends, many of them attesting to close emotional attachment. Why did Lee Richmond say she was "disappointed" at Heffernan's sudden departure? And who was Mrs. Archer, who seemed so interesting? This note seems suggestive in part because there is so little evidence of Heffernan's personal life in these years, but also because it is typical of the pattern of close personal ties with women that defined Heffernan's later life.

Whatever the nature of her personal and emotional life, Heffernan's energy and professional abilities were soon evident. She was an active participant in the California Rural Supervisors Association. In 1924 she began a preservice education program for teachers at Fresno State Teachers College in which student teachers completed their teaching practicum in Kings County.[39] In the fall of 1925 she taught an evening course entitled "Rural School Problems" for Kings County teachers. According to her description of her work as rural supervisor in her master's thesis, Heffernan visited every schoolroom in Kings County an average of ten times in the school year, holding individual and group conferences; she also taught extension courses, and held office hours from nine to twelve every Saturday morning.[40] The success of the Kings County schools was noted by California commissioner of rural education Mamie Lang. After her visit to the county in 1926, Lang wrote to Richmond that the county's "system of supervision is splendid. The latest and most up-to-date methods are being used. The educational surveys and classification of pupils are very worth while pieces of work and reflect much credit upon the department.... The work of Miss Heffernan is fine."[41]

In 1924, Heffernan was a founding member of the California Rural Supervisors Association, a group that would provide her with a network of supportive and like-minded colleagues throughout the state. At its inception, the California Rural School Supervisors Association had just over one hundred members, thirty-three men and seventy-five women. This ratio of men and women supervisors remained roughly the same throughout the 1920s and 1930s until 1936, when the Rural School Supervisors Association was disbanded and incorporated into the California School Supervisors Association, a group that included both rural and urban supervisors. Women dominated the Rural School Supervisors Association. At the 1926 annual convention, for example, eleven of the twelve speakers were women, as was the president of the organization, Ethel Ward. This gender balance can be compared to the California Teachers Association, in which men predominated in leadership positions and as speakers at annual conventions.[42]

In 1926, State commissioner of elementary education Mamie Lang died in an automobile accident. The position of commissioner of elementary education had been held by a woman since it was established in 1914, doubtless reflecting the view that elementary teaching was women's work. Nonetheless, when Mamie Lang died, a number of men as well as women were invited to apply for the position, including Charles Waddell, head of teacher training at the University of California at Los Angeles, and Roy Cloud, who later became president of the California Teachers Association. That Helen Heffernan was also invited to apply was a remarkable tribute to her accomplishments in only three years in Kings County. Heffernan later frequently told the story of her interview, claiming she got the job because she had spent forty dollars on a new hat. The new hat may or may not have mattered, and the fact that the position had been viewed as a woman's job doubtless helped her. Still, surely the deciding factor must have been her recommendations and performance at the interview. Despite her young age and relatively limited experience, she was appointed to the position of overseeing all the public elementary schools in California.

Commissioner of Elementary Education

Helen Heffernan was just thirty years old in 1926 when she was appointed commissioner of elementary education for the state of California. Heffernan's formative years had been spent in small towns and cities in the mining and farming West. Now she was a key official in a complex and rapidly urbanizing state. Heffernan's activities in her first few years in office showed the energy and initiative that would mark her public career for forty years. A major part of her time was spent visiting schools, speaking at institutes, conferences, and teachers colleges across the state. Beginning in 1927, she began teaching in summer schools. Throughout her career she continued her summer teaching: at Caroline Swope's private summer school for teachers, at Stanford, the University of California at Berkeley, San Francisco State, and later with Corinne Seeds at UCLA.[43] Soon after her appointment as state commissioner of education, she became involved with national organizations and activities. Between 1927 and 1931 she participated in National Education Association (NEA) and PEA conferences in Dallas, Boston, Minneapolis, St. Louis, Detroit, Atlanta, and Atlantic City and conducted workshops in Nevada, Utah, Idaho, and Oregon.[44]

When she began her tenure as commissioner of elementary schools, Heffernan was most concerned with rural school reform, not surprisingly given her experience as a teacher and rural school supervisor. Building upon her work in Kings County and her contacts with the Rural Supervisors Association, in her first few years as commissioner Heffernan focused on the supervision of rural teachers and founding new organizations and means of communication for teachers, principals, and supervisors. Her talent for creating networks of like-minded educators and for inspiring teachers was immediately apparent. One school superintendent remembered that "she could listen...to sixty persons introduce themselves and tell [about] the school district in which they worked. From then on she would call each by name, and...talk about what was going on in each of the districts! She never forgot a name, a face, or a situation."[45]

Upon taking office, Heffernan looked first for support to the rural supervisors and superintendents she had known during her years in Kings County. Describing the October 1926 meeting of the California Rural School Supervisors Association, Beulah Hartman, secretary-treasurer of the association, wrote, "We have met Miss Heffernan at all meetings of the association in which she has taken an active part and have come to know her. Supervisors throughout the state rejoiced to have one of 'their own' chosen for this high honor."[46] The members of the Rural School Supervisors Association were Heffernan's earliest supporters and formed the nucleus of the network of educators who continued to support her through the years.

One of Heffernan's first official actions was to establish the *California Exchange Bulletin in Rural Education,* which began publication in November 1926. The *California Exchange Bulletin in Rural Education* was intended to be a forum for the exchange of ideas between classroom teachers and rural supervisors. In practice, as might have been expected, most of the pieces published in the *Exchange Bulletin* were written by Heffernan, members of her office, or by university professors, country superintendents, and rural school supervisors sympathetic to her views. Although the *Exchange Bulletin* did not turn into a forum for the voices of classroom teachers as Heffernan had hoped, it was a means of introducing the democratic and progressive ideas she was beginning to embrace. Various articles in the *Exchange Bulletin* advocated the project method popularized by William Heard Kilpatrick and celebrated the advantages of the one-room school for more open and creative teaching.[47] When the *California Exchange Bulletin in Rural Education* ceased publication, Heffernan introduced a monthly column in the *Western Journal of Education* called "Department of Rural Education," which ran from 1928 to 1929. Heffernan wrote some of these columns; others were written by supervisors and teachers with her encouragement.

Within a few years, Heffernan moved from a focus on rural schools to a broader concern with urban as well as rural classrooms. And, although she retained her belief in the need to monitor children's progress and to provide guidance, she also moved beyond the Thorndike tradition of scientific measurement and testing she had been introduced to at Berkeley to become a strong advocate of the new education. The impact of these new ideas and the evolution of Heffernan's own thinking can be followed in her columns in the *Western Journal of Education* as well as in her speeches from the late 1920s. Heffernan now frequently cited nationally known progressive educators. In her discussion of the "pupil-directed" rural school in the December 1929 issue of the *Western Journal of Education,* for example, Heffernan noted that there were many models for this kind of school, citing Evelyn Dewey's *New Schools for Old*, Ellsworth Collings's "Experiment with the Project Curriculum," and Fanny Dunn and Marcia Everett's *Four Years in a Country School*.[48] Heffernan repeated her vision of progressive education in a number of speeches she gave in 1929. She described California schools as "voluntarily putting themselves through a metamorphosis from the old type of education to the new."[49]

In 1930, Heffernan organized five regional conferences for the elementary administrators of the state—740 supervising principals or district superintendents and 1600 teaching principals—in order to encourage this group to "stimulate and promote a progressive program of elementary education."⁵⁰ In a 1929 address given at the Rural School Supervisors Conference, Heffernan emphasized the advantages of the small rural school for progressive practices. Heffernan herself loved gardens and the natural landscape of California. She argued that the natural environment, with its "trees, crops, fruit, flowers, birds and animals," had not been adequately explored. With the guidance of a sympathetic teacher, the country child could "be led to appreciate the beauty in the natural environment—the honey colored hills, a row of dancing eucalyptus, the delicate tracery of early spring growth on the vines."⁵¹ The open spaces surrounding country schools allowed for games and activities in the fresh air that would build healthy bodies in country children, while the natural beauty of California would inspire their creativity and joy.

Heffernan was aware that not all rural children were equally able to enjoy the natural beauty of California—most obviously the children of migrant agricultural workers. Schooling for migrant children became a problem for California educators in the 1920s, with the influx of Mexican families working as migrant farmworkers. Earlier, most migrant farmworkers were single men, usually Asian or Mexican, but by the late 1920s, families, primarily from Mexico, were increasingly employed as farmworkers. These families moved throughout the West, following the crops.⁵² In 1928, Lillian Hill, chief of the California Bureau of Attendance and Migratory Schools (formerly the Commission on Immigration and Housing), estimated that there were 40,000 children of migratory workers in California, moving from school to school; most of these children spoke Spanish.⁵³ One teacher noted that her school, formally called a School for Migratory Children, was commonly referred to as the "Mexican cotton school."⁵⁴

Heffernan first expressed concern about these children in a 1929 article in the *Western Journal of Education,* where she wrote that no problem facing California was more pressing "than that of providing education for migratory children...This problem is a challenge to the humanitarian impulses of growers, citizens, and educators. Shall these children, deprived of a children's right to a home, also be neglected and allowed to suffer educational deprivation?"⁵⁵ Heffernan's depiction of these children was sympathetic, but she did not address the practice of segregating them from other children, a practice widespread across the state. School officials across the state tended to justify the practice of segregation not only on grounds of language, but also because of assumptions about Mexican children's intellectual inferiority. As Alexandra Stern has documented, eugenicist ideas of the supposed mental inferiority of children of Mexican descent and the widespread use of IQ testing were used to justify the establishment of "Mexican schools" and the shunting of Mexican children into vocational tracks throughout these years.⁵⁶ In other communities, Japanese children were put in separate schools simply because of their race. Although she spoke eloquently of the poverty faced by rural migrant children and the responsibility of the state to meet their needs, Heffernan did not directly address the issues of racism and segregation until the 1940s.

National Activities

In the late 1920s, Heffernan became increasingly active in national organizations. She was more and more in demand as a speaker. In June 1930, she gave an invited address to the National Congress of Parents and Teachers Conference in Columbus, Ohio, on "Parent Education as a Function of the School." Also in the spring of 1930 she participated in a three-day conference on the topic of education and mental hygiene sponsored by the Julius Rosenwald Fund at Hot Springs, Virginia. Heffernan was one of a handful of public school officials present. Most of the other participants were university professors (including Harold Rugg and William Heard Kilpatrick) or heads of private progressive schools.[57] This invitation to the Hot Springs conference was a clear sign of her growing visibility in the progressive education movement.

In 1930, Heffernan was elected president of the Division of Rural Education of the NEA.[58] The most prominent woman in the Division was Mabel Carney, the head of the Department of Rural Education at Teachers College, Columbia, who in 1929 became the first woman to be elected president.[59] During Heffernan's presidency, over half the presentations of the Rural Education Division—sixteen of twenty-nine—were by women speakers. Perhaps even more striking in that year were the number of presentations using the word "progressive" in their titles.[60] In 1931, a Committee on Resolutions of the Rural Education Section headed by Mabel Carney inserted its report into the NEA's Addresses and Proceedings. The report concluded by endorsing two basic principles—progressive or child-centered education and "the responsibility of the state for the adequate education of all its children both rural and urban." It concluded by expressing "our special appreciation of the untiring efforts of our President, Miss Helen Heffernan, in making this convention...a notable contribution to the history and achievement of the Department."[61]

Heffernan and Seeds: First Contacts

By 1930, Corinne Seeds and Helen Heffernan were following parallel but separate paths. At UES, Seeds was gathering a supportive faculty around her and developing the methods and curriculum for which she became renowned. While Seeds was developing her interpretation of what progressive education meant in practice in her own school, Heffernan was spreading the word through her speeches, publications, and workshops at the statewide level. The two must have been aware of each other's work, but they do not seem to have met until the late 1920s or early 1930s. The only mention of their first meeting is in Seeds's oral history. In Seeds's account, she first saw Heffernan during the UCLA Summer School:

> For a long time, we didn't seem to have anything in common to share, but finally, one summer during the summer session, she visited the University.... She

came to the University to give a talk on training and she didn't know as much as we did....Well, we all sat there in Royce Hall and looked at this very, very handsome and beautiful woman. Her dress was made from un-cut velvet, and it was cerise color. Of course, we thought she was very poorly dressed to make a business speech and, just like a lot of kittens, you know, we just discussed her and made up our minds, I guess, that we didn't like her very well.[62]

Given the similarity of their writings and speeches of this period, Seeds's comment that "we didn't have anything in common to share" surely referred more to personality than to philosophy.

It is not clear when Seeds and Heffernan first met, but they came into contact around the 1930 volume, *The Teachers' Guide to Child Development*, a book prepared by the California Curriculum Commission and published by the State Department of Education.[63] The California *Guide* is an early example of the innovative curriculum bulletins published by a number of states in the 1930s.[64] Its publication provides a kind of benchmark of the ascendancy of progressive education in California. The *Guide* was a celebration of the new education and included the work of teachers, supervisors, and university professors throughout the state who were attempting to put the ideas of progressive education into practice in public school classrooms. Ethel Salisbury and Francis Giddings contributed chapters describing the work of the UES. Although she was not an author, Corinne Seeds was cited as the source of the programs and activities of the school.

The Teachers' Guide to Child Development was not really about child development. It was essentially a guide to organizing kindergarten and primary classrooms around "the activity program," justified by a psychological theory of children's emotional and cognitive growth. The suggested readings for teachers included the classics of the movement, including Rugg and Shumaker's *The Child-Centered School,* John Dewey's *School and Society* and *The Child and the Curriculum,* Stanwood Cobb's *The New Leaven,* and pamphlets describing specific activities published by the Lincoln School at Teachers College and the Francis Parker School in Chicago. *The Teachers' Guide to Child Development* was not a state course of study to be imposed upon teachers. Instead, the introduction stated: "It is hoped that teachers will find it not something imposed upon them or required of them, but a sincere, conscientious attempt of a group of fellow teachers to cooperate in the development of a reliable point of view and of greater professional skill."[65]

In many ways, *The Teachers' Guide to Child Development* remains a stimulating volume. The descriptions of classrooms, the argument that teachers themselves must master a wide range of material and be conscious of the needs of individual children, and the examples of projects and activities remain fresh and pertinent. But the *Guide*, like many of the texts advocating child-centered schools of this period, is also striking in its assumption that the classroom is a self-contained world in which all children will respond in the same basic manner to the opportunities presented to them. There was no discussion of class conflict or privilege, poverty, race or racism, sexism or gender. "The child" was generic; the activities assumed to be appropriate for all children. On the one hand, this absence of assumptions about children is refreshing. There were few claims that certain children "learn differently" because of their gender or ethnicity, that they are innately lacking because of their social location and identity. On the other hand, California in 1930 was hardly an egalitarian utopia. It was profoundly shaped by racism, class differences were extreme, domestic violence and the objectification of women were as widespread as today, and white men controlled virtually all aspects of politics and the economy. But in the *Teachers' Guide,* as in virtually all the discussions of progressive classrooms in this period, children were imagined as somehow untouched by these forces. There was no indication that children themselves might bring any of the violence, privilege, or oppression of the larger society into the classroom.

The Teachers' Guide to Child Development included accounts of a wide range of schools and communities and was illustrated by many photographs. While the classrooms from the majority of urban and suburban districts tended to show well-dressed white children, those from rural schools and from the Bridge School in Los Angeles included Mexican and African American children, many of whom showed signs of poverty. But these social and economic differences were not acknowledged or questioned; they were simply presented as the way the world is. The one place in the *Teachers' Guide* in which cultural and social difference was acknowledged was in the section "A Developmental Program of Activities for the Language Handicapped Child." In many ways, this section reflected commonly held assumptions about immigrant, non-English-speaking children. Assuming a culture of poverty, the homes of these children were described as "inadequate, unattractive, ill-fitted to provide experiences and materials which will result in their all-round development."[66] Thus these children entered school with a double disadvantage: their families had not provided them with adequate "experiences and materials," and they did not speak English. On the other hand, the children themselves were presented as having the ability to overcome these disadvantages. The writer of this section noted that anyone who has tried to learn another language knows how difficult it is. The teacher should acquaint herself with the "home life, environment, racial interests, and customs of her group. It will be of great help to her also to know their racial history, and something of their great achievements." And for the only time in the *Teachers' Guide,* racism was acknowledged: "Teachers who are troubled by feelings of race prejudice should not undertake to guide such groups unless they are sure these feelings can be overcome."[67]

The Teachers' Guide to Child Development reflected the limited attention to race and class typical of white progressive education of the time, but it was also a considerable achievement and was probably the first publication from a State Department of Education advocating the adoption of progressive methods by all public school teachers. Corinne Seeds might have been expected to welcome and celebrate the publication of the *Guide.* But Seeds had serious reservations. In a typescript of what seems to have been a speech delivered to an audience of teachers soon after the publication of *The Teachers' Guide to Child Development,* Seeds presented her own critique.[68] Seeds made a point of recognizing the achievement of the *Guide,* calling it "the finest piece of cooperative work that has yet appeared in the country from a State Dep't of Ed."[69] Nonetheless, Seeds had criticisms. Her main complaint was that the classroom activities described were too controlled and directed by the teacher and too focused on outcomes rather than the process of learning. Seeds's critique of *The Teachers' Guide to Child Development* does not seem to have been well received by Helen Heffernan. According to Seeds in her oral history, despite Seeds's praise for the overall accomplishments of the *Teachers' Guide,* Heffernan was deeply hurt by Seeds's criticism, and "then it took years, just years, for things to settle down, and I didn't care."[70]

Conclusion

Heffernan and Seeds had both accomplished a great deal by 1930. According to the *Western Journal of Education, The Teachers' Guide to Child Development* was "a monumental work" whose success was primarily due to the direction provided by Helen Heffernan.[71] And by 1930, Corinne Seeds was firmly in control of the newly located University Elelmentary School in Westwood. Supported by Charles Waddell, she was actively engaged in implementing her version of the activity or project method, which came to be called units-of-work. Increasingly, the achievements of Seeds and Heffernan were recognized both within California and nationally.

Seeds and Heffernan were charismatic figures. Of the two, Seeds was at the same time more theoretical and more concerned with pedagogy. Heffernan was a powerful speaker and clearly a gifted institution builder. Neither was really an innovator. Seeds attempted to put into practice the ideas that she had first encountered at Teachers College, while Heffernan was influenced by the embrace of the new education in the liberal press and in the work of progressive rural educators like Fannie Dunn, Marcia Everett, Mabel Carney, and Elsie Ridley Clapp.[72] In their first few years in positions of power and influence, Seeds and Heffernan became passionate advocates of the new education and built the institutional foundations to support the approach that they would continue to defend throughout their careers. By 1930, each of them had become committed to the child-centered and democratic wing of the progressive education movement. Although their work centered on the lives of children, it was already evident and would soon become even clearer that their work was in every sense political.

CHAPTER 3

Dare the School Build a New Social Order?

The Depression of the 1930s led many Americans to reconsider the nature of their political, social, and economic institutions. In California, the social and economic crisis of the Depression raised significant challenges for Corinne Seeds and Helen Heffernan, including financial cutbacks, the beginning of attacks from conservatives, and the need to respond to the entry of increasing numbers of impoverished children into the schools.[1] As was true throughout the United States, California was deeply affected by the Depression: local economies suffered, tax revenues shrank, and unemployment reached extraordinary levels. But unlike the Midwest or East, California also experienced an influx of migrants from other states seeking work in its rich agricultural counties, a migration documented by such well-known figures as Dorothea Lange, John Steinbeck, and Carey McWilliams. Through Lange's photographs and the 1940 film "The Grapes of Wrath," images of white migrant farmworkers became icons of the Depression. At the same time, under the New Deal, California received substantial federal aid; it was the site of large public works projects such as the Golden Gate and Bay Bridges in San Francisco and was the recipient of federally supported programs for the unemployed, farmworkers, and children. This increased federal aid led to an increased federal presence and influence in the state.

Nationally, progressive education underwent significant changes in response to the crisis. In these years it took on a more political cast, particularly through the influence of a group of left-leaning professors at Teachers College who formed what came to be known as the social reconstructionist movement. Along with Dewey and Kilpatrick, the two best-known members of the movement were probably Harold Rugg and George Counts. The stock market crash of 1929 and the onset of worldwide depression led members of the group to have deepening doubts about capitalism and to consider more radical conceptions of how education might help create an alternative social order. In February 1932, at the PEA convention in Baltimore, George Counts delivered his speech "Dare Progressive Education Be Progressive?" in which he attacked the lack of social and political commitment of the PEA. Later that year, Counts spoke before the NEA and the National Council of Education on the topic "Dare the School Build a New Social Order?" Counts subsequently published a pamphlet under the same name. In it he proclaimed that if it were truly progressive, progressive education would "emancipate itself from the influence of [the ruling class], face squarely and courageously every social issue, come to grips with life in all of its stark reality, establish an organic relation with the community, develop a realistic and comprehensive theory of welfare, fashion a compelling and challenging vision of human destiny, and become less frightened than it is today at the bogies of imposition and indoctrination."[2] The immediate response to Counts's speeches was dramatic. The PEA formed a committee on social and economic problems with Counts as chair. The committee issued "A Call to the Teachers of the Nation" (1933), urging teachers to "throw off their slave mentality."[3] "Dare the School Build a New Social Order?" proclaimed a radical shift to the left in educational thinking.

The Division of Rural and Elementary Education

Like many other progressive educators, Helen Heffernan began to explore more radical political ideas in the early 1930s. At the Department of Education, Heffernan reported directly to the elected state superintendent of public instruction, Vierling Kersey, but although Kersey was her immediate superior and she was supposed to carry out his suggestions and orders, in practice she seems to have had almost complete autonomy to shape the state's elementary program. Heffernan's influence was spread not only through her speeches and public appearances across the state, but also through the pamphlets, journals, and bulletins published by the State Department of Education and made available free to all classroom teachers. By the early 1930s, these publications, which had enthusiastically promulgated the ideas of the new education of the '20s, began to reflect the more critical stance of the social reconstructionists in response to the crisis of the Depression. In the summer of 1933, for example, Heffernan wrote to Kersey, recommending that the department's magazine for teachers, *California Schools,* include an article on "California's answer to the challenge: 'Dare the School Build a New Social Order?'"[4]

Heffernan herself vigorously defended a democratic conception of education. In a 1932 speech, "Interpreting the School Program to the Public," Heffernan attacked what she saw as "insidious" elitist views that questioned all children's right to a challenging education. She asked: "Must we accept the aristocratic division of people into two classes, one of which can be trained to understand while the other is doomed by its own incapacity to remain forever outside the field of intelligence?"[5] Instead, she argued that all children must have access to a challenging curriculum. She wrote, "Much new material must be introduced to interpret the essential ideals of a democratic society.... Educational progress demands the right of teachers to present all the facts on vital and controversial issues in American life; American youth should be guaranteed the right to learn all the pertinent facts and upon them to make their own judgments."[6] Just as in the 1920s she used the phrases of John Dewey, in 1932 in the depths of the Depression, Heffernan took up Counts's call for the schools to build a new democratic social order.

Although Heffernan was an eloquent speaker and proclaimed the need for schools to contribute to social transformation, she remained an employee of the California State Department of Education and worked within its bureaucratic structure. The Department of Education had undergone a number of organizational changes in the late 1920s, but throughout Heffernan had retained her position of leadership. In 1931, the Department of Education was again reorganized and Heffernan's title changed from chief of the Division of Rural Education to chief of the Division of Elementary and Rural Education. With the 1931 reorganization, Heffernan's attention moved from her initial concern with rural school reform to include urban schools as well. As part of the reorganization, Heffernan added an assistant division chief, Gladys Potter, formerly a rural supervisor from San Bernardino County.

The activities of the Division of Elementary and Rural Education were wide reaching. By 1932, there were over 780,000 children in 4,052 elementary schools in California, taught by 24,000 teachers. In the broadest sense, Heffernan was responsible for overseeing the work of all of these teachers. A list of the professional relationships Heffernan maintained as division chief shows the complexity of her position. She was to stay in close contact with the other nine departments within the state bureaucracy, but also to reach out to professionals in the field—superintendents, supervisors, principals, and teachers—as well as to lay groups such as the Parent Teachers Association, the American Association of University Women, the Daughters of the American Revolution, and religious organizations.[7] Heffernan kept up a challenging schedule of activities in the 1930s, organizing conferences, encouraging the progressive transformation of the curriculum, supporting rural demonstration schools, writing, and speaking at institutes and conferences across the state and nation. For the first time, she also moved into an international arena, traveling to Mexico in 1932 to study Mexican rural education.

Heffernan's progressive vision for the future of California education was evident in several presentations she gave at the Annual Convention of Superintendents and Rural Supervisors held at the Fairmont Hotel in San Francisco in October 1932. The program of the convention overall reflected the impact of George Counts's electrifying speech to the NEA that year. At the convention, talk of the "new education" and of the need for "reconstruction" was widespread. Even Superintendent Vierling Kersey, a Republican and member of the Optimist Club, the Masons, and the Sons of the Revolution, spoke approvingly of the state's "new educational program" that sought to address the "social demands of contemporary life."[8]

Support for the schools remained strong in California, even in the darkest days of the Depression. In the early 1930s, a number of groups, including the California Taxpayers Association, demanded cuts in funding for education.[9] Opposition was led by the California Teachers Association, local school administrators, and the State Department of Education. These groups organized to support Proposition One, which transferred the bulk of fiscal responsibility for the schools from the local districts to the state. Voters passed Proposition One in June 1933. To meet this new obligation, the state instituted a series of new taxes that provided a relatively strong base for public education for the rest of the decade. Although California teachers suffered a decline in salaries in the Depression, schools were not forced to close and few teachers lost their jobs.

Throughout the 1930s, Heffernan maintained close ties with women superintendents and rural supervisors across the state. The Rural Supervisors Association continued to be her strongest source of support. An account of the group's 1931 convention at Riverside in the *Western Journal of Education* captures something of the atmosphere of this close-knit organization and of Heffernan's sociability and enjoyment of like-minded friends and colleagues: "Helen Heffernan was the life of the party at the Mission Inn and the several hundred rural supervisors of the state who were present enjoyed her talks, and are in hearty sympathy with her progressive program for the improvement of the rural school."[10] Heffernan clearly had a powerful personality and had intense personal relationships. Although she did not leave a diary and there are few remaining personal letters written by her, the letters written to her provide evidence of the strong emotional responses she called forth.

The letters from the 1920s and early 1930s are scanty compared with those from the 1940s, and it is impossible to know the nature of the relationships described in them, in part because we do not have Heffernan's side of the correspondences, but the letters that remain certainly suggest deep emotions. For example, one of Heffernan's colleagues at the Department of Education was Lillian Hill, the chief of the Bureau of Attendance and Migratory Schools. Hill and Heffernan frequently appeared on the programs of state conferences and shared similar concerns. Hill's letters to Heffernan suggest a deeper personal involvement than just an interest in the schooling of migrant children. One letter began: "I haven't had any news, haven't seen anyone and all I know is that I love you and wish you were here."[11] In another letter Hill wrote, "It seems ages since you went away, and it's only two days, I wonder if it seems as long to you as it does to me. I shall be very glad when this long dreaded trip is over and you are home again. Will you, love girl?" After some discussion of events in the Department of Education, the letter ends, "I love you and want you every minute of the day and night."[12] While women expressed their love for one another in these years with much less self-consciousness than is true today, the tone of these letters is quite different from other letters Heffernan received from colleagues.

Personal correspondence from this period in Heffernan's papers also includes four letters written in October 1933 from an unnamed correspondent (the letters are not signed). It is unclear whether they were from a man or a woman. The letters were addressed either to "Darling girl" or to "Darling." Internal references suggest that the writer was either a state official or perhaps a representative of a publishing company. They begin with a description of trips taken, everyday chores, a "Supts convention" and contain references to textbooks. But the letters quickly change tone. One letter continued, "I'm so anxious to see you and talk that I can't think of it too much. I never in all my life have ever wanted to see anyone a thousandth part as much as I want to see you."[13] With the exception of these unsigned letters (which may also have been from a woman), all of the romantic letters in the Heffernan papers are from women who were educators or closely involved with education. It was widely known that Heffernan had attracted a large and loyal following across the state, mostly among women, but the intensity of her personal relationships was kept private.

THE CALIFORNIA JOURNAL OF ELEMENTARY EDUCATION

In 1932, Heffernan initiated a new journal, the *California Journal of Elementary Education*, which replaced the earlier outlets for her ideas, the *Exchange Bulletin in Rural Education* and her monthly column on rural education in the *Western Journal of Education*. The *California Journal of Elementary Education* was more ambitious than the earlier publications. The influence of the social reconstructionists and the new education on the *California Journal of Elementary Education* was evident from the beginning. In "A Statement of the Philosophy and the Purposes of the Elementary School," the first of many articles she would publish in the journal, Heffernan stated the political stance that would guide the journal for the next thirty years. She began: "The philosophy of John Dewey is basic in the thought and practice of most advanced schools today. He maintains that education is life; education is growth; education is a social process; and education is a continuous reconstruction of experience."[14] Other articles in the *California Journal of Elementary Education* reinforced Heffernan's progressive stance. The August 1933 issue included an excerpt from George Counts's "A Call to the Teachers of the Nation," demanding that teachers "emancipate themselves completely from the domination of the business interests of the nation."

Beginning in 1934, the journal began to publish articles describing the exemplary work of UES That year, Corinne Seeds's article "An Interpretation of the Integrated Program in the Elementary School," summarizing the work of UES, appeared.[15] In February 1935, Natalie White's "Painting in the Schools as One More Means of Sharing Worthwhile Experiences" described the role of art in the UES curriculum, and in May 1935, Laverna Lossing explored the use of music.[16] In November 1935, Elizabeth Bruene, a counselor at UES, published an article called "The Activity Procedure and the Fundamentals," describing the results of the new Stanford Achievement Test given to UES children in May 1934.[17] Corinne Seeds contributed two more articles—"The School and its Task" in 1937 and "Next Steps in the Preparation of Teachers" in 1938.[18]

Building the "Kingdom of God" in Westwood

By the early 1930s, UES was well established in its new location in Westwood. With the support of Provost Ernest Moore and Charles Waddell, Seeds was in complete control of the school. In her 1932–33 report to Waddell, Seeds provided a sweeping vision of her work. In her school, she wrote, children were building a small society, "providing for the acquisition of attitudes which will urge and compel social reconstruction for the good of each and all, knowledge of what is necessary for such social improvement and techniques which bring about successful group living—all of which eventually must make changes for the good in this, our world."[19] One of the most important venues for spreading Seeds's ideas was the annual UCLA summer session.[20] Students at the Summer School observed classes at the summer demonstration program at UES and took two courses taught by Corinne Seeds—Education 131A and 131B. These two courses were versions of Seeds's course ED 390, which introduced the progressive method based on units-of-work to undergraduate UCLA students in elementary education during the regular academic year. In his 1932–33 and 1933–34 reports to the Provost, Waddell wrote glowing accounts of the school's progress "under the splendid leadership of our principal, Miss Seeds." The University Elementary School was becoming increasingly well known throughout the state and the nation.[21]

Seeds began to publish accounts of her method in the early 1930s. Her most significant achievement in this period was the 1932 publication of *Major Units in the Social Studies,* which she coauthored with Charles Waddell and Natalie White.[22] *Major Units in the Social Studies* began with introductory chapters by Waddell and Seeds on the "Point of View" of the school. In a list of "some of the writings which have been particularly helpful in shaping this point of view," Seeds and Waddell included five works by Dewey, including "Progressive Education and the Science of Education," the six articles in the *New Republic* series "The New Education Ten Years After," and four pieces by Kilpatrick, including his major work *Foundations of Method.*[23] Waddell and Seeds's introduction was followed by chapters on art, music, and rhythmic expression, then by three chapters on specific units-of-work that had been developed at UES for fourth, fifth, and six grades. These three chapters included a detailed discussion of materials and resources, transcriptions of the conversations between students and teachers, and a description of the children's activities. The fourth graders made paper and miniature Chinese houses, read stories, learned songs, and prepared Chinese foods; the fifth graders built an 8x10 foot log cabin; the sixth graders studied aeronautics and created model gliders and a hot air balloon. In all three of these units, the children read extensively and produced both creative and academic writing.

As well as providing detailed examples of actual classroom units, *Major Units in the Social Studies* set out the school's philosophical and political goals. In her chapter, "Our Present Educational Point of View," Seeds cited the problem of unemployment, the need to abolish war, "Nationalism versus

'Worldism,'" and the "crises brought about in the struggle between Labor and Capital." For her, the solution to these problems was only to be found in educating a new generation in schools where they would "learn to solve the problems which arise in their group and individual living in an unselfish, thinking way."[24] She also set out her demanding expectations of teachers. Seeds wrote that teaching should be chosen "only by those who can truly say with genuine feeling, 'My teaching is my life. Through it I find my greatest satisfaction, joy and happiness'—only those should enter into this profession, the members of which should always strive to be 'prophets of the true God and Sharers in of the true kingdom of God.'"[25] This last phrase was from Dewey's "My Pedagogic Creed."

Personal and Professional Relationships

Seeds was a charismatic figure, but her work at UES would not have been possible without the support of a nucleus of women educators who were close to her both personally and professionally. The faculty at UES were all women, many of whom had worked with Seeds for years. The most influential members of her staff were probably Natalie White, who taught art and had coauthored *Major Units in the Social Studies* with Seeds and Waddell, and Diana Anderson, who taught physical education at UES between 1931 and 1958. Anderson, who was interviewed in 1988, when she was ninety-seven, praised Seeds's vision of education, but added, "It was a challenge to teach there...[It was] not exactly easy under Corinne Seeds."[26] Also closely associated with UES was Martha Deane, who taught dance in the Physical Education Department. Following Seeds's suggestion, in the mid-1920s Deane had studied at Teachers College with Kilpatrick. When she returned to UCLA, Deane applied the ideas she encountered at Teachers College to dance and creative movement; in 1933 Seeds asked if Deane could be assigned to work with UES.[27] Deane subsequently worked with teachers and students at UES for many years, although she was never a full-time member of the staff.

The women of UES had close personal and professional ties. Seeds, White, Deane, and Anderson remained single all their lives. Despite the beginnings of fears about "mannish lesbians" and the spread of Freudian ideas, single women teachers like the women of UES were still able to live with other women and move in a women's social world in the early 1930s, in part because their professional identity had been established earlier, and in part perhaps because in the public imagination respectable middle-aged professional women were asexual. Seeds continued to share a home with her parents, who in 1933 moved from Pasadena to 1416 Holmby Avenue in Los Angeles, doubtless to be closer to Seeds's work at UCLA. But other UES teachers shared households with one another. Helen White lived for many years with Helen Read, another UES teacher. Seeds herself may have had a close emotional relationship with Diana Anderson. But Seeds's circle of friends in the early 1930s did not include Helen Heffernan, even though it is obvious, comparing Heffernan's speeches, articles, and editorials in the *California Journal of Elementary Education* with Seeds's writings, that Heffernan and Seeds were natural allies. They relied on the same figures for inspiration, often used the same phrases, and saw themselves as part of the wider national progressive education movement. For both Seeds and Heffernan, the political implications of their shared vision of democratic education were challenged by the dramatic political events of the mid-1930s.

1934: YEAR OF CRISIS

As the Depression deepened, conflicts between organized labor, particularly in agriculture, and business and growers' organizations, often supported by local police, made California a kind of theater of the conflict between the radical Left and what Kevin Starr has called "embryonic fascism."[28] According to Carey McWilliams, the farm and cannery strikes of 1933–34 were "without precedent" in terms of "scale, number and value of crops affected."[29] Local growers brought in strike breakers; there were beatings of journalists and lawyers attempting to defend strikers, and eventually violent deaths when strikers were attacked by local vigilante groups. Police responded with mass arrests under the state's criminal syndicalism laws. These confrontations culminated in the San Francisco general strike of the summer of 1934. The 1934 California campaign for governor both reflected and heightened this social and political crisis.

California's voters had long been influenced by issues and ideological differences rather than traditional party loyalties. The state had a tradition of nonpartisan voting as well as strong local centers of liberalism, primarily in the Bay Area, and of conservatism, particularly in Southern California and the Central Valley. In 1933 Upton Sinclair, a well-known Socialist and head of the EPIC (End Poverty in California) Party, changed his registration to the Democratic Party and declared his candidacy for governor. Despite accusations that he would "Russianize" California, Sinclair won the Democratic primary. The Republican candidate was Frank Merriam, whom one commentator called "reactionary to the point of Medievalism."[30] The campaign between Sinclair and Merriam was acrimonious, with charges and counter charges of Communism and Fascism. Although Sinclair clearly spoke to the anxieties and disillusionment of large segments of the California populace, he failed to gain the support of more traditional Democrats, and the national Democratic Party refused to support him. His opponents were able to take advantage of his advocacy of vegetarianism and free love and his rejection of organized religion as well as his vaguely "socialistic" ideas to attack him as a dangerous and eccentric radical. In the end, Merriam defeated Sinclair, winning 49 percent of the vote to Sinclair's 38 percent, with a third-party progressive candidate winning the remaining votes.[31]

The political passions raised by the events of 1934 continued after the election. While the Left attracted followers among workers, intellectuals, and university students, conservative and right-wing groups organized in response. In 1934, the Associated Farmers of California was founded, an organization Carey McWilliams later termed "farm fascism" for its support of vigilante violence in breaking strikes. That same year, suspicions of dangerous subversives led to the UCLA controversy over free speech. A group of students, including the student body president, wanted to create a free speech forum totally under their own control, without including faculty or administration. Provost Ernest Moore, who suspected the leaders of the group of being associated with the National Student League (closely connected with the Communist Party), called UCLA "a hotbed of Communism" and suspended five students. There was a nationwide outcry, including an editorial in the *New Republic* attacking Moore. John Dewey sent a telegram, urging Moore to reinstate the students.[32] Eventually, Chancellor Sproul did reinstate the five students, but the incident exacerbated the tensions between Right and Left on campus and brought UCLA to the attention of local conservative groups as politically suspect. Although there is no indication that Corinne Seeds was involved in this controversy, it reveals the highly politicized climate at UCLA in these years.

Some left-wing educators began to take a more radical stance. In 1934, the social reconstructionist group at Teachers College founded the journal the *Social Frontier*. The editors of the *Social Frontier*, following George Counts, argued that schools could and should help build a new social order, one based on collectivist and democratic principles; the obligation of progressive teachers was both to create democratic classrooms and to encourage social critique. Although the *Social Frontier* gained only a few thousand subscribers, its impact was considerable in 1935 and 1936. In the column "Keeping Informed" in the February 1935 issue of the *California Journal of Elementary Education,* for example, Murray Lee and Dorris May Lee wrote of the *Social Frontier:* "In less than six issues it has become one of the most important periodicals on the American educational scene. After reading the January number on indoctrination and the February number on Hearst, there is little doubt that the *Social Frontier* has arrived."[33] The Lees recommended that all California teachers would benefit from a close reading of the *Social Frontier*.

The Impact of the New Deal

Heffernan was deeply influenced by the ideals of the New Deal. Although it has been argued that the New Deal failed to articulate a coherent educational policy and that its programs were conceived as temporary solutions in the face of a national social crisis, in practice, these programs set a precedent for future federal involvement in education.[34] Heffernan's vision of the role of the school combined the New Deal embrace of government responsibility for social welfare with the pre–First World War progressive idea of the school as social center. In her 1935 article "Health Problems in Rural Schools," for example, she called for an alliance between departments of education and departments of health and social agencies to construct clinics, conduct medical inspections, provide better training in health education in teacher education programs, and support the "closer integration of health service, health instruction, physical activities, and recreation programs within schools and with homes."[35]

In June 1934, Heffernan attended the Washington, D.C., Conference on Youth and Unemployment organized by the U.S. Office of Education. Heffernan's long memo describing this conference shows her concern for the suffering caused by the Depression, her distrust of business, and her support of the New Deal. Heffernan noted that over 4,000,000 youth between the ages of sixteen and twenty-five were unemployed in 1934.[36] Discussing the question of jobs for youth, Heffernan was sharply critical of the status quo: "Even before the depression, many of the jobs which were available were mechanical and blind-alley jobs.... The mere return of business conditions existent four years ago will not solve the problem or ameliorate the situation." Instead, she said, "The solution of the problem lies in a reorganization of our industrial economy."[37] Heffernan's suggestions, though, hardly called for the complete overthrow of capitalism. She supported the Civilian Conservation Corps, called for higher education to be made available to all youth, and argued that public education address questions of citizenship and individual needs as well as vocational preparation. She suggested adult education programs in crafts, dramatics, and choral work as a way of "saving adults and youth alike from being demoralized during these times."[38]

The mid-1930s saw the first criticisms of Heffernan from more conservative local school administrators and the first open expression of antagonism between Heffernan and state superintendent Vierling Kersey. Kersey had supported Heffernan in the early years. When she reported on her participation in the 1934 Washington Conference on Youth and Unemployment, for example, he responded that it was "an excellent statement" and hoped "that very soon I can visit with you and chat about something we, in California, should be doing about the situation which evolved in Washington."[39] But at heart, Kersey was a cautious and conservative figure, very different in both temperament and political sympathies from Heffernan. The first overt conflict between them centered on the rural supervisors, who were among Heffernan's strongest supporters and included many of her old friends and colleagues. In the face of the fiscal crisis of the Depression, some local counties tried to use state money intended for rural supervisors for other purposes. Although Kersey sent a letter to all county superintendents urging them to use the state's funds to "the best possible advantage for rural school children," he did not want to come into direct conflict with the local county authorities.[40] In a memo to Heffernan, he cautioned that this was not the time "when there should be further centralization of control of any educational activities in the State Department of Education."[41] Heffernan responded by defending the rural supervisors and asserting the state's leadership. Kersey was hardly willing to confront the local superintendents, but perhaps as a way of making peace with Heffernan, the next month he sent her a memo praising her "excellent statement" at the superintendents' conference in October.⁴² Heffernan continued to respond politely to Kersey, but it seems clear that their relationship was strained.

Paul Hanna

In 1934 Heffernan began to take graduate courses at the Stanford School of Education. The next year Paul Hanna joined the Stanford faculty as professor of elementary education. Hanna came to Stanford from Teachers College, where he had been acquainted with the major figures of the social reconstructionist group. After receiving his doctorate from Teachers College in 1929 at the age of twenty-seven, Hanna had been immediately hired as an assistant professor. While at Teachers College, Hanna had been involved with the experimental Lincoln School in New York and worked on the Virginia Curriculum Study with the well-known progressive educator Hollis Caswell, who had been a graduate student with Hanna at Teachers College. When he arrived at Stanford, Hanna immediately became the best-known academic associated with the progressive education movement in the state. Heffernan was now in a contradictory position. On the one hand, she was older, more experienced, and had more power over actual classrooms than did Hanna; on the other, she was now a graduate student in a department where Hanna was a prominent professor. And then there was the issue of gender. The parallel careers of Hanna and Heffernan provide a window into the gender dynamics of the progressive education movement in these years.

It may have been Hanna's reputation and association with the social reconstructionists at Teachers College that encouraged Heffernan to continue on at Stanford. In his first years at Stanford there was considerable interaction between the two of them. Immediately after Hanna arrived at Stanford in 1935, Heffernan appointed him to the newly formed Committee on Scope and Sequence in Major Learnings in the Curriculum, a committee that also included Corinne Seeds. In July 1936, Heffernan was one of the keynote speakers at a Stanford Conference on Curriculum and Guidance organized by Hanna and Dean Grayson Kefauver, a conference that attracted almost 900 participants from across the country, approximately half of whom were teachers. The other speakers included John Studebaker, the U.S. commissioner of education, state superintendent Vierling Kersey, George Counts of Teachers College, and Hollis Caswell of Peabody Collage. The account of the conference in the *Western Journal of Education,* a journal deeply sympathetic to Heffernan, suggested that the attendance of so many teachers may have been "a reflection of the growing feeling throughout our educational world that our very foundations are being challenged."⁴³ But also, the article suggested, the success of the conference reflected the ongoing work of California educators and state officials, particularly Helen Heffernan: "Indeed, it was the expressed opinion at Stanford that the work of Miss Heffernan in the rural and elementary schools of California explains to a considerable degree the response of the classroom teacher to the opportunities of this conference."⁴⁴ While the *Western Journal of Education* may have celebrated Heffernan's progressive leadership, there is no indication that Paul Hanna shared this view.

In November 1936, Hanna published an article, "Master Teachers and Modern Education," in Heffernan's *California Journal of Elementary Education*.[45] The article began (typically for Hanna) with sweeping generalizations about the differences between "ancient man" and "modern man." Unlike ancient man, modern man—through the power of science and technology—now could control nature and society. Youth today, Hanna argued, must not only master new knowledge, but they must have experience practicing "the principles of cooperation in the pursuit of commonly held goals."[46] Thus elementary schools needed to provide the experience of collectivity and teach children about the contemporary world. But in this call for democratic elementary schools, Hanna failed to provide any specific examples. Hanna's failure to mention the ongoing work being done in California is striking, particularly since Heffernan was his student, because she had spoken at the Stanford conference the summer before, and because the article appeared in Heffernan's own journal.

Heffernan failed to complete the work for her doctorate at Stanford, only receiving a certificate of her attendance in the School of Education between 1934 and 1937. Heffernan did not leave any explanation for her abandonment of her studies, but she may have found it difficult to take on the role of student to someone like Hanna, who was considered an expert on the elementary curriculum but whose only experience in the public schools was a year and a half as principal of the high school at West Winfield, New York, a position for which he was recommended by his professor George Strayer of Teachers College because Strayer thought Hanna should have a little experience in the schools before entering the academy.[47] And despite his early association with the social reconstructionists at Teachers College, Hanna was a life-long Republican with close contacts to elite networks, including membership in the exclusive all-male Bohemian Club, a world closed to Heffernan. Corinne Seeds certainly seemed distrustful of Hanna's influence at Stanford. In 1941, she wrote to Heffernan: "Emily DeVore told me today that Stanford is filling most of the places in their college at San Jose and that the men in the Dept. there seem never to have heard of either Dewey or Kilpatrick."[48]

In July 1938, another summer conference was held at Stanford, this time on the theme "Social Education," but Heffernan did not participate. Papers from the conference were published under the title *Social Education*. All of the contributors to this volume were male academics. Hanna's essay, "The Problem of Social Education," which introduced the collection, was typically abstract, filled with broad generalizations about "man" and his culture and the progress of science and technology.[49] Again, there was no reference to Heffernan's work in California. That Hanna would have ignored Heffernan's work—and that of Corinne Seeds—might have been based on his judgment of them as individuals, but it is consistent with a wider pattern of ignoring the work of women educators in this period. Despite the participation of progressive women professors in schools of education, male progressive educators like Hanna tended to call for the schools to become the site of social transformation without considering the fact that most teachers were women or acknowledging the ongoing contributions of women like Heffernan and Seeds. The prevalence of attitudes like these suggests that the women's world in which Heffernan and Seeds moved may have been both a personal choice but also a professional strategy in the face of male condescension or hostility.

In contrast, Heffernan was well aware of the contribution of women educators. In a 1935 keynote speech at the Conference of Supervisors and Directors of Instruction and Supervisors of Child Welfare and Attendance in San Francisco, Heffernan celebrated the role of women in progressive education, noting the importance of the kindergarten movement and citing as examples of leadership Jane Adams, Ella Flagg Young, Susan Dorsey, and Patty Hill.[50] Heffernan also continued to depend on and support a network of like-minded women, particularly in the rural counties of California. An example of gendered nature of Heffernan's network is the 1935 State publication "Suggested Course of Study in Reading and Literature for Elementary Schools." In her introduction, Heffernan cited the important work of a number of California teachers and supervisors—all of them were women.[51] It is instructive to compare this publication to Paul Hanna's writings of the same period, which failed to include any reference to the work of women educators.

An example of Heffernan's supportive network was her friendship with Ruth Edmands of Colusa County, who seems to have been both a personal friend and a professional ally.[52] In 1936 Edmands had published an article entitled "The New Educational Program" in the *California Journal of Elementary Education* discussing progressive methods and arguing that schools should prepare children to live in "our changing social order."[53] A series of letters from Edmands to Heffernan shows both their close professional relationship and a sense of personal loyalty and friendship. Edmands, for example, felt free to write to Heffernan about an incident in which Heffernan was perceived to be autocratic in her dealings with the school supervisors association. Edmands wrote: "You have gone such a long way in a manner of democratic procedures that it would be too bad to seem to do even one thing which denied any of the principles which you and your committee have set up as desirable practices." It is not clear from the correspondence what exactly this conflict was or how it was resolved, but it was a mark of Edmands's closeness with Heffernan that she felt free to raise the issue with her. And the close social network among women educators is suggested in her closing lines: "It was nice being with you girls the other day, and I wish I had a mountain lodge with a gurgling stream where I could take you for rest and some fun."[54]

Teaching for Democracy at the University Elementary School

Although Corinne Seeds was not a part of Helen Heffernan's intimate circle of friends in the mid-1930s, they gradually began to work together more closely.

In these years, Seeds published more extensively on the methods being developed at UES. Her ideas closely paralleled those of Helen Heffernan, who gradually began to acknowledge Seeds's work.[55] Describing her attendance at a July 1933 conference of elementary school principals held at UCLA in a memo to State Superintendent Kersey, Heffernan noted, "One of the most valuable presentations was made by Miss Corinne A. Seeds, Principal of the University Elementary School."[56] In her position at the Department of Education, Heffernan began to reach out to Seeds. In May 1934, Heffernan appointed her to a joint committee of ten librarians and ten elementary school people to work on producing manuals about children's literature and the use of books and libraries.[57] And beginning with her 1934 article, "An Interpretation of the Integrated Program in the Elementary School," Seeds began publishing in Heffernan's *California Journal of Elementary Education*. In 1935, the California Department of Education published a bulletin called "Community Life in the Harbor," based on the UES first-grade unit-of-work. It was written by Clayton Burrow with the assistance of Corinne Seeds, Laverna Lossing, and Natalie White of the UES teaching staff and with a preface by Helen Heffernan.[58]

Despite her advocacy of progressive ideas, Seeds and her school seem to have escaped the attention of right-wing groups in the mid-1930s. But education in general was becoming a charged topic among the radical-right fringe in California, particularly in Southern California. Nationally, such books as Elizabeth Dilling's *The Red Network* claimed that a "red menace" was trying to take over the public schools.[59] In Southern California, such ideas were spread through small groups alarmed at what they saw happening in schools. A flavor of this highly politicized climate is captured in a series of long memos sent by Mrs. Arthur Heinemann, state assistant superintendent, to Superintendent Vierling Kersey, describing her travels around the state in 1935, defending the public schools against charges that they were Communistic. In late April 1935, Mrs. Heineman visited Los Angeles. In her memo to Kersey, Heineman described her visit as "in many ways the most amazing week I have ever spent. Wherever one goes or looks one sees or hears evidence of the 'red' scare."[60]

The panic over subversives soon led to worries about the schools. Heineman described a small group called the Los Angeles County Advisory Council. According to a letter from one of the participants, the group met to discuss "an effective campaign to combat the serious menace endangering our entire school system. We feel it has become a question of Communism or Americanism, in which there is evidenced a definite movement to destroy the traditions of our country."[61] Heineman wrote to Kersey that she did not know how to respond to organizations like these: "There is evidence throughout this country that these organizations are taking as facts not only the propaganda spread from the police department but also from such books as Elizabeth Dilling's *The Red Network*."[62] Heineman found some hope in a meeting held by the League of Women Voters attended by fifty people opposed to the anti-Communist campaign, among them Tom Rice of the local American Legion, who headed a new organization called the Los Angeles County Committee on Americanism and declared himself as having "enormous faith in the schools and their soundness." Nonetheless, Heinemann wrote, "All over town there are huge billboards covered with signs urging the vote against communism in our Council and in our schools." Altogether, Heineman concluded, "It is an amazing picture that Los Angeles presents."[63]

Although Seeds and UES seem to have escaped the notice of this early Red Scare, in the late 1930s the school began to face criticisms from both UCLA faculty members and from the Westwood community. With the retirement of Provost Ernest Moore in July 1936 Seeds lost one of her strongest supporters. Perhaps because Moore was no longer there to defend Seeds, in the fall of 1936 Marvin Darsie, the dean of the Teachers College, wrote to Charles Waddell about a letter he had received "from academic instructors" complaining "that Miss Seeds continues to require students in Education 390 to make observations regardless of their other class obligations." Darsie was concerned about Seeds's attitude in general. He added, "I honestly think that her unwillingness to cooperate with her colleagues is developing into an extremely serious situation—one which may well jeopardize her status and the work she is doing."[64] Seeds defended herself in a strongly worded letter to Waddell five days later. She denied the accusations against her, claiming that her students were required to miss other classes only once during the semester and that she was often asked to excuse her students for other professors' field trips. But for Seeds the issue was more than scheduling conflicts. The question was, she wrote: "Shall Education 390 be taught or not be taught? Is it worth the effort it takes to try to help students who have been dead for twelve years come to life enough to teach children more vitally than they were taught?" This confidence that through her teaching she would bring to life students she considered to be intellectually dead was typical of Seeds, as was her response that any criticism was a personal attack. She told Waddell she was not willing to continue to teach the course "if this persecution is not stopped."[65] There is no doubt that Seeds saw criticisms of herself or her method—however mild—as personal attacks. In one letter to Heffernan she described a meeting at which a local superintendent of schools had told UCLA students that not all school superintendents were committed to Seeds's unit-of-work approach and that there were many excellent teachers who used other methods. Seeds was outraged: "It made me plain mad to think that T[eacher]s who refuse to teach democratically can feel so secure! The lazy brute!"[66] It seems a bit extreme to call someone who disagreed with her educational philosophy a "lazy brute," but Seeds simply couldn't accept that there could be other useful approaches than her own.

For his part, Waddell wrote to Darsie strongly supporting Seeds. Waddell noted that Seeds, like everyone, made mistakes. But, he argued, she was also a person of strong convictions and honesty and this brought her into conflict with others on the faculty. Waddell wrote that he had "tried to help her to cultivate more tact but I am convinced that we should consider her very great service to teacher training and take her as she is as if we cannot change her. She is certainly not one of those who makes no mistakes and no enemies because she never *does anything*." Waddell went on to suggest some changes in scheduling that might resolve the conflicts around ED 390, but more broadly, he acknowledged that there were members of the faculty who "do not like Miss Seeds personally and perhaps because they do not hold her philosophy of education, no opportunity to put her in a bad light seems to get by. I have wondered whether there is not a set determination to force her out of the university if possible." Waddell concluded by suggesting to Dean Darsie that "perhaps a little more recognition of the difficulties of her situation and a little more help to correct some of them might go a long way to relieve what so frequently comes to be a tense situation."[67]

The complaints about Seeds even reached University of California president Robert Sproul. Faculty salaries for Seeds and her staff, along with other UCLA faculty salaries, had been cut in the early1930s in response to the economic crisis. But in July 1937, when other members of her staff had their salaries returned to the level of 1932, Seeds was only offered $3,500, still $100 less than she was earning in 1932, even though Waddell had recommended that her salary be raised to $3,800. In his recommendation, Waddell noted that UES had gained "national and international recognition and respect," that Seeds's work was "more widely known throughout the country and more highly regarded than anything else done by the Teachers College," that her classes had the highest attendance of any summer school courses, and that visitors paid for "single admission tickets" to attend her lectures, bringing the Summer Session a "*net profit of something like $3500.*" She had published widely and had "consistently worked harder and more creatively than anyone in our entire Teachers College faculty." Waddell conceded that "Miss Seeds has some faults," but argued that "her virtues far outweigh them."[68]

When she received the news about her salary, Seeds herself went to complain to Sproul. In his "Memoranda" entry Sproul noted, "Miss Corinne Seeds expressed her disappointment at failing to receive an increase in the 1937–38 budget. I explained to her that, as in all similar cases, I had made no increase because there had been a conflict of testimony concerning her."[69] Seeds then asked Sproul about the future of the Teachers College itself. Sproul replied that no decision had been made, but that opponents of the Teachers College included "(1) certain of the State College people who feel that we should be out of the field of elementary education, (2) certain of the more academic professors who feel that elementary teacher training has no place in a university, and (3) certain influential members of the Teachers College who feel that we should have a School of Education."[70] Seeds did not receive her raise.

In the late 1930s, Seeds began to hear other complaints. One source of tension was the confusing status of the school—neither private nor completely open to the public. This led to complaints from Westwood parents whose children were not admitted to the school.[71] These criticisms of the school and other issues began to come to the attention of President Sproul. In a 1936 memo, Sproul described a meeting with Mr. Dixon of the Westwood Business Association and Mr. Cunningham, a member of the Los Angeles City Council. The two men complained to Sproul that "great numbers of children in the area surrounding this campus must go miles to school, whereas the Training School admits children from other districts." When Sproul related this complaint to Waddell, Waddell responded that he did not think that "there was much to this statement, although it might have been true three or four years ago."[72]

As a way to address the complaints of local parents, in 1937 UES worked out a set of criteria on which to admit children, since it had more applicants than it could accommodate. The first criterion was a preference for children of residents of the UES school district.[73] While it was a common practice to favor children from local neighborhoods, in this case, this policy meant that the great majority of children at UES were from Westwood and nearby Bel Air, an area described in a later report as "a highly restricted residential area. Chinese, Japanese, Mexicans and Negroes do not reside there. Due to their appreciation of attractive surroundings, there is an increasing number of Jewish people settling in the community."[74] The decision to admit more local children created a student body similar to that of an exclusive private school, and it also provided the school with a loyal group of wealthy and powerful parents willing to support it.

The other source of discontent was a small group of UES parents. While Seeds enjoyed the support of the majority of UES parents, in the late 1930s some parents began to voice criticisms. One issue was the firing of one of the school's teachers, a Miss Ringer, in 1938.[75] Three UES parents—Mrs. Phillip Davis, Mrs. Walter Allen, and Mrs. Frank Cowgill, met with President Sproul about the case. The three women claimed that Miss Ringer was forced to resign because of Corinne Seeds's jealousy and that Seeds had "lied directly about various matters concerning which they had consulted her." They also complained that their concerns about the school were ignored by Seeds and by Charles Waddell. When Sproul asked the three women if they thought Seeds should be replaced, only Mrs. Allen agreed.[76] In the end, nothing more was done by Sproul, and the dissatisfaction of the three women, particularly Mrs. Walter Allen, was not assuaged. At the time, Mrs. Allen's anger did not seem of great significance.

Spreading the Gospel of Progressive Education

Progressive ideas were widely disseminated and discussed in California in the mid-1930s. In April 1936 the Northern California Conference of the PEA met in San Francisco and at the University of California, Berkeley. It was one of a series of regional meetings sponsored by the PEA. The speakers at the

Northern California conference included the stars of the progressive movement, among them Boyd Bode and Laura Zirbes of Ohio State University and Harold Rugg of Teachers College, who was so popular that he gave his speech at the Greek Theater on the University of California campus in Berkeley. At the Southern California Regional Conference of the PEA the next April in Los Angeles, speakers included the well-known figures Lois Meek and Rachel Davis DuBois.[77]

The progressive education movement continued to attract followers, but political divisions were becoming apparent in the movement. A number of progressive educators, including major figures such as Elsie Clapp, William Kilpatrick, and Boyd Bode, were beginning to distance themselves from the radical rhetoric of the *Social Frontier,* in particular around the question of indoctrination. In his 1935 article, "Karl Marx and the American Teacher," in the *Social Frontier,* Theodore Brameld, one of the sharpest critics of the schools as tools of the ruling class, claimed that "the teacher must abandon his 'illusion of neutrality,' acquire 'class consciousness,' and become an effective participant in the class struggle." Rugg, Dewey, and Kilpatrick all sharply critiqued this article in subsequent issues of the *Social Frontier.* But while many progressive educators were beginning to retreat from the more radical criticisms of capitalism, the idea that the schools should contribute to the building of democracy and a belief in the power of a child-centered approach continued to hold sway at both the national and state levels. The PEA's journal, *Progressive Education,* was widely read. Although legally limited to providing statistical and other information about the schools, in practice the U.S. Office of Education became a major advocate of progressive methods in the 1930s, while the meetings of the NEA became an important site for advocates of progressive education to present their ideas.[78] The California Department of Education played a similar role.

One of the strongest expressions of the California State Department of Education's commitment to the new education was the 1936 publication of *the Teachers' Guide to Child Development for Intermediate Grades,* prepared under the auspices of the California Curriculum Commission as a compliment to the 1930 *Teachers' Guide to Child Development,* which had been addressed to kindergarten and primary grade teachers. Like the earlier volume, the 1936 *Teachers' Guide* was not in fact a guide to child development, but a curriculum guide, providing both a justification of the new education and rich and detailed examples of curriculum and methods. It also included a 114-page bibliography of resources for teachers.

Heffernan and Gladys Potter, her colleague in the Department of Elementary Education, were the coauthors of the introductory chapter, "Point of View," which set out the overarching philosophy guiding the subsequent chapters. This chapter began by citing the educational philosophy of John Dewey that education should prepare for democratic citizenship.[79] "In the modern school," Heffernan and Potter claimed, "knowledge is no longer poured in and given back in the formal recitation, but problems are solved, judgments are made, and the child develops through active participation in real life situations."[80] Heffernan and Potter recommended what they called the integrated curriculum, a model very similar to Kilpatrick's project method and the units-of-work of Seeds's UES, although Seeds did not contribute a chapter to the *Teachers' Guide.*

The publication of the 1936 *Teacher's Guide* was a triumph for Heffernan, but she was also facing challenges. Heffernan lost a long-time source of support when on March 10, 1936, the California Rural School Supervisors Association changed its name to the California School Supervisors Association.[81] In practice the rural and urban supervisors had been meeting together for a few years, so the creation of the new organization was an acknowledgement of the closer collaboration of rural and urban educators and a reflection of the growing urbanization of the state. But the dissolution of the close-knit Rural Supervisors Association also meant the end of the organization that had long been Heffernan's strongest support. The end of the Rural Supervisors Organization was doubtless stressful for Heffernan, and her enrollment in classes at Stanford added to her many obligations. In the summer of 1936, she wrote to Superintendent Vierling Kersey asking for sick leave, claiming to have contracted lead poisoning. She added, "My doctor further states that I am suffering from nervous exhaustion."[82] There is no record of a reply from Kersey, and it is not clear how much time Heffernan took for sick leave.

There is also evidence of continued conflict between Heffernan and Kersey over the school supervisors. In September 1936, a month after Heffernan's request for sick leave, Monterey County superintendent of schools James Force wrote to Kersey to complain about Heffernan's program. Force wrote, "It seems to me that we have a dual supervisory set-up which is neither conducive to harmony or efficiency and I would like to see the situation clarified so the county superintendent may know where he stands." Although there had been no public controversy, Force wrote that he heard occasional "rumblings of disapproval, particularly to recent trends in the activity program."[83] Instead of defending Heffernan and the state's policies, Kersey replied: "It is not the policy nor is it ever an assignment to a staff member of the State Department of Education for [the] activities of the State Department of Education to conflict or substitute for the administrative and supervisory activities of local educational authorities. I too have heard of the situation which is reported in your letter and am doing everything possible to correct it."[84]

It is not clear what steps if any Kersey took in response to the Monterey superintendent's letter, but Heffernan must have been pleased when, four months later, on February 1, 1937, Kersey suddenly resigned as state superintendent of public instruction to take the position of Los Angeles city superintendent of schools. Kersey's resignation as state superintendent coincided with a developing controversy over possible improprieties in the awarding of a state textbook contract, although Kersey's involvement was never proven. Soon after his appointment as Los Angeles superintendent, Kersey began to talk of setting up a teachers college and demonstration school to be run by the city of Los Angeles.[85] Such a school, of course, would be in direct competition with UCLA and the University Elementary School.

Kersey was replaced as state superintendent by Walter Dexter, who was subsequently elected to a four-year term in 1938 and reelected in 1942. Heffernan must have been eager to create a better relationship with Kersey's successor. Soon after Dexter took office, Heffernan sent him a comprehensive memo describing the activities of her division and listing her activities, accomplishments, and needs for more office space and more staffing.[86] She also outlined her plans to ask the progressive education group of the California Teachers Association to work more closely with the state. In March, she sent Dexter a note describing how pleased Dr. Bess Goodykroonz, the assistant commissioner of U.S. education, was about Dexter's appointment: "The particular thing she said was so gracious and discerning that I shall pass it on even at the risk of making your face red. She said 'People's faces light up when his name is mentioned.' Than which there is no greater compliment!"[87] There is no response to this note but it would be natural for Dexter to be pleased, no matter how obvious the flattery.

The appointment of Walter Dexter as state superintendent did not have an immediate impact on Heffernan's work. She followed her usual challenging schedule. In 1937 she helped found the first Berkeley summer demonstration school, which seems to have been modeled on Seeds's UES demonstration school at UCLA. John Hockett, a protégé of Heffernan's who had published several articles in the *California Journal of Elementary Education* in the late-1930s, served as director, Heffernan was associate director, and Gladys Potter served as Principal.[88] Heffernan also was directly involved in the publication of several state curriculum bulletins, particularly for science education.[89] Heffernan also worked with Gladys Potter on a work entitled "Effective Learning in Rural Schools." This was apparently never published, although it eventually comprised a 358-page manuscript.

By 1938, Heffernan showed an increasing concern about the plight of the children of migrant agricultural workers, reflecting a growing national awareness. In previous years, the children of migrant workers had been assumed to be Mexicans who did not speak English. By 1938, attention was turning to the English-speaking children of the native-born, white families from the Dust Bowl who had come to seek work in California.[90] In November 1938, a conference on the education of children of seasonal workers was held in Fresno. Heffernan's report on the conference in the *California Journal of Elementary Education* included summaries of a number of presentations. These ranged in tone from those who saw the migrant children as a social menace to those who saw them as suffering from the effects of poverty and the national economic crisis. R. T. Neideffer of Bakersfield saw the children as a threat to existing schools, claiming that "the social habits and background of children of seasonal workers may often, if not carefully supervised, lower or break down the pupil morale of the entire school. Examples of chewing and smoking tobacco in lavatories, and sex conduct on the playground, together with social diseases in the elementary level, have become evident with the greater advent of the children of seasonal workers."[91]

In contrast, Heffernan presented a powerful defense of the rights of the children of migrant workers, tying the hostility these children met to broader patterns of racism in California. In her address, Heffernan argued that the state's position on the education of migrant children had been clearly established over twenty years ago: "Wherever there are children of school age, it is the responsibility of the constituted educational authorities to establish and maintain schools of a quality equal to that of schools provided for the permanent residents of the community." She argued, "[Migrant children] and their parents are not wanted in the regular schools because of considerations of cleanliness, health, or social status; and some socially myopic adults who would decry long hours of labor as barbarous for their own children, actually advocate labor rather than education for the migratory child." These "myopic adults" included local growers, members of school boards, and sometimes even local school authorities. It was the responsibility of public spirited citizens to protect these vulnerable children from exploitation. But, Heffernan claimed, it was also the responsibility of the federal government to provide support for education, housing, and decent working conditions.[92]

Conclusion

By the late 1930s both Heffernan and Seeds had developed educational philosophies that built upon their commitment to the child-centered education of the 1920s to incorporate the more socially critical ideas of the 1930s. Both were shaken by the collapse of the world economy in the Great Depression. Like many other progressive, liberal educators, Heffernan and Seeds moved to a more radical critique of capitalist institutions in the mid-1930s. But they retained their fundamental belief in a strong state, human reason, and the basic goodness of human nature. Seeds never deviated from the basic ideas she had acquired from John Dewey and William Heard Kilpatrick; Heffernan remained fully committed to the idea that the school should observe and guide students' behavior. Basic to their vision for education was a belief that all children were capable of becoming responsible citizens who would recognize the truth if only their natural rationality were encouraged and allowed to flourish in publicly supported schools. These assumptions were fundamental to the educational and political vision not only of Heffernan and Seeds but of progressive educators across the nation. Unspoken and unexamined in this vision of the good society was the possibility of alternative discourses and suppressed knowledge that might challenge the figure of benevolent teacher and the wisdom of the educational state.

CHAPTER 4

Was Progressive Education Progressive?

The story of Helen Heffernan and Corinne Seeds provides a well-documented example of how progressive education was enacted at the local and state levels. Their work was specific to California, but at the same time was typical of the way progressive ideas were implemented across the country. In this chapter I turn from a narrative of their activities to an analysis of their thought. While they did not yet work closely together, their writings provide evidence not only of their own thinking but of the educational vision of liberal progressive educators more generally in the years before the Second World War. The ideas of Seeds and Heffernan reveal the competing and overlapping discourses of freedom and control, equity and unacknowledged privilege, that marked progressive education in these years.

DEWEY AND DEMOCRACY

The ideas of John Dewey and William Heard Kilpatrick were fundamental to Heffernan and Seeds's politics and educational philosophies. Phrases from Kilpatrick and Dewey appeared frequently in their speeches and writings. The curriculum and methods at UES, Seeds wrote, were "a direct result of the efforts of teachers in the field to apply the thoughts and utterances of the great educators, philosophers, and leaders of all time such as Dr. John Dewey, Dr. William Kilpatrick and others of today to the actual situation."[1] In each of her courses, Seeds required students to memorize part of Dewey's "My Pedagogic Creed."[2] Heffernan frequently cited Dewey as her inspiration and guide. Both Seeds and Heffernan shared Dewey's belief in the key role of public education in a democracy. For Dewey, democracy meant a political and social system based on the active participation of a community of citizens. Deweyan democracy was, in Benjamin Barber's terms, a "strong democracy," one that entailed more than simply voting for representatives every two or four years, but called for the active engagement of citizens in making the decisions that affect their lives.[3] This strong democracy relied upon an educated citizenry, able to judge and evaluate issues and make wise choices informed by not just narrow individual interests but a sense of the collective good. The Deweyan schools would help produce these citizens by being organized as small democratic societies in which children would discuss significant issues and participate in making decisions about the group and their own learning. As Seeds described the ideal school: it should be "arranged as to be a *simplified, purified,* and *balanced replica of life*—an environment in which children living together can grow through the acquisition of ever better and finer ways of behaving."[4]

A key concept in Dewey's educational philosophy embraced by both Seeds and Heffernan was the somewhat amorphous idea of growth. "Growth" referred to children's positive intellectual, emotional, and social development. Progressive educators like Seeds and Heffernan argued that the organization of the school around group activities, particularly around Kilpatrick's idea of activities or "purposeful acts," would encourage this kind of growth. Seeds, for example, argued that the task of progressive teachers was to "stimulate the children to activity," which would "reveal to the children needs and desires which can only be satisfied through *purposeful acts* which necessarily guarantee character and behavior changes in each child in knowing, feeling, and doing which, then leads to real growth."[5] The key terms here are "purposeful acts," a phrase from Kilpatrick's *Foundations of Method*, and Dewey's "growth." In her courses, Seeds passed out a handout entitled "The Growth Pattern." It began: "To LIVE is to ACT! To ACT PURPOSEFULLY is to grow! To ACT PURPOSEFULLY IN WORTHY WAYS is to live the GOOD LIFE!"[6]

By the late 1920s, both Seeds and Heffernan were committed to the ideas of Dewey and Kilpatrick, but like others in the progressive education movement, they wrestled with the balance between children's autonomy and teachers' control. The accusation that the new schools lacked content and direction raised concerns even for the original proponents of the new education about what exactly "freedom" in these schools really meant. The best known of these cautions were those raised by John Dewey himself, who first expressed his concerns in two pieces published in 1928 and 1930, "Progressive Education and the Science of Education" and "Too Much Freedom in the New Schools?"

In "Progressive Education and the Science of Education," Dewey's 1928 speech to the PEA, Dewey cautioned against what he saw as a romantic and sentimental view of children and a lack of structure and direction in the new schools. Dewey continued to defend the political goals of the new education, arguing that if what was desired was to "perpetuate the present order," then mastering an existing body of knowledge made sense, but if the goal was to build a true democracy, to educate "with social change in view," then encouraging students to question, to seek new knowledge and new ways of thinking became the primary goal.[7] But he made a point of disassociating himself from the idea that progressive education should leave all decisions about learning up to the individual child.[8] This did not mean the subject matter was to be presented to students to be memorized and mastered; but it did mean that materials and activities were organized by the teacher so that children could engage and explore significant intellectual questions. Dewey repeated these views in "Too Much Freedom in the New Schools?" part of a symposium entitled "The New Education Ten Years After" published in the *New Republic*.[9] In "Too Much Freedom in the New Schools?" Dewey agreed that the child's natural curiosity and eagerness to learn was fundamental to all good education, but "in some progressive schools the fear of adult imposition has become a veritable phobia."[10] Forecasting the more radical concerns of progressive educators in the 1930s, Dewey emphasized the need for the curriculum to address "the social realities—including the evils—of industrial and political civilization."[11]

Seeds and Heffernan were well aware of the emerging criticisms of the new education as lacking content and structure and shared Dewey's concerns. While they remained committed to the idea that all children could learn through experience, they also agreed with Dewey's insistence on the centrality of a well-prepared teacher, a rich learning environment, and a commitment on the part of the school to both "scientific" reasoning and scholarly content. Seeds, for example, frequently cited Dewey's "Progressive Education and the Science of Education" to distinguish her own approach from what she called "extreme child-centeredness."[12] And in an undated speech that from internal evidence must have been delivered in 1931 or 1932, Heffernan favorably cited Dewey's "How Much Freedom in the New Schools?" agreeing with his condemnation of "unrestrained freedom of speech and action, and lack of manners."[13] But despite their awareness of the dangers of "extreme child-centeredness," both Seeds and Heffernan were unwavering in their belief that the new education offered the key to a better future.

The University Elementary School

The UES provides the most extensively documented example of the actual classroom practices advocated by Heffernan and Seeds. Seeds called her method the integrated or activity curriculum, organized into what she called "units-of-work." Heffernan explained and defended the idea of the activity curriculum in terms very similar to Seeds's in her 1937 article, "The Guiding Philosophy of the Unitary Type of Curriculum Organization." Heffernan wrote that progressive educators were "now building a new curriculum, the unit of which is 'not a specific lesson of subject matter, as was formerly held, but a person facing an actual situation.'"[14] This approach, sometimes called the "unit of work," Heffernan explained, excited children's interests and stimulated their curiosity. Units-of-work should address significant aspects of contemporary life, be developmentally appropriate, provide opportunity for first-hand experiences, and include individual and group activities such as art, music, drama, and modeling, the stimulus of critical thinking, and "the sharing of worthwhile enterprises in a democratic school environment."[15]

Central to this conception of learning was the idea of sensory experience. In this too Seeds and Heffernan followed Dewey and Kilpatrick, who both emphasized that children are only motivated to learn in an authentic way if they are physically engaged with the world. Although Heffernan was not as involved with actual classrooms as was Seeds, she shared Seeds's belief that children needed to experience the world through the senses. For example, in her description of the unit "Community Life in the Harbor," Heffernan praised the way the teacher led the children to be aware of sights, smells, and sounds when they took a field trip to the harbor. When the teacher returned to the classroom, she asked the children, "Now, you remember that Ted said...the 'creaking' of the winches. Oh, let's say that. The 'creaking' of the winches. Isn't that good? Can you hear it?"[16] Seeds provided a similar celebration of the senses. She wrote that children should notice "how the seagull banks his wings when he turns and how he soars and glides; they should *listen* to the bang of the hammers, the whine of the saw, the whirr of the motored power-planes at the building of the new house; they should *smell* the odor of the upturned earth as potatoes are dug from their hills, the salt of the sea as the tide rolls in."[17] This belief in the importance of sensory experiences underlay Seeds's advocacy of what she called "rhythmic expression," in which children created movements, dances, poetry, and music to express their feelings about the subject they were studying.

At UES, rhythmic expression was led by Diana Anderson, who taught physical education at the school, and by Martha Deane, who taught dance in the UCLA Physical Education Department. In her 1934 article, "Rhythmic Expression: An Outgrowth of Learning," published in the journal *Progressive Education,* and in her 1937 book, *Creative Expressions,* Seeds offered numerous examples of this method. When UES children studied the Pueblo Indians, for example, they would grind corn, make piki bread, and "perform their ritual dances for rain." Eight-year-olds studying "the kayak of the Eskimo" made miniature kayaks, wrote poems, painted pictures, or created a play of Eskimos hunting a polar bear. As Seeds described the scene: "The final struggle between the polar bear and the hunter was rhythmic in movement. With the aid of the pianist, who created music to help the children sustain their bodily expression, this became one of their favorite rhythmic patterns of the year."[18] Although we cannot recapture actual classroom practices, the extensive documentation of units-of-work at UES provides an invaluable record of the school's methods and goals. Numerous examples of units-of-work exist, including units (called "Seeds boxes") that student teachers prepared for Seeds's courses, California State Department of Education *Bulletins,* articles describing specific units, a mimeographed annual collection of materials called *Sequences,* and Seeds's lecture notes for her introductory course on elementary education. The curriculum at UES was very similar to that of Dewey's laboratory school in Chicago at the turn of the century and of many other progressive schools—the study of the home and community in the early grades, moving to studies of "primitive civilizations where life, by contrast to ours, is simple," and finally to an examination of aspects of contemporary society with the goal of providing "our citizens of tomorrow a growing understanding of the basic causes of the evils of industrial and political civilization and, we hope, an increasing disposition to act for their removal."[19] This curriculum was organized around themes, not traditional academic subjects. For Seeds, the academic disciplines themselves were the result of human classification of experiences and knowledge into "subject matter compartments."[20]

Seeds provided extensive discussions of units-of-work in her many speeches and publications. One of the most useful sources for Seeds's methods is her handwritten lecture notes for EDS131a and EDS131b, the summer versions of her introductory courses on elementary education.[21] Students in these courses were required to spend mornings observing classes at the UES Summer Demonstration School. Course readings included a mimeographed collection of materials used at UES, Dewey's "My Pedagogic Creed," the State Department of Education Bulletin "Community Life in the Harbor," and one of the chapters in Seeds and Waddell's *Major Units in the Social Studies*. The major assignment was the creation of students' own units-of-work—their "Seeds boxes." A Seeds box was expected to contain "a collection of sources of information, a file of audio-visual aids correlated with proposed activities, a statement of desired outcomes, and a sequence of activities arranged to foster continuity between desired learning experiences and designed with consideration for the stage of growth and development reached by the learners."[22] Seeds also emphasized that students should consider how to teach basic skills, a major concern of critics of progressive education. Another detailed description of UES units-of-work can be found in a collection of bound mimeographed texts entitled *Sequences of Activities, University Elementary School*, covering the years between 1934 and 1945.[23] These volumes contain a summary of the activities of each grade. The first volume of the bound curricula for the year 1934–35 is typical of those that followed. Each unit of work included the initial introduction to the topic, the children's responses, and the materials and activities created by the teacher. Descriptions of different units of work varied in length and detail, but it is clear that they all followed the same schema. By grade three, the units-of-work moved from the focus on local communities and aspects of life that the children had experienced themselves (milk, bread, boats) to historical topics. The older grades had a longer study period in the morning in "centers of interest," which provided ample resources for children to read about their topic. But older children also had an hour "drill period" after lunch, with attention given to arithmetic, language, and penmanship. In the afternoons, between 2:30 and 3:30, the older children took up different activities, including gardening, study in the library, or classes in art, drama, or music.[24] According to the description of the UES unit-of-work on the early Hebrews, for example, after children engaged in group discussions, rhythmic activities, and imaginative play, they had a spelling lesson in which they "learned how to spell words used in our discussions," practice in manuscript writing, and "drill on the forming of correct and complete sentences." They also studied and traced maps of the Middle East "to outline all the routes of the Hebrews from Abraham to Joshua."[25]

According to Seeds, her school always included an hour of drill in subjects that benefited from memorization and direct instruction, such as arithmetic, spelling, and handwriting. The ways in which "drill" was balanced with the activity curriculum at UES is elaborated in Seeds's article, "The Language Arts and Elementary School Activities," which appeared in the journal *Progressive Education*. In this article, Seeds showed how writing, which traditionally had been conceived of as a separate subject, could be made an integral part of the integrated or activity curriculum.[26] In the traditional curriculum, she maintained, writing was an artificial activity and teachers dreaded the hours they had to spend on corrections. The writing assignments "had almost nothing of the children themselves in them."[27] The activity curriculum changed all this. Now writing was the expression of children's lived experiences and activities. Seeds pointed out that outside of the school, writing was primarily used for either communication or recording. In the integrated classroom, children wrote letters arranging field trips, thank you letters, invitations to speakers in addition to engaging in creative writing and compiling academic reports. Of course for the teacher to help the children express their feelings and knowledge, she had to understand "what constitutes the elements of good verse, prose and drama."

For Seeds, teaching was not just a job; it was a calling, which she saw as "second to none in its significance to mankind as the agency most responsible for the promotion of the 'social betterment.'" The new education demanded much, but it gave back extraordinary rewards. In a 1934 article, Seeds proclaimed: "This new teacher will be alive! She will be fired with the enthusiasm of making her contribution in bringing about a social order which is democratic and which, by virtue of the fact that it is democratic, changes itself to meet its own needs."[28] In practice, Seeds expected that teachers would prepare materials for activities in advance, have various plans in mind to be able to respond to children's interests as they developed, and keep careful records of how each activity worked out for each group of children. This combination of a child-centered approach and an emphasis on the mastery of spelling, grammar, and mathematics made extraordinary demands on UES teachers. One UES teacher noted that students at the school "probably did more reading in the morning than most schools with a formal reading program do all day long.... We had a formal reading program [too]." And spelling was taught through memorization. The teacher recalled, "when it came to spelling, brother, you'd better teach spelling. If the kids didn't show up well on the spelling lists, spelling tests, she was concerned.... As I said, Miss Seeds talked Dewey and she talked Kilpatrick, but she taught Seeds."[29]

Disciplinary and Pastoral Technologies

While the term democracy was frequently invoked by both Heffernan and Seeds, they both believed they already knew what was best for children, just as they were confident about the capacity of the liberal state to guide individuals in correct ways. Heffernan and Seeds's acceptance of the benevolent state and their view that a properly organized school could produce a certain kind of self-regulating subject ignored the disciplining power of the state or the school. A growing body of theoretical analysis, influenced in large part by Foucault, sees schooling, including progressive education, as a modern form of discipline and surveillance. The Foucauldian perspective emphasizes the disciplinary nature of all discourses, but particularly those that seek to produce subjects by internalizing norms and behaviors.[30] As Foucault put it in *Discipline and Punish*, "The success of disciplinary power derives no doubt from the use of simple instruments: hierarchical observation, normalizing judgment, and their combination in a procedure that is specific to it—the examination."[31] From this perspective, the qualities of surveillance or "hierarchical observation" and covert control through "normalizing judgment" in progressive classrooms are of central concern. Critics influenced by Foucault have critiqued progressive educators for their unproblematic acceptance of the positive role of the state and belief in the ability of educators to measure and assess students' abilities and needs and to guide their development.

As is well known, Foucault argued that modern forms of liberalism entail the production of subjects who ideally discipline and regulate themselves. Thus, although the discourse of liberalism emphasizes freedom, to the extent that individuals have already internalized proper and acceptable choices, they do not need external mechanisms of discipline. Following Foucault, Nikolas Rose has argued that "the general strategic field of all those programmes of government that regard themselves as liberal has been defined by the problem of how free individuals can be governed such that they enact their freedom appropriately."[32] And Tom Popkewitz has pointed out the irony of the "fundamental promise of the welfare state and mass schooling of the past century" that institutions could "produce an individual's own freedom."[33] Valerie Walkerdine has called this "the romantic promise of progressivism in education."[34] In Walkerdine's view, progressive pedagogies have served the ends of those who control and benefit from existing arrangements of society by teaching middle-class children to be self-directed, preparing them for future class positions, and encouraging all children to adjust to the values of existing class society and to accept the judgment of the school as the truth about themselves. These practices are not obvious because the form of power they employ is invisible. Their power comes from a reliance not on overt and authoritarian practices, but on the concept of normalization.[35]

Nikolas Rose has distinguished between pastoral relations, which aim to create internalized practices such as confession, self-disclosure, and self-inspection, and disciplinary relations, which rest on the practices of surveillance, naming, classifying, and sorting. This distinction between pastoral and disciplinary techniques is similar to the difference between policies framed around ideas of care and those around what Jacques Donzelot called policing. The idea of policing, like that of social discipline, views the modern state as an institution based on an unproblematic belief in its own beneficence and ability to know what is best for the population. For this process to work, the state requires extensive knowledge of individuals—what Donzelot describes as the "ordering, standardizing, and making of the individual who is legible and administratable."[36] Most schools employ disciplinary relations, particularly those based on sorting. But Foucauldian critics like Popkewitz and Walkerdine argue that while progressive schools like those advocated by Heffernan and Seeds rejected the more obvious forms of disciplinary technologies such as competitive academic examinations and formal grades, at the same time they embraced the less overt disciplinary mechanisms of surveillance, guidance, and normalization. Through these measures, the schools were intended to produce students who would enact pastoral techniques of self-inspection and self-policing.

It is obvious that there is a process of selection and control in any school; what is difficult is acknowledging this control and reconciling it with dreams of freedom.[37] This contradiction between the valuing of democracy and the practices of knowledge-gathering and surveillance was central to the wider discourse of progressive education. Despite the rhetoric of individual choice, Seeds and Heffernan were very clear about the authority and responsibility of the teacher to select, observe, and guide the student into an already conceived path. As Seeds explained: "We arrange an environment, rich in things we believe are of interest to children, allow them to explore it and then guide the interaction into worthwhile living. If we believe the children need to know about a butterfly we catch him and put him into the environment—we don't depend on his flying in thru the window!"[38] Similarly, Heffernan and Gladys Potter argued in the 1936 *Teachers' Guide to Child Development for the Intermediate Grades* that schools needed to be organized so children would have "an opportunity to exercise desirable social relationships; to develop powers of thinking through problems; to cultivate individual interests and aptitudes" as well as engage "subject matter which makes living a rich, colorful, cultural adventure in the realms of art, music, and literature." For schools to provide this education, they must employ "watchfulness over every environmental influence which might be subversive to the child's complete physical, mental, social, and spiritual realization."[39] It is the term "watchfulness" that stands out here, with its implication of surveillance and assumption that the watcher knows what is best for the child.

Watchfulness appeared as well in Seeds's writings. She called for teachers to create stimulating learning environments and to serve as both resources and guides, but once they created that rich and challenging classroom environment, teachers were to watch the children carefully in order to encourage their proper growth. Seeds wrote of her school: "The children are given the opportunity to explore or interact with this arranged environment. The teacher watches this interaction most carefully, for out of this will develop the children's first needs and desires, which she may guide into worthwhile purposeful activity."[40] Here Seeds presented watchfulness as a way for teachers to meet individual needs, but teachers also were to categorize which needs were useful or not useful. In an unpublished typescript, "Guide to Recording Attitude Development," Seeds argued for the need for close observation and record keeping of every child's "attitude." She wrote, "Ideally such records should include a complete picture of each child for it is only through seeing the whole child in the total situation that we are able to understand and guide his growth." Seeds recommended that teachers focus on one area of growth, one that will be "important to both the child's present and future adjustment."[41] In order to follow each child, she recommended careful record keeping, including descriptions of specific incidents. She then gave an example of an "attitude chart" that consisted of columns with dates and incidents indicating the need for improvement.

In lectures to her students in ED 131, Seeds spoke directly of the paradoxical need for teachers to control children and their environment in order to achieve democratic goals. Seeds wrote that a belief in democracy meant respecting the rights of others to live to their highest capacities. But, she noted, "Unless all cooperate this cannot be done. This demands control. Prog[ressives] believe in democ[racy] therefore they believe in control—but they approach it in a diff[erent] way from those who believe in dictatorships. The dictator says do right because I say so—the democrat says do right because we have thot it thru together and decided that for us at this time this is the approved plan of action." Despite the reference to thinking things through together, there is little recognition here that there might be conflicts of opinion or interests in this process. This is similar to Seeds's shift from "I" to "we" in her lecture notes. For example, at one point Seeds summarized her past few lectures: "On Wed.... we decided that the Dem[ocratic] way of life belonged to us here in America and that T[eachers]s can help to make it a realization." Seeds did not explain how this consensus that "we decided" was achieved. Nor did she mention any invitation for students to disagree or present a different point of view. Although Seeds presented a method based on "Democratic Living," her assumption that she and her own students were as one was itself hardly democratic.

Both Heffernan and Seeds were comfortable with their own authority and judgment. For example, in speaking of the question of what environment and content should be presented to children, Seeds wrote that the school needed to make sure the child was learning, but more than that, the school was to select "out of all of the child's social heritage those influences which shall affect the most changes in him for good and place them in his immediate environment, so that *when* and *as* he needs them he can make them an integral part of himself."[42] Seeds showed no sign of uncertainly or hesitation in deciding which aspects of the child's social heritage were desirable. She defined social heritage as including physical knowledge of the world and its people, skills such as reading, writing, and mathematics, and the realm of the aesthetic. But, Seeds continued, slipping from the "social" to the "racial," "not all of this racial heritage is good." The teacher had to decide what was most appropriate and useful to the growing child.[43] There was an assumption here of a unified cultural heritage that the teacher (as authority/agent of the state) already knew. The teacher decided what was valuable knowledge—the knowledge of the school. If the child's family or culture valued different knowledge, then that "racial heritage" was not good.

Seeds's lack of self consciousness about her authority to define what culture is good is captured in this passage about the moral responsibility of the school to shape the child's culture. She wrote, "Because the world as it is, the world of the alley, the pool hall, with the homes of the dance-mad, liquor-mad, and race-mad people, does not provide for the acquisition of the finest ways of behaving possible the school must arrange for life which is fairly ideal." For Seeds, "The language of the street, alley, radio, sound picture, and dime novel must be offset in school by the use of good, effective English and by the reading of that which is good in literature."[44] It is not clear what Seeds meant by "race-mad," but the rest of the passage makes clear that debased popular culture must be countered by the high culture of the school.

Mental Health

Heffernan and Seeds were typical New Deal liberals. Gary Gerstle has pointed out that although liberalism in the United States has historically been "protean" and not easily captured by a single definition, it has always rested on "three foundational principles: emancipation, rationality, and progress."[45] The belief in rationality in the 1930s meant a belief in the power of science and technology to transform lives, and in education, that meant a trust in the authority of psychology.[46] It was because of their faith in psychology that Heffernan and Seeds embraced the use of standardized tests to categorize and guide students. Intelligence testing, a form of testing that claims to measure innate ability, became widely used in the United States beginning in the 1920s. Testing had been enthusiastically embraced by Charles Waddell at the UCLA Training School in the 1920s; Corinne Seeds continued to rely on standardized tests to monitor and place children at the UES throughout her career.[47] In Heffernan's rural demonstration schools in the 1930s, children were tested to "determine aptitudes, interests, abilities, improvement, and for diagnostic purposes." The results of the tests were then used to create activities that would meet each child's needs.[48]

While Heffernan shared the language of Deweyan democracy and a confidence in psychological testing with Seeds, Heffernan was much more indebted to ideas of mental health. One of the major goals of education, Heffernan said, was "the integration of personality." The activity curriculum contributed to that goal by "helping the individual to understand his social relationships" that in turn prevented "the disintegrating influence of unresolved conflicts in his behavior patterns." Heffernan claimed that "modern education is not primarily concerned with 'How much did this child *learn* today?' as it is concerned with 'What kind of human being is this child becoming?'"[49] Thus the first purpose of the elementary school was "to develop a sound body, normal mental attitudes, and controlled emotional reactions." This theme—that the school was responsible for encouraging mental health and happiness—was a constant in Heffernan's statements about the goals of education.

Heffernan's vision of schooling as a form of overseeing children's mental health was intertwined with her conception of education as the foundation of democracy. This was a contradictory position, advocating methods that would lead children to "adjust" themselves (which assumed the status quo) and at the same time arguing that education should be the grounding for progressive social transformation (which assumed change). Heffernan moved back and forth between these positions beginning in the early 1930s. In one 1932 speech, she suggested that children should "become active propagandists for the school program in every home throughout the commonwealth." This support would be achieved if the schools achieved the goal of making "the child's school experience one that is pleasurable and satisfying to him, or we might express it in a slogan, 'Send the children home happy.'"[50] This speech, which called for children to become "active propagandists" for the progressive approach and emphasized the importance of pleasure must have infuriated more conservative educators. Passages like this provided support for the accusation that the schools were becoming therapeutic rather than academic and that progressive education emphasized mental hygiene, social adjustment, and the search for happiness to the detriment of learning. These concerns were central to the conservative opposition to Heffernan that began to form in the mid-1930s and to the later claim that she advocated "fads and frills" instead of "the three R's."[51]

Mental health and social adjustment increasingly became central themes for Heffernan in the mid-and late-1930s. The California Department of Education's 1936 *Teachers Guide to Child Development for Intermediate Grades,* for example, emphasized the responsibility of the school to encourage personality adjustment and mental health, echoing Heffernan's statements in other publications and speeches from this period.[52] Heffernan's belief that the school was responsible for children's mental health and happiness underlay her enthusiastic support of the school guidance counselor. In her 1938 chapter, "The Principal's Responsibility in Guidance," Heffernan explained: "The process by which education helps children to become happy, wholesome, self-controlled, self-directed and socially minded personalities is called guidance. The purposes of guidance and the purposes of education are identical because education is guidance." This statement captured her deep belief in educators' ability to know the child and their duty to shape the child according to a notion of the social good. Heffernan argued that the elementary school principal must first of all acquire knowledge about the child: "his out of school life, his family background, the economic and social status of the family, the dominant standards or ideals maintained in the home." In order to serve children, Heffernan argued, the schools needed to develop "a more effective use of a cumulative record based upon a recognition of the need of modern education to know everything possible about the nature and needs of the human beings it serves."[53]

The conflation of a rhetoric of valuing individual differences and the embrace of normative ideas of mental health and adjustment can be clearly seen in Heffernan's rejection of ABCDF report cards, a stance that would later become a major focus of conservative attacks on her programs. As early as 1932, Heffernan was denouncing the dangers report cards raised of creating "undesirable mental traits." Instead, she advocated the use of narrative reports that indicated "the quality of the child's work in relation to native capacity" rather than those "based on competition with his fellows."[54] In her 1936 article, "Classification and Promotion Policies in Some City School Systems," Heffernan presented more evidence to justify the elimination of ABCDF report cards. This article examined a study of seven urban districts that were experimenting with different forms of elementary school organization by eliminating academic promotion and grade levels. In her enthusiastic depiction of these new methods, Heffernan claimed: "In an education stressing cooperation there is no place for the traditional report card based upon competitive marks which disregard individual differences."[55] Justifying these changes, Heffernan argued: "An education conceived as personality development and social adjustment requires organization and procedures quite different from a type of education conceived as subject-matter to be learned."[56] This use of the terms "personality development" and "social adjustment" as the guiding aims of education would be repeated again and again in Heffernan's arguments for the new education.

Heffernan's move from the evaluation of children's accomplishments against a set standard to an evaluation based on the teacher's judgment of their "physical, mental, social, and emotional" growth seemed more responsive to individual difference. But in practice it replaced adherence to a uniform standard with a much more overarching and subtle form of surveillance and judgment. For Heffernan, the school was responsible for addressing children's mental and emotional condition, whether the result of personal relationships or social situation, and its goal was the happy child. She wrote, "The child will be, in the final analysis, the best agency for educational interpretation if and when education preserves for him his inalienable right to happiness—when the school sends the child home happy, never discouraged, never defeated!"[57] This liberal belief in the school's obligation and ability to create happiness has had many critics. From a conservative point of view, of course, the school cannot guarantee happiness. Life is a competition; children should learn to cope with defeat and unhappiness as well as happiness. From a radical-Left perspective, on the other hand, many aspects of individual unhappiness have their roots in social inequality and exploitation; society is marked by conflicts over resources and power; oppression must be addressed and combated, and this process is not necessarily going to result in children who are always happy.

Gender, Class, and Race

The belief in mental hygiene and the acceptance of psychological testing and ideas of normative intelligence in the writings of Heffernan and Seeds are examples of the kind of social discipline and surveillance that Foucault identified as characteristic of modern societies. What are obscured in these practices are existing hierarchical structures based on class, race, and gender privilege and power. By failing to explore or even acknowledge these structures, the universal claims of progressive educators like Heffernan and Seeds tended to replicate and even encourage existing hierarchies. For example, while they moved among networks of other women and acknowledged male privilege in their private writings, Heffernan and Seeds failed to problematize gender among boys and girls in the progressive classrooms they described. While they spoke of class inequities and were supportive of the labor movement, they ignored the implication of class as a lived culture or the impact class location might have on children's lives in schools. And, like most white liberals in the years before the Second World War, Heffernan and Seeds tended to accept existing racial categories in the United States even when they called for tolerance.

As was true of other progressive educators of the 1930s, Heffernan and Seeds tended to discuss their pedagogical goals without reference to the social identities of either children or teachers. Their claims were set out as universally true, although at times they did show a clear recognition of the power of gender, class, and race. Seeds and Heffernan were particularly aware of male privilege, as shown in Seeds's frequent references to the male UCLA faculty as "the boys on the hill," her comment in her oral history that "the men" all hated Heffernan, or Heffernan's references to the men at the State Department of Education as "the boys." But while they moved among networks of other women and were well aware of male privilege in their professional lives, Heffernan and Seeds failed to discuss the workings of gender among boys and girls in the progressive classrooms they described. As was true of progressive educators more generally, gender did not appear as a category of analysis or concern in their writings in the 1930s.[58] This failure to problematize gender is clear in Seeds's discussion of children's choices for dramatic play. For example, she described one UES classroom filled with pictures of trucks, airplanes, trains, and autos. There were also boxes, blocks, and other materials that could be used to build cars, planes, or boats. When the teacher asked the children what they would like to play with or make, many of them wanted to make airplanes. From this beginning, the teacher led the children to build an airport, oil refinery, then an entire town. According to Seeds, these steps both followed and guided each child's interests. The end result was not preordained; it followed from the children's interests, stimulated by a rich classroom environment.

This approach celebrated individual choice. But Seeds did not consider that moving things like trucks, boats, and airplanes might be more interesting to little boys than to little girls. On the one hand, it is possible to argue that this kind of gender-blind activity opened up possibilities for girls; on the other, it may be that an activity that was more traditionally associated with boys encouraged their leadership. That some gender dynamic was in fact at play in this classroom is suggested by Seeds's description of the children's roles in the community they ultimately built. The boys built airplanes and became pilots. The girls' activities were domestic: "During one of the last days in the semester when community living was at its fullest and best it was thrilling to see some of the little girls cleaning house, marketing, ringing for a taxi and then gathering the family and the lunch-basket together and taking them in the taxi to the park for a picnic."[59] It may have been "thrilling" to Seeds to see little girls pretend to clean house and make lunch for their families, but it raises again the question of how free the free classroom really was from social expectations.

When they discussed the progressive classroom, both Heffernan and Seeds tended to take the differences between boys and girls as natural. For example, Seeds described the relationships between boys and girls at the UES: "Boys play harder, tumble, wrestle and are noisy, boisterous, rough, and unkempt. Therefore the girls tend to avoid them."[60] When Seeds described rhythmic expression, she noted the different ways in which boys made use of music and rhythm. While boys might have been dismissive of "interpretive dancing," she wrote, they were quite willing "to ask for music to aid them in manning and building Viking ships, in fighting with drawn swords in the mortal combats of Castle Days,...pitting in battle Romans against Carthaginians, Trojans against Greeks, Aztecs against Toltecs, etc. in playing Greek games, and in other pursuits which they consider 'manly.' "[61] Here Seeds simply accepted boys' understanding of masculinity as the expression of war, violence, and aggression, rather than calling this into question or considering how to challenge it.[62]

The only questioning of the social construction of gender in Seeds's writings appears in her discussion of an experiment she had her students in ED 330 conduct. She asked the students to observe and record the activities of 109 children (fifty-four girls and fifty-five boys) for three hours on a single morning. Although both boys and girls equally participated in strenuous physical activities, there were differences in dramatic and imaginative play. Girls still played with dolls among themselves, Seeds reported, but "when boys and girls played together the play centered on cowboys, Indians, pirates, and the like. Rarely did they play house or with dolls." In class, boys tended to ask questions about other people and issues. Girls, on the other hand, were more concerned with personal matters. Boys were interested in mechanical, scientific, and natural history questions, whereas "only eleven instances of girls' interest in science were recorded." In a rare moment of questioning these gender differences, Seeds commented: "Even at such an early age women seem to confine their questions to the personal and social rather than to things and ideas! Is this the effect of culture on girls? At least, this is a variant which merits further investigation."[63] But Seeds herself did not carry out any further investigation of these issues.

Heffernan and Seeds also held contradictory views of class. Like most New Deal liberals, they were sympathetic to the labor movement, which they saw as central to democracy. Both of them had grown up in families supportive of working-class struggles. And by the late 1930s, both Heffernan and Seeds took a critical view of the existing capitalist system. In her 1937 article "Supervision Appropriate for Progressive Schools" in the *California Journal of Elementary Education,* for example, Heffernan argued that schools needed to be redesigned "to provide for the needs of all the people rather than the profit and privilege of a few." Education was central to this process of progressive change by providing young people with facts and "by developing attitudes of social justice which will make it possible for them to participate with civic competency in an orderly reconstruction of our institutions."[64] While Heffernan and Seeds were sympathetic to the labor movement and argued for a more equitable social order, they rarely addressed the implications of class culture and class privilege.[65] Seeds, in particular, failed to mention the fact that the majority of the children of the UES came from wealthy and well-educated families in Westwood and Bel Air when she celebrated the success of her methods. Her own unspoken class and cultural assumptions are suggested in a series of model "write-ups" done by her staff of student teachers. For example, she wrote that "Miss... is an unusually able young woman. She has good presence, a rich academic background, and true culture." Of another, that she was "always becomingly groomed, knows the social niceties (member of Greek letter sorority). She has a thorough and practical knowledge of the laws of learning."[66] The emphasis on grooming, social niceties, and poise surely speaks to class as much as the ability to work with children. This emphasis on appropriate manners and dress was common in Seeds's descriptions of the student teachers, all of whom were women. The gendered nature of these judgments was also unmentioned.

Unconscious cultural and class assumptions also operated in Seeds's idea of what was considered to be appropriate attitudes toward children in the classroom. One student teacher, for example, was criticized for her classroom manner. Although this teacher was "noticeably attractive in manner and dress at all times" and was "happy, courteous, and responsive," she was criticized for being "too demanding and negative in her attitude and language in approaching the children." For example, Seeds wrote, the teacher gave commands such as "Don't go up on the jungle gym now" instead of "Now we're all going for a walk," or "Come right down as fast as you can; you know we don't take toys on the jungle gym with us." In this instance, the student teacher was criticized for giving clear and direct instructions to the children. Of course, scholars of color such as Lisa Delpit have argued that the use of this indirect approach is an expression a certain kind of white, middle-class culture and that many children of color (and presumably teachers of color) are accustomed to and prefer straightforward and firm directions.[67] We know nothing of the race or class identity of these student teachers, but since there were very few students of color in the teacher education program at UCLA in this period, and since those who were not white were almost always marked ("a Negro teacher," "a Japanese teacher"), we can assume these students were white. Whether there was a class difference between the poised member of the Greek letter sorority and the young woman who gave too many direct commands to children we cannot know.

Even more problematic than the acceptance of middle-class culture as superior were Heffernan's and particularly Seeds's views about race. When speaking of children in general, Heffernan and Seeds often celebrated the idea of individual difference, but in the 1930s that conception of difference ignored racial, ethnic, or other factors, and instead conceived of difference only as emotional or intellectual. In their coauthored essay, "Point of View," in the 1936 *Teacher's Guide to Child Development for the Intermediate Grades,* for example, Heffernan and Gladys Potter argued that the purpose of education should be to encourage "individual talents and abilities as completely as possible."[68] They asserted that all children were unique and rejected the idea that achievement should be geared to the "mythical 'average child.'" Instead, they argued, "the interests and purposes of each individual child are important, and it is the function of the school to find ways and means of carrying them out."[69] This focus on the individuality of each child was typical of progressive discourse in the 1930s and in many ways was democratic and respectful of all children. But it also revealed one of the lacunae of progressive discourse. White Californians outside of Heffernan and Potter's ideal classroom did not treat all individuals as different and equal in value; quite the contrary, they categorized and treated individuals as different within a rigid social hierarchy according to their race, ethnicity, religion, gender, and class.

When Heffernan acknowledged racial difference in these years, she advocated a tolerant appreciation of different heritages, but accepted stereotypes and did not explore the effects of white racist practices. Heffernan's 1939 children's book, *Desert Treasure,* for example, included chapters on the Mojave and Piute and on the Chinese.[70] The Piute and Mojave peoples were presented as close to nature, wise, and stoical. The Chinese were responsible and nurturing. The chapter "Chinese People in California" did mention the Chinese Exclusion Acts and the discrimination the Chinese had experienced in the past, but in general the Chinese were presented as loyal and devoted servants. Contemporary Chinese were presented as "graduates of our universities, and are doctors or dentists or nurses." There was no mention of ongoing racism against Asian Americans. This book was published three years before the beginning of the Japanese internment.

Seeds's unselfconscious assumption of white superiority, which was so striking in her account of her experiences as a young teacher at the Avenue 21 School, continued to be evident in her discussions of the UES curriculum in the 1930s. The assumption that white experience was the norm can be seen clearly in the UES unit-of-work, "Westward Movement to the California Gold Fields," which was concerned solely with the perspective and experience of the "pioneers." They were the center; native peoples were part of the obstacles they overcame. Although the unit included some information about the lives of the Plains Indians and made reference to "their feeling of hostility toward the pioneer settlers who would change their way of life," and though one of the desired outcomes was "a more sympathetic understanding of the American Indian," these points did not challenge the overall grand and heroic narrative of white conquest. For Seeds, native peoples at their best were seen as noble primitives.

Seeds not only assumed the centrality and superiority of white culture, she also held more stereotypical and racist views. One example of the simple and emotional Negro is found in a student's piece titled "A Negro Prayer," published in Seeds's 1937 book *Childhood Expressions,* a collection of poems and other writings by UES students. This piece of work by a twelve-year-old girl was written in what she imagined was dialect. It was accompanied by a photograph of white UES children in blackface, "playing" at being black:

> Come, all ye niggers for to praise the Lawd! Oh Lawd, my God, our almighty and merciful Lawd, bless the houses where we so humbly lib....Lawd bless our little chillens dat dey may enter de gates ob Heben unharmed. Oh, dese golden gates ob Heben and dese pearly streets ob Heben. Lub dese little chillens down here in de front row, Lawd, Praise de Lawd! Sammy, if yo want de Lawd to lub you, yo better stay out ob Br're Sam's chicken coop! Oh Lawd, bless us ole niggers. Though our skin is black as de night, make our souls as white as de day![71]

Seeds chose to publish this poem without commentary as an example of exemplary student work. In her review of *Creative Expressions,* Heffernan singled out this poem as a "dignified interpretation of the emotional life of Negroes."[72]

Even when African American authors such as Langston Hughes and Paul Lawrence Dunbar were brought into the curriculum at UES in the 1930s, it was in the context of viewing black people as simple farmers in the rural South. The unit on "the cotton workers" for seventh graders described in the 1934–35 issue of *Sequences* is a good illustration. The teacher began the unit with the question of where cotton was grown and the location of the cotton belt. She then provided pictures, movies, and books for the children to read. The students first focused on the boll weevil, but then explored who picked the cotton and "why Negroes make the best cotton pickers." From this amazing starting point, they read books and pamphlets and the poems of Hughes and Dunbar among others. But they also read Joel Chandler Harris and wrote "poems and stories about Negro life" and learned "some Negro songs." Among their activities was a sharing of "their own ideas as to whether the Negro was better off in bondage or free and why."[73]

Not only was there an acceptance of racist stereotypes in the UES curriculum, but also in the school's attitude toward black students. UES was overwhelmingly white, but it did include a few African American and Asian American children. Although there is no record of opposition to their inclusion in the school, there is evidence that these children were viewed as different by white teachers. In "Rhythmic Expression: An Outgrowth of Learning," published in 1934 in the journal *Progressive Education,* Seeds mentioned a "Negro boy" in the context of discussing a seventh-grade performance about travel in the desert. She described the audience's astonishment at seeing "a huge, very black Negro boy, draped in a snow-white sheet, lead the procession of camels and men across the floor....It was an unusual performance—a Negro boy was in command of a group of white children."[74] Seeds then quoted the teacher, who said that the boy, Henry, "had been the problem-child of the school! Being a Negro, not very quick to learn, and being so large he has been a source of much trouble both for teachers and children during his whole school career."[75] Once he entered into the rhythmic expression of his ideas, he came to enjoy school and the other children came to appreciate him. Seeds accepted without comment the teacher's view that Henry was a source of trouble because he was a Negro, and that he was "not very quick to learn." The implication seemed to be that rhythmic movement and dramatic expression were areas where he could succeed, a confirmation of the stereotype of the dancing and singing black performer.

In the 1930s, an acceptance of white privilege, the unquestioned assumption that white experience was the norm, and the stance that "others" should at best be tolerated were widespread among U.S. liberals like Heffernan and Seeds. And overtly racist views like those evident at UES were all too common. It was only in the face of the growing threat of war and in particular the racist ideology of National Socialism that white liberal educators would begin to articulate greater consciousness of and concern about racial discrimination and to call for intercultural understanding and tolerance. The acknowledgment of racism would challenge progressive educators like Heffernan and Seeds to consider who they envisioned as belonging within their imagined social democracy.

Democracy and Freedom

Democracy was a central concern of both Seeds and Heffernan. But their failure to consider the realities of class, race, and gender privilege and oppression undercut their claim to speak for all. Neither of them expressed any doubt about what democracy meant in the classroom, but in practice their vision of the democratic school did not invite input from either children or their parents. Seeds's description of the democratic classroom captured this stance very well: "Teachers need not only to give lip-service to the building of a democratic social life but every hour of the day they should strive to guide their children into *living* democratically—into living an ethical life, one which all would choose if they only knew enough."[76] This belief that the progressive teacher knew better than families what the ethical life consisted of was a central contradiction in the progressive claims of Heffernan and Seeds and would become a major source of opposition to their ideas.

While Seeds asserted the need for the teacher to control the classroom, she did not seem to see the contradiction between teacher control and the promise of individual freedom and choice, a central problem for theories of democratic education. For Seeds, the solution to this dilemma was found in the idea of group welfare or the common good (similar to Rousseau's idea of the general will). Seeds argued that choices should be made "in the light of whether they will promote the common good, or at least not interfere with it." The "welfare of the social group" was of great importance, but the group also had to "consider the highest development of each individual, as only through the continual contributions of its individual members working toward the common good does society grow toward ever higher levels of living."[77] But it was not always easy for children to achieve the finest levels of group living. As Seeds noted, "Teachers realize that each child and each group cannot be expected to reach an ideal without continual guidance."[78] And at times the idea of "guidance" verged on coercion. As Seeds explained, "If [the child] responds to nothing but coercion, the group under teacher guidance must coerce in order that the social order may be as fine as possible for each and all."[79]

Seeds and Heffernan framed their defense of progressive pedagogy in terms of the needs of democracy. They saw the experiences of children as central to their roles as future citizens. But despite their commitment to the idea of democracy, there seems little doubt that they were speaking through a discourse that allowed for only one political and pedagogical truth. The goal of their pedagogy was to lead students to incorporate the specific set of values underlying the activities and materials they encountered in the progressive classroom. The conflict in the writings of Seeds and Heffernan between their celebration of democracy and their desire to control and create a certain kind of subject was not unique to them. The debate over indoctrination in the mid-1930s raised the same issues. Heffernan and Seeds enacted many of the principles of progressive education in the 1930s. Underlying their claims was a belief in the goal of self-discipline and a belief in rationality that made possible the more open classroom practices they advocated and that they assumed would lead to democratic consensus. At the same time, they accepted normative ideas of mental hygiene, observation, record keeping of children's behavior and "attitudes," and the use of standardized testing—practices that imply the kind of social discipline and surveillance that Foucault identified as characteristic of modern disciplinary societies.

Conclusion

Helen Heffernan and Corinne Seeds, as Deweyan progressives, held a deep faith in the ability of the liberal state to lead citizens to an enlightened view of collective social needs and to provide the services that would allow all citizens to participate actively and responsibly in a democratic society. The Foucauldian critique of progressive education challenges this unqualified acceptance of the positive power of the state, pointing to the inherent contradiction between the desire to measure and control outcomes and the claim of democracy. Discourses are not unitary; they incorporate multiple voices, traces of past histories, competing desires. The educational vision of Heffernan and Seeds rested on a desire to educate active citizens who could regulate themselves and participate in an ideal democratic society. This meant the uneasy juxtaposition of disciplinary practices of scientific measurement and pastoral techniques of surveillance and self-regulation with democratic discourses emphasizing children's freedom.

From a Foucauldian perspective it is easy to accuse the progressive educators like Heffernan and Seeds of being utopian, of encouraging the disciplinary power of the schools whose ultimate function is to produce self-policing subjects who will not challenge or even be aware of the surveillance of an omniscient modern state or the power of the discourses that construct and police them. Heffernan and Seeds celebrated individuality and embraced the idea that all children bring different interests and abilities to the classroom, but the benevolent state schools they envisioned did not acknowledge existing privileges of class, gender, and race. The most striking aspect of Heffernan and Seeds's writings from the 1930s is their failure to address racist injustice or to recognize the different social positions of children, families, and teachers. Because they did not fully address these realities, they did not consider the ways in which the schools and school practices were implicated in the production and reproduction of privilege and oppression. It can be argued that Helen Heffernan and Corinne Seeds were idealists who sought to create an education that would encourage individual expression and growth for children who in reality were going to grow up into a society in which their futures were already shaped by their class, race, and gender, in which their work would be divorced from their pleasure, and in which they would increasingly be seen as consumers whose desires could be manipulated rather than reflective citizens. When "progressive methods" focus only on the individual child in the self-contained classroom and fail to address structural issues such as these, they may serve simply to maintain an unequal system by providing an illusion of freedom.

The Foucauldian critique of progressive education highlights these forms of social discipline and power, but it does not consider the ways public school systems can further democracy in the Deweyan sense—by offering access to knowledge and skills for all children, not just the privileged, and by providing a site for the critical engagement with ideas and the opportunity to create new knowledge. It does not directly address the political nature of educational struggles—the nature of curricular knowledge and who controls it, the struggles of groups to gain access to an education that has been denied them, the implications of seeing children not as future consumers or workers, but as citizens. Underlying debates over education are fundamental conceptions of what constitutes the good society, who has power and who deserves power, human nature, the possibility and meaning of democracy. From a contemporary vantage point, the stance of progressive educators like Seeds and Heffernan looks decidedly more complex and problematic than it did to liberals in the 1930s or 1940s. They argued for the right to education for all children and in coming years would defend democracy against Fascism abroad and at home. Is their work a deeply flawed example of cultural imposition, or does their defense of the rights of all children to an education challenge Foucauldian ideas of the disciplining and oppressive state?

CHAPTER 5

Love and War

January 1939 must have seemed like a new beginning to progressive Californians. On January 2, Culbert Olson was inaugurated as governor, the first Democrat to hold that office in the twentieth century.[1] Immediately after assuming office Olson took the symbolic action of freeing accused Socialist Tom Mooney (who had been imprisoned for over twenty years on almost certainly trumped-up charges) and appointed the radical journalist Carey McWilliams as commissioner of housing and immigration. Political tensions were still high in California, particularly around the question of farm labor. Both McWilliams's book on California agriculture, *Factories in the Fields*, and John Steinbeck's *Grapes of Wrath* were published in 1939. Once he took office, McWilliams began to investigate and document the living and working conditions of migrant farm workers.[2] As one radical labor organizer remembered 1939: "We used to say that when Culbert Olson was elected governor, socialism came to California. It was a joke, of course, but it did make a big difference.... It was a very different atmosphere from before. It was a Culbert Olson atmosphere. It was a Carey McWilliams atmosphere."[3] Although Olson would last only one term as governor—he was defeated by the Republican Earl Warren in 1942 and faced hostility from right-wing legislators throughout his term—his election heartened radicals and liberals alike.

In February 1939, the Golden Gate International Exposition opened on Treasure Island in San Francisco Bay, celebrating the possibilities of a Pacific culture and the achievements of the New Deal in San Francisco. The Golden Gate exposition, which continued through 1940, captured that brief moment of hope between the Depression and the onset of war. But if progressives welcomed Olson's New Deal and many Californians saw hope for a new future in the Golden Gate exposition, internationally things looked quite different. The fall of Madrid in May 1939 marked the Fascist victory in the Spanish Civil War. The Nazi-Soviet Pact of August 23, 1939, shocked both liberals and Soviet sympathizers and confirmed the suspicions of the Right. The Nazi invasion of Poland a week later led to the declaration of war on Germany by Britain and France, thus beginning the Second World War.

Both Seeds and Heffernan were increasingly concerned about the international situation. Even before the outbreak of the war, they had begun to frame the progressive values of democracy, cooperation, and respect for individual difference in opposition to Fascism and to a lesser extent to Soviet Communism. In a 1938 presentation to a teachers' institute, for example, Heffernan justified teaching topics like the Westward Movement as a way to lead children to appreciate "their forefathers' achievements," since "if the children of today are to appreciate democracy fully, we must emotionalize their feeling toward democracy just as determinedly as Fascist and Nazi leaders are emotionalizing their future citizens."[4] In a 1938 paper, "Some Philosophical Considerations Which Are Basic to Curriculum Building," Corinne Seeds and Lorraine Sherer contrasted democratic living to "living in a country such as Italy or Germany or Russia today where the way of living is determined not by the people themselves but by dictators."[5] In defending Dewey's conception of the school as a small society to her 1938 summer school class, Seeds commented, "Dewey's Kingdom of God is not a commune as we have it today in Russia—nor is it a dictatorship as we have it in Italy and Germany today. I believe it may be defined as a Social Democracy."[6]

In the spring of 1939, the University of California radio station broadcast a series of programs on the UES. One May 1939 broadcast, entitled "The Little Red Schoolhouse is Gone," advertised the coming UCLA summer session for teachers.[7] In the context of rising concern about war in Europe, the announcer of the program made a point of comparing the old education to Fascism. He commented to Seeds that when he was young "we kids didn't know what it meant to be free in school. We had about as much freedom as Hitler allows the German people today. We sat in our seats, each one doing exactly as he was told—each one seeking to outdo the others—each one doing exactly the same thing." The summer session, Seeds responded, was designed to challenge such authoritarian teaching methods and to show "teachers working with children in a democratic way." She continued, "It is hard to change from a dictator to a promoter of the democratic way of life. But every summer miracles do happen! Classrooms everywhere are slowly being transformed from teacher-dominated autocracies to child-willed democracies."[8] Heffernan also spoke of the importance of teaching the value of democracy in an address to the Bay Area Regional Conference of Elementary School Principals and District Superintendents held only two months after the declaration of war between England and France and Nazi Germany. According to the *Western Journal of Education*, Heffernan celebrated the accomplishments of democratic educators, but she also made clear her sense that the world was at a crisis point. She concluded: "We will either win at this juncture and make the world a decent place in which to live, or civilization will be destroyed."[9]

Heffernan and Seeds were at the height of their influence in 1939. Heffernan was chair of the committee in charge of preparing the 1939 *Yearbook* for the National Education Association's Department of Supervisors and Directors of Instruction. Of the sixteen chapters in the *Yearbook*, nine described California schools.[10] In April 1939, Heffernan spoke at an education conference in Oregon to an audience of 1,000 on the topic "What Society Has a Right to Expect of the Modern School." The other speaker on the program was the governor of Oregon.[11] The year 1939 saw the publication of Heffernan's children's book, *Desert Treasure*, which she coauthored with Irmagarde Richards and Alice Salisbury.[12] The first joint meeting of the California Elementary School principals and district superintendents, long supporters of Heffernan, was held in April, 1939. At that initial meeting, the president of the Elementary Principals' Association proclaimed: "Miss Heffernan is to be commended as the leader who, perhaps more than any other one person, has encouraged the growth of a progressive philosophy of education."[13]

In the late 1930s, Seeds's work was widely recognized in California and beyond. She trained large numbers of teachers, many of whom became disciples of her progressive approach and spread it throughout California. Helen Heffernan reached out to Seeds, inviting her to participate on statewide committees, most significantly including her on the Committee on Scope and Sequence in Major Learnings in the Curriculum, which was established in 1935 to identify the common goals of all levels of education in the state and to help develop a "more unified school system."[14] Seeds and Heffernan met at conferences and institutes, sometimes appearing on the same platform, as was the case at the 1938 School Supervisors Conference at the Biltmore Hotel in Los Angeles.[15] Seeds continued to enjoy a national reputation as an innovative educator and the support of an active and influential group of UES parents.

In September 1939, Helen Heffernan, along with a number of other California educators, including Lillian Hill and Gladys Potter, spoke at several teachers' institutes in Idaho, traveling for the first time by plane.[16] Only a few weeks later, Potter abruptly resigned from her position as assistant chief of the Division of Elementary Education to become supervisor of Primary Education in the Long Beach City Schools.[17] Potter and Heffernan had worked closely together since 1931, when Potter was appointed assistant chief. The two women were often presented as coleaders of the progressive movement in the State Department of Education.[18] Given her close association with Heffernan and her many activities speaking at conferences, publishing articles, and serving as principal of the summer demonstration school at Berkeley, it is surprising that Potter would resign from her influential state position to become a supervisor in the Long Beach public schools. No reason was given for Potter's decision to resign, but it may be no coincidence that in the fall of 1939, Helen Heffernan and Corinne Seeds began an intense romantic relationship.

To Think of You Makes My Heart Sing

Knowledge of Seeds's and Heffernan's personal relationship comes from a collection of over 400 letters Seeds wrote to Heffernan between 1939 and 1946 found in Heffernan's private papers after her death. Although

Heffernan kept a number of personal letters addressed to her, very few of Heffernan's own letters remain, and none of the letters she wrote to Seeds have survived.[19] The letters to Heffernan provide evidence of a wide group of women—professional colleagues and allies—who lived in a world of intense same-sex relationships. There is evidence to suggest that both Seeds and Heffernan had had previous close bonds with women, and after her romantic involvement with Seeds ended, Heffernan entered a long-term relationship with another woman. Tricia Franzen has noted that the stories of the lives of women in same-sex relationships, especially those touching on "their full emotional and sexual lives, have been lost to several generations of historians, feminists, and lesbians."[20] In many cases, the letters and diaries documenting the emotional lives of women were intentionally destroyed. Estelle Freedman has pointed out the striking phenomenon of the "burning of letters" by women in close same-sex relationships in the 1940s.[21]

The surviving letters from Seeds to Heffernan provide an invaluable resource for understanding their own stories and suggest a wider community of women. In this world, personal connections strengthened and shaped political alliances. The letters document the public political struggles of the time, but they also reveal a powerful intimate reality, a woman's world in formation in the years before gay liberation. Letters as evidence are hardly transparent.[22] Like diaries and unlike autobiographies, letters describe a present moment of time, but unlike diaries (written to oneself) or autobiographies (written to a public audience), letters are composed to an audience of one other person—and are thus both public and yet at the same time private.[23] Personal letters like those from Seeds to Heffernan thus must be read with a consciousness of the relationship of writer and recipient in mind. Like any other form of writing, letters are constructions, but, as is the case for many other genres, what is being constructed is not only a view of the external world, but of the letter-writing subject herself. In her letters to Helen Heffernan, Corinne Seeds constructed herself as loyal, loving, and passionate.

Fall 1939 is mentioned in several of Seeds's letters as the beginning of her intense relationship with Heffernan. The romantic nature of that relationship is suggested in the first letter from Seeds to Heffernan that can be dated, from October 12, 1939. The letter begins: "To think of you driving through Southern Oregon at this time of year, fleeing from year-books and stacks of mail makes my heart sing!" And later in the same letter: "Arriving at school I found exactly four letters from you which ought to be enough. Four 'Helens' and four 'Corinnes' and best of all your itinerary! Letters from the State Department, for some reason seem to have a rather rosy hue these days!"[24] That this October letter was written very early in their intimate relationship is also suggested by later references, as in this passage from a letter Seeds wrote to Heffernan two years later, on September 28, 1941. Mentioning an upcoming October conference, Seeds wrote: "Yes, dear, the conference *is* week after next. It is anniversary *two* for us."

The narrative line of Seeds's letters is one of absence and desire. The two women lived in cities separated by about 400 miles, Heffernan alone, but Seeds with her parents. They only spent time together at professional meetings or on holidays. A consistent theme in Seeds's letters is the pain of absence and the power of memory of past times together. On January 5, 1941, Seeds wrote to Heffernan: "Beloved I hope you do miss me—for I have been bereft without you. In my bedroom I feel as if someone had died and left it with much unfinished."[25] Another theme that occurs again and again is a mutual love of nature and the California landscape. The letters frequently refer to the beauty of the California countryside, their mutual enjoyment of wildflowers, the mountains, and the ocean. This love of nature is intertwined with their political and educational alliance. In one letter, Seeds wrote: "I loved our trip to Sacramento, talking about democracy in education and seeing the spring burst in the Sacramento Valley."[26] Descriptions of nature were also connected to expressions of love. For example, in one 1942 letter to Heffernan, Seeds wrote that she wanted to remind Heffernan "that in every beautiful thing my love for you pours forth—in the delicate orange slip of moon hanging suspended over a magnificent eucalyptus tree, in the gorgeous orange sunrise of the late autumn, and in the burst of orange fire which lights the western sky as the great ball of life for us sinks beyond view in the Pacific. I love you so!"[27] Nature also represented sensuality, as in this description from a letter from April 1941: "Of course many, many times today my spirit returned to Dana Point with the breeze blowing about your hair and the sand squishing up between your toes as hand-in-hand we walked along the water's edge. Together, yes—but really *one*!"[28]

Several of Seeds's letters suggest a physical desire. In a letter to Heffernan about her anticipation of a weekend they were to spend together at a conference in Bakersfield, for example, Seeds wrote: "Wherever you believe we will be happiest we shall stay. Tell me where to go as I will probably arrive first. I may not be able to sit thru' that last meeting without leaving early. It seems that there are nice looking motels—but sometimes they are noisy and not overly private. But, anyplace with you will do!" Another example of sensuality is this passage from Seeds commenting on Heffernan's relationship with Gladys Potter: "I'm sure all of the others felt honored to be one with you. No wonder Gladys Potter kissed you and sat on your lap. You lifted her head and shoulders above the crowd—with the caress you have in your voice when speaking of her and to her. She has missed it more intimately and you gave it back. She will look less old from now on. As for myself, I care for you so much and want you to care for me above all else." As previously mentioned, Gladys Potter had suddenly left her position as Heffernan's assistant only the year before. Seeds's description of Potter's kiss, her sitting on Heffernan's lap, and the use of the term "caress," even though it referred to a tone of voice and not physical touch, was highly sexual. And of course Seeds's comment about Potter that "she will look less old from now on..." was a rather transparent expression of Seeds's jealousy and competitiveness for Heffernan's affection.

Seeds's understanding of her relationships may well have been influenced by her experience with psychoanalysis. In 1941, several members of the UES staff, including Seeds, began psychoanalysis with Lydia Sicher, a Viennese follower of the Austrian psychoanalyst Alfred Adler. Sicher had directed Adler's Clinic for Nervous Diseases in Vienna from 1929 until 1939, when the Nazis closed the clinic and she escaped to the United States.[29] Naturally we have no idea what the experience of psychoanalysis was for Seeds, but given the nature of most psychotherapy in this period, it is highly probable that sex would have been raised in her sessions with Dr. Sicher. And it also seems likely that in the early 1940s Seeds would have understood women's sexuality in a very different way than had women at the turn of the twentieth century, when close relationships between middle-class women were accepted and seen as nonthreatening. Such relationships, often known as Boston marriages, frequently entailed the establishment of households and life-long partnerships. But by the 1930s, the single woman was becoming a dangerous figure, in part through the dissemination of the work of late nineteenth century sexologists such as Krafft-Ebing and Havelock Ellis and the spread of Freud's belief that same-sex relationships were "arrested" and thus unnatural.

Lillian Faderman sees the 1928 publication of the novel *The Well of Loneliness* as marking the beginning of social anxieties about women's same-sex love, captured in the popular figure of the "mannish lesbian."[30] After the publication of *The Well of Loneliness*, a number of popular novels depicting lesbians as sick, self-hating, and sexually voracious were published. Public acceptance of Boston marriages, "smashing," or women "romantic friends" gradually began to be replaced by fear and suspicion of the sexually deviant lesbian.[31] When single women had been viewed as harmless spinsters (the object of pity or amusement), they had been accepted, but as it became clear that they were able to support themselves and live outside the patriarchal family, and particularly when they became sexualized (that is, when the lesbian identity became possible to think), they were increasingly seen as deviant, dangerous, and subversive to the social order. The early 1940s, when Heffernan and Seeds's relationship was at its most intense, was a transitional period. Although there was increasing anxiety about the dangers of the "mannish lesbian," close relationships between middle-class women, particularly professional women, seem still to have been accepted. Corinne Seeds's parents, for example, seem to have embraced her close friendship with Helen Heffernan. Evidence from letters and autobiographies indicates that women-identified women fell in love, set up households together, and often moved in woman-only social groups. In her 1929 study of the sex lives of 2,200 women, Katherine Bement Davis found that 50 percent had experienced "intense emotional relationships with other women" and about ten percent had sexual relations with other women.[32] Similar results were presented in Lura Beam's 1934 study, *The Single Woman: A Medical Study in Sex Education*. But these books were not taken up by the media and did not reach popular audiences. It was only with the 1948 Kinsey report, which reported that 25 percent of women reported sexual attractions to other women and between 3 and 12 percent were lesbians, and the aggressive homophobia of the Cold War, that lesbianism became widely seen as a social problem.

As was true of other women, Heffernan and Seeds kept their personal lives private. There was no public political movement with which they could identify as women who loved women, even though as John D'Emilio points out, at the end of the Depression approximately 30 percent of all "white, native-born, college-educated women between the ages of forty and forty-five had never married."[33] Lillian Faderman provides evidence that independent professional women in this period created households together and were accepted as respected members of their communities if they "enjoyed enough status to be beyond reproach in the world in which they moved."[34] Although Heffernan and Seeds did not directly address the political implications of this women's world, they were acutely aware of male privilege and hostility toward women, particularly toward single women. In one letter to Heffernan, Seeds responded to the idea that unmarried women teachers lead "unnatural" lives: "Helen, I'm sick of hearing that school teachers do not live normal lives—especially the unmarried ones. I've yet to see that marriage alone is the answer. In my experience I'll take the unmarried ones who have found satisfaction in contributing to the reconstruction of society in ways other than reproducing themselves."[35]

In her letters, Seeds often referred to a wider group of women educators in California who had intimate same-sex relationships, but, as was true of other romantic letters between women from these years, Seeds's letters never mentioned the term lesbian. This seems typical of the time. Liz Kennedy has noted that the personal letters, diaries, and memoirs of women in same-sex relationships have usually continued a "pattern of discretion created during a lifetime of 'never talking.'"[36] The only reference I have found to either Heffernan or Seeds as a lesbian is a comment in Helen Heffernan's FBI file, where "an informant" stated that "rumors had been persistent for years that Miss HEFFERNAN is a lesbian, and that, while these contentions had never been proved, many circumstantial events tended to support the suspicions."[37] But if Seeds did not use the term "lesbian," she did describe close same-sex relationships, using the terms "special friend" or "best friend" to describe them, as in one letter to Heffernan: "Did you know that [Miss Holt's] *special* friend is Pearl Middlebrooks? I refrained from making any derogatory remarks about my friend 'Hepsie' who was my 'Betsy's' best friend."[38] In another letter, Seeds described two women who had attended the summer supervisors' conference two years earlier: "They are both salt-of-the-earth types, good hearted, a bit catty, but talk so much that it is hard to know what they think. Edith is more brilliant—Mimi more social. But, they found each other twenty years ago (or more) and have made a wonderful two-some."[39]

The bond between Heffernan and Seeds was domestic as well as passionate. Both Seeds and Heffernan had rich and busy separate private lives. They lived in their own homes and had wide circles of women friends. Tricia Franzen has argued that although they have too often been overlooked, women-centered communities were central to the success of women in the professional world in the years before gay liberation.[40] The personal and political alliances among Heffernan and her supporters do suggest a kind of family. For example, Seeds wrote to Heffernan imagining a bridge party Heffernan was going to have at her Sacramento house for some of her friends: "Yes dear, I would have been bored to distraction with bridge but from a great distance, through a telescope I would like to have witnessed your joy at having your family reunited in the midst of the beauty you had created for its members. All of them are greatly honored and blessed to be loved by you, dear!"[41]

Heffernan, Seeds, and their friends enjoyed playing cards and drinking whiskey. One friend wrote to Heffernan about an upcoming party with a "Mrs. L.," who was "Scotch, in spite of her name, and really fun. She plays a particularly virulent form of rummy instead of bridge, but she serves good whiskey and good conversation, so it may not be a bad evening."[42] This social world suggests the circle of women friends in San Francisco described by a lesbian professor in an oral history collected by Lillian Faderman. The group was made up of "psychologists, teachers, professors, librarians" who "held salons and dinner parties regularly, to which most of the women wore navy blue suits and pumps, almost as much a requisite uniform as butch and femme dress in the gay bars."[43] In the interwar years, the representation of the single-woman professor, teacher, or social worker, established and accepted in the late nineteenth century, still had purchase, particularly when the woman was careful to wear navy blue suits and pumps.

Heffernan collected tiffany glass, was an avid gardener, and entertained frequently. Seeds's letters to Heffernan were filled with questions about the state of the garden. In Fall 1942, Heffernan sent the Seeds family preserved quinces from her own tree.[44] Heffernan's garden was clearly a source of pleasure, but Seeds felt the burden of meeting the demands of both her domestic and professional life. In a letter to Heffernan, she described the difficulties of managing both her obligations at home and her duties at work. One night she described frying a young chicken for dinner, "but," she wrote, "it isn't easy to work at school and at home as you know!" In another letter she described her day: "I have several chores to do after this letter is finished—making a custard pie with the good crust I made this morning and sewing the clean covers on the sofa cushions. Then, I shall read carefully the opening Chap. of the Year Book and see what I can do to shorten ours."[45]

Beginning in 1940, Seeds and Heffernan created a kind of domestic life together, even though they lived in separate cities. Heffernan stayed with the Seeds family when she visited Los Angeles and Seeds stayed with Heffernan when she was in Sacramento. In one letter, Seeds imagined that she was with Heffernan, arriving at Heffernan's home at 3416 Land Park Drive in Sacramento: "We did not unpack the car—merely opened the door wearily, turned on the light, looked for mail on the little corner table by the fireplace, then moved to the kitchen for a drink and on up the stairs and into the bedroom where I soon folded myself in beside you under the white blankets! It was *all* so real! I could actually smell the shut-in-ness of the house and feel the cool air as you opened the bedroom door."[46] Seeds's letters describe a settled domestic routine when Heffernan visited Los Angeles. Heffernan, Corinne, and Sherman Seeds played cards together; Heffernan did jigsaw puzzles with Sherman Seeds. In the early 1940s, Heffernan spent every Thanksgiving with the Seeds family in Los Angeles.

The closer personal relationship between Seeds and Heffernan led to a much stronger professional alliance. Heffernan and Seeds both spoke at the March 1940 joint meeting of the California School Supervisors' Association and the Elementary School Principals' Association, organizations that were powerful supporters of Helen Heffernan. In her presentation, Seeds was effusive in her praise for Heffernan. Her vision, Seeds said, "will bring real education into every classroom in California and along with it enriched living for our children and tremendous growth for ourselves and our teachers."[47] For her part, in her 1940 article, "How Can We Make a Rural School Democratic for Children, Teachers, and Parents?" Heffernan used examples from UES to illustrate the power of creative expression as fundamental to democratic education.[48] This personal and political alliance with Heffernan would become invaluable to Corinne Seeds in the political struggles in years to come.

Conflict at UCLA

The early 1940s brought significant changes at UCLA. Seeds's protector Charles Waddell had retired in 1939. Later that year, the UCLA Teachers College had been disbanded and a school of education established in its place, focused on research and offering doctoral degrees. In January 1940, Marvin Darsie, the first dean of the newly established School of Education, died unexpectedly. Edwin Lee, a professor at Teachers College, Columbia, was appointed to replace him. Lee remained dean of the UCLA School of Education until he retired in 1957, the same year that Corinne Seeds retired. On June 30, 1940, Jesse Bonds was named to replace Seeds's long-time supporter Charles Waddell as director of training programs. Seeds was probably the best-known educator at the new UCLA School of Education, but she did not have a doctorate and was not a full-time member of the faculty. Her relationship with Bond and Lee seems to have been uneasy from the beginning. In his previous position as director of secondary training, Bond had little contact with Seeds, but once he replaced Waddell as overall director of teacher training in 1940, conflicts with Seeds developed almost immediately. And Seeds and Edwin Lee had little in common. Although Lee had received his MA and PhD from Teachers College, Columbia, he did not study with Dewey and Kilpatrick. His specialty was vocational education. These two men—Lee, the dean of the School of Education, and Bond, the director of teacher training—would become central figures in the coming drama of the University Elementary School.

Seeds was particularly sensitive to gender politics in education and was distrustful of Lee's attitude toward women. That she may well have had reason for this distrust is suggested by Lee's 1934 speech, "Woman's Education as a Man Sees It." What mattered most for Lee was not women's minds, but their maternal bodies. Lee wrote that the most important aspect of education for a woman was to guarantee "that her body shall be as nearly perfect as possible for the function which is her biological reason for existence—call it physical education, personal hygiene, health education, what you will. I care not what the name so long as you teach this girl the beauty, the sanctity, and the total care of her beautiful body."[49] Lee concluded, "Woman is a mate, and the mate of a man and not of another woman." It is doubtful that either Heffernan or Seeds knew of Lee's speech on the education of women or his ideas about who should be "woman's mate," but they certainly sensed his views. Seeds commented to Heffernan in one letter, "I had an appointment with Dean Lee at eleven.... He resents a woman telling him anything."[50] In another she mentioned the upcoming superintendents' conference organized by Lee: "Not a woman appears as speaker.... I'm not going to remind [Lee] that he has ignored women. I know you turned them down. You must have been the only woman invited to speak."[51]

In 1940 Seeds faced not only a new and less supportive administration at UCLA, but the hostility of Los Angeles superintendent of schools Vierling Kersey. From the beginning of his tenure as Los Angeles superintendent Kersey had been suspicious of Seeds and her school. He wanted to eliminate UES and instead build a demonstration school under the direct control of the Los Angeles city school system. In a letter to Los Angeles School Board member Fred Good in June 1939, Kersey complained that, although the Los Angeles School Board loaned the university the site and buildings, it had virtually no control of UES, which was in essence run as a private school. Kersey continued, "This has not been an entirely satisfactory arrangement and I believe we are all glad that the time is at hand when the city is to take over this school."[52] It is clear Seeds deeply distrusted Kersey. In one letter to Heffernan, Seeds mentioned that she made sure Kersey was excluded from a banquet she was organizing: "I wouldn't sit at the banquet with that traitor as an honored guest."[53] In another letter, she wrote: "Bond says that Kersey says the U.E.S. is going one way while the *City* is going the other! Pretty true—I would surely lead the U.E.S. in a direction away from *him*!"[54] Seeds later described seeing Kersey at a conference: "Kersey made the opening address. It was a masterpiece for him—short sentences finished and well composed. He is thinner—but still disgusting."[55]

The conflict over the status of UES was already under way when Edwin Lee became dean of the School of Education in 1940. Lee had been brought in with the expectation that he would strengthen the academic offerings of the new School of Education, particularly by introducing a doctoral program in School Administration.[56] He had little experience with elementary education. Heffernan and Seeds, who were uncertain of Lee's position, seem to have encouraged their supporters to write to University of California president Robert Sproul to defend Seeds and her program. The letters argued that teachers trained at UCLA were superior to those coming from other institutions. One teacher wrote, "We teachers out in the field look to these experimentations in reading, in rhythms, and in creative writing for our background. We point out with pride: 'at the Training School it is done in this manner. We know it's right because it has worked there.'"[57] Heffernan herself wrote Sproul on May 28, 1940, strongly supporting UES. Sproul responded with some exasperation: "I am a little late in acknowledging this letter because it is, literally, one of hundreds which have come to me in the last week on the same subject. In reply, I can only say that I know of no present proposal to permit the control of the University Elementary School to be taken over by the Los Angeles Board of Education."[58]

In the 1940 debate over the future of UES, Lee and Bond both cautiously supported the school. Despite his lukewarm support of women educators in general, Lee backed Seeds and saw UES as contributing to UCLA's prestige and status. Bond, while personally unsympathetic to Seeds, was at this point impressed by the level of support the school had elicited. In a January 30, 1941, letter, Bond noted that before he had taken his present position, he believed UES should become simply a public school controlled by the Los Angeles School Board, but after being "deluged by such a mass of testimony from school men outside of the University concerning the worth of the school," he had changed his mind.[59] Bond's use of the term "school men" here is interesting. Although of course there were some men among Seeds's supporters, the majority of her followers were women, led by the powerful and charismatic Helen Heffernan.

In the summer of 1941, a third UCLA administrator with authority over Corinne Seeds was appointed. This was John Hockett, who was named director of elementary training in July 1941, replacing Charles Waddell. Apparently the male administrators at UCLA assumed that Waddell's replacement should be a man, despite the overwhelming preponderance of women in the field of elementary education. As Ernest Horn, a professor at the University of Iowa, wrote to Edwin Lee, "Unfortunately, the young men capable of directing such work in elementary education are scarce as hen's teeth."[60] Hockett, who had obtained his PhD from Teachers College, Columbia, and had been on the faculty of the University of California at Berkeley since 1927, had worked closely with Helen Heffernan at the Berkeley summer demonstration school. He and his wife Ruth Hockett seem to have been personal friends of Heffernan's.

Given his close connection with Heffernan and his seeming dedication to progressive ideas, John Hockett should have been a natural ally for Corinne Seeds. But there was tension between Hockett and Seeds from the beginning. Some sense of this is shown in a letter Ruth Hockett wrote to Helen Heffernan in January 1941, during the negotiations to bring John Hockett to UCLA. Ruth Hockett believed that Seeds herself might have wanted the position of director of elementary training and that Seeds viewed John Hockett as some kind of threat to her own position.[61] That Ruth Hockett was correct in her suspicion that Seeds did not welcome John Hockett's appointment at UCLA is made clear in the letter Seeds had sent Heffernan a few weeks earlier. Seeds wrote, "The more I think of John the more disgusted I get. To think that by doing little at Berkeley for fourteen years he can be rewarded by a title of Assoc. Prof. and a place in *my* sun down here. He has all the characteristics of a *small* man, small in stature and otherwise....While he owes everything to *women* he gives no one of them any credit!"[62] This letter captures many aspects of Seeds's character: her sensitivity to men in leadership positions (Hockett "owes everything to *women,* but gives them no credit"), her egotism (Hockett should not have a place in *her* sun), and her resentment and anger at those she considered rivals.

The tension between the School of Education and the Los Angeles City schools over UES continued into the early 1940s. Vierling Kersey was openly hostile to UES, and President Sproul was lukewarm. Only Dean Edwin Lee continued to defend the school. One contentious issue was the question of repairs and maintenance. Kersey and the Los Angeles School Board were reluctant to provide funds to repair a school that was not under its control. On the other hand, President Sproul did not want to spend money on a building owned by the City of Los Angeles. Lee tried to convince Sproul of the school's significance: "The University Elementary School...is to the School of Education what the hospital is to the Medical School—a laboratory for study and investigation as well as training."[63] Although Lee told Sproul that "no arrangement can be worked out with Kersey which will not scuttle the elementary school as an experimental institution," Sproul was still reluctant to end the connection with the Los Angeles public schools.[64] Kersey did finally agree to provide $2,000 for "ground improvements" for the 1942–43 school year, but this hardly addressed the major needs of the school.[65]

Suspicion that male hostility to a woman in a position of power underlay the threats to Seeds and her school is most clearly expressed in an exchange of letters between Madeleine Veverka, the former director of elementary curriculum for the Los Angeles City Schools, and Helen Heffernan in October 1941. Veverka, who herself had studied at Teachers College and who had retired in June 1939, wrote in response to what she saw as the threat to Seeds's life work. Veverka wrote to Heffernan:

> A situation is developing or has developed among us here in California which it seems to me is the business of all women in Education....There came to me a rumor some days ago, indeed it was more than a rumor, that Miss Seeds at U.C.L.A. is becoming less and less secure in her position, in short that there are forces set in motion to "get her." This you and I know is prompted by professional jealousy for it is no secret that she stands head and shoulders above some of the Educational staff of her College. It is also strengthened by that insidious thing all women feel and that is the underground effort to eliminate or at least to minimize women in positions of responsibility and leadership in education. As soon as this rumor came to me, I asked about the attitude of our own City Superintendent. You and I know even without inquiry what that attitude would be. I was told we could hardly expect much help from that quarter.

The Los Angeles City superintendent, of course, was Vierling Kersey. As Veverka saw the situation: "A fine woman [Seeds] is possibly being attacked in ways against which she can not well defend herself. How can we use our wits and influence to keep a colleague from the claws of self-seeking jealous men?"[66]

Heffernan wrote back thanking Veverka for her support. Heffernan emphasized her debt to Corinne Seeds: "I have not hesitated to state publicly and privately the deep professional debt I owe [Seeds] because she has influenced my professional thinking as I believe she has influenced the thinking of all of us." The situation was particularly troubling to her, Heffernan wrote, because "over the past two years...my long professional acquaintance with Corinne Seeds has flowered into a deep friendship." In those two years, Heffernan said, she had been diligent in "efforts to strengthen [Seeds's] position and to bring an understanding of the high regard in which she is held to the attention of the President of the University, Dean Edwin Lee, and the Regents of the University." Although she was careful not to mention specific names, Heffernan called the group mobilizing against Seeds "a conspiracy." Moreover, she wrote, "Some of the persons who have entered into the conspiracy occupy high places in education in your area. I shall be glad to mention names which I know will not come as a surprise to you. But personally, I have the greatest faith in the integrity of Dean Lee."

The mention of persons in "high places in education in your area" seems an obvious reference to Vierling Kersey. Heffernan continued, "The opposition comes largely from one wicked man who would impose his stupid will on educational progress and prevent movement in the direction of what is right and good for human beings." Moreover, "he really is not even representing his own beliefs but is the paid mouthpiece of financial interests which fear the outcomes of education in producing the day when every man will truly have opportunity to achieve his potentialities." Heffernan then tied the threat to Seeds to the broader struggle between democracy and the forces of reaction and, eventually, of Fascism. Just as there would always be resistance to Fascist dictatorships, Heffernan wrote, there would always be those who would defend democratic education.[67]

Heffernan's faith in Dean Lee was justified. In late 1941 Lee appointed a "committee of six" to evaluate the school. His choice of the newly retired Charles Waddell to chair the committee was almost certainly a sign of Lee's positive view of the school, since Waddell was one of Seeds's strongest supporters. Bond and Seeds were also appointed to the committee. On April 8, 1942, the committee presented a report strongly supportive of UES. In response to the continuing tension over the Warner Avenue site, the committee recommended that a new school facility be built on the UCLA campus. While the university should provide "maintenance, support, and control" of the school, the school would continue to be a public school with funding from the state based on average daily attendance.[68] The committee report basically recommended everything Corinne Seeds wanted.

Strong-Willed Women Together

Seeds survived the crisis over the future of her school in the early 1940s, in part because of the support Helen Heffernan was able to mobilize. The professional alliance between them was strengthened that year when the annual Summer Conference on Supervision moved from Berkeley to UCLA. Seeds had taught her summer courses Education 131A and 131B and directed the summer program at UES at the UCLA summer school for a number of years. Beginning in 1941, Heffernan, working closely with Seeds, led the summer conferences on Elementary Supervision at UCLA, integrating observation of UES into the supervisors' program. Seeds and Heffernan planned the 1941 conference together and led sessions, as did their allies Natalie White, Martha Deane, and Gretchen Wulfing, who was also president of the California School Supervisors' Association that year.[69] After the first conference, some thirty participants wrote a group letter to Sproul, Lee, Bond, and Dexter, with copies to Seeds and Heffernan, "to voice our appreciation of two great educational leaders, Miss Helen Heffernan and Miss Corinne Seeds."[70]

In the early 1940s, the summer conferences on Supervision drew more than 200 educators annually, many of them teachers and supervisors who already had worked with Heffernan or had studied with Seeds at UCLA.[71] Participants observed classes at UES in the morning, sat in on meetings with student supervisors and teachers, and participated in group discussions and analysis of what they had observed in the afternoon. Heffernan claimed that over 80 percent of California elementary school supervisors had attended one of the summer workshops by 1943.[72] In these years, the UCLA summer supervisors' conferences were among the most important venues for building a network of educators supportive of their ideas. And for Seeds at least, they also offered her a chance to spend time with Heffernan privately. She wrote to Heffernan in 1941 that the conference was hard, but "it was most satisfying, particularly to me because I saw *you* every day. It is just as much joy to work with you as it is to play with you—and that is Heaven's own bit of recreation! To me we have twice demonstrated that two very strong-willed women can work together and like it!"[73]

Despite the professional alliance between Heffernan and Seeds and Seeds's continued declarations of love, there were tensions between them almost from the beginning. One major source of tension was Heffernan's ongoing other relationships. Heffernan was clearly a charismatic and attractive person who called forth deep loyalty, affection, and sometimes passion. A number of personal letters from other women educators in the Helen Heffernan papers at the University of Riverside testify to the intensity of these relationships.[74]

There is some evidence that Seeds also had earlier romantic relationships. In one letter to Heffernan, Seeds referred to Natalie White's jealousy of Seeds's relationship with Heffernan: "I *don't understand*! She's always encouraged my other friendships—aided and abetted the Diana episode!"[75]

It is unclear what Seeds meant to imply by her "other friendships," but the reference to aiding and abetting the "Diana episode" is suggestive. It seems most likely that the "Diana" mentioned here is Diana Anderson, who taught physical education at UES for many years. Seeds's use of the phrase the "Diana episode" seems to imply something more than platonic friendship. In another letter to Heffernan, Seeds wrote: "Diana used to say, 'Two women can't make it'.... I know now that Diana never could 'make it' with anybody—but thank God we're not all alike."[76] Seeds obviously thought she and Heffernan could "make it" together. She wrote to Heffernan that she wished they could take a trip to their childhood homes: "I so much want to do *Goldfield* with you and would like then to drive on over the Rockies for a sojourn in *my* birth place with you!"[77] Although Seeds continued to worry about losing Heffernan, she was optimistic about their future. She wrote: "I wish to make myself worthy of your love all my life! I wish *that* more than anything in life. Surely, together we can make it work—even two 'prima donnas' together."[78]

The romantic relationship between Seeds and Heffernan was at its most intense in the early 1940s, but even then Heffernan continued to have involvements with other women. The most serious of these was with Gretchen Wulfing. Wulfing, who also participated in the 1941 Supervisors' Conference, was a Phi Beta Kappa graduate of Stanford who had worked as a school supervisor in a number of districts since the mid-1930s. She had worked with Paul Hanna at Stanford during the 1935 summer session when Heffernan was a graduate student at Stanford, and this may have been where Heffernan and Wulfing met. But they also must have known one another through the articles Wulfing published in Heffernan's *California Journal of Elementary Education*.[79] In 1940 and 1941, they worked closely together as coeditors (along with Wilhemina Harper) of a children's reader, *All Aboard for Storyland*.[80] Heffernan's contribution was a story called "Fun Gardening Indoors," about a boy named Richard who brought his teacher a bag of tulip, daffodil, and hyacinth bulbs, doubtless based on her memory of the bulbs she had planted as a young teacher in Goldfield many years earlier. Wulfing sent Heffernan a series of passionate letters beginning in 1940.[81] Heffernan's letters to Wulfing have not survived, but she also seems to have written frequently.

The relationship among Seeds, Wulfing, and Heffernan was complex. For example, Wulfing sent a letter to Heffernan in late December 1940, care of Corinne Seeds at 1416 Holmby Avenue. The letter began, "My own angel." Wulfing wrote, "Tomorrow evening I'll phone you at Corinne's, as you suggested.... I should hate to upset plans Corinne is making for you in L.A., so please consider her first."[82] In this letter, Wulfing both expressed her love for Heffernan, yet acknowledged Heffernan's closer relationship with Seeds ("please consider her first"). Seeds, on the other hand, expressed a great deal of concern about Wulfing's relationship with Heffernan. In August 1941, after the completion of the Supervisors' Conference, Seeds wrote Heffernan: "Dear, both you and G. looked *very happy* this morning. G. looked as if she were in heaven! That's what four weeks with you will do! When we planned the Conf. I had no idea that it meant three weeks with G, for you!!!"[83]

Heffernan's relationship with Wulfing continued for several more years. For Christmas, 1942, Heffernan gave Wulfing a piece of tiffany glass. But, by 1943, there was increasing tension between them. Perhaps because of her conflicted relationship with Wulfing, Heffernan began seeing a psychiatrist. When Seeds found out about this, she was disturbed and disapproving, despite her own analysis with Lydia Sicher. She wrote Heffernan: "I am quite alarmed over your sudden concern over psychiatry. I could never dream of *you*, H.H., sitting by the hour telling even Sicher *all* of your life activities from the time you can remember!—placing undue emphasis upon dreams and the like—only to learn the old old story of 'love thy neighbor as thyself.' In your case it would mean letting the *boys* shine in their dumb glory while Calif. Education suffered. I can't reconcile H.H. and psychiatric treatment."[84] It is not clear how long Heffernan saw a psychiatrist. But however troubled she was in her personal life, she certainly did not intend to retreat from her commitments and allow California to suffer while "the boys" shone in all "their dumb glory."

THE INSIDIOUS ENEMY WITHIN

Heffernan's and Seeds's personal relationships may have been a source of anxiety as well as support, but national and international political events brought both Seeds and Heffernan problems of an entirely different sort. In the early 1940s, public criticism of Heffernan and Seeds had not yet emerged, but there was growing unease about contemporary education in the popular press. At the October 1940 School Supervisors' Conference in Pasadena, at which Heffernan and Seeds both spoke, John Sexson, the progressive Pasadena superintendent of schools, gave the opening address on "The Role of Education in the Defense of Democratic Principles." Sexson argued that "only by having accurate knowledge, right attitudes, sane thoughts and a spirit of sacrifice can the insidious enemy from within and belligerent forces from without be combated."[85] This reference to the "insidious enemy within" was doubtless a reference to the attacks on public education that began to emerge in these years.

Beginning in the mid-1930s the attack on progressive public schools had been instigated by fringe right-wing groups, often dominated by single individuals. These groups claimed that the permissive and collectivist nature of progressive education weakened the moral fiber of youth and made them vulnerable to Communism. Individuals like Elizabeth Dilling in Chicago, who in 1934 privately published *Red Network: A 'Who's' Who and Handbook of Radicalism for Patriots* and organizations like the American Legion and the Daughters of the American Revolution became increasingly alarmed about the schools. One focus of right-wing concern was around social studies textbooks. As early as 1933 state superintendent Vierling Kersey had asked Heffernan for her response to criticisms he had received about Teachers

College professor Harold Rugg's popular textbook series, "Man and His Changing Society."[86] Rugg's series, which was extensively used in school systems across the country, encouraged students to consider contemporary social problems by providing what Rugg called "an honest and intelligible description of our social order."[87] Heffernan submitted a strong defense of Rugg, arguing that the series represented more than just "Dr. Rugg's opinions and those of the authors associated with him; it is really the result of the greatest experiment carried on in the United States in developing a course of study, and in producing a series of textbooks to fit this course of study."[88] Heffernan's defense seems to have convinced Kersey, and California schools continued to use the books.

But the Rugg series was not forgotten. In 1940, the American Legion began a concerted campaign against the books, which had sold close to four million textbooks, workbooks, and teachers' guides during the 1930s.[89] The attack on the Rugg books began with a 1939 article in *Forbes* magazine charging that the series was biased against private enterprise and sympathetic to collectivist ideas. The next year the American Legion and the Hearst newspapers joined the battle against the series, as did the Advertising Federation of America and National Association of Manufacturers. Although not all members of the American Legion or the business community joined the attack, those who opposed the series were able to mobilize enough popular support to have the textbooks dropped by local school boards across the nation. Now aware of the dangers of subversion in public school classrooms, the American Legion turned its attention to other materials. The September 1940 issue of the *American Legion Magazine,* included an article, "Treason in the Textbooks," naming the *American Observer,* the *Weekly News Review,* the *Junior Review,* the *Civic Leader,* and *Scholastic* as "objectionable" publications. The *Legion Magazine* subsequently retracted and apologized for the article, but it did not end its suspicion of what it saw as a dangerous liberal bias in public education.[90] In this political climate, the conflation of progressive education with subversion became much stronger.

In response to the Rugg controversy, in 1941 the NEA formed the Committee for the Defense of Democracy Through Education to defend teachers and public schools from "misunderstandings and unjust attack."[91] Several speakers at the NEA's 1941 convention noted the emergence of anti-Communist attacks on the schools.[92] Heffernan, of course, was an active member of the NEA's Department of Supervisors and Directors of Instruction and attended the 1941 convention. In defense of the schools, Heffernan published the results of a national survey done by the NEA in the May, 1941 issue of the *California Journal of Elementary Education,* showing strong public support for education. Heffernan suggested that all those associated with public education in California should become familiar with this survey, since "all articles on education carried by certain widely circulated magazines direct unfavorable criticism toward the schools."[93] This advice to prepare themselves against unfavorable criticism was particularly appropriate for progressive California educators who also were faced with the California legislature's newly formed Joint Fact-Finding Committee on Un-American Activities, later known as the Tenney Committee after its most flamboyant chairman, Jack Tenney.[94]

The establishment of the California legislature's fact-finding committee echoed developments in Washington, where the House Un-American Activities Committee had been established in 1938 under the chairmanship of conservative Democrat Martin Dies. It also reflected the wave of anti-Communist sentiment called forth by the Nazi-Soviet alliance of 1939. In 1940, for example, Congress passed the Smith Act, which made it illegal to advocate the violent overthrow of the government and which was used to persecute members of the Communist Party USA. But the establishment of the fact-finding committee was also the result of the 1940 California legislative elections, which brought control of the Assembly to a new bloc of Republicans and right-wing Democrats. The principal sponsors of the committee were Sam Yorty and Jack Tenney, who had both begun as New Deal Democrats and had been reborn as rabid anti-Communists.[95] When the California Fact-Finding Committee on Un-American Activities was created in 1941, the danger of subversion in education—both in the universities and in the public schools—was one of its central concerns.

At the Annual Conference of the California State Supervisors in October 1941, Corinne Seeds presented a resolution about the need to defend democratic education against its enemies. She described the threat of war as the "German totalitarian machine ruthlessly bombards the strongholds which lead to Moscow in the East and relentlessly continues its attacks upon the British Isles in the West."[96] But the enemies of democracy and democratic education were not only abroad, but within the United States as well. Educators, Seeds continued, needed to fight to "safeguard the children of California and their educational rights against attacks made either by those who are uninformed concerning the purposes of public education, who would reduce the cost of education in their selfish interest, or who are fundamentally opposed to the democratic principle of equality of educational opportunity."[97] Democratic educators should seek allies in other groups loyal to democracy such as organized labor and those concerned with "the socio-economic welfare of the people." The leader of this fight in California, Seeds's resolution concluded, was Helen Heffernan.

Heffernan herself warned of the danger that those hostile to progressive education would take advantage of wartime patriotism. She argued that progressive educators needed to be vigilant and strong in their defense against "attacks from groups who have long been sharpening their knives...under the guise of 'defense,' 'economy,' and 'Americanism.'" Heffernan warned, "I am not calling on educators to be martyrs but I am asking that we do not go to the other extreme and content ourselves to be rabbits. We might reinforce the idea by bringing to the attention of those who would prefer to be rabbits that even rabbits sometimes end as hassenpfeffer."[98] Heffernan may have sensed that she faced enemies who were "sharpening their knives" against her, but the threat they posed was soon eclipsed—at least for the moment—by other events.

THE OUTBREAK OF WAR

On December 7, 1941, the Japanese attack on the U.S. military base at Pearl Harbor brought the United States into the war against Japan, Germany, and Italy. In a vivid passage, Corinne Seeds described Los Angeles on Christmas Day, 1941, less than three weeks after Pearl Harbor:

> On Christmas morning we heard the blast of our guns as they sank a Japanese submarine. We have watched the night-long glow of the lights from the Douglas, Lockheed and Northrop airplane factories and have seen the dog-tired employees staggering home after long, long hours of labor. We have seen the mile-long freight trains composed of flat-cars carrying tanks, machine guns and military conveyances of all kinds slipping toward the harbor under cover of night where their loads are placed on transports bound for the Orient. We have seen the moonless night made bright as day as twenty searchlights at once played upon the flight of a lone airplane through the sky.[99]

The war brought immediate changes to California. The growth of shipbuilding and aircraft manufacturing and California's location as the major base for the war in the Pacific transformed the California economy.[100] Jobs in the defense industries brought about a mass migration of Americans, including many African Americans, from the South and Midwest to Los Angeles and the San Francisco Bay area. The wartime migration meant that schools were faced with an influx of new students, and educators had to grapple with the role of schools in a wartime democracy.

Schools in California as across the nation were encouraged to contribute to the war effort by selling war stamps and bonds, and by making school buildings available for defense. Teachers were expected to work in civil defense and war-related activities. Seeds and the teachers of UES, for example, were asked to help with gas rationing. Seeds described her assignment in a letter to Heffernan: "My shifts will be Thurs., Fri. 5–8 p.m. and Sat. 4–8 p.m. You see we'll run school and then ration at night.... After awhile we shall find it difficult to run schools—with coffee, clothing etc. all waiting to be rationed. Isn't it odd that the Elem. Schools should be the agency to such work?"[101] From the perspective of the military, teachers were expected to teach patriotism and prepare young men for service in the military. As General Somervell said at a 1942 conference on education and the war: "There must be an all-out effort on the Education Front. Every able-bodied boy in America is destined at the appointed age for the armed services."[102]

For Seeds and Heffernan, as for many others on the left, education in war time meant more than the cultivation of future soldiers; it was a key site in the struggle between social democracy and authoritarian Fascism. As Seeds put it in a speech delivered in early 1942: "The whirring motors of the mighty axis planes have grown steadily louder, more ominous and closer to us, until on December 7th at Pearl Harbor the whirring became a bombing which made *us* participating members in this world struggle to decide the fate of democracy, *our* social faith."[103] This conception of democracy included not only personal freedom, but equal opportunity and social welfare. Seeds continued, "The whole people in a democracy must look after the health of its members. This involves changes in our economic structure which will enable all people to have adequate food, clothing and shelter, with competent medical advice."[104] Both Seeds and Heffernan used the rhetoric of the war as the defense of democracy to defend their conceptions of progressive education. They made the point over and over again that if children were to grow up to defend democracy, they needed to experience democratic schooling. The alternative was the kind of authoritarian education used by the Nazis. Seeds made this point forcefully: "Hitler is making Nazis with every means at his disposal. We must consciously work to make democratic Americans."

Heffernan made similar arguments in her 1942 speech "Shall the Modern Educator Recant? The Darkness beyond Tomorrow." Like Seeds, she tied education to politics. She noted that critics had complained that progressive schools lack discipline: "We might ask these critics if they would prefer young people with a spirit of independence to young people who have no minds of their own, who must have a strong leader and who avow only such convictions as have been imposed upon them by external authorities." Heffernan then made one of her strongest claims for the importance of a progressive, democratic education: "My major thesis is this: *Education and Democracy are to each other as roots are to the plant.* Without education, there can be no democracy. If democracy disappears wholly from our earth, its demise will be coincident with the death of modern experimental education." She concluded by considering what makes a period of history a "dark age": "At least one factor of darkness is this: that in such an age all teaching proceeds on authority from above, that all premises are given, and that in the end a supreme education must be regarded as faithful adherence to accepted dogma. Is this what the critics of modern education want? Perhaps not, but this is what they may get."[105]

CHAPTER 6

Prejudice

The Second World War transformed U.S. society. The mobilization of twelve million into the military, the mass internal migrations of those seeking work in the war industries, the short-lived celebration of the abilities of women workers on the home front, and the creation of new gay and lesbian spaces and identities all intimately touched individual lives. The war also raised profound questions about the meaning of democracy in the United States in response to the two poles of Fascism and Communism. Heffernan and Seeds continued to write, teach, and advocate for progressive ideas during the war years, but they faced new challenges and new responsibilities as well. The early 1940s saw the first attacks specifically directed at Heffernan and Seeds. As a state official, Heffernan was faced with the problem of educating a new population of children whose families were drawn to California to work in the defense industries. But perhaps most fundamentally, Heffernan and Seeds, like other white liberals, were challenged by the events of the war to face the deeply entrenched racism of U.S. society.

The lack of discussion of racist injustice in Heffernan's and Seeds's writings in the interwar years was typical of liberals in those years. Race or ethnicity was only mentioned if a child was not white. Like many other white progressive educators, Seeds and Heffernan had tended to ignore structural racism, calling for tolerance and the value of cultural difference while accepting ethnic stereotypes. And, like virtually all white liberals of the period, they failed to see whiteness as a privileged social identity. White children were the norm and children of color the outsiders—only they bore race. It was only with the ascendency of Hitler and National Socialism in Germany that many American liberals began to address racism within the United States. The historian Gary Gerstle has argued that the shift in liberal thinking about race, which in the 1930s had been "subtle," achieved "seismic proportions" in the 1940s.[1] Among progressive and liberal educators, the concern with race was first expressed in the intercultural movement, particularly the Service Bureau for Intercultural Education, which was dedicated to fostering tolerance and mutual understanding among different ethnic and racial groups.[2] By the late 1930s leading liberals were beginning to see the parallels between Nazi ideology and racism in the United States. John Dewey, for example, made a number of speeches in which he denounced Nazism and called on U.S. schools to teach tolerance and mutual understanding. In a 1938 speech before the New York Society for Ethical Culture, Dewey noted that people in the United States condemned "the narrow, bigoted and cruel practices of Nazism." But, he asked, "how far are we free of racial prejudice? What of our attitude toward Negroes, toward aliens within our gates, our anti-Semitism? And what are our schools doing to create tolerance, good will and mutual understanding?"[3]

While white liberals were beginning to grapple with American racism, the African American community was becoming more assertive. Even before the United States joined the war against Fascism, A. Philip Randolph and other African American leaders called for fair and equal opportunities in the defense industry, proposing a march on Washington to publicize their demands. In response, in June 1941, President Roosevelt created the Fair Employment Practices Commission, which at least nominally asserted that the federal government would fight discrimination in hiring. But long-standing racist practices continued, not only in the South, but in the rest of the country as well. The United States armed forces, for example, remained segregated by race. With the entry of the United States into the war, the Nazis and the Japanese used U.S. government treatment of Native Americans and African Americans to argue that the United States was racist against all people of color. In her book *American Unity and Asia*, Pearl Buck warned that the discrimination of the armed forces against "colored soldiers and sailors, the exclusion of colored labor in our defense industries and trade unions, all our social discriminations, are of the greatest aid today to our enemy in Asia, Japan. Japan is saying to millions of listening ears: 'Will white Americans give you equality?'"[4] Liberal magazines and newspapers inside the United States soon began to echo this argument that racial discrimination was a danger to the war effort. Assumptions about race and democracy would be tested almost immediately after the United States entered the war on December 8, 1941.

So Many Tragedies

In his State of the Union address in January 1942, President Franklin Roosevelt emphasized the dangers of racism: "We must be particularly vigilant against racial discrimination in any of its ugly forms. Hitler will try again to breed mistrust and suspicion between one individual and another, one group and another, one race and another."[5] But less than three months after the United States joined the war against Fascism, on February 19, 1942, Roosevelt issued Executive Order 9066, authorizing the removal and internment of all West Coast Japanese Americans and Japanese nationals from the West Coast military zone.[6] California elected officials, including Democratic governor Culbert Olson and Republicans Senator Hiram Johnson and Attorney General Earl Warren, supported Roosevelt's actions. In a February 5, 1942, radio broadcast, Los Angeles mayor Fletcher Bowron claimed that

Los Angeles had become "the hotbed, the nerve center of the spy system of planning for sabotage" by Japanese Americans and demanded that all people of Japanese descent be removed from Los Angeles.[7] Pronouncements like these drew on the tradition of racism against Japanese and Japanese Americans in California.[8]

Corinne Seeds was very sympathetic to Japanese Americans, particularly those she personally knew as students at UCLA. Immediately after Pearl Harbor she wrote, "Yes, in California we know that the war is here. We also know what it means to see the blanched faces of our Japanese friends trying to live above the suspicion that surrounds them."[9] Although Roosevelt signed the evacuation order in February, the difficulty of rounding up thousands of families, keeping them in guarded assembly centers, and then building permanent camps in which to hold them meant that the removal did not begin until late March and continued through the spring of 1942. Los Angeles Japanese were first taken to Santa Anita and Hollywood Park race tracks where they remained for up to two months, many living in whitewashed stables, awaiting transportation to permanent internment camps. In April 1942 Seeds wrote to Helen Heffernan of her concern about "our little Kaoru Kumai," a student whom Heffernan seems to have supported at UCLA, and who was being held at Santa Anita. Kumai had completed her undergraduate work in education at UCLA, but still needed a teaching credential. Seeds wrote to Heffernan: "If she secures her certificate is there anything that you as Chief of the Division of Elementary Education in California can do to enable her to assist in a classroom directed by an American teacher instead of being placed in the fields to work?" Seeds clearly was deeply affected not just by Kumai's situation, but also by the injustice and personal suffering of the Japanese Americans in general. She wrote to Heffernan, "There are so many tragedies connected with this evacuation that it is almost unbearable to think about them."[10]

Seeds was unable to help Kaoru Kumai, but in May 1942, she did what she could to help interned Japanese American families at the Santa Anita racetrack. In her oral history, Seeds described the incident. A Japanese American student teacher from UES (probably Kaoru Kumai) wrote to Seeds from Santa Anita. According to Seeds, she described babies "dying because of lack of milk, and that the children were getting clear out of hand. She wondered if the nice people in our district wouldn't send toys to them." In response to this request, on May 26 Seeds sent a mimeographed letter home to UES parents, describing harsh conditions at Santa Anita and asking for donations of toys and other supplies. In her oral history, Seeds commented, "I thought it was a good letter and sent it home with the children. We got five truck-loads of toys, fruit, milk, and things that were taken to Santa Anita."[11]

On May 31, a *Los Angeles Times* article entitled "Santa Anita Center Officials Defended" appeared. The *Times* quoted extensively from Seeds's letter, which must have been obtained from a UES parent. In the letter, Seeds wrote: "The suggestion has been made that those who are interested in having these Japanese people (many of whom are American citizens) retain their loyalty and belief in the United States, should write to Major General DeWitt of the United States Army to ask that an investigation be made regarding the food conditions at Santa Anita." The *Times* article then cited a number of "officials and local citizens" who strongly denied Seeds's description. The *Times* also noted that there had been a "conference with university officials" after the letter was sent that led to a second letter to parents from Seeds. The *Times* quoted from this second letter: "Most of you received a letter from me written on May 26 regarding the needs of the Japanese children at Santa Anita. The statement should in no way be construed to mean that the situation there is bad. The note merely suggested that certain rumors regarding food conditions might be investigated in order that the children be protected."[12]

The *Times* article called forth immediate responses from the army and local officials denying Seeds's description of conditions in the camp. It also led to a visit to Seeds from an FBI agent, who, according to Seeds in her oral history, spent three hours interviewing her and then interviewed her parents. Seeds recounted that the agent "came down to home and talked to Mother and Dad, and scared Mother nearly to death."[13]

The FBI were not the only ones concerned about Seeds's letter and the story in the *Los Angeles Times*. Immediately after the *Times* article, outraged letters arrived at the offices of UCLA provost Hedrick, President Sproul, and the University of California Regents. According to Sproul, Hedrick himself was indignant about Seeds's actions and thought she should be reprimanded and made to apologize to the military.[14] A number of letters to the regents and to Sproul demanded that she be fired. For example, Walter K. Mitchell (certified public accountant) wrote to the Board of Regents demanding that "if the article is true, and I have no doubt that it is, I think that Miss Corinne A. Seeds should be discharged from her position. The country is at war and this is no time to criticize our army officers, particularly about a matter such as was made the subject of Miss Seeds' letters."[15] The regents immediately sent the letter to Sproul. Sproul responded to Mitchell that although he shared Mitchell's "indignation" about Seeds's letter, he did not believe it would be "a punishment proportionate to the crime to discharge her from her position after some thirty years of faithful and effective service. All of us are sorry for Miss Seeds's indiscretion, and have taken steps to see that it is not repeated."[16]

The controversy over Seeds's letter led to a meeting of Sproul, Dean Edwin Lee, and Director of Training Jessie Bond. According to Sproul's "Memoranda," Lee and Bond took this opportunity to discuss Seeds's future. They described Seeds as "temperamental, dictatorial, and uncooperative," but admitted that she was "also a brilliant teacher, a leader in the devising of elementary school curriculum and methods, and a potent influence in the school administrations of various communities in this area." According to Sproul, Lee and Bond took somewhat different positions. Not surprisingly, Bond wanted to use this incident immediately to remove Seeds and replace her with John Hockett. Lee, on the other hand, suggested that

Sproul severely reprimand Seeds, but allow her to retain her position. Both Bond and Lee suggested that Sproul should encourage Seeds to take a year off and return to Teachers College for her doctorate, which would be "physically, intellectually, and spiritually good for her."[17]

Almost immediately after the letter to UES parents about conditions at Santa Anita, Seeds left to conduct a three-week workshop for teachers in Albuquerque, where she worked with Marie Hughes, a progressive educator who later testified against the segregation of Mexican American children in the 1946 *Mendez v. Westminster* case.[18] When Seeds returned in late June, she was called to a meeting with President Sproul. According to Sproul's "Memoranda," Seeds agreed that she had made a mistake in writing the letter to the UES parents, "although she had done it with the best possible motives." Sproul then told her of criticisms he had heard "not only from people feeling strongly on the Japanese issue, but also from many parents of children in the school, who had taken advantage of the occasion of the letter-writing to attack her on the ground of uncooperativeness, dictatorial attitude, etc." Seeds, of course, denied these charges. Sproul then raised the issue of her position at UCLA, which had been a concern to the UCLA administrators since the founding of the School of Education in 1939.[19] A 1940 School of Education report had recommended that she not be promoted to associate professor, noting that although she had contributed community and university service, she did not have a doctorate and her publications tended to be celebratory descriptions of her own methods rather than scholarly research.[20] When Sproul raised these concerns to Seeds, she said that she was satisfied with her present situation. Sproul then suggested that she take a year off to study for her PhD. But, according to Sproul, Seeds was unwilling because "(1) she feels that she is now too old, and (2) she has an invalid mother to support and can not afford to take leave. She said that she was thoroughly happy in her work with children and that I could be sure that she would cause neither me nor the University trouble again."[21]

Sproul seems to have believed he had chastised Seeds. Seeds, however, saw the interview in a different light. Describing the incident later in her oral history, Seeds presented Sproul as indulgent and protective: "He treated me like a child who had strayed, and, thereafter, I always went over Lee's or Bond's head whenever I pleased."[22] Seeds provided a similar account of the meeting in a letter to Heffernan. She wrote that she had feared she would be fired, but instead "Dr. Sproul has always liked me a little and was very nice. Of course he scolded me for getting *him* and the Univ. into trouble. He also said that *10* of our 425 parents had written to him telling him I was uncooperative, etc. It gave me an opportunity to tell him about some of those parents."[23] Heffernan's response to this letter has not survived. She may well have provided a sympathetic ear, but she was not present to provide more support. Despite the outbreak of war, in January 1942, she took a prearranged six months leave from the California Department of Education to serve as a field representative for the Inter-American Demonstration Project in the Division of Inter-American Educational Relations at the U.S. Office of Education.[24]

Between January and July 1942, Helen Heffernan's energies were focused on establishing Inter-American Demonstration Centers throughout the West. These centers were intended to provide teaching materials and encourage schools and colleges to teach about Latin America.[25] Seeds also threw herself into the inter-American work. In March 1942, a conference on inter-American education, at which Heffernan spoke, was held at UCLA under the joint sponsorship of the UCLA School of Education and U.S. Office of Education.[26] Seeds sent Heffernan materials on Latin America developed for a UES unit-of-work. Despite her support of Heffernan's project, Seeds had a somewhat cynical view of U.S. policy toward Latin America. In a letter to Heffernan, Seeds noted the irony that the Inter-American Demonstration Project was partly supported by the Rockefeller Foundation, owners of Standard Oil. "It amuses me that Standard Oil money is now to be used to create attitudes which are designed to prevent further exploitation: Will *that* be done?—or will the work simply build interest in the Arts, etc.? I know if you have your way the H[igh]S[chool] children at least, will face the *real* facts!"[27] In her own articles on the inter-American project, however, Heffernan avoided an economic analysis and instead described the importance of education in building cultural understanding among all the peoples of the Americas.[28]

Heffernan's public writings supporting American democracy might have been seen as evidence of her patriotism, but the progressive methods she and Seeds advocated were increasingly viewed with suspicion and hostility by those on the Right. In October 1942, Hearst's *Los Angeles Examiner* ran a series of articles attacking progressive methods and calling for a return to "fundamentals" and suggesting—none too subtly—that progressive methods were in essence subversive. The *Examiner*'s series claimed to represent widespread dissatisfaction among teachers. One article entitled "Teacher Reveals Need for Training in 3 R's" was prefaced by an editorial comment claiming that teachers, too, wanted "a change, a shift to REAL STRESS on workable fundamentals, the 'three R's' which open the way to all the fields of education."[29] Later that October, the PEA of Southern California met to try to organize what Seeds called a "counter attack to the *Examiner* campaign against public school education." She wrote to Heffernan that the Steering Committee was "seeking the real source of the attack. Some believed it to be subsidized by the Nat. C. of C. [Chamber of Commerce] and M. and Mf. Assoc. [Merchants and Manufacturing Association]—and also by those who would destroy public education in favor of private schools (Catholics, etc.)."[30]

Corinne Seeds had other, more personal concerns in the fall of 1942. She was consumed with the care of her terminally ill mother. Her father did the housework and cooked during the week, but on weekends Seeds took over. In one letter to Heffernan, she described her Sunday morning chores—"dusting, cleaning the medicine cupboard, changing all the beds completely, sweeping the kitchen, dressing mother." Seeds was very close to both her parents, but that fall, for almost the only time in her letters to Heffernan, she expressed the need to get away: "In my life I've had relatively few days away from home and some way those I have now seem extra precious. Does this sound terribly selfish to you? I think you know more than anyone in the world how much I love my parents—but it's good to be away occasionally."[31]

Seeds's mother died on Christmas Day, 1942. Seeds wrote Heffernan after her mother's death: "Sometimes I am gripped with the terrible fear that she did not believe I loved her. Strange how our minds work. Dad said that he wanted to be sure mother's ashes were in the ground before his were ready. You may know how that makes me feel. Someday, I know I shall never be able to bear bravely his leaving."[32] In early January 1943, Seeds and her father buried her mother's ashes in Inglewood Cemetery. Seeds wrote to Heffernan: "Dad and the man laid the box in the cement case and Daddy placed six lovely camellias on top of it. They closed the casing and slowly the good, black earth again filled the opening—and the grass was fitted into place. The sun shown warmly upon us all. At last mother is at rest permanently and forever in 'the peaceful spot' for which she asked."[33] Seeds was deeply distressed by the death of her mother. But she did have the continued support of her loyal father and her friends, most importantly, her friendship with Helen Heffernan.

The Lanham Act and Child Care for California Children

When Heffernan returned from her six-month leave at the Inter-American Demonstration Project in the summer of 1942, California was beginning to feel the consequences of the extraordinary expansion of war industries in the state. Given the severe labor shortage, industry turned to women, who were needed if factories were to produce the planes, ships, and weapons necessary to win the war. In Southern California, the number of women workers in six major aircraft factories increased from 143 in 1941 to over 65,000 in 1943.[34] The figures were similar in the Northern California shipyards. But the increased numbers of working women created another pressing problem: the need to care for their children. In fall 1942, just a few months after Heffernan returned from the Inter-American Demonstration Project, the heads of the California Departments of Social Welfare, Education, and Health met to discuss the need for wartime child care.[35] They recommended that public schools and child care centers apply for federal funds under the federal Lanham Act, which provided federal support to local communities affected by the war effort, including funding for programs to provide care for the children of workers in the defense industries, and that the program be overseen by the State Department of Education. On December 30, 1942, the California Department of Education received notification that they had received emergency federal funds under the Lanham Act to appoint six field representatives to work with local school districts to provide extended care for the children of women working in wartime industry.[36] Heffernan nominated the representatives, among them Bernard Lonsdale and Fred Trott, two of her longtime supporters.

In January 1943 the California legislature passed a bill establishing childcare centers in school districts in order to address the emergency.[37] This "Plan for the Care of Children of Working Mothers" relied on local school districts to provide two programs: six- or seven-day-a week nursery schools for children two to five, and extended school care for children five to sixteen.[38] Under the Lanham Act, local school districts could then apply to the State Department of Education for federal funds to help support the programs. While Heffernan did not receive a formal appointment to administer the child care centers, requests for information about the program and applications for Lanham Act funding went to her in the Division of Elementary Education.[39] By the end of the war, California had enrolled 25,000 children in child care centers, more than any other state.[40]

Throughout 1943, Heffernan was deeply involved with the work of administering the child care centers. She responded to the child care crisis with her usual energy. In her foreword to the 1943 Yearbook of the California Elementary School Principals' Association, *The Elementary School Faces the Problems of Migration,* Heffernan framed the arrival of a new population of war workers to California positively. The new migrants, she wrote, "represent everything America has achieved in its various regions.... With all these people added to those who have driven their roots somewhat deeper, the school can be the instrument of preparation *now* for the extension of democracy after the war in exact proportion as it provides opportunity for children to practice democracy now."[41] Seeds continued to support her, largely through letters filled with UES gossip, descriptions of her domestic routine, and expressions of love. In 1943, Seeds, who seems to have been partially deaf from an early age, finally got a hearing aid. She wrote to Heffernan: "Long ago I faced the fact that I could never do what I would like to do because of my miserable type of deafness. Forever I must seem a person who *tells* rather than one who *teaches*. Forever must I lose many things that children say which would help me to evaluate teaching more clearly."[42]

By late spring, Heffernan was becoming discouraged by the difficulties of working with the Federal Works Agency around the child care centers. She objected in particular to the agency's decision that local school districts had to provide 50 percent of the funding for the child care centers.[43] This was particularly difficult since the Lanham Act specifically stated that the child care centers could not use tax revenues if they were to receive federal support; instead, the centers were to be supported by parental fees and "local contributions other than taxes."[44] By the spring of 1943 the fee in California child care centers was $1.00/day/child. Heffernan had recommended 50 cents a day. Apparently Heffernan failed to receive much support from State superintendent Walter Dexter. In a letter to Heffernan, Seeds wrote reminding Heffernan of those who saw the child care centers as an "attempt on the part of the State to secure *control* of the children.... It is from that group and like groups that Dexter has heard. Since *they* are his masters he must heed their chatter, but not *you!*"[45]

Heffernan may have been frustrated by Dexter's lack of support, but she also faced another, unexpected enemy. On January 29, 1943, conservative Republican state senator John Harold Swan of Sacramento introduced Senate Bill No. 693, which called for the elimination of the Division of Elementary Education. Swan, who was a member of the Senate Standing Committee on Education and a defender of "fundamentals," may have been encouraged by the *Los Angeles Examiner* series attacking progressive education. Swan made quite clear that his bill was specifically directed against Helen Heffernan, stating in the *Senate Daily Journal:* "Senate Bill No. 693 abolishes the position now occupied by Miss Heffernan, because there is no other way to remove her pernicious influence."[46] In response to Senate Bill No. 693, Heffernan seems to have mobilized a major letter-writing campaign. On March 17, 1943, Swan issued another statement in the *Senate Daily Journal* complaining that he had been "deluged with communications from teachers and teacher groups attacking his bill." Swan described these letters as "hysterical and vituperative" as well as "libelous." He continued, "The whole campaign against the bill is, in my judgment, inspired and directed by Miss Helen Heffernan of the State Department of Education." Swan claimed that "the people of the State have lost all control of their schools if an individual with this bureau chief's philosophy can, under the protection of the civil service, impose her visionary and impractical experimentation upon the children of the State."[47] He particularly recommended that everyone should read Heffernan's 1941 article, "What Practices are Defensible in Time of Crisis," to see how outrageous her ideas were.[48]

In "What Practices are Defensible in a Time of Crisis," written just before the United States entered the war, Heffernan described what she saw as two pressing issues facing educators: first, the Fascist victories in Europe; and second, the "numerous criticisms of public education" that had appeared in 1941 during the campaign against the Rugg textbooks. Heffernan argued that schools, including elementary schools, should address the social and economic challenges facing the nation. These problems, she argued, constituted "a threat to democracy as genuine and foreboding as any inherent in foreign aggression."[49] Heffernan went on to argue that original, critical thinking, and not a rigid emphasis on fundamentals was essential to education in a democracy: "No slavish memorization of the pages of a textbook will equip America's children to face America's problems."[50]

It is easy to imagine the reaction of a conservative like Swan to this article. Heffernan's emphasis on the need to bring an analysis of the country's social problems into the curriculum, her support of educating the whole child, and her call for critical thinking instead of "the slavish memorization of the pages of a textbook" confirmed right-wing suspicions of progressive education as irresponsible, left-wing education. Despite Swan's fulminations, Heffernan was able to mobilize her allies.[51] Harry Lantz, a Los Angeles superintendent, wrote to Swan (with copies to Heffernan and state superintendent Walter Dexter) defending Heffernan, concluding, "Very few of us, no matter how long we stay in the field of education, will ever grow to the educational stature of Miss Helen Heffernan of our State Department. Few people in the history of California education have made the contribution that she has."[52] In the end, Swan was unable to gather enough support to get his bill out of committee.

Swan was unable to unseat Heffernan from her position in the State Department of Education, but he may have been influential in removing her from the child care program. It seems clear that the child care centers took a great deal of Heffernan's time in 1943. In one September 1943 letter to a friend she noted: "I have had responsibility for the development of child care center programs in addition to my other work. Since the first of July I have had no assistance in the child care program and...the position as assistant chief in this division was also terminated."[53] Whether because of Heffernan's workload, because of her criticisms of the Federal Works Agency policies, or because John Harold Swan was one of three members of the Senate committee investigating the child care centers, in December 1943 administration of the child care program was transferred from the Division of Elementary Education to the Bureau of Homemaking Education, which became responsible for overseeing the educational programs, and to the Bureau of School Accounts and Records, which was given responsibility for financial oversight of the programs.[54]

Although she was no longer directly involved with the child care programs, Heffernan remained strongly supportive of the idea of publicly supported early child care. In a 1944 article in the *California Journal of Elementary Education* Heffernan described the positive accomplishments of the child care centers. Not only did the preschool programs provide nutritious meals and, at least in some centers, preventive health care such as immunizations and physical and dental examinations, they had other benefits: "In learning to let the other child take his turn at the swing or with the toy, to lie quietly on his cot though he cannot sleep, while others nap, perhaps the child has caught the first glimmer of a philosophy that will broaden his outlook and deepen his understanding of life."[55] While the California child care program may not have met all of Heffernan's goals, it provided a model for state-supported early education. And unlike most other states, which dismantled their child care programs with the end of the Lanham Act in 1946, California continued to provide some publicly supported child care centers for years after the war.[56]

Brothers Under the Skin

Heffernan's involvement with the child care centers for the children of defense workers preoccupied her throughout 1943, but there were other tensions on the home front during this year, most significantly around race and the limits of American democracy. In her speeches and articles in the early days of the war, Heffernan put forward a celebration of democracy that ignored race. In her article, "A Heritage of Freedom," for example, published in the October 1942 issue of the *Western Journal of Education,* she argued that children needed to understand the "great periods and events in our history." These included the story of the English colonists who came to North America seeking religious freedom and "the dream of political rights which led to the great American Revolution." She concluded, "Human freedom has always been the cherished goal of the New World." Of course, this picture of the commitment to human freedom as the "cherished goal of the New World" overlooked the institution of slavery or the genocidal treatment of indigenous peoples in both North and South America. A similar blindness can be seen in Heffernan's celebration of the Westward Movement, which she described as a "heroic epic... in which we expanded our living area from ocean to ocean, exploited our tremendous natural resources and became a great industrial nation." Heffernan described the heroes of this epic as "folk from all parts of the world attracted by the lodestar of freedom," a claim that surely would have seemed hollow to many African Americans, Japanese Americans, and Mexican Americans.[57]

The events of the war years, particularly the emphasis on American racism by both the Nazis and the Japanese, challenged this race-blind picture of the United States. Although the Bureau for Intercultural Education had called for cultural understanding and tolerance in the 1930s, the 1940s saw a sharp increase of books and curriculum units on intercultural education.[58] Like other progressive educators, Heffernan began taking a sharper tone. In "Education for Inter-American Friendship," written after her time with the Inter-American Demonstration Project, Heffernan condemned the practice of de facto segregation, which was widespread in California, particularly in areas with high Mexican American and African American populations. She wrote, "Segregation in our schools whether frankly made because of racial bias, or concealed behind a program of district gerrymandering prevents the acculturation of new Americans and denies to all the experiences which provide the basis for genuine tolerance."[59] Heffernan emphasized the consequences of racist practices for U.S. relations with Latin Americans, who, she wrote, would have "little confidence in our friendly overtures while the people of their culture suffer from exclusion, discrimination, and lack of opportunity as members of our society."[60] In her analysis of the international consequences of U.S. racism, Heffernan was echoing the increasing concern about the consequences of the hypocrisy of the United States, which, while claiming to fight anti-Semitic and racist Nazism, tolerated racist laws and institutions within its own borders. This argument underlay Carey McWilliams's 1943 book *Brothers Under the Skin,* in which McWilliams argued that racism should be understood globally as "a clash between the idea of racial superiority (central to the Nazi doctrine) and the idea of racial equality (central to the concept of democracy)."[61]

Brothers Under the Skin became a best seller. Its message was prescient. Only two months after its publication, in June 1943, in Los Angeles, white servicemen from nearby military bases attacked "pachucos," young Mexican and African American men, some wearing zoot suits and some simply there, in what came to be known as the Zoot Suit Riots. The Los Angeles police responded by arresting those who had been attacked. The riots did not dissipate until the military authorities declared Los Angeles off-limits days later.[62] The Zoot Suit Riots, along with the previous year's Sleepy Lagoon murder case, in which twenty-four young Mexican American men had been arrested and accused of murder on shaky evidence, heightened awareness of racism against Mexican Americans among California liberals. After an irregular and biased trial, twelve of the men in the Sleepy Lagoon case had been found guilty and three of them sentenced to life imprisonment. The anti-Mexican prejudice revealed by the case led to the creation of the Sleepy Lagoon Defense Committee, led by Carey McWilliams, which managed to generate wide support from the liberal Hollywood and Los Angeles community and raised white awareness of discrimination against Mexican Americans in California. In contrast, the Hearst papers—the *Los Angeles Evening Herald* and the *Los Angeles Examiner*—covered both the Sleepy Lagoon murder case and the Zoot Suit Riots as examples of the criminal nature of Mexican Americans. An editorial in *The Herald And Express* on the Zoot Suit Riots, for example, claimed that servicemen "promise to rid the community of its newest evils—those zoot-suited miscreants who have committed many crimes and have added a very serious side to juvenile delinquency problems."[63] The Zoot Suit Riots were followed less than three weeks later by the even more violent Detroit riots of June 20–21 and later that summer by the August riots in Harlem.

The 1943 riots raised the problem of race in ways that were difficult to ignore. In California, various civic organizations against discrimination were formed, among them the Bay Area Council against Discrimination, the Los Angeles County Committee for Interracial Progress, and the Los Angeles Council for Civic Unity, which included a number of well-known Hollywood liberals. In April 1944, the Council for Civic Unity organized a program at the Philharmonic Auditorium featuring Orson Welles and Dalton Trumbo, the performance of a play, "Divide and Conquer," a group singing of "We're in the Same Boat, Brother," and a pledge of unity which included the line, "I PLEDGE myself to refrain from any thought, speech or action based on prejudice or discrimination against a race, a creed or a class."[64] One victory for the liberals was the reversal of "*The People v. Zammora*" case in October, 1944, in which the Sleepy Lagoon defendants were freed from prison because of the irregularities of their trial.

THE SCHOOL AT MANZANAR

Californians were made acutely aware of the power of race not only by the Sleepy Lagoon case and the Zoot Suit Riots, but by the continuing reality of the Japanese internment. By late 1942, permanent camps had been built to hold the internees. Only two of the camps were located in

California—Manzanar and Tule Lake. The camps were under the joint control of the military and the War Relocation Authority (WRA), a civilian authority created by executive order. Military units patrolled the perimeter fences, controlled the gates, and were responsible for maintaining order inside the camps, while the WRA provided social services, including education. A "Memorandum of Understanding" between the California Department of Education and the WRA created two unified school districts for Manzanar and Tule Lake, but the hiring of teachers and the curriculum were under the control of the WRA.

The first head of the WRA's Education Section was Lucy Adams, who in the 1930s had been educational director of the Navajo reservation, where she had introduced a progressive curriculum for Navajo children emphasizing good citizenship and vocational education. In an article she published in the *California Journal of Secondary Education*, Adams presented the internment as a move into temporary "small cities," which were intended to become self-supporting and provide "a reservoir of labor which can be drawn on to assist other communities outside the military areas." The school curriculum would focus on vocational education—"work experience" in the camps would become a major focus of the school curriculum. The "school enterprises" Adams advocated included poultry raising, hog raising, growing small specialty crops, and construction. These activities would become the "major textbook and provide an important part of the learning material." Children over sixteen could spend half of their school time as members of work corps and receive school credit.[65]

Adams was in contact with Paul Hanna at Stanford, whose graduate students conducted a study of education in the camps in the summer of 1942. Hanna and his students proposed guidelines for a "democratic" progressive education for the incarcerated children. These guidelines were disseminated to education directors in all the camps, although it is not clear to what extent they were implemented. The irony of teaching students the value of democracy behind barbed wire, or of making the camp "community" the focus of study while organizing the curriculum around physical labor has not been lost on later observers; nor was it lost on the incarcerated Japanese themselves. Most Japanese parents seem to have rejected the progressive, vocational approach for a more traditional academic curriculum for their children. But one Manzanar parent reflected on the "progressive" curriculum: "The Hearst papers in Los Angeles are always criticizing progressive education and saying it is no good. We know how the Hearst papers handle news and lie about us Japanese here. If the Hearst papers knock progressive education, then it must be all right."[66]

Heffernan, who was not responsible for the curriculum at the Manzanar and Tule Lake camps, did not publicly comment on the internment, but her statements about the threat to civil rights in time of war suggest that she was well aware of the contradiction between claiming to defend democracy and the mass incarceration of American citizens. In her 1941 article, "What Practices are Defensible in Education in Time of Crisis," for example, she had argued that schools needed to teach the values that would "keep institutions functioning democratically in spite of the immediate exigencies. They must serve to keep alive civil rights that are basic in the ideology of democracies. If guaranteed liberties are denied, even in time of crises, democracy is already defeated and lost."[67] Responses to the Japanese internment from conservative and nativist groups, the Hearst newspapers, the House Un-American Activities Committee, and the California legislature's Tenney Committee justified Heffernan's fears. These ranged from accusations that the Japanese were enjoying a luxurious vacation in the camps, to calls that they all be forced to work as agricultural laborers, to the demand that they all be repatriated to Japan at the war's end. Heffernan did not speak out publicly against such attitudes, but her correspondence with Genevieve Carter, the superintendent of education at the Manzanar camp, suggests her views.

Heffernan visited the school at the Manzanar camp in September 1943 at Carter's invitation. Carter had invited both Heffernan and Seeds, but Seeds, who was much more open than Heffernan about her opposition to the internment, did not go. Seeds wrote to Heffernan, "Yes, it is too bad to disappoint Dr. Carter, as all too many people forget efforts made in behalf of our Japanese Americans. I hope you will have the time to devote to an examination of the 'education-in-schools' of these children. (I fear their *attitudes* are being formed in the *out-of-school* education!)."[68] Heffernan's response to the "out-of-school education"—a reference to the lessons learned by the racially motivated imprisonment of American citizens in desolate camps—has not survived, but she seems to have been favorably impressed by what she saw in the Manzanar schools. She wrote to Carter in October after her trip: "On the basis of this observation, may I take this opportunity to state that I believe the quality of education which I observed in the schools at Manzanar compares favorably with the educational program in the schools from which these children came."[69] Carter in return thanked her for her visit and "the interest you have always shown toward the education of the Japanese American children."[70]

Heffernan remained concerned about the education being offered to the incarcerated children. In a November 1943 letter to Carter, Heffernan noted that no teachers from Manzanar had attended the October Supervisors' Conference. Along with Heffernan, who gave the opening statement at the conference, other speakers included Carey McWilliams, an outspoken critic of American racism, who spoke on "Sociological Problems Confronting Postwar United States," and Corinne Seeds's friend, UCLA professor of physical education Martha Deane, who brought a group of her dance students to perform.[71] Heffernan wrote to Carter that she was sorry Carter had been unable to attend: "I think you would have been particularly pleased with the fine attention which was given to the problem of education of minority groups by Carey McWilliams and many of the other speakers."[72] Heffernan acknowledged the continuing practice of segregation based on race. She continued, "It will take years to break down this practice, but it is my belief that it must be broken down if any true acculturation of minority groups is to take place in this state."[73] Heffernan's assumption that the solution to racism was the "acculturation" of those discriminated against was typical of white liberals of this period. Nonetheless, given the context here—the forced incarceration of Carter's students because of their race—Heffernan's discussion of segregation and her references to Carey McWilliams seem particularly pointed.

Mobilizing against Prejudice

The year 1944 saw a growing acknowledgement of racism in United States media and a continued concern about its impact on international politics. Wendell Wilkie, who had unsuccessfully run against Roosevelt in the 1940 presidential election, published a series of syndicated newspapers articles on race relations, condemning the existence of segregation and discrimination in the United States. In one column, Wilkie wrote: "When we talk of freedom of opportunity for all nations, the mocking paradoxes in our own society become so clear that they can no longer be ignored."[74] Both Gunner Myrdal's *An American Dilemma*, an extensive analysis of race in the United States commissioned by the Carnegie Foundation, and Carey McWilliams's *Prejudice: Japanese Americans, Symbol of Racial Intolerance*, a study of the history of Japanese settlement on the West Coast and the Japanese internment supported by grants from the American Council of the Institute of Pacific Relations and the Guggenheim Foundation, were published in 1944. *An American Dilemma*, which documented discrimination against African Americans and called for the legal enforcement of equal rights, sold over 100,000 copies.

A powerful indictment of white racism against Japanese Americans, McWilliams's *Prejudice* was published while fighting continued in Europe and the Pacific and Japanese Americans were still being held in the camps. McWilliams outlined the attitudes and events leading up to the internment, pointing out that most German and Italian nationals were not subjected to the treatment meted out to American citizens of Japanese descent. The only explanation for the difference, McWilliams argued, was racism. McWilliams used the experience of the Japanese Americans as a way to examine the underlying dynamic of racism in United States society more broadly. He wrote, "A comparison of the racial creed of the West Coast on the Japanese with the racial orthodoxy of the Deep South will reveal the existence of the same fallacies, stereotypes, and myths."[75] Like other liberal commentators during the war years, he condemned American attitudes toward race not only on moral grounds, but also in terms of international politics, as undermining the country's democratic claims.

Heffernan echoed McWilliams's arguments. In her 1944 Report for the Division of Elementary Education, Heffernan spoke of the "Problem of Acculturation of Minority Groups."[76] In an article in the *Western Journal of Education* that same year, Heffernan again emphasized the need to address discrimination and to meet the needs of different groups of California children. As Heffernan noted: "Not only is the problem hideous but also it is a disruptive and divisive factor in our internal life; witness the Harlem and the Detroit riots, the Pachuco zoot suit phenomenon." She went on to discuss the existence of current prejudice against "any person of Japanese ancestry," and the historical intolerance of Jews and the mutual distrust of Catholics and Protestants. But the most powerful prejudices in the United States, she said, were against "our 13,500,000 Negroes and our 3,500,000 persons of Mexican ancestry." The most pressing problem in California, Heffernan argued, was the discrimination facing those in the Mexican community. Schools needed to make sure they offered adequate opportunities for Mexican children, that there were teachers trained in teaching English, and that they eliminated "policies and practices of segregation in schools and communities."[77]

While Heffernan's views on race clearly evolved during the war, Corinne Seeds's stance was more ambiguous. Like Heffernan and other white liberals, Seeds was increasingly conscious of racial discrimination, but she continued to assume that racism against African Americans was a southern problem. In 1944, she wrote to Heffernan of reading Lillian Smith's best seller *Strange Fruit,* a denunciation of lynching in the South. Seeds wrote: "Last night I couldn't put it down so anxious was I to find out whether the lynching actually took place. It is a powerful book...Darling, you can't afford to miss it because of its sociological and psychological analyses of the forces at work in the South."[78] Despite her condemnation of southern racism, Seeds clearly still saw African Americans as different and possibly dangerous. For example, in another letter to Heffernan she recounted that she was reading *Twelve Million Black Voices,* a collection of photographs from the Farm Security Administration of black life in the United States. "Of course," she wrote, "the black horde has every right to rise against the degradation and exploitation which they have suffered for the last three hundred years but it seems a terrible thought that at *this* time they may seek to throw off the shackles." Here she was referring to the widespread concern that African Americans might support the Japanese in the war because of their common experience of white oppression. Seeds continued: "Who knows what may happen within our borders because of our own sins of cruelty, selfishness and greed!"[79] In this fascinating passage, Seeds acknowledged white racism and its effects (the "degradation and exploitation" experienced by African Americans, the "sins of cruelty, selfishness and greed" of whites) but at the same time, she referred to African Americans as "the black horde."

Seeds's attitude toward Jews showed a similar ambivalence. She was well aware of Nazi anti-Semitism and had been in analysis with Lydia Sicher, a Jewish refugee. There were a number of Jewish families at the UES. But despite her awareness of Nazi anti-Semitism and her claim of fighting discrimination, Seeds held conventional views about Jews. In one letter, for example, she described the son of one of her Jewish teachers: "David is a lovely boy—He is quite precocious, spoiled and of course a typical Jew in features."⁸⁰ Describing another of her Jewish students, she wrote to Heffernan of a visit to the child's home where she met "her father who is a very *fine* Jew." Seeds praised his daughter, noting "some of her outstanding qualities, among which was her rare ability to get along with people." The father replied, "I would rather my children would know that that is the most important thing for us in life than that they display unusual intelligence!" Seeds commented to Heffernan, "Apparently M. comes from a Jewish family that recognizes the sins of the Jewish people."⁸¹

Seeds was resistant to bringing an analysis of race or racism into the curriculum. For example, she argued that elementary-age children should "work together on projects of interest to them, without attempting to focus directly upon problems of any one minority." Thus, she argued, children should learn to see "Mexican, Negro and Italian workers in early years, speak of them as *workers,* not as Mexicans, Italians, etc. thus tying up respect to the *worker,* not to the color of his skin or his race, religion or what have you." This passage captures Seeds's long-standing support of workers, but also her essentially color-blind approach to race. And she did not question her own cultural superiority. Consider, for example, her attitude toward African Americans' contribution to discussions about curriculum. Seeds wrote to Heffernan: "I believe that when negroes have *ideas* to share with others that they will be received and welcomed on *that basis.* It is our job to create a situation where the children of the minorities can develop ideas of worth and feel *free* to express them."⁸² The condescension here—that African Americans would only develop valuable ideas if the school created the right environment and the implication that they did not yet have any ideas worth sharing—is evidence again of Seeds's ignorance of African American intellectuals, cultural institutions, and political leadership.

There is some evidence that Heffernan encouraged Seeds to be more self-conscious in her attitude toward race. In one letter to Heffernan, Seeds wrote: "Once you said that you never made a change in my thinking! You see you have. So much so that I will tell you that you are absolutely right in saying that nationalities and races are not *inferior.* The reason why our Mexicans seem so hard to teach is not that the Mexicans are an inferior nationality—but that we coax into our country for the purposes of cheap labor the inferior strata of Mexican society. Perhaps no other strata could be so exploited!"⁸³ Here again, although Seeds described a "change in her thinking" about race, she still described Mexican American immigrants to the United States as an "inferior strata of Mexican society." The inferiority she was referring to of course was the impact of class—the need for poor and working-class families to find work in the United States. Seeds, with her strong sympathy for labor, did not refer to white American workers as an "inferior strata." The underlying dynamic of her treatment of race or ethnicity continued to assume essential, innate differences (implying superiority and inferiority) among groups of people. Even when she saw injustice, she did not escape these assumptions.

Education for Cultural Unity

The growing awareness of race and racism in California education in these years is most clearly seen in the 1945 Yearbook of the California Elementary School Principals' Association, *Education for Cultural Unity*. The yearbook included Seeds and Heffernan's article "Intercultural Education in the Elementary School," probably the best expression of their thinking about race in the mid-1940s. The yearbook also included articles by Holland Roberts of the American-Russian Institute, Berkeley Professor of Sociology Paul Taylor, Alaine Locke of Howard University, and Rachel DuBois of the Intercultural Education Workshop in New York. Afton Nance, a Southern California school supervisor known to both Seeds and Heffernan, contributed an article on the Japanese American children reentering the schools from the camps.[84]

Afton Nance had been a critic of the Japanese removal from the beginning, had visited the camps at Poston and Gila River, and had remained in contact with her former students during their incarceration.[85] In her article, "The Return of the Nisei," in *Education for Cultural Unity*, Nance discussed the responsibility of teachers to the returning Japanese American children. She wrote that the Japanese were not "returning on sufferance because of the great tolerance of the American people" or because "Jap-lovers-do-gooders" had exerted a mysterious influence on Washington. She pointed out, "They are coming back because they have the *right* to come back—the right guaranteed by the Constitution of the United States."[86] Nance pointed out the returning children might be angry and confused. After all, before the war they were taught that all people had rights in a democracy. "Then," Nance wrote, "a whole people, accused of no crime, was uprooted, confined for three years in desolate spots, subjected to endless questioning and the racist drumbeating of fascist elements. Injurious effects on the personalities of growing children were inevitable." Nance concluded that there would still be those who opposed the return of the Japanese. These people, she said, were driven by two motivations: "race prejudice and economic gain."[87]

In their article "Intercultural Education in the Elementary School," Heffernan and Seeds did not take as strong an antiracist stand as Nance, but they did put forward their most developed argument for the need to address cultural and ethnic differences in the public school curriculum.[88] This article demonstrated both the strengths but also the limitations of their understanding of culture and race. They began the article by stating the need for goodwill, international understanding, and peace, since "learning to live harmoniously within our country is crucial to learning to live in peace with the other peoples of the world." Given the political events of the time, this emphasis on peace among the peoples of the world was not surprising. The conference to establish the Charter of the United Nations was held in San Francisco in June 1945, and both Heffernan and Seeds strongly supported the United Nations from the beginning. But the focus of their article on intercultural education was not on international understanding, but on the situation inside the United States. They pointed out that there were numerous racial, religious, and national groups in the country, leading to the potential for "intergroup tensions and inharmony." The two most vulnerable groups were "Negroes" and "persons of Mexican background." These two groups, Heffernan and Seeds wrote, were "victims of the most serious intercultural dislocation with which the United States is confronted."[89] Their choice of the term "serious intercultural dislocation" rather than racism or even discrimination suggests their relatively cautious approach.

Heffernan and Seeds argued that intercultural understanding could be achieved only in democratic schools, where through "social sensitivity" and an appreciation of different cultures, children could "come to recognize the common humanity of mankind."[90] In addition to these broad and abstract principles, Heffernan and Seeds acknowledged that occasionally it was necessary "to deal directly with problems of racial difference." But their focus was on changing the attitudes of white children, not addressing the experiences of children of color. They gave the example of a kindergartener, "Lionel, a Negro child," who was called Little Black Sambo by a second grader during assembly. The second-grade teacher overheard this comment and noticed that Lionel's "eyes filled with tears." When her second-grade class returned to the classroom, the teacher discussed the incident with her class, focusing on differences in skin color. She led her class to recognize that skin color says nothing about a person's worth. "Subsequent to this discussion no comment regarding color was heard from any child."[91] There was no mention of what happened to Lionel.

Seeds and Heffernan's discussion of how teachers should handle diversity in classrooms similarly focused on white children. They recommended children's books that provided positive images of minority children and suggested studying the cultures or nations represented by children in the classroom.[92] But the goal of these approaches was not to support children of color but to build cultural understanding and tolerance among white children. They wrote, "If children of minority groups are actually members of the class, the teacher may skillfully but unobtrusively indicate their personal qualities of unselfishness, cooperation and industry, to counteract derogatory generalizations which are frequently attached to the minority groups the children represent."[93] Not only was the focus here on changing stereotypes held by the white children, but there was also the assumption that the "minority" children would be model students. Heffernan and Seeds acknowledged the historical practice of segregating school districts in California, "thus preventing the interaction of the minority and majority groups." They argued that "nothing but actual contact will make children understand that a wide range of individual traits and abilities exists in every group; that every culture has individuals capable of making important contributions"[94] On the other hand, they did not advocate immediate steps to eliminate the practice of segregation. School districts should eliminate segregation "gradually through processes of community education," which would eventually lead to the end of discriminatory practices.[95]

Conclusion

Helen Heffernan and Corinne Seeds, like other progressives, were made much more aware of American racism by the events of the war years. Nazi claims of racial superiority were condemned as undemocratic, but once the issue of racism was raised, it was difficult for white liberals to ignore the profound racial injustice within the United States as well. The Japanese internment was perhaps the most dramatic instance of homegrown racism in practice, but the continued segregation of the United States armed forces, legal segregation and inequality in the American South, and informal practices of discrimination and racist violence throughout the country were hard to ignore once the issue was raised. And the growing resistance of communities of color and their demands for civil rights and social justice forced white progressives like Heffernan and Seeds to address the reality of a segregated and unequal society, even if they did not examine their long-held assumption of their own cultural and racial superiority. By the end of the war calls for racial justice were increasing rapidly. Carey McWilliams claimed that nationwide, hundreds of organizations against discrimination and advocating racial tolerance were formed and that in the last three years of the war the "number of forums, programs, conferences, seminars, and institutes...on 'the racial problem' would invite disbelief today."[96] But the end of the war against Fascism was soon replaced by the war against Communism. In the context of this new struggle, demands for racial justice, along with calls for open discussion and political dissent, themselves could be denounced as subversive. The limits of democracy in this new world would soon be put to the test at the University Elementary School.

CHAPTER 7

The Battle of Westwood Hills

The debate over the schools was muted during the Second World War, but the tension among competing visions of both politics and education was only repressed, not extinguished. One of the earliest expressions of the political struggles over education in California was the controversy that emerged in the mid-1940s over the University Elementary School, which *Time* magazine later called "The Battle of Westwood Hills." Although the conflict originated in the complaints of a small number of disgruntled parents, the attack on the school and its defense soon hardened into battle lines between Los Angeles conservatives and liberals. Critics of the school raised the question of whether Seeds and her methods were not only academically suspect but political subversive as well. It was probably the most difficult and formative episode in Corinne Seeds's career.[1]

On the surface, the future of Corinne Seeds and UES seemed to be assured at the beginning of 1945. Seeds had considerable strengths. Her school had a national reputation for educational innovation, and the many teachers she had trained at UCLA were fiercely loyal to her methods. The appointment of the liberal Clarence Dykstra as the new UCLA provost brought her a powerful ally within the university. Her political alliance with Helen Heffernan remained strong, even if their personal relationship seems to have cooled. In spring 1945, Seeds wrote to Heffernan: "Dad was remarking that you hadn't really been with us since Christmas. As I went thru' my 'engagement' books since '40 to find out what professional activities I had engaged in I realized that your visits of this year are not in line with those of the year before. We miss you, dearest."[2] In December 1944 Seeds was elected to a one-year term as president of the California School Supervisors' Association, an organization that strongly supported Helen Heffernan and her programs. In her inaugural speech, Seeds told the audience, "As we work with teachers, parents, and children, let it be done in accord with the democratic process, keeping ourselves emotionally stable as we work to meet the challenge of a world-community in the throes of becoming a world brotherhood."[3] This advice, particularly the need to remain emotionally stable, was something she could well apply to herself in the coming year. Criticisms of progressive education on the part of conservative groups and newspapers like the

Los Angeles Examiner and the *Los Angeles Times* were gaining strength, her old enemy Vierling Kersey was still Los Angeles superintendent of schools, the disgruntled parents at UES were emboldened by the growing criticisms of progressive education, and powerful male administrators at the UCLA School of Education remained suspicious and antagonistic.

THE BOYS ON THE HILL

Seeds was always very aware of male privilege and the ways in which men were favored in education. She frequently referred to the male professors and administrators at the UCLA School of Education as "the boys on the hill" and claimed that they favored other men. Seeds wrote to Heffernan describing the visit of an old friend, Ethel Salisbury, who "spent nearly two hours telling me that the men on the campus are going to rid themselves of *all* women." Salisbury singled out John Hockett, who, she said, wanted to "reorganize the whole of the Elem. School program soon with the aid of *all* of the men. She says that the survey will provide a reason for reorganizing me out and putting a *man* in my shoes!"[4] Seeds was suspicious of Jesse Bond and Dean Edwin Lee as well as Hockett. She especially resented Bond's authority over her. Describing one meeting, Seeds wrote Heffernan: "My interview with Bond was a warm one. He was quite nasty!... Of course both men *hate* me! However, I shall work on!"[5] Even though in fact Dean Edwin Lee was quite supportive of Seeds and UES in his interactions with university president Robert Sproul, in Seeds's eyes Lee was just as untrustworthy as Bonds. In one letter to Heffernan Seeds wrote: "Helen, Dean Lee is a *terrible* person—one whose practices are undemocratic, one whose principles of administration are questionable—and, in fact he is one bloated, conceited toad! He merely confirmed the general impression most people have of him. This is said *only* to you darling—but I am not mistaken!"[6]

The tensions within the School of Education were exacerbated by the complaints of the small group of discontented parents at UES. In both her oral history and in letters to Heffernan, Seeds repeatedly mentioned UES parents George Bagnall, Frank Cowgill, and Marcus McClure, referring to them as enemies numbers one, two, and three. Eleanor Allen, another UES parent, was enemy number four. Although these parents had begun to express dissatisfaction with the school in the late 1930s, in 1943 their complaints grew stronger. In her oral history, Seeds described a conversation with Marcus McClure at a school open house in which McClure stated that his children "hadn't learned a thing." When Seeds mentioned that his son Arthur was the best student in the fifth grade, McClure responded, "Don't congratulate yourself; that's because of what he learns from us at home."[7] In March 1943, George Bagnall met with Sproul and Dean Lee to complain about Seeds's treatment of his son, who had been suspended from UES for discipline problems.[8] In his "Memoranda," Sproul noted, "Dean Lee and I agreed after he had gone that there might be a good deal to what he said, but that Miss Seeds' brilliant direction of the school should lead us to support her, and to try to keep Mr. Bagnall happy until his oldest boy graduates this June."[9] That spring, Seeds held a series of four meetings with UES parents to discuss the philosophy and practices of the school, but these meetings seem to have created even more unrest among the dissatisfied parents. In May, Bagnall, Cowgill, and McClure wrote to Jessie Bond again complaining about the school.[10]

Unlike Dean Lee, who had discounted the complaints of Bagnall, Cowgill, and McClure, Bond took their criticisms seriously. In fall 1943, Bond met with Seeds to discuss their complaints. Bond told Seeds that he and John Hockett would now begin to monitor the educational program at UES much more closely.[11] Seeds responded with a ten-page letter to Bond, defending herself against Bagnall, Cowgill, and McClure's criticisms.[12] The parents' accusations and Bond's response clearly infuriated Seeds. In October, she wrote to Heffernan that she didn't believe she could "'buck' the game at U.C.L.A. much longer."[13] For his part, Bond sided with the disgruntled parents. In an October letter to Frank Cowgill, Bond wrote that he and John Hockett had "started a campaign of visiting throughout the school and are 'pulling no punches' in talking directly with individual supervising teachers, students teachers and pupils." He concluded, "We thank you, Mr. Cowgill, and those you represent for your interest and attitude in this whole situation. We shall inform you from time to time relative to progress made and shall appreciate any information and comments you have to offer."[14] From the tone of this letter and from Bond's later suggestion to Sproul that Seeds be removed as principal, it seems clear that Seeds's suspicion that Bond was seeking to undercut her was justified.

Seeds also had powerful allies. There was strong support for UES both from other UES parents, led by the Family School Alliance, and from UCLA faculty, a significant number of whom sent their own children to her school. The UES teaching staff was also loyal to Seeds. In November 1943, the staff sent a group letter to Dean Edwin Lee, defending Seeds and criticizing Bond. The letter claimed that Bond had invited the group of dissatisfied parents to meet at his home without any of the UES staff present and encouraged the parents to write a letter setting out their complaints. The staff saw Bond's actions as unprofessional and "contrary to the best interests of the school."[15] Seeds was clearly well aware of the staff's letter. She wrote to Heffernan, "Darling, the staff 'crossed the Rubicon' this a.m. when *the letter* was mailed. I expect the Dean to hold me accountable for that insubordination on the part of the staff. Being a *man*, he will rise to avenge *men*! By now, I care not what he does!"[16] That Helen Heffernan was also involved in the drafting of this letter is suggested by a copy of the letter in Heffernan's papers with a note in Seeds's handwriting: "Thanks to you, the original is much improved. Here is the latest draft! The staff has decided to mail it directly to Dr. Lee without notifying 'the boys.'"[17]

There was no direct response from Lee to the staff's letter, but he did call Seeds in for a meeting. Seeds wrote Heffernan that she had such a strong reaction to the meeting that she was "unable to write—sleep, or even eat!"

She continued, "He is truly a terrible fascist! He began by telling me that we had a big problem to solve—but that first I must know that my *superiors,* Drs. B. and H. [Bond and Hockett] always had acted with sincerity to protect both the school and me—that he tho't I must know that I had to get along with my superiors." According to Seeds, Lee also demanded that she had to "get along with *all* the parents." Seeds concluded, "When I refused to accept the role of a bad little girl acting cross for no reason he promptly said he and I must solve the problem. I told him it could never be solved unless B. and H. changed some of their ways."[18] But Bond continued to attempt to undercut her. In June 1944, Bond met with President Sproul to discuss parents' complaints about the school and to express his own concerns about Seeds. Sproul's impression was that "relations between Miss Seeds, and possibly Dean Lee, on the one hand, and himself and Mr. Hockett on the other, were strained badly." According to Sproul, Bonds urged him to replace Seeds with "a man [presumably Hockett]" while Seeds could be "made, as it were, the research head of the institution."[19] Sproul did not record his own opinion.

In addition to her enemies in the School of Education and the antagonistic clique of parents at UES, Seeds faced the hostility of Los Angeles superintendent of schools Vierling Kersey. One source of tension was the continued wrangling between the Los Angeles City Schools and UCLA over the funding, maintenance, and repairs of the Warner Avenue buildings. UCLA claimed that the city received state funds based on average daily attendance (ADA) for the school but provided nothing for maintenance, while Kersey denied that the city received funds from the state.[20] In July 1944, Kersey wrote to James Corely, the university comptroller, stating that he would not sign the next year's lease until a provision was written guaranteeing that UCLA would pay $1,500 for maintenance. Kersey then brought up the issue that really concerned him—the educational philosophy of Corinne Seeds. He wrote to Corley: "The Warner Avenue School is not a Los Angeles City School. It does not conform to our educational philosophy nor does it conduct the type of educational program that we would support were it a school in the Los Angeles School System." Kersey went on to argue that if UCLA wanted this kind of program it should build its own school.[21] After continued negotiations, the city did sign the 1944 lease, but the school's relationship with the Los Angeles city system remained strained.

The small group of discontented UES parents also continued to voice their dissatisfaction. Both Frank Cowgill and Marcus McClure wrote to President Sproul in 1944 complaining about the school. Sproul told them to meet with Dean Lee instead. Seeds was elated that Sproul had refused to meet with Cowgill and Bagnall. She wrote to Heffernan, "No more 'under cover' meetings with the Boys on the Hill."[22] But in the end, Lee agreed to a private meeting with Cowgill at Lee's home. Lee described the meeting to Sproul: "It was an interesting discussion lasting until one o'clock. My guess is that you will hear nothing more about the matter, unless Mr. C. wishes to express satisfaction."[23] Cowgill may have been temporarily placated, but the controversy around UES was not resolved. Finally, in September

1944, Lee appointed an internal committee, chaired by UCLA professor Lloyd Morrisett and including Professor of Education Frank Freeman of the Berkeley campus, President Frank Thomas of Fresno State College, and Pasadena superintendent of schools (and longtime ally of Helen Heffernan) John Sexson, to evaluate the UES program.[24]

Despite the appointment of the Morrisett Committee, missives from the disgruntled parents continued into the fall. In October 1944, Marcus McClure wrote complaining about a mimeographed letter his daughter brought home from UES asking parents to help their children with spelling. In his opinion, teaching spelling was the school's business. He went on to criticize the teacher training program at UES and then moved to a denunciation of teacher preparation programs in general.[25] In response, Lee told McClure that an investigating committee had been appointed under Professor Morrisett and assured McClure that "as a patron of the School you will be informed of the progress and findings of the study." In a handwritten note to Sproul accompanying a copy of this letter, Lee wrote that McClure's letter was filled with "misinformation and personal bias," and added, "This is not an easy letter to answer without saying something that will elicit in response another long epistle from Mr. McClure, who seems to have studied letter writing with the same instructor as Mr. Cowgill."[26]

The End of the Warner Avenue Lease

In April 1945, a new and unexpected danger emerged. Eleanor Allen, a former UES parent and ally of McClure, Bagnall, and Cowgill, was elected to the Los Angeles School Board. Allen was one of three parents to complain about Seeds's treatment of a UES teacher to President Sproul in 1938. Her children had attended UES, but she was not pleased with the education they had received, and she had removed her daughter from the school. Allen was a member of Moral Rearmament, a controversial Christian organization accused of having been sympathetic to Hitler in the 1930s, and of Pro-America, a women's organization founded in 1933 to respond to "the threat to the freedom of the individual" raised by the election of Franklin D. Roosevelt. Initially, Seeds had not been overly worried about Allen's decision to run. She wrote to Heffernan, "As Mrs. Allen is really stupid, I believe we have a chance of showing her up along with her tactics.... Those boys, Cowgill, McClure, and Bagnall, should use a more reliable cat's paw!"[27] But as the campaign wore on, Seeds became more concerned. She wrote to Heffernan: "My main purpose is to keep enemy #4 [Eleanor Allen] off.... However, the F.S.A. are doing the work!! And what better business could they be engaged in than to help arrange for a board that will oust V. K. [Vierling Kersey]?"[28] But in the end, Eleanor Allen won the election, and the new Los Angeles School Board was much more sympathetic to Vierling Kersey than they were to Corinne Seeds.

Eleanor Allen's term on the Los Angeles School Board began July 1, 1945. The next day, she attended her first meeting. The topic was the annual question of renewing UES's lease of the Warner Avenue School, which UCLA rented from the city for the nominal fee of one dollar. Despite the opposition of Superintendent Vierling Kersey, the board had unanimously voted to renew the lease for many years. But this year, the vote was not unanimous. Mrs. Allen, the new member, voted no. The lease for 1945–46 still passed, five votes to one, but the question of UES and the Warner Avenue lease was now publicly raised. At the next board meeting, on July 5, Frank Cowgill read a statement signed by himself, Marcus McClure, and George Bagnall, asking for an investigation of the progressive methods used at the school and demanding the board terminate the lease for the following year. Accounts of Cowgill's, Bagnall's, and McClure's testimony in front of the School Board appeared in articles in both the *Los Angeles Times* and the *Los Angeles Examiner*. The report in the *Examiner* identified the three men by occupation: "Frank H Cowgill, baking company executive; Marcus A. McClure, head of an insurance firm, and George L. Bagnall, vice president of a motion picture studio."[29] According to the *Times'* account, Cowgill, the spokesman for the group, testified that although the school had "many commendable features," he, Bagnall and McClure "and many others in the community" believed it also had "many objectionable features." When he was asked later to explain what was meant by "objectionable features," George Bagnall said, "I don't question the university's right to conduct a school as it sees fit, but I don't want my children to be the 'guinea pigs.' "[30]

At subsequent meetings in July, numerous speakers representing the Family School Alliance and the League of Women Voters testified before the board supporting UES and the continuation of the Warner Avenue lease. According to the *Los Angeles Times*, a delegation of nearly fifty UES parents attended the July 9 Board of Education meeting, led by Mrs. William A. Fort, president of the Family School Alliance, the parent-teacher organization that had consistently supported Seeds. In her statement to the board, Mrs. Fort argued that, although there were "a few disgruntled parents," at UES, overall, most parents were very satisfied.[31] But there were more than a few disgruntled parents involved. Seeds was opposed not only by Eleanor Allen and the three dissatisfied UES parents but also by the powerful Los Angeles superintendent of schools, Vierling Kersey.

In response to the conflict over the school, the School Board asked Kersey to prepare a memorandum on the issue.[32] On July 10, Kersey met with Dean Lee wanting to know if the "present educational program" at UES would be continued and how long the school needed the Warner Avenue site. On July 14, Lee wrote to Kersey reiterating that he supported the present UES approach, which he called "important and necessary," and that although there were plans to build a school on the UCLA campus, these were not finalized and the university still needed the Warner Avenue site.[33] On July 18, Kersey wrote to James Corley, the comptroller of the University of California, setting out his reasons as to why the present situation was untenable, among them that UES was not a Los Angeles City School and "does not conform to our educational philosophy nor does it conduct the type of educational program that we would support were it a school in the Los

Angeles School System."[34] He went on to suggest again that UCLA should build its own school. On August 2, 1945, the Los Angeles School Board reviewed Kersey's report. In it, Kersey recommended that the connection between the Los Angeles School District and UES be ended. The board then voted unanimously not to renew the lease for 1946–47. UES could continue to use the site through the 1945–46 school year, but in July 1946, Warner Avenue would revert to being a public school under the control of Los Angeles School officials and UES would have to find a new home.

That summer Helen Heffernan was as usual in Los Angeles participating in the UCLA conference for school supervisors. Although that August saw momentous world events—the bombing of Hiroshima on August 6 and Nagasaki on August 9 and the subsequent Japanese surrender—Heffernan and Seeds were preoccupied with the struggle to save UES. When Heffernan heard the news of the Los Angeles School Board vote ending the Warner Avenue lease, she immediately sprang into action. According to Seeds's account, Heffernan first spoke to Lee, demanding that the school be saved. Seeds described the scene: "Helen said [to Lee], 'What have you been doing? You're the one who should be sending the letters out.'" Instead, Seeds recounted, Heffernan immediately took action and sent out a letter "to all the supervisors and all the administrators. She did it without permission and her head might have been slashed off at any time, but she roused the whole state."[35]

Heffernan's mimeographed letter addressed "Dear Co-worker" was sent to educators throughout California. In her usual concise and clear style, Heffernan described the board's vote, and explained the need for widespread support of the school. She asked, "Please write a strong letter urging the continuance of the University Elementary School as a part of the University of California at Los Angles School of Education." She then offered some specific suggestions: "Include in your letter statements regarding the influence of the University Elementary School on education in California, the quality of its graduates, the curriculum material produced. Now is the time to act!"[36] The results of Heffernan's appeal were immediate. The files of the UCLA School of Education contain hundreds of letters from across California supporting the school—all dated mid-August 1945.[37] One day after sending the mimeographed letter, Heffernan wrote directly to UCLA provost Clarence Dykstra, supporting UES. She wrote that "the quality of instruction provided for the children is unequalled in any school I have visited in a long career in the field of professional education." She concluded, "It would be difficult to find a school system in California which has not been influenced by the curriculum materials developed at the University Elementary School and generously shared by the Staff with educators throughout the State and Nation."[38]

Seeds also found unexpected support from Dean Edwin Lee. In an August 13 memorandum to Provost Dykstra, Lee described the board's decision as "the culmination of efforts by a small but determined group of residents of the Westwood area." The situation was made worse by the critical attitude of School Superintendent Vierling Kersey, who was "at present riding the wave of 'return to fundamentals' and following Hearst's lead in 'emphasizing the three R's.'" Lee went on to defend the accomplishments of UES, noting that studies showed that UES students scored above grade level and outperformed other Los Angeles public school students. He also noted that he had received letters from some eighty Southern California school administrators and over 400 supervisors of elementary education from all over California favoring the continuance of the school, as well as a petition supporting the school from the ninety participants at the Summer Supervisors Conference at UCLA, and another signed by 91 percent of UES parents. He added, "Miss Heffernan speaks of the wide influence of this annual conference in her letter to you of August 10, 1945." Lee concluded that if President Sproul and the regents decided to discontinue the school, "it would be a most unwise decision and could only have most unfortunate consequences."[39]

In the wake of the School Board's August vote, tensions within the UES community became even more heightened, with members of the Family School Alliance defending Seeds and those opposed to her continuing their attack. Although Allen, Cowgill, Bagnall, and McClure were successful in forcing UES from the Warren Avenue site, they represented a minority (although a vocal and powerful minority) of parents of children in the school. The majority of UES parents were strong supporters of Seeds and of her vision of progressive education. Liberal residents of West Los Angeles rallied behind the school. Nelda Salisger, the executive secretary of the board of the Beverly-Westwood Citizens Committee wrote to Provost Dykstra in 1945 that the controversy "was negligible and the 'tensions' non-existent until a handful of dissidents tried to provoke trouble."[40] But in the fall of 1945, those tensions were high. The opposing factions clashed in a number of meetings. A meeting of the West Los Angeles Coordinating Council in early September 1945 had to be adjourned because of the heated discussion about the methods used at UES.[41] In her oral history, Seeds noted that "every social event they went to in that neighborhood was ruined by battles between those who believed in the school and those who didn't."[42]

Some UES parents still thought they could convince the Los Angeles School Board to renew the Warner Avenue lease. But others, including the leaders of the Family School Alliance, pressured the regents and the legislature to pass a special bill authorizing funding for a new school on the UCLA campus. Both Dean Lee and Provost Dykstra supported a new building. The key question was what President Sproul would do. The most powerful development in favor of UES was the September release of the Morrisett Committee's "Report of the Survey of the University Elementary School, University of California, Los Angeles." The Morrisett Report was overwhelmingly positive, concluding that the school was successful in demonstrating "an effective interpretation of the Dewey-Kilpatrick philosophy of education," and noting the high esteem in which the school was held by other educators in California and across the nation. What's more, a comparison of the standardized test results showed that the overall achievement of

UES students on standardized tests was higher than any school in the Los Angeles city system.

The report did have criticisms. Despite the school's achievements, teachers' salaries were low and the facilities were "deplorable." The school consisted "of a few shacks which house one of the most interesting and significant school programs in the nation. The plant consists of ten small, worn-out bungalows, a crafts room, a small sanitary building, and a tent."[43] The Morrisett Report saw room for improvement in the organization of the school as well. It called for greater "scientific evaluation or control" over the school and was critical of the current administrative structure, which led to "conflict and confusion...between the office of the director of training [Jesse Bond] and the principal and staff of the University Elementary School."[44] The Morrisett Report concluded with a number of recommendations, among them that the principal of UES report directly to the dean of the School of Education and be given "full responsibility...for the organization and administration of the school and for the supervision of the work done there, including the educational program for the children, as well as the professional preparation of prospective teachers."[45] In other words, Jesse Bond and John Hockett should no longer have any administrative control over the school. In essence, the Morrisett Report was a complete vindication of Corinne Seeds.

After the Morrisett Committee issued its report, Sproul wrote to UCLA provost Clarence Dykstra for advice about the UES situation. Dykstra replied that he concurred with the Morrisett Committee's conclusion that the school was a "vital, significant educational undertaking." Dykstra reported that he had received letters from "almost every district of the State" in support of the school. He concluded, "It is clear that the school is one of a very few outstanding institutions of its kind and I have been amazed at the furor created by the action of the Los Angeles Board of Education."[46] Dykstra met with Sproul on September 17, 1945. According to Sproul's "Memoranda," Dykstra believed the Los Angeles School Board would not reverse their decision. He urged Sproul to support the construction of a new school on the UCLA campus. Sproul responded cautiously, advising Dykstra to continue to negotiate with the School Board for the Warner Avenue site.[47] But Sproul had not calculated on the impact of the school's well-connected supporters. In September 1945, the UES Family School Alliance presented the regents a petition with over 1,100 names (including such well-known figures as composer Arnold Schoenberg and journalist Carey McWilliams), demanding that funds be allocated for permanent school buildings.

Eventually, in October 1945, the regents voted to continue the school. This vote doubtless reflected the organized campaign in support of UES on the part of the Family School Alliance as well as the active involvement of Helen Heffernan. Heffernan wrote to a friend that before the regents met, "we planned a little bombardment of telegrams urging the immediate establishment of the University Elementary School. I will pray that all of the telegrams had thinly veiled threats about meeting the University Authorities in the Legislature next January, unless they moved ahead on the erection of the building."[48] But while the regents voted their support of the school, they did not vote on the question of funding. Instead, they asked Provost Dykstra to reopen negotiations with the Los Angeles School Board to try to renew the Warner Avenue lease until a permanent home for the school could be found.[49]

The question of the new home for UES dragged on. Between December 14 and 19, 1945, more than a hundred letters from UES parents, other California teachers and administrators, and local businessmen were sent to the regents urging that the university quickly build a facility on campus for UES. It seems obvious that this was a coordinated letter writing campaign. The correspondence to the regents includes many prepared postcards that read: "Dear Sir: For better education in California I join with others in urging you to exert your utmost influence to obtain at the coming special session of the Legislature, an emergency appropriation for the UCLA Elementary School buildings and support. Sincerely, Name: Address:"[50] The social capital of the Family School Alliance is shown in UES parent Peggy Kiskadden's recollections of the strategies used to influence the Board of Regents. Letters of support were solicited from such well-known figures as Aldous Huxley, Igor Stravinsky, and Arnold Gessell. Kiskadden even wrote her old friend Bertrand Russell, who, she recounted, replied he would be glad to defend the school, but "that a letter from him could only do harm; that, as he had no respect for the Regents, nor they for him, I was at liberty to use this letter but he didn't think I'd better."[51] Finally, in December 1945, the regents announced that they would seek an appropriation from the State Postwar Building Fund for $600,000 to build a new school for UES on the UCLA campus.[52] But although the school could complete the 1945–46 school year at the Warner Avenue site, the new UCLA facility would not be ready for several years. There were no buildings provided for the 1946–47 school year.

American Russian Friendship

The year 1946 brought Seeds more trouble. In January she was called before Jack Tenney's Fact-Finding Committee on Un-American Activities to defend herself against accusations that she was a Communist sympathizer and was teaching subversive, Communist-inspired doctrines at the UES. During the war years, the Tenney Committee had held hearings on a broad range of issues, including the Zoot Suit Riots, possible subversion in the Japanese-American community, and leftist groups such as the Hollywood Writers' Mobilization. But by 1945, the committee's attention turned almost exclusively to the dangers of Communism. The committee was also deeply concerned with both public schools and higher education. In the mid-1940s, hearings were held on such targets as the YMCA, individual high-school teachers like Francis Eisenberg and Blanche Bettington of Canoga Park High School, and what were viewed as culturally subversive curricula, such as the sex education program at Chico High School.[53] In the fall of 1945, the committee turned to the political activities of students and professors at both the Berkeley and Los Angeles campuses of the University of California. Hearings were held on student radicalism at UCLA and on faculty members who lectured at the People's Educational Center.[54]

Among the groups cited by the Tenney Committee as a Communist front organization was the American Russian Institute. The institute, which had been founded in 1926 to provide information and cultural exchange with the Soviet Union, promoted cultural events and was supported by a number of liberal artists and intellectuals.[55] In June 1945, for example, the Southern California branch of the institute organized a performance of Prokofiev's Alexander Nevsky Cantata conducted by Otto Klemperer at the Los Angeles Shrine Auditorium.[56] Events sponsored in San Francisco included a performance of Othello with Paul Robeson at the Geary Theater, receptions and banquets for Soviet dignitaries, exhibits of photographs, and the showing of films about the Soviet Union.[57] The president of the American Russian Institute was Holland Roberts, a Stanford professor of education who was involved in a number of left-wing causes, including the San Francisco Labor School.

Both Heffernan and Seeds were involved with projects supporting the Soviet Union during the war and both were associated with the American Russian Institute. Seeds's FBI file lists her membership in a number of anti-Fascist and liberal groups including the Citizens' Committee for Better Education, American Youth for Democracy, the Civil Rights Congress, and the Southern California Chapter of the National Congress of the Arts, Sciences, and Professions.[58] But it was Seeds's membership in the American Russian Institute that was of particular interest to the Tenney Committee.[59] The committee also was interested in Seeds's attendance, along with Heffernan, at a conference sponsored by the American Russian Institute that took place on December 7 and 8, 1945, at UCLA to discuss students' rights to free speech. Among the speakers at the December 1945 conference were the novelist Thomas Mann and the liberal UCLA provost Clarence Dykstra.[60]

Seeds may well have been influenced by Heffernan's close association with the American Russian Institute during the war. Heffernan had first been contacted by the American Russian Institute around the development of curricular materials on the Soviet Union for public schools.[61] She was enthusiastic about the project and unsuccessfully tried to convince state superintendent Dexter to support a statewide conference tentatively to be called the "Conference on Education for American-Soviet Understanding."[62] In January 1945, Heffernan wrote to Holland Roberts that the conference would not be held because those "opposed to friendship between the U.S.S.R. and the United States of America have been effective in creating fear concerning this enterprise."[63] Because of her support of the curriculum project, Heffernan was invited to join the board of the institute, an invitation she accepted.[64]

Eventually, in the spring of 1945, a curriculum for fourth-, fifth-, and sixth-grade children called "Boy of Leningrad" was produced. Heffernan wrote to Holland Roberts that she was looking forward to seeing the curriculum and mentioned that "the sixth grade at the University of California at Los Angeles is carrying forward a study on Russia. I am sure that Miss Seeds would make the wisest possible use of this material, and would produce a valuable critical review."[65] Seeds wrote to Heffernan that she was eager to use the materials.[66] In its 1945 Annual Report, the American Russian Institute listed ten California schools that used "Boy of Leningrad," including UES. Among the testimonials attached to the Annual Report were two enthusiastic statements from UES sixth graders.[67]

The "study of Russia" that Heffernan referred to in her letter to Holland Roberts was a fourth-grade unit-of-work focused on a Ukrainian collective farm, the fictional Hammer and Sickle Collective, used at UES since 1943. Although Seeds did not teach the unit, she was actively involved in its preparation. The unit was developed during the darkest days of the war, when the Soviet Union was an American ally and bore the brunt of the Nazi war machine. To gather material for the unit, Seeds met with a Miss Alexander, who had done research for the 1943 pro-Soviet film "North Star," set on a Soviet collective, and Malbone Graham and his wife, who showed Seeds the Russian children's books they had brought back from their visits to the Soviet Union in 1930 and 1938. Seeds wrote to Heffernan that Mrs. Graham's "descriptions of Lenin's black marble tomb lined with white marble shot with revolution-red marble and of the fourteen mile subway, also of marble and constructed *free* by the people of Moscow left me sitting speechless on the edge of my chair.... She would be grand to speak to our Supervisory Group at a Sec. meeting when we visit the children at work to understand Russia (or the Soviet Union)."[68] Although Seeds was enthusiastic, there is evidence that she was also aware of political dangers. In one 1943 letter to Heffernan, for example, she described a favorable article on UES that appeared in the *People's World*: "I had quite a *fight* with the writer to keep her from using my name. I see she used *U.C.L.A.*—and I'm keeping my fingers crossed hoping our enemies do not find the article."[69]

Playing Ukrainian Farmer

Seeds's concerns that her enemies might find out about the curriculum at UES seem to have vanished by 1945. She favorably mentioned the Ukrainian Farmers unit in "Intercultural Education in the Elementary School," the 1945 article she coauthored with Helen Heffernan, and she discussed the curriculum in greater detail in her article, "Playing Ukrainian Farmer," which appeared in *Progressive Education* in May 1945. Seeds framed "Playing Ukrainian Farmer" around the issues facing the world now that the war was ending. Primary among those issues was the question of peace and how to create a world of understanding and cooperation among all peoples. Seeds explained that "knowing, that in the world of the future, the citizens of the United States must engage democratically in friendly relations with the peoples of the USSR," she had decided to engage in a study of a Ukrainian collective farm as a way of coming to understand the lives of Soviet people.

Seeds described the classroom for the unit as "rich in materials and ideas" that could provide the children what they needed to fully understand the life of Ukrainian farmers. The classroom was transformed into a room on the collective with "an *izba* with its copper tank and plunger containing water for washing the face and hands, pictures of Stalin and Lenin, small-paned windows filled with geraniums in blossom.... On the opposite wall was a huge back-drop showing the farmers at work in the fields belonging to the Hammer and Sickle Collective." The children made clothes, examined the political organization of a collective farm, and studied agriculture and methods of distribution and export. The culminating event was a dramatic play for parents called "A Day on the Hammer and Sickle Collective," which included such scenes as "The Drovsky Family at Home," "Working in the Fields," and finally "The Soviet Meeting in the Collective." At this meeting, "a prominent scientist receives an award from Stalin; another scientist lectures on 'How to Raise Better Sugar Beets'; members join in recreational activities." The children's parents then had a chance to examine the materials the children had created. Seeds concluded her article: "At nine years, the children had created the beginning of an interest in a land which is rapidly coming to the front.... From this small beginning may grow increasingly the understanding and appreciation out of which will emerge strong patterns of action in the promotion of friendly relationships with the Soviet neighbors of the United States."[70]

At the same time that Seeds was publicizing the Ukrainian Farmers unit, she was also enthusiastically supporting a scheme to have American children "adopt a hungry foreign child" and send them food packages. The children of UES were paired with Dutch children in the town of Ryskoff. Seeds saw no difference between having Dutch pen pals and the unit-of-work on the fictional Hammer and Sickle Collective. For Seeds, all were equally valuable classroom activities, meant to teach children about the wider world and to encourage a sense of political and social responsibility. But encouraging children to write to Dutch pen pals and turning a classroom into a Soviet collective farm with large pictures of Lenin and Stalin had quite different meanings in 1940s Los Angeles. Building friendly relations between the United States and the Soviet Union was hardly the primary goal of Jack Tenney's fact-finding committee.

In addition to her article in *Progressive Education*, Seeds proudly discussed the Ukrainian Farmers unit at public presentations. The well-known Los Angeles photographer Valeska took hundreds of photographs of UES including several of the Ukrainian Farmers unit.[71] In her oral history, Seeds described a presentation on the unit at a conference sponsored by what she called the "Association for the Promotion of Russian Friendship"—doubtless the American Russian Institute—in which she showed enlargements of the photographs Valeska had taken of the unit. Seeds described the scene: "I had all those pictures behind me when I made that speech on how to promote

Russian friendship. I said that we could do it with the children by introducing them to an interest in Russia as a friend of ours, because she was losing more men than we were, you know, in the Stalingrad days, etc."[72] Seeds was pleased with her presentation and with the power of Valeska's enlarged photographs. But those photographs attracted other attention. One of her friends told her later that an investigator for the Tenney Committee was in the audience that day and had closely examined the photographs.

THE TENNEY COMMITTEE

On January 2–6, 1946, the Tenney Committee held hearings in Los Angeles. Six professors who had lectured at the People's Educational Center were subpoenaed as were Santa Monica superintendent of schools Percy Davis, UCLA provost Clarence Dykstra, and Corinne Seeds.[73] Dykstra and Seeds testified on January 4, 1945. Dykstra was called first and was subjected to extensive and hostile questioning. In the afternoon Seeds went on the stand. An article in the *Westwood Hills Press* noted she had been called before the committee "because she had described, at the U.S.-Soviet conference, how children at her school had studied the lives and customs of—among others—the Russian people."[74] Seeds submitted a written statement for the committee setting out the goals of UES and describing the various units-of-work in which students studied different cultures through reading, drama, and dance; these included the Pueblo Indians, the Samoans, the Mexicans, the Chinese, the rubber-gatherers of the Upper Amazon, the Ukrainians of the USSR, colonial life on the Atlantic seaboard and in early California, pioneer life, and life in the industrial United States. Seeds showed the committee enlarged photographs of children in costume acting out scenes from a collective farm. According to the *Westwood Hills Press,* Seeds said, "Children should understand the way of life the Russians have—which is not often undertaken in American schools, and now I am beginning to see why." She then showed the committee the newspaper, "The Red Star Gazetteer," that the children had produced as part of the unit. Tenney entered it as Exhibit A.[75]

According to Seeds's later account in her oral history, she was in control of the exchange. She wrote that by the time she testified, "those old boys (there were about seven of them and most of them had been asleep all afternoon) finally straightened up when I went up with my pictures. They began to be quite interested, you see, because there was something to look at." After Seeds described the Ukrainian study, Tenney asked where she got all her information: "I said, 'Why, we read.' That brought the house down. It just fairly shook—it was a packed court room.... Tenney pounded on the desk and he said, 'Quiet! Quiet! The next person who makes a fuss in the court room will be escorted out.'" At the end of this testimony, Tenney, who was at that point more interested in the activities of Dykstra and other UCLA professors, allowed her to go.[76]

Seeds did not curtail her political activities immediately after her testimony before the Tenney Committee. The April 29, 1946 issue of the *People's*

World noted that she spoke at a Hollywood Writers' Mobilization Forum event for the American Society for Russian Relief. Nonetheless, it seems clear that the experience of testifying before the Tenney Committee was more frightening than Seeds admitted. Seeds tried to defend the Ukrainian Farmers unit, noting that when the forty-seven children who had completed the Ukrainian Farmers unit that year were asked, "Of all the countries of the world, which one do you like best?" Forty-five children responded "The United States," one responded "Alaska," and one Germany ("because they have good scientists there.")[77] But in the end, the unit on Ukrainian farmers was removed. As Seeds recalled the decision: "Well, when I got through with all this, I promised the staff that I'd just never get them into the dither again. You know, I suppose they thought they'd be next...Natalie said to me, 'Oh, Corinne, please do let us have a little breathing spell now before you begin again.' I said, 'Well, I'm not going to do any Russian study until this school is settled.'"[78] That question, of what the future held for UES, was still unanswered in the spring of 1946.

Saving the University Elementary School

Although the regents had voted their support of UES in December, there remained the problem of making sure the legislature appropriated funding for new school buildings. The Family School Alliance was centrally involved in this campaign. On January 14, 1946, Mrs. Eliscu, then president of the FSA, phoned President Sproul proposing that a separate bill be filed for the new school building. According to his "Memoranda," Sproul tried to dissuade her, but Eliscu would not be moved and pressed Sproul about what the university was going to do once the Warner Avenue lease was over.[79] Although Sproul clearly did not want to become involved with the struggle over UES, he was no match for the Family School Alliance and the network of supporters mobilized by Helen Heffernan. Once again, hundreds of letters from supporters throughout California were sent to the legislature and the regents in support of the school. Finally, in early February 1946, an omnibus bill for the postwar building program, including $600,000 specifically appropriated for new UES buildings on the UCLA campus, was passed by the legislature. Governor Earl Warren later reduced this to $300,000.

Despite several attempts to convince the Los Angeles School Board to allow UES to remain at the Warner Avenue site until new buildings could be constructed, by the spring of 1946 it was clear that the board would not revoke their decision. In March, President Sproul acknowledged that the university would not be able to lease the site. He wrote to the Los Angeles School Board, "I want you to know that we have accepted your decision with good grace and without any rancor whatsoever."[80] A few weeks later, in April, Provost Dykstra established an Advisory Committee on the Elementary School charged with the mandate to find a temporary home for the school. UES moved out of the Warner Avenue buildings in late June and the city reoccupied the property on July 1, 1946.[81]

Now there was a very real possibility that UES would not be able to reopen in the fall. Despite this uncertainty, Seeds taught her summer course and served as principal of the UES summer demonstration school in 1946. Heffernan joined her for the usual three-week conference for school supervisors.[82] While Seeds and Heffernan attempted to conduct their summer program as usual, they were deeply involved with the struggle to find a new home for UES. And Seeds was not free of the attentions of Eleanor Allen, who had proven a formidable presence on the Los Angeles School Board. Because of her urging, in December 1945, the Los Angeles School Board had issued a "Directive on the Teaching of Moral and Spiritual Values in Education," stating the board's conviction that there "must be a new and strong emphasis on the teaching of moral and spiritual values in the schools of Los Angeles." These values included a "recognition of a Power greater than our own."[83] In June 1946, Allen published three articles in the *Los Angeles Times* on the "moral and social crisis of today." Los Angeles schoolchildren needed moral education, she wrote, because "our schools are becoming the battleground where the materialistic and the moral ideologies are fighting to win the future citizens of America.... It is important that every citizen recognizes this war of ideas."[84]

Even though the Warner Avenue lease was now ended, Eleanor and Walter Allen continued to complain about Seeds and UES. In July 1946, just two weeks after UES left the Warner Avenue site, Walter Allen wrote to Dykstra and Sproul, accusing Seeds of defaming his wife. He claimed that Seeds had called Mrs. Allen a poor choice for a member of the Board of Education and had characterized Mrs. Allen's educational philosophy as "contrary to progress" and as advocating "(among various things) that the whip should be used in schools." Allen called Seeds's comments a "libelous attack" and pointed out that the university was responsible for her comments.[85] Dean Lee asked Seeds to reply in writing to Walter Allen's accusations. On July 30, 1946, she replied to Lee, with copies to Provost Dykstra and President Sproul. It took her a week to respond, she wrote, because she "sought the counsel of friends," who recommended that she consult an attorney, which she had done. Seeds completely denied Allen's accusations of her in-class comments and noted that her attorney believed the content of the letter was slanderous.[86] The next day, Dykstra wrote to Walter Allen, quoting extensively from Seeds's letter. He recommended to Allen that he drop the issue, since "it would seem to me quite unseemly and a magnification of the charges to take this conflict to the courts."[87] Allen wrote back on August 5, 1946, insisting that his information came from teachers and students, although he did not provide the names of these informants. He concluded, "Since the slanderous remarks have stopped and my purpose has been accomplished, I am not interested so much in the past as...that they will not continue in the future."[88]

While the Allens continued to complain, Seeds and her allies were frantically busy trying to find a home for UES so it could open in the fall. Jean Trapnell, then president of the Family School Alliance, wrote to Sproul that UES parents were ready to support the school and had already raised pledges of $26,000 at one event. She continued, "We are still ready to assist in every way: with money if necessary, and with such aid as cutting the red tape in Washington, in the state highway department, and even in supplying the University with the name of a contractor who is familiar with the buildings."[89] This reference to providing money and to "cutting red tape" suggests the kind of political as well as monetary resources of the parents in the Family School Alliance. But there were still no buildings available for UES. Various options for a temporary site were pursued: a local military academy, a small college, local military police barracks. Helen Heffernan wrote Dean Lee about some one hundred war surplus portable buildings at Camp Lathrop that might be available, but this plan fell through.[90] In July, surplus buildings were located in Santa Ana, but they would have to be moved. The first proposal was to move them to a site in Santa Monica to be provided by the Santa Monica School Board. But there was resistance in Santa Monica to any involvement with UES, led by Marcus McClure's *Santa Monica Evening Outlook*.[91] At its July 22 meeting the Santa Monica School Board turned down UES's request.

The Family School Alliance continued to put pressure on Sproul and the UCLA administrators. In late August, Jean Trapnell wrote to Dykstra pointing out that "the parents pledged this money to open the school this fall, not to give it as a gift to the University to use some time in the future" and asking for a guarantee that the funds allocated by the legislature would be used.[92] In the end no buildings were found, and in early September 1946, Seeds announced that UES would not be able to provide a full program for the 1946–47 school year, although they would try to offer a kindergarten and sixth-grade class in private homes.[93] UCLA University Counsel reported that holding first- to sixth-grade classes was forbidden by zoning ordinances, although they could hold kindergarten and nursery school classes.[94] Ultimately, only kindergarten and nursery school classes were held during the 1946–47 school year.

Despite the fact that classes were not held in the fall of 1946, Heffernan and the Family School Alliance continued their campaign to guarantee support for new school buildings. Heffernan sent a telegram of support to the regents just before their October 1946 meeting. The Minutes of the Family School Alliance summarized their plan to send letters to "each member of Regents asking for 'redress of grievances' and if we get no answer we will go to the legislature and ask them to investigate fiscal policy of Univ. (Miss Heffernan's suggestion)."[95] The pressure from the Family School Alliance was successful. At their October meeting, the regents appointed Robert Alexander, a leading Los Angeles architect and UES parent, to design the new school. The Family School Alliance Bulletin reported that "the Regents also authorized a budget for temporary buildings for the school and the procurement, if possible, of government surplus buildings as temporary structures."[96]

On June 23, 1947, UES reopened for summer school in temporary buildings transported from the Santa Ana airbase to the UCLA campus.[97] Three days later, the *Westwood Hills Press* ran a story on the results of a survey it had conducted in cooperation with the UCLA School of Education and the

Los Angeles city school system comparing UES graduates with graduates of other Los Angeles public schools.[98] The survey compared the achievement of three groups of students at Emerson Junior High School, a Los Angeles city school attended by many UES graduates. The first group consisted of eighty-one children who had graduated from UES. The second group consisted of eighty-one children who were matched by age, grade, sex, IQ, and "social background" with the UES graduates and who had attended other Los Angeles city public schools. The third group of eighty-one was chosen at random from the Emerson student body. The results of the survey showed that the students who had attended UES did better in terms of grades than either of the other two groups.

This story then made its way into the influential national magazine *Time*, which ran a story, "The Battle of Westwood Hills," in its July 14, 1947 issue. In the *Time* account, Seeds was presented as a passionate "schoolmarm" dedicated to children, but with no strong political views. The story began, "Corinne Seeds looks like a mild-mannered schoolmarm.... She once taught Mexican women in a boxcar; and she has a zealot's faith in the wonders of progressive education."[99] According to *Time*, the current controversy was attributed to parents "who discovered that fourth-graders could not hold their own in a spelling bee." It then referred to "an irate parent"—Mrs. Allen—who was elected to the Los Angeles school board. Parents rallied to support Seeds, but "when left-wingers gave Miss Seeds some unsought backing, she found herself before California's Legislative Committee on un-American Activities." But, *Time* noted, Seeds was cleared of being "un-American." *Time* then reported on the state legislature's commitment of $300,000 toward the construction of new school buildings on the UCLA campus and referred to the study carried out by what it described as "the carefully neutral" *Westwood Hills Press*: "Miss Seeds' students did as well as the others, if not better, in almost every subject—even on the non-progressives' home grounds (reading, arithmetic). Said Miss Seeds: 'It was a great victory. Besides, our children are world-minded, too.'"

In this article, the general outline of events is there, but Seeds is presented as a charming eccentric with no political ideas of her own, simply the pawn of "left-wingers." *Time* clearly meant this as a defense. The well-connected parents in the Family School Alliance may well have been the source of this relatively positive story. Although Helen Heffernan mobilized educators across California in her defense, ultimately Seeds's survival was doubtless the result of the energy and resources of the Family School Alliance. The parents of the children of UES included wealthy and well-known figures from the business, artistic, and intellectual elites of Los Angeles, many with connections to powerful media. The struggle over UES was a contest over pedagogy and curriculum; but even more, it was about class. With the publication of the sympathetic story in *Time*, it was clear that the University Elementary School was going to survive.

CHAPTER 8

Exporting Democracy / Defending Democracy

Helen Heffernan marshaled her energies and resources to support Corinne Seeds in the fight to save UES, but she also faced opportunities and dangers of her own in the immediate postwar years. In June 1945 Heffernan's old enemy state senator John Harold Swan, who had unsuccessfully attempted to pass legislation eliminating Heffernan's position, inserted a statement into the Senate *Journal* repeating his earlier accusations that the "products" of the public schools were not being adequately trained because of "those who have infected public education with the pernicious doctrines of so-called 'progressive education.'"[1] The major source of these doctrines, Swan wrote, was an individual who was "in many quarters recognized as an able, intelligent educational leader," but who was leading in the wrong direction. Swan pronounced: "Until such leadership is changed, elementary education will be in an increasingly desperate plight." He therefore recommended "an immediate change in the chief of the Division of Elementary Education in the State Department of Education."[2] Swan then inserted passages from Heffernan's writings into the Senate *Journal* as proof of her dangerous and irresponsible ideas.[3] Swan was unsuccessful in the attempt to have Heffernan fired, but she soon came to the attention of other foes.

Living Democratically in an Atmosphere of Cooperative Effort

Like other liberals, Heffernan was heartened by the victory over Fascism and the founding of the United Nations. With many others on the Left, she was committed to international peace, the need to address ongoing injustice, particularly racism, and the values of cooperation and group effort. In 1945 and 1946 she articulated these ideas in two articles, "Methods in the Social Studies" and "Discussion, a Technique of Democratic Education," and in a position paper on the state's proposed social studies curriculum frameworks, "Implementation of the Frameworks of the Social Studies in the Elementary School."[4] In "Methods in the Social Studies," she advocated that schools should teach the values of "international collaboration and co-operation."[5]

In "Discussion, a Technique of Democratic Education," she argued that the responsibility of the school was to make "democracy function by helping children to think collectively."[6] Heffernan also advocated the discussion of topics that brought forth differences of opinion. For high-school classrooms, for example, she suggested such topics as "Should the United States yield any of her sovereignty in order to become a part of an international organization?" and "Should a study of the Soviet Union be carried on in the public schools of the United States?"[7] Heffernan approvingly called group discussion "a technique in social engineering" that "provides an opportunity to face the problems that confront individuals as well as groups and to arrive at mutually acceptable conclusions. It accepts no dictation by authority." Most importantly, she wrote, "It is the forerunner of new social methods in the process of replacing 'rugged individualism' with cooperative effort and interest in group welfare."[8] Everything about Heffernan's stance was offensive to conservatives: education as "social engineering," the direct rejection of "authority," the need for "new social methods," openly debating the value of the United Nations and Soviet Union, and of course replacing individual interests with cooperative effort and group welfare. Even raising such political questions was seen as inappropriate and even subversive.

On October 21, 1945, state superintendent Walter Dexter died of a heart attack.[9] A few days before his death, Seeds sent Heffernan a newspaper clipping entitled "Dr. Walter Dexter's Condition Critical." Seeds's view of Dexter was made clear in a note she attached to the clipping: "Death may solve one of your major problems!—according to the above clipping."[10] After Dexter's death, there was uncertainty about who would be named to replace him. In Seeds's eyes the obvious candidate to replace Dexter was Helen Heffernan, but obviously not everyone agreed. An October 27, 1945 *Los Angeles Times* editorial entitled "Let's Have a Strong Man in Dexter Post!" argued that what both parents and "those who hire the products of our public school systems" wanted was "a basically solid educational program" with children drilled in "the Three R's."[11] On November 6, 1945, Republican governor Earl Warren appointed Roy Simpson, a Southern California superintendent of schools and former president of the Association of California Public School Superintendents, to complete Dexter's term.[12] Soon after his appointment, Helen Heffernan introduced Roy Simpson at the annual conference of the California School Supervisors' Association. Simpson read from the Sermon on the Mount and talked about the importance of spiritual values.[13]

Simpson was a cautious figure with no strong political allegiance. But he soon was faced with political choices. The first crisis came with the publication of the new state social studies frameworks. Attempts to develop a set of curricular guidelines or frameworks had occupied the California Department of Education for years.[14] When in 1942 the National Education Policies Commission had asked each state to create a "master plan" for curriculum, the State Curriculum Commission had appointed yet another committee to develop frameworks, beginning with the social studies. Doubtless through Heffernan's influence, Corinne Seeds was named chair of the committee.

Seeds and Heffernan had consulted frequently about the frameworks committee in the years between 1942 and 1945.[15] Finally, in spring 1946, the document describing the new social studies frameworks was almost complete. In May, state superintendent Roy Simpson asked Heffernan to present a summary of the new frameworks to the curriculum commission.[16] In response, Heffernan prepared a statement entitled "Implementation of the Framework of the Social Studies in the Elementary School."

"Implementation of the Framework of the Social Studies" was a kind of manifesto of Heffernan's beliefs about the role of education in a democratic society. It began with the claim that the social studies were central to developing a conception of citizenship based on "active opposition to all forms of political, social and economic injustice" and "intelligent cooperation."[17] Heffernan then went on to describe what she saw as successful methods for teaching the social studies, methods very similar to the units-of-work developed at UES.[18] Heffernan's statement in "The Implementation of the Frameworks" was uncompromising about highly charged issues—the need for educators actively to oppose injustice, the advocacy of cooperation and world government, the rejection of disciplinary boundaries, and the emphasis on a flexible pedagogy based on children's interests and activities. Although the eventual statement issued by the curriculum commission was a bland three-page statement listing the topics to be studied in each grade, basically repeating the course of study that had been in place for many years, Heffernan's defense of the frameworks was not overlooked by those on the Right.

The Sons of the American Revolution

Heffernan's 1945 and 1946 articles, along with her defense of the social studies as a means to build a cooperative world order in "Implementation of the Frameworks for the Social Studies," confirmed for right-wing observers what they already suspected—Heffernan was the leader of a concerted plot to undermine traditional American values. On June 27, 1946, Aara Sargent of the Sons of the American Revolution wrote to state superintendent Roy Simpson and Jay Conner of the curriculum commission demanding that a statement he had prepared be brought to the attention of the California State Curriculum Commission at its next meeting in Los Angeles on June 28–29, 1946.[19] In his statement, Sargent rejected the frameworks, whose purpose, he argued, was to inject political propaganda and teach international socialism in the public schools in violation of Sections 8273 and 8274 of the Education Code. More specifically, he cited Helen Heffernan's statement, "Implementation of the Framework of the Social Studies in the Elementary School," and her two articles, "Methods in the Social Studies" and "Discussion, a Technique of Democratic Education," to support his accusations. In his statement, Sargent cited the "revolutionary ideas originating from a group of educators at Teachers College at Columbia University in New York City," who, Sargent claimed, wanted to make the public schools the means of creating a new social order, a reference to Counts's "Dare the School Build a New Social Order." Heffernan's "Implementation of the Framework of the Social Studies in the Elementary School," Sargent continued, showed that the frameworks were "a deliberate attempt at indoctrination of the children in our public schools, beginning even with the kindergarten and the first grade." When Sargent introduced his protest to the July 12 State Board of Education meeting, Heffernan responded with a petition signed by eighty teachers, principals, and supervisors declaring that the signers were "in full accord with the philosophy expressed by Miss Helen Heffernan in her statement entitled 'Implementation of the Framework of the Social Studies in the Elementary School.'"[20]

Heffernan weathered this storm, but Aara Sargent did not give up his campaign to transform California education. Three weeks later, he and the Sons of the American Revolution turned their complaints to the *Building America* series, the set of supplementary social studies materials that was widely used in schools in California and nationally in the early 1940s.[21] The series, illustrated by the extensive use of photographs, addressed contemporary social issues in the United States, including poverty, racism, and other pressing social problems. The State Curriculum Commission had unanimously recommended to the State Board of Education that *Building America* be adopted as a supplementary textbook in history and geography for Grades 7 and 8.[22] In early August, Sargent appeared before the Board of Education to demand that the board reverse the curriculum commission's decision. The board listened to Sargent's complaints but in the end issued an innocuous resolution supporting the idea that the history of the United States and California should be taught along with civics.[23] Sargent next appeared at the joint Los Angeles meetings of the curriculum commission and the State Board of Education on August 24, 1946 to demand that *Building America* be removed from the list of approved textbooks. The commission equivocated, voting to postpone their next scheduled meeting for "several weeks" in order to "examine the recommendation and textbooks involved."[24]

Heffernan, however, was not to be involved in the ongoing controversy over *Building America*. In July 1946, she learned that she had been recommended for the position of primary schools officer on General MacArthur's staff in occupied Japan.[25] Heffernan did not hesitate. Not only was she faced with the attacks by Swann and Sargent, but she had recently been put in charge of a new program to provide educational services to children with cerebral palsy. In June, she wrote to a friend, "This has been an unusually strenuous year for me, with the administration of the cerebral palsy program added to an already killing schedule."[26] The prospect of participating in building a new democratic school system in Japan was not only an adventure and challenge, but it also provided a respite from this "killing schedule." Heffernan was granted a one-year leave of absence, retaining her civil-service status. Bernard Lonsdale of her staff was appointed acting chief of the Division of Elementary Education while Heffernan was away.[27]

Heffernan would be missed, not only at the State Department of Education, but by many others. One person who would particularly miss her was Afton Nance, the Southern California teacher and supervisor who had contributed the article on the treatment of returning Japanese American children, "The Return of the Nisei," to the 1945 volume *Education for Cultural Unity*, which also included Heffernan and Seeds's article, "Intercultural Education in the Elementary School." Nance had received her undergraduate degree from Mills College and her MA from the University of Southern California and had taught at the Shanghai American School in China before returning to the United States after the Japanese invasion of China. From the time Nance returned from China she had been deeply concerned with questions of social and racial justice. In 1943, Seeds mentioned in a letter to Heffernan that Nance, who had her supervisory credential, was looking for a position to "render service in areas where there are either Mexicans or Nisei Japanese.... Do you have anything in mind for her?"[28] Perhaps with Heffernan's help, Nance found a position as school supervisor in Riverside. She was a member of the Friends of the American Way, a group that worked with the American Friends Service Committee to support the incarcerated Japanese Americans.[29] In 1945, Heffernan recommended her for a scholarship so she could attend an intercultural workshop at the University of Chicago sponsored by the National Council of Christians and Jews.[30]

Nance and Heffernan began to correspond in the summer and fall of 1946, as Heffernan was preparing to leave for Japan. The early letters from Nance were addressed to "Miss Heffernan," but by the summer they had moved to "Helen" and "Afton." In August, Heffernan wrote to "Dear Afton" about the appointment of an African American teacher in San Bernardino: "It is a real victory to have San Bernardino City appoint a Negro teacher. I cannot see how we can continue to give lip service to democracy and practice discrimination against the Negro group."[31] In October, when news of Heffernan's appointment to MacArthur's staff in Tokyo was made public, Nance wrote to "Dear Helen" that she was pleased to hear that Bernard Lonsdale would serve as acting chief: "It is a relief to know that the liberal educational policies which you have set over the years will continue, but we will certainly miss you, just the same."[32] Heffernan responded, thanking her and mentioning an upcoming conference: "You and I know that people don't go to conferences just for the fun of it. That is, I mean not altogether.... Of course, I can't hesitate to add that it would be fun if you were going to be there."[33]

Heffernan would be missed by the supporters of UES as well. The bulletin of the Family School Alliance noted her departure and her contribution to the fight to save UES.[34] And she would be missed in a more personal way by Corinne Seeds. In a letter written only a few weeks before Heffernan left for Japan, Seeds wrote her: "Tonight there is a little, new moon! By the time it grows into a large, round-faced fellow—and then wanes—it will be time for the plane to carry you to Japan where the same moon will continue to bring back memories of moonlight, clear and bright—moonlight, hidden behind dense, black clouds! The month will soon pass—too soon!"³⁵ On October 26, 1946, Heffernan boarded a military flight to Tokyo.

Bringing Democratic Education to Japan

In her first published "Letter from Japan," Heffernan described the forty-two-hour flight from California to Tokyo, stopping at various Pacific bases to refuel.³⁶ It must have been a relief to leave the increasingly contentious political scene in California. But Heffernan did not escape political tensions when she joined the Occupation. Although the Americans constantly spoke of democracy, neither the occupiers nor the Japanese were united in their conception of what democracy meant for the future of Japan. The Occupation, which lasted until 1952, soon felt the effects of the growing tension between New Deal reformers and anti-Communist groups who more and more dominated politics in the United States. Nor were the Japanese united politically. Despite the wartime ascendancy of ultranationalist and militarist ideals, Japan had a liberal and left tradition of its own. After the war the political differences within Japanese society were revealed and heightened. Heffernan approached her time in Japan seemingly unaware of these fault lines. Deeply disturbed by German and Japanese fascism and militarism and naturally unaware of the coming political repression of McCarthyism in the United States, she held a deep faith in American democracy and the power of progressive schools to build democracy. In an early letter she wrote of the Japanese, "Actually, I believe the people were worn out with the military domination and welcome the development of democracy in Japan. In my opinion a political, social, and economic revolution unprecedented in modern history is being accomplished."³⁷

Heffernan arrived in Japan more than a year after the end of the war. Although Japan had an elected government, in practice the U.S. military under General Douglas MacArthur had the final say in virtually all aspects of life. The goal of the Occupation was not only to maintain order, but also to create new institutions that would foster democracy in what was seen as a deeply authoritarian culture.³⁸ The Occupation government (formally known as the Supreme Command of the Allied Powers and informally, as SCAP) was comprised of various sections responsible for different aspects of Japanese culture, society, and government. The Civil Information and Education Section (CI&E), established on September 22, 1945, was itself divided into six divisions, among them the Education Division, to which Heffernan was assigned.³⁹

When Helen Heffernan arrived to join the Education Division of CI&E, the foundations of education reform were already in place. In the early months of 1946, the Education Division had issued four major policy directives. These included the prohibition of nationalist or ultranationalist ideology, the elimination of militarist and nationalist material from textbooks, the removal of "ultranationalist" teachers, and the elimination of any Shinto materials from the curriculum. In the spring of 1946, General MacArthur invited 27 U.S. educators to form an Educational Mission to Japan to survey the existing

Japanese educational system and to make recommendations for its reorganization on a democratic foundation.[40] The Educational Mission spent a month in Japan, interviewing officials, visiting schools and universities, and attending conferences. Their final report, which was submitted to General MacArthur on April 6, 1946, was described by one historian as "a small manifesto on 'progressive education' for 'personal development, citizenship, and community life.'"[41] The report emphasized that democratic education must take place in an atmosphere of freedom. It proclaimed: "The unmeasured resources of childhood will bear rich fruit only under the sunshine of liberalism. It is the business of the teacher to furnish this, not its opposite."[42] The source of the "sunshine of liberalism," the report suggested, could be found in the Charter of the United Nations and the draft Constitution of UNESCO. After the mission's visit, the Japanese Government appointed a Japanese Education Reform Council (JERC), which was given cabinet rank and the task of implementing the new democratic reforms.

Educating Self-Respecting People among the Peoples of the World

When she arrived in Tokyo, Heffernan was billeted at the Hotel Osaka, which in early December still did not yet have heat. The food was good, but had to be shipped in from the United States, since the Japanese could barely feed themselves. Heffernan lived and worked in what was called "little America" in downtown Tokyo. There the Americans created their own world, driving through the military traffic on newly renamed MacArthur Boulevard and attending shows at Ernie Pyle Theater.[43] Heffernan wrote that she tried to save one day a week "for the re-creation of H.H." She visited a temple, which was beautiful, but her feet still felt "the effects of walking in nylons on the frigid floors of this temple." Her initial impressions emphasized the terrible conditions under which the Japanese were living. She wrote, "The poverty is great. It gets me down to see children cold and hungry but I am comforted to think that work is now in progress which will ultimately restore the economy of Japan and make it possible for them to be self-respecting people among the peoples of the world."[44]

Shortly after she arrived in Japan, Heffernan read Ruth Benedict's newly published *The Chrysanthemum and the Sword*, a study of Japanese culture written as part of Benedict's work with the Overseas Intelligence Division of the Office of War Information. *The Chrysanthemum and the Sword* was meant to be "a kind of cultural guidebook for American officials overseeing the reconstruction of Japan." It was based on a reading of published works in English (Benedict did not know Japanese) and on interviews with Japanese Americans.[45] Heffernan wrote to Afton Nance that Benedict "certainly has analyzed the cultural pattern of the Japanese with her usual discernment. Just at present, I am struggling with the revision of the School Edict and fully realize what she says about the adherence to the idea of hierarchy in the Japanese cultural pattern."[46] Like other Americans in the Occupation,

Heffernan seems to have taken Benedict's idea that there are "patterns of culture" to heart in trying to understand the Japanese.

Heffernan was one of a number of women, both American and Japanese, on the CI&E staff. By spring 1946, there were 453 women and 3,760 men working in General Headquarters. Many of the American women were members of the Women's Army Corps (WACs)who provided service and clerical work, but others were influential in setting policy. American women in CI&E wrote what was called the Japanese Equal Rights Amendment in the new constitution, argued for the establishment of a women's bureau in the Ministry of Labor, and created publications and radio programs supporting gender equality.[47] Japanese women with a knowledge of English—members of the educated Japanese elite—were recruited to work as translators for American women. Heffernan herself had a personal interpreter, Yoshiko Kunugi, who later spent a year in California where she worked with Corinne Seeds at the UES.[48]

Although women were active within SCAP, men held all the significant leadership positions. Mark Orr was chief of the Education Division during Heffernan's time in Japan and remained in that position until March 1949.[49] While the leaders of the Education Division were men, the division also included a number of women specialists. Captain Eileen Donovan, a graduate of Boston Teachers' College, was a specialist in secondary education; Dr. Lulu Holmes, who had taught at the Kobe Women's Academy for two years before the war, was the head of the Higher Education branch; Dr. Verna Carley, who had a doctorate in Education from the University of Colorado and had been assistant professor of education at Stanford, was a specialist in secondary education and teacher training.[50] Heffernan joined this group as a specialist in elementary education. There were eight officers in the Education Division, including Heffernan. Heffernan wrote in a "Letter from Japan" published in December 1946, that she was "only in the process of orientation" and was acquainting herself with the work done by CI&E in helping the Japanese Ministry of Education to develop a new course of study for the schools.[51] Her first responsibility was to conduct "a weekly seminar in elementary education for 32 elected leaders in elementary education from the Tokyo area." Heffernan described her work with the seminar: "Last Thursday night we developed the basic concepts on the objectives of education in a democratic society. This coming Thursday we will devote the two hours to a discussion of what are the obstacles in the way of realizing these objectives in the schools of Japan."[52]

In her first few months in Tokyo, Heffernan worked most closely on a new educational psychology textbook for preservice and in-service Japanese teachers. According to an Education Division report, the two-volume *Kyoiku Shinri* (Educational Psychology), edited by the Ministry of Education and intended to "introduce teachers to modern points of view," was published in March 1947 and subsequently used as a textbook in both normal schools and in-service teacher training programs.[53] After the educational psychology textbook was completed, Heffernan spent the majority of her time working with three groups: a Seminar in Elementary Education, a Committee on Early Childhood Education, and a group focusing on the education of "handicapped children." The groups met once a week with the goal of encouraging and building leadership. Heffernan apologized to Afton Nance for not writing more frequently: "I'm really pretty busy and making speeches, arranging workshops, writing law, holding committee meetings, and the like—pretty dry fodder for the reading public."[54]

One aspect of Japanese education that Heffernan rarely mentioned was the role of teachers' unions. SCAP's October 1945 "bill of rights" had allowed labor unions and political parties, including those dominated by socialists and Communists, a policy that was in line with the emphasis on democracy and freedom of expression in MacArthur's early proclamations. The Japanese teachers' unions that formed after the war were dominated by left-wing groups, since the purge of nationalist and militarist teachers in 1945 had eliminated most of the openly right-wing teachers and thus provided an opening for socialist or Communist union leaders. In her first published letter from Japan in December 1946, Heffernan referred sympathetically to the struggles of the Japanese Educational Workers Union, which she noted had a membership of 320,000, to improve teachers' low salaries, but she did not mention the crisis around the proposed general strike called for February 1, 1947. The Japanese teachers' unions were deeply involved in the planning for the strike. But in the end SCAP banned it, a stark reminder of where true power lay. After the failed strike the left-of-center teachers' groups merged into the Japan Teachers' Union (Nikkyoso) and by June 1947 most teachers had unionized.[55] Nikkyoso enthusiastically embraced the democratic educational reforms initially proposed by the Education Division of SCAP, but it was closely associated with the Japanese Communist Party and its radical stance meant that it frequently clashed with the Japanese Ministry of Education. Heffernan must have been aware of these tensions around the teachers' unions and the struggles of the Japanese Left to establish democratic institutions, but she did not refer to them in her letters or published accounts.

Throughout the spring and summer of 1947, Heffernan was busy organizing and participating in conferences for Japanese teachers, administrators, and professors of education. In March 1947, the Japanese Diet passed the Fundamental Law of Education and the School Education Law. The School Education Law established the 6-3-3 structure for public schools and set the school leaving age at fifteen, while the Fundamental Law of Education essentially replaced the 1890 Imperial Rescript as the basic statement of Japanese education.[56] "A Tentative Suggested Course of Study: General," issued by the Japanese Education Ministry, showed the influence of progressive tenets. It proclaimed that "real learning does not result from memorizing...facts. The teaching methodology must be contrived on the basis of the understanding that real knowledge and skill will never be acquired through other means than the child's activities...[It is necessary] to satisfy the wants springing from the purposes set up by the child himself."[57] This focus on the child rather than the curriculum clearly reflected central beliefs of progressive educators in the United States and doubtless the influence of American officials in the Education Division of SCAP.

In the next few months Heffernan was involved with a number of projects. She oversaw and consulted on the completion of various projects in both social studies and language arts and helped develop a new course of study in fine and practical arts that emphasized "the relation of art to the social studies and science curriculum." She also helped establish an Advisory Committee in the Language Arts Curriculum for Elementary and Junior High Schools. Finally, clearly drawing on her California experience, she was asked to help the Seminar in Elementary Education prepare a brief bulletin to be called *How to Develop a Unit of Work*.[58] In a letter to Afton Nance, Heffernan described the seminars and meetings she held with Japanese educators: "My meetings seem to go better when I have something for the people to eat and smoke and I am glad that my figure precludes candy and my taste precludes smoking." She gave her weekly ration of candy and cigarettes to the members of her groups, who were "starved for sugar." She wanted "to give them a cup of coffee and a good stout sandwich" but that was impossible. She asked Nance for any professional books she could spare, since many of the Japanese educators read English and books were "taken with great enthusiasm."[59]

Heffernan shared the assumption of other members of SCAP's Education Division that the Japanese uniformly followed a rigid and authoritarian theory of education and that she would be introducing them to new and strange educational ideas. In a description of her presentations before Japanese teachers and administrators, for example, she wrote, "I have been trying to get across ideas of democratic administration and supervision but most of the teachers in Japan think their principals are unassailable little autocrats."[60] One of her responsibilities was to check the scripts of daily radio broadcasts produced by the Japanese Ministry of Education for school children. She wrote of one script: "The sentence which arrested my attention was: 'Japan has entirely given up War forever, and she is now to start on her new career as a peaceful and pacific nation, all *dominated* by the noble ideals of democracy.' The italics are mine!"[61]

Heffernan's view of the underlying patterns of Japanese culture echoed the ideas of Ruth Benedict. In analyzing the reasons for the success of the Japanese militarists, for example, Heffernan spoke of Japanese "mental characteristics" and their "indigenous tendency" to act in unison. Thus it was a characteristic of Japanese culture, not just the control of the militaristic clique, that led to the disaster of Japanese imperialism. She wrote: "*Esprit de corps* becomes dangerous when no individual can express ideas contrary to those held by the total group. With this mental characteristic it was little wonder that the people of Japan were deceived by and blindly followed a small group of leaders."[62] Although she continued to view Japanese culture as hierarchical and authoritarian, by the summer of 1947 she had made the acquaintance of Japanese educators with more progressive ideas.

Contrary to the original assumptions of the Americans in SCAP's Education Division, there was a progressive educational tradition in Japan, in part influenced by John Dewey, who had visited Japan in 1919. Although, as Victor Kobayashi points out, the progressives "operated in a hostile and precarious environment" and faced constant opposition from the traditionalists in the Ministry of Education, a number of Japanese educators had sought to introduce progressive ideas to Japanese schools in the 1920s in what was called the "New Education Movement."[63] Alice Miel, who spent seven months in Japan in 1951 and 1952 as a consultant for the Institute for Education Leadership in Occupied Japan, claimed that "for many of the participants in [the Institute] and those who addressed them, the new education in Japan meant resumption of work along progressive lines begun twenty-five or more years ago but interrupted by the militarists."[64] Kobayashi, who interviewed several former members of CI&E, agrees that "many Americans working in the occupation's educational reform program discovered that Japanese teachers and educationists were acquainted with Dewey's ideas as well as with the various theories and methods popular in the American progressive education movement in the twenties and thirties."[65] Heffernan seems to have become acquainted with at least some of the Japanese progressive educators. She worked particularly closely with a Mr. Isaka from the Education Ministry, who published a book entitled *The Teacher and the New Elementary School* and who worked with Heffernan and a group of elementary school principals and supervisors on the new social studies texts for the elementary school.[66]

In the fall of 1947, Heffernan's attention turned to the production of a new handbook on administration and supervision intended to be a "guide to democratic education" for Japanese educators.[67] This became the *Handbook on the Administration and Supervision of Elementary Schools*, which was eventually published in 1948 after Heffernan had left Japan. In October 1947 the first draft of the *Handbook* was completed. Heffernan participated in a number of regional conferences held to discuss the new *Handbook*, which in essence was a blueprint for a progressive, child-centered system of elementary education for Japan, much like the one Heffernan had shaped in California. At the conference at Beppu, she told the Japanese that "the democratic ideal does not sanction the imposition of the will of the supervisor on his colleagues." Echoing Dewey, she emphasized that "the modern school aims at a program of living as well as learning. Children learn democracy not through verbalism but by living democratically day by day in the program the school provides."[68]

Heffernan spent just over one year in Japan. In October, 1947, as she was preparing to return to California, she submitted a summary of her work over the previous year, listing what she saw as the major accomplishments in elementary education: the creation of new elementary social studies textbooks, the publication of the two-volume textbook on educational psychology, the conferences, extension courses, and workshops jointly conducted with the Japanese Ministry of Education intended "to acquaint teachers with the new curriculum and modern educational practices."[69] Heffernan made a particular point of mentioning the summer workshop she organized for approximately 180 teachers of blind, deaf, and mentally retarded children in Tokyo in the summer of 1947. She then summarized the publications she had helped develop in her year in Japan: the first three chapters of a volume for teachers entitled *The Guidance and Evaluation of Learning in the Elementary Schools*, which was to be completed in 1948; a bulletin called *The Education of Children Two to Six*, which should soon be published; and most importantly, the *Handbook on the Administration and Supervision of Elementary Schools*, which Heffernan clearly regarded as her most significant accomplishment in Japan.

Heffernan was still concerned about what she saw as excessively centralized control by the Japanese Ministry of Education. In her final summary of her work, she warned that the ministry needed to learn to exercise "functions of leadership, stimulation, and encouragement rather than authoritarian controls over the educational program."[70] Building on her work in California, Heffernan saw continuing in-service teacher education and the support of progressive supervisors and administrators as the key to creating democratic schools. Thus she strongly recommended that the Education Division pursue the following steps: (1) a nationwide study of the *Handbook* by individual principals and supervisors; (2) the group study of the *Handbook* by professional groups to adapt to local conditions; (3) summer conferences and workshops; (4) having principals and supervisors visit one another to see successful leadership and "democratic cooperation"; (5) continued research; (6) the publication of professional literature on administration and supervision; (7) support for professional associations of administrators and supervisors.[71] Essentially, Heffernan recommended replicating the progressive system she had developed in California.

It is difficult to judge Heffernan's influence on the progressive reforms proposed by the Americans. Heffernan led seminars and workshops, but she was not part of the formal leadership of the Education Division of CI&E. The two examples put forward by CI&E officials as model Deweyan programs were the curriculum programs of the states of California and Virginia. The Virginia curriculum was instigated by Hollis Caswell, a well-known progressive educator. Victor Kobayashi claimed that "a comparison of the ministry's social studies course of study of May 20, 1947, with the Virginia plan indicates that there was great similarity between the two."[72] Yet in the *Dictionary of the New Education*, published by the Japanese ministry in 1949, the progressive approach is called "the California plan."[73] The *Handbook on the Administration and Supervision of Elementary Schools*, Heffernan's most ambitious undertaking, clearly was modeled on the practices she put into effect in California. Heffernan herself did not complain about the lack of recognition of her work as the key architect of California progressive education, but she came to believe that the Education Division badly needed experienced progressive educators. She wrote to Afton Nance: "Finally I broke down and recommended some Californians to come over to work on this job."[74]

Heffernan left Japan in late December 1947. By early 1948 what came to be called "the reverse course" of the Occupation was rapidly gaining momentum, part of the growing aggressive anti-Communism of the Cold War. In his analysis of the internal politics of the Occupation, Herbert Passin argues that "New Dealers were increasingly pushed aside by technocrats and by pro-business advisers and staffs. Many reform programs began to slow down or grind to a halt, the emphasis shifting to making Japan economically self-supporting and politically part of the Free World."[75] The reverse course was emphasized in the March 1948 visit of George Kennan to Tokyo to discuss the new U.S. policies. Radical labor unions were stifled, war crimes trials were abandoned and antitrust policies were eliminated. In terms of education, John Dower noted that "by 1948, distraught SCAP officials were traveling the country to denounce "Red" influences in the schools."[76] By 1949, the purge had clearly turned against Communists rather than militarists.

It is not clear whether Heffernan met open opposition during 1947, when she was in Japan. The only indication of criticism of Heffernan's work within SCAP is found in one obscure memo from June 1949, over a year after Heffernan had left Tokyo and at a point when the reverse course was fully under way. The memo, from JRM, "Chief of Section," to Alfred Loomis, then chief of the Education Division, refers to a controversy over the direction of the Education Division's educational reforms. The issue seems to have been Heffernan's influence. The memo refers to an ongoing controversy over instructional material: "This matter was discussed in great detail with the Ministry of Education as early as five months before Miss Heffernan arrived in Japan. It was done with full knowledge and approval of the present chief, CIE." Moreover "there was little evidence in the textbook manuscripts submitted and passed by both the Japanese and by us, of influence from California which are alarming in character." It is clear that someone saw Heffernan's California influence as "alarming" and that pressure of some kind was put on the Education Division to temper her reforms. JRM himself was caustic about these complaints. He wrote, "If the presence of one former staff member at a few meetings of a Japanese committee two years ago is sufficient cause to bring about unhappiness, it would seem as if we should stop about 90% of the activities of the Education Division because of the risk that unhappiness might pile up in 1951."[77] Whether these criticisms of Heffernan's programs came from within the Occupation or from figures back in the United States is unclear. The chief of the CI&E Section in 1949 was Lt. Colonel Donald Nugent, who, according to Eiji Takemae, "coordinated a steadily escalating assault on Communist influence in the labor movement, the schools, and the mass media that culminated in the Red Purge of 1949–50."[78] But it is certainly also possible by this time that right-wing politicians in California may have raised alarms about Heffernan's possibly dangerous influence on Japanese education.

In her final letter from Japan, Heffernan reflected on what she saw as the overall success of the Occupation. She praised General MacArthur's "wise, firm, and consistently humane direction to the reconstruction of Japan."[79]

Heffernan wrote, "You know that it is with great regret that I am turning my back on Japan in what seems an hour of greatest need. I have loved working with the Japanese people. It has been a source of real inspiration to work out some of the many problems with them."[80] Years later, at her eightieth birthday celebration, a friend reported: "When I asked Helen recently what she felt was the greatest honor she had received, there was a long pause before she replied: 'To be asked to do the job in Japan.'"[81] Heffernan's time in Japan seems to have been deeply satisfying, despite the growing political divisions within Japanese society and within the Occupation itself. While she ignored politics in her accounts of her time in Japan, she would not be able to escape the impact of the changes in the political landscape once she returned to California.

Postwar California

When Helen Heffernan returned from Japan in January 1948, she found a world in transition, both politically and personally. Culturally, the country was in the midst of a backlash against women's participation in public life. The wartime woman worker, exemplified by the image of Rosie the Riveter, was now encouraged to return to the home. Popular works such as Ferdinand Lundberg and Marynia Farnham's 1947 *Modern Woman: The Lost Sex* echoed the claims of Philip Wylie's misogynistic *Generation of Vipers* and Helene Deutsch's *Psychology of Women* that women needed to follow their true destiny into heterosexual marriage and motherhood within the patriarchal family. Politically, the nation was in the midst of equally dramatic political changes. On March 12, 1947, President Truman asked for military aid for Greece and Turkey to combat Communism in those countries. The arguments put forward to justify this decision came to be known as the Truman Doctrine, based on the idea that the United States must oppose Communism everywhere. Nine days after the request for aid to combat Communism abroad, Truman issued Executive Order 9348, requiring loyalty oaths of government employees. In October 1947, the House Un-American Activities Committee held widely publicized hearings in Los Angeles about possible Communist infiltration in Hollywood. The Hollywood Ten, writers and directors who refused to cooperate with the committee, were jailed for contempt of Congress. In California, although the popular moderate Republican Earl Warren was reelected governor in 1946, at a local level, right-wing politicians, particularly in Southern California, flourished. Richard Nixon's defeat of the liberal Democrat Jerry Voorhis in a 1946 congressional campaign marked by Nixon's vitriolic anti-Communist rhetoric was a sign of the growing strength of the Right.

A number of historians have analyzed the growth of conservative and radical Right groups in the immediate postwar years, particularly in Southern California. In the Cold War, California politicians and policy makers were active in developing a military economy in California, encouraging military bases, the aircraft and other war industries, and military research centers.[82]

In her study of the growth of the Right in Orange Country, Lisa McGirr has argued that the dependence on defense and the military "deeply penetrated the consciousness of local elites, reinforcing the sense of connection between capitalism, prosperity, and anti-communism."[83] Southern California, with its large tracts of empty land near a metropolitan area served by federally financed highways, was particularly well suited to suburban tract development. In these white suburbs, almost everyone had come from somewhere else and was isolated from traditional networks of family and ethnic community. New social networks developed around churches (often the large evangelical churches) and right-wing political groups.

In the late 1940s, California public schools still retained widespread support. Between July 1945 and July 1947 more than a million people moved to California, resulting in sharply increased public school enrollments. To address the problem of overcrowding, in 1947 a series of propositions were passed providing funding to build new schools.[84] In the *Mendez v. Westminster* decision, a forerunner to the *Brown v. Board of Education* case eight years later, the California Supreme Court outlawed the formal segregation of Mexican American children.[85] The Mendez case was brought by five Mexican American parents who claimed their children's rights were violated when they were forced to attend "Mexican schools." After the court's decision, the state legislature overwhelmingly passed a bill, signed by Governor Earl Warren, making school segregation by race illegal in California. Despite the liberal Mendez decision and the voters' willingness to fund public education, the right-wing attack on the schools and on progressive education continued to gain momentum. The most dramatic issue in California during 1947 while Heffernan was in Japan was the continuing controversy over the *Building America* series.[86] Although the *Building America* materials were approved by the State Board of Education in January 1947, when the California legislature met to vote on appropriations for public school textbooks, Jack Tenney submitted an amendment, subsequently made law, stating "that no part of this appropriation may be expended for the purchase of any textbook or supplement thereto which is in any way a part of the 'Building America Series.'"[87] This meant there would be no future purchases of *Building America*.

Even though no new funds were allocated to purchase the series, in February the Sons of the American Revolution filed a petition with both houses of the California legislature claiming violation of the law and misconduct by the State Board of Education, the Curriculum Commission, and Roy Simpson, the state superintendent of public instruction. The Senate Committee on Education then met to consider these charges. Eventually, the senate committee presented two reports on the *Building America* controversy.[88] The majority report stated that no illegal action by state officials or the State Board of Education had taken place and that *Building America* was not subversive. The minority report, signed by state senator Nelson Dilworth and three others, agreed that there was no conspiracy, but asserted that the series was in fact subversive. As a result of this controversy, the Senate established the Special

Investigating Committee on Education in April 1947. This committee, which came to be known as the Dilworth Committee after its first chairman, Nelson Dilworth, was charged with the task of analyzing "all facts relating to the public school system.... and particularly (without limitation by reason of the specification thereof) all matters pertaining to the *Building America* textbooks."[89] The committee was renewed every year until 1963.

THE DILWORTH COMMITTEE

Nelson Dilworth, a Riverside Republican, had been a member of the Tenney Committee in the early 1940s and served on the Standing Education Committees of both the Assembly and the Senate. The Dilworth Committee would become one of Heffernan's most powerful enemies. Dominated by staunch anti-Communists and doubtless encouraged by the publicity generated by the House Committee on Un-American Activities (HUAC) and Jack Tenney's joint fact-finding committee, the committee held hearings and issued sensational annual reports about California education, condemning what it claimed were subversive elements and defending patriotic American values.

The controversy over *Building America,* the formation of the Dilworth Committee, and the continued activities of the Tenney Committee changed the educational and political landscape in California. Moderate establishment figures were now put on the defensive. The power of the anti-Communist crusade led to the addition of a new staff position in the State Department of Education in the late 1940s. According to George Fisher, chairman of the Un-American Activities Committee of the California American Legion, in his testimony before the Tenney Committee, the duties of this staff member was "to make investigations for this Department of all applications for teaching credentials where there is any indication of reasonable doubt concerning the fitness of the applicant for a teaching position in California schools, not only as it relates to subversive interests, but also to interests that may be illegal or immoral."[90]

A CHANGED WORLD

Heffernan took up her new position as assistant division chief, Elementary Education, within the Division of Instruction in the revamped Department of Education on January 4, 1948. A reorganization of the Department of Education had been put into place in the fall of 1946, just as Heffernan left for Japan.[91] She returned to a completely new bureaucratic structure, in which her autonomy as an assistant division chief was sharply curtailed. Heffernan may have chafed at the new levels of bureaucracy on her return, but she immediately picked up the projects she had left when she went to Japan. Soon after she returned Heffernan sent a memo to state superintendent Roy Simpson advocating a stronger state program of child care centers and arguing that the Department of Education was best equipped to oversee such a program.⁹² In March 1948 she spoke at the state conference of elementary superintendents and principals in Long Beach on the topic "A World Community—Its Implications for the Curriculum."⁹³ This speech captured Heffernan's commitment to global justice and her hope that the United Nations, and particularly UNESCO, could provide a means for achieving this end.⁹⁴

In terms of national concerns, Heffernan spoke of the upcoming 1948 election in which Republican Thomas Dewey, Democratic incumbent Harry Truman, and Progressive Henry Wallace vied for the presidency. Heffernan did not directly support any candidate, but her comments on the issues reflected Wallace's positions more closely than those of the other candidates. In a typescript of an undated speech from this period, she considered the question of what American citizens should ask of their government. She answered: "Certainly greater social justice and stability. The economic system must guarantee an annual wage which will provide an adequate standard of living. The basic acceptable minimum must include proper food, clothing, housing, health, recreation, and education for all our people."⁹⁵ Statements like this, which would have been acceptable in the 1930s, met a very different response in 1948.

If Heffernan returned to a changed political and professional world, she also was in the midst of significant changes in her personal life. The letters from Seeds to Heffernan that so vividly document their relationship and the political struggles between 1938 and 1946 end with Heffernan's departure to Japan in late 1946. No letters from Seeds to Heffernan while she was in Japan or subsequently have survived. After 1946, the contours of their relationship become blurred. In the late 1940s, Seeds was consumed with overseeing and monitoring the construction of her new school on the UCLA campus. Between January and June 1949, she took a semester's sabbatical leave, perhaps in part to recover from the stress of the previous three years. She wrote on her application that the purpose of her leave was her "wish to finish a book on *Elementary Education* which is to be a summary of 24 years of experimentation in the curriculum of the Elem. School at U.C.L.A."⁹⁶ The leave was approved, but the book never appeared, and Seeds retreated more and more into the world of her school. Both Seeds and Heffernan must have felt satisfaction in 1948 when the Los Angeles School Board voted unanimously not to renew the contract of their old adversary Vierling Kersey as superintendent of Los Angeles city schools.⁹⁷

Heffernan remained close to Seeds throughout the rest of Seeds's life, frequently staying with Seeds and her father when she visited Los Angeles, but their relationship clearly had moved to a new phase. Even before she had left for Japan, Heffernan had become closer to Afton Nance. Nance and Heffernan had continued to correspond while Heffernan was in Japan, although Heffernan made it clear that she still had a special relationship with Seeds. Describing her attempts to get a flight home in early December, for example, Heffernan wrote to Nance: "Please don't tell Corinne that I may return by air. She doesn't like air travel for me!" But Heffernan's relationship with Nance was deepening. Her last letter to Nance from Japan ends: "Will save many impressions of Japan to share with you on a real gab-fest soon. The little talisman has gone with me everywhere. Maybe it was responsible for one of the most satisfying years of my life. Love and love, Helen."[98]

After Heffernan's return, Nance and Heffernan continued to write about school matters throughout the spring of 1948. Nance seems to have been considering applying for a position in Tokyo working in the Occupation's Education Section. Heffernan herself contemplated going to Germany to work with the U.S. Occupation in much the same position she had held in Japan, but when she discovered that she needed to stay in her position for several more years in order to qualify for her pension she decided not go to Germany. Nance wrote to Heffernan, "The news that you are to remain in California is both good and bad; good for California, and bad for the international situation." She asked Heffernan to lunch with her at the upcoming supervision conference "to discuss current matters in strategic education and otherwise."[99] In June, Nance was still trying to decide what to do. Heffernan encouraged her to take the civil service examination for a position on Heffernan's staff at the Department of Education. Nance was interested, but also applied for a position as West Coast Director of Educational Programs for the National Conference of Christians and Jews, a move that would have allowed her to pursue her interest in intercultural education. Heffernan agreed to write a reference for the position at the National Conference of Christians and Jews, but encouraged Nance to consider the position with the state instead: "Interesting as such an opportunity [to work for the National Conference of Christians and Jews] would be, it seems to me that education offers a far greater opportunity to build attitudes of social justice and social responsibility."[100] In the end, Nance applied for the position at the State Department of Education and was appointed Consultant in Elementary Education on November 20, 1948, working directly under Helen Heffernan.

Tensions within the Department of Education

Nance took up her position just as a new chief of the Division of Curriculum and Instruction was appointed. This was Jay Conner, the former assistant superintendent of San Diego public schools, who became Heffernan's immediate superior. Heffernan seems to have clashed with Conner from the beginning. In a February 1949 memo to state superintendent Roy Simpson, Connor reflected on his first three months as division chief, including his initial dealings with the assistant division chiefs. Conner claimed to be pleased with most of the assistant division chiefs working under him, but he was less positive about the assistant chief of the Division of Elementary Education, Helen Heffernan. He wrote to Simpson that the Elementary Division was "still very much a question mark." He went on to describe his interactions with Heffernan: "The assistant chief has responded promptly and cooperatively to every request. No contact has been initiated *from* the source, however. I 'feel' a definite 'climate' that is very real but difficult to describe.... I am concerned."

Conner's uneasiness with Heffernan and her views may have been behind his suggestion, only four months after he took up his position, that the *California Journal of Elementary Education,* one of the most important outlets for Heffernan's ideas, be transformed into a broader educational journal. According to the minutes of the March 30, 1949, meeting of the Division of Instruction administrative staff, Connor suggested that the title of the journal be changed to *The California Journal of Education,* thus "omitting the elementary aspect of it, that funds for its publication be sought from some source other than the elementary textbook fund, that the employment of a person to edit it be requested, and that the editorial board be entirely reconstituted."[101] Since the *California Journal of Elementary Education* was completely under Heffernan's control, this was clearly a direct threat to her power. She must have quickly mobilized her allies in opposition to Connor's suggested change. The idea of changing the focus of the journal and finding a new editor did not reappear.

A sense of Heffernan's attitude to Conner and to Superintendent Roy Simpson is captured in an undated letter from Heffernan to Afton Nance from this period. Describing a conflict over the wording of a document, she wrote that she was expecting an "order to come to Sacramento at which time 'the boys' will try to bulldoze me into changing the document."[102] But one of "the boys," Superintendent Roy Simpson, confounded her suspicions when he gave her a glowing evaluation in 1949, perhaps because she had just been appointed to the Advisory Committee of Fifteen to the U.S. Office of Education, which he called "a merited recognition of your stature in Education."[103] Heffernan may have appreciated Simpson's positive words, nonetheless, her conflicts with authorities in the State Department of Education, and particularly with Jay Conner, continued.

Despite her loss of autonomy within the State Department of Education, Heffernan continued to write articles, organize conferences, and give speeches arguing for an expanded role for public schools. In a number of speeches in the late-1940s, Heffernan described inadequate school buildings, double sessions, lack of qualified teachers, and large enrollments and argued that teachers needed to fight for better teaching conditions so they could meet the needs of all children. In a speech entitled "The Elementary School of 1975," she set out her vision of what elementary schools could be in the future. They should be social centers with free nursery schools, clinics providing medical care for children, prenatal care for mothers, a modern guidance program, health examinations, a nutrition program, and free lunches for all children. Segregation by race would be completely eliminated. Smaller elementary schools would replace "our large urban monstrosities." Class size would be between ten and twenty for younger children and no more than twenty five for six- to twelve-year-olds. Schools would have larger classrooms, gardens, shops, libraries, a place for housing pets, and museums and would be administered by administrative councils of children, teachers, supervisors, and specialists. There would be no set grades; children would be placed in the group that best met their needs.[104]

Heffernan never deviated from her commitment to schools as central sites in a social democracy. But by the late-1940s she was well aware that this vision of what schools could be was threatened by lack of public support and by the increasing attacks from the Right. In the present, she wrote, teachers were "being harassed unbearably by the constant scrutiny to which they are subjected. No other group in our society has to carry on such difficult work under such an ominous cloud of suspicion." She described the critics of public schools as "certain self-constituted guardians of 100 percent Americanism" who subjected teachers to a "noisy verbal barrage." Heffernan continued, "Why certain individuals feel that their brand of patriotism is purer or more soundly based in democratic ideals and principles than that of devoted American school teachers is beyond understanding."[105] But the patriotic guardians of Americanism had just begun their barrage on public education in California.

CHAPTER 9

"Progressive" Education Is Subverting America

The 1950s were years of intense political struggle in the United States, as different groups vied to assert their competing visions of the good society. This political struggle over the direction of American democracy changed the educational landscape in California and throughout the nation. Despite the active struggle of the African American freedom movement, which was laying the groundwork that would develop into the social movements of the 1960s, political discourse in the 1950s was dominated by the Right and marked by the paranoid atmosphere of the Cold War. The educational vision of Helen Heffernan and Corinne Seeds, shaped by their early experiences in the working-class West, their embrace of Deweyan ideas, and their unwavering commitment to New Deal liberalism, was deeply at odds with the world of the 1950s, in which claims that had earlier seemed the rantings of an extremist fringe were increasingly accepted as common sense. In the early 1950s, Corinne Seeds was coming to the end of her career. She had survived the attack on her school and the investigation of the Tenney Committee. After the dedication of the new school building on the UCLA campus in 1950, Seeds retreated more and more to the world of the University Elementary Schol. Helen Heffernan, on the other hand, continued to be a powerful public voice defending the progressive vision of public education and was more and more the target of virulent right-wing attacks.

THE ANTI-COMMUNISTS AND THE SCHOOLS

By the end of the Second World War, powerful groups such as the NEA, the U.S. Department of Education, and the faculties of the prestigious schools of education had embraced the basic tenets of progressive education. But this seeming consensus was short lived as the paranoia and hysteria of the Cold War came to dominate all aspects of life in the United States. The dramatic events of 1949—the Communist victory in China, the trials of Harry Bridges and Alger Hiss, and the explosion of the Russian atomic bomb—were followed by the outbreak of the Korean War in the summer of 1950. That year, Senator Joseph McCarthy claimed that the State Department was "riddled with Communists." Congress, following President Harry Truman's Executive Order 9835 requiring loyalty oaths from U.S. government employees, passed a new Internal Security Act, forcing members of the Communist Party and other Left organizations to register with the Justice Department and threatening the internment of suspected subversives during periods of national emergency.

In this climate of fear, precipitated by legislative witch hunts, the introduction of loyalty oaths, and the international successes of Communist China and the Soviet Union, the idea that the schools were vulnerable to subversion or even themselves a danger to America gained purchase. The Right continued to hammer away at its major themes of the weakness of "fads and frills," the need to return to fundamentals, and the schools as the frontline in the battle against Communism. Thus physical education should prepare for military service, schools should emphasize competition and grades in preparation for the free market economy, and Christianity should be taught in opposition to "atheistic Communism." The popular campaign against progressive education in the 1950s, led by journalists, academics, and school board members, was grounded in and intertwined with this anti-Communist crusade. Critics employed the language and claims of the radical Right to focus attention on the public schools, the institution that most intimately affected families in the United States. In the context of national anxieties over Communist subversion and fears of imminent atomic attack, these views of education seemed to make sense. Concerns about public education thus reflected social anxieties that had their origins in quite different arenas. Recognizing the power of anti-Communism in these years is key to understanding the panic over the public schools and the backlash against progressive education.

Educators responded slowly and cautiously to the mounting criticism of the schools. In a 1948 article in the journal *School and Society,* Frederick Redefer described liberal educators' silence as a kind of paralysis "in the face of Red scares and widespread personal confusion."[1] Many groups, including the NEA, sought to distance themselves from earlier progressive political stands and to demonstrate their anti-Communist credentials. In 1949 the NEA passed a resolution stating that members of the Communist Party should not be allowed to teach in American public schools. The Educational Policies Commission, which had accepted the basic concepts of progressive education just one year earlier in its bulletin *Education for All American Children,* issued a new document in 1949 entitled *American Education and International Tensions,* emphasizing education as a key institution in the fight against Communism.[2]

Others did try to defend the schools. The National Citizens Commission for the Public Schools, founded in 1949 with the support of the Rockefeller and Carnegie Foundations and the General Education Board, established local citizens' committees and undertook an advertising campaign to build support for the public schools. The National Education Association's National Commission for the Defense of Democracy Through Education—popularly known as the

Defense Committee—which had been established in 1941, became probably the most effective defender of public education.³ Another vocal supporter was the Association for Supervision and Curriculum Development, whose 1953 yearbook, *Forces Affecting American Education,* included a series of articles analyzing the right-wing offensive and proposing possible strategies for school people.⁴ But these responses by established educational organizations had little impact compared to the sensationalistic and highly publicized books and articles attacking the schools.

The early and mid-1950s were the peak of the Red Scare. The witch hunts of the congressional and state investigating committees targeted individuals and ruined the lives of both public school teachers and professors.⁵ There was a striking increase in attempts to censor "subversive" textbooks and teachers. In 1949, Lucille Cardin Crain began *The Educational Reviewer,* an influential newsletter dedicated to uncovering and forcing the removal of "subversive" books from the schools. That same year the House Un-American Activities Committee issued a series of five pamphlets on "100 Things You Should Know About Communism," including "100 Things You Should Know About Communism and Education," which claimed, among other things, that Communists had always found "the teaching group the easiest touch of all the professional classes for actual Party zealots and fellow travelers." Readers of the pamphlet were encouraged to work in their own communities to "get rid of Communists and Communist influences, whether in the school system or anywhere else."⁶

The claim that the schools were dominated by collectivist and socialist ideas was publicized by patriotic organizations like the American Legion. Articles such as Irene Corball Kuhn's "Your Child is Their Target," and "Why You Buy Books that Sell Communism," both first published in the *American Legion Magazine,* were widely distributed.⁷ The writings of anti-Communist liberal intellectuals like Sidney Hook, who argued that Communism implied the loss of independent critical thought, provided a rationalization for the purge of Communist and socialist teachers. As Robert Iverson pointed out in *The Communists and the Schools,* by the late 1940s the offensive against the schools moved from the search for subversive teachers to "the more general and intangible area of educational philosophy and 'atmosphere' about which almost anything could be said with some justification."⁸

A number of critiques of the philosophical foundations of progressive education were published in the late 1940s and early 1950s, among them Milo McDonald's "'Progressive' Poison in Public Education" and "American Education: The Old, the Modern, and the 'New,'" Frederick Rand Rogers's "Progressive Education: Irresponsible and Immoral Pedagogy," and, probably most influential, Allen Zoll's "'Progressive' Education is Subverting America."⁹ These publications shared the basic themes of conservative politics—American patriotism in opposition to internationalism and world peace; traditional standards of morality versus humanistic relativism and pragmatism; Christianity as opposed to atheism; academic discipline instead of child-centered irresponsibility; individualism and the free market in contrast to collectivism and socialism. Although most right-wing critics condemned Dewey as the source of the failings of the public schools, they rarely engaged with his actual writings. Zoll and Rogers, on the other hand, took up and contested Dewey's central philosophical tenet of pragmatism.

Frederick Rand Rogers, former dean of the School of Education at Boston University, saw pragmatism as "consummate atheism joined to utter selfishness."[10] Progressive education, Rogers wrote in an astonishing statement, was "the natural child of an intellectual rape: of Bright Freedom by Black Atheism."[11] Like Rogers, Allen Zoll saw the philosophical origins of progressive education in pragmatism. Zoll, a well known anti-Communist, had been a supporter of Father Coughlin in the 1930s and had testified before the Senate Judiciary Committee in 1939 to oppose the appointment of Felix Frankfurter to the Supreme Court on the grounds that Frankfurter was Jewish.[12] In "'Progressive' Education is Subverting America," Zoll wrote that pragmatism led inevitably to the belief "that no unchangeable, always valid, religious doctrines or moral standards can possibly exist."[13] In opposition to atheistic and immoral pragmatism, Zoll defended the Christian moral principles, which he claimed were the bedrock of true Americanism. These principles included the belief that life "should be lived in the light that streams upon us from God Himself, and that man was made for an eternal destiny," and that independence, self-reliance, and a distrust of government were basic to the American way of life.[14]

Zoll pointed to "the powerful individuals and organizations in control of the training of prospective teachers" who sought to create a new kind of society based on collectivism. And of course many progressive educators held precisely the view that Zoll attributed to them—that the schools should help build a new society with collective social values. Thus Zoll saw correctly that progressive educators hoped that the relationships and methods of the progressive school would become a model for a reconstructed society. But, for Zoll, collective values meant mind control. What was the result of the embrace of progressive methods, he asked, but "a tragically misshapen generation without the essential elements of education, without the ability to think for themselves, filled only with the desired herd ideas—fit only to be citizens of the authoritarian state? In actuality, this is the very purpose behind the whole diabolical scheme."[15] Ideas like those proposed by Rogers and Zoll, previously considered the expression of a radical fringe, had an impact that would have been hard to imagine only a few years earlier.

Loyalty and Subversion

In the 1950 California elections the Republican Party won overwhelming victories. Republicans now controlled the governorship and both houses of the California legislature, thirteen of twenty-three representatives in Congress, and, with Richard Nixon's victory over the liberal Democratic candidate Helen Gahagan Douglas, both U.S. Senate seats.[16] The right-wing attack on the schools in California continued to gain momentum, although one adversary was removed from the scene. This was state senator Jack Tenney, chair of the Joint Fact-Finding Committee on Un-American Activities. There were various reasons for Tenney's downfall, but his increasingly wild accusations that other legislators were Communist dupes were surely significant in his loss of support in the California legislature. Tenney's removal, however, did not mean the end of the joint fact-finding committee. After Tenney withdrew, Senator Hugh Burns, another strong anti-Communist, was appointed chair, and the committee continued its investigations and hearings.[17]

Heffernan attempted to mobilize the State Department of Education to defend the schools in the midst of growing intimidation. In early February 1950, a two-day conference on public schools and public relations was held at the offices of the State Department of Education under the direction of the Office of Elementary Education. Organizations represented at the February meeting included the California PTA, the California Federation of Women's Clubs, the California Teachers Association, the California Elementary School Administrators Association, the American Association of University Women, the California Youth Authority, and the Rosenberg Foundation.[18] In her remarks at the conference, Heffernan called for what she described as "a program of public enlightenment" to unmask the actions of "certain forces" that were opposed to accessible and democratic education as a threat to their own "special privilege."[19] This statement, tying the attack on the public schools to groups who wished to protect their own advantages, was an unusually sharp analysis of the entire campaign against the public schools. But Heffernan did not discuss why ordinary people would be convinced by this campaign, or why their anxieties and vulnerabilities in postwar America might coalesce around what they saw as a threat to their children. Typically, Heffernan was convinced that a strong public relations campaign could bring about "public enlightenment." Once people saw the truth, they would support the schools. Heffernan's warnings about the dangers facing the school were prescient. Only a few months later, California saw some of the most extreme challenges to progressive education and to the civil rights of teachers: the crisis over the Pasadena schools, the loyalty oath controversy at the University of California, and the passage of the Levering Act.

The Pasadena affair was probably the best-publicized of the 1950s school controversies. It erupted in late spring 1950, precipitated by the request of the Pasadena superintendent of schools, Willard Goslin, for a property tax increase. Goslin, who had been appointed Pasadena superintendent in 1948, was a respected and experienced administrator who served as president of the American Association of School Administrators; he was a well-known supporter of progressive education. Goslin's progressive ideas doubtless raised antagonism from conservatives, but a powerful subtext of the controversy was Goslin's proposal to rezone school boundaries, which would challenge the de facto racial segregation then in place in Pasadena schools. In response, a small number of Pasadena taxpayers founded the School Development Council. At a public meeting held in May, the chairman of the School

Development Council denounced the proposed tax increase and attacked Goslin, quoting extensively from Allen Zoll's 1950 pamphlet, "Progressive Education Increases Delinquency."[20]

In the June 1950 Pasadena special election, the proposal to increase taxes was defeated 22,210 to 10,032. But the controversy did not end with the special election. In November 1950, the Dilworth Committee held two days of highly publicized hearings in Pasadena. The week before the hearings, the Pasadena school board asked Goslin to resign. The incident attracted nationwide attention. The report of the NEA's Defense Committee, "The Pasadena Story," which defended Goslin, appeared in June 1951. In *This Happened in Pasadena,* also published in 1951, David Hurlburd, a journalist at *Time* magazine, also supported Goslin, framing his account as an expose of sinister and authoritarian forces that had taken over a successful public school system.[21]

At the same time that the Pasadena school crisis was making headlines, the simmering controversy over the loyalty oath at the University of California came to a head. The loyalty oath controversy had begun in June 1949, when the regents of the University of California inserted a new sentence, requiring a denial of membership in the Communist Party, to the already existing loyalty oath.[22] There was widespread protest over the new oath, and in August 1950, thirty-six professors at the University of California who refused to sign the oath were dismissed by the regents. The loyalty oath controversy and the growing panic about hidden Communists in public life led to the passage of the Levering Act by the California legislature in October 1950. Named after its author, Republican assemblyman Harold Levering, the Act required public employees to swear that they were not and had never been "a member of any party or organization, political or otherwise," that advocated the overthrow of the government "by force of violence or other unlawful means."[23] Although in 1952 the California Supreme Court struck down the regents' oath for the University of California, it ruled that faculty had to sign the Levering loyalty oath required of all public employees. The Levering Act oath was finally repealed as unconstitutional in 1967, but in the 1950s it was a powerful tool limiting the civil liberties of teachers and other state employees and a sharp reminder of the move to the right in California politics.

Defending the Schools

Heffernan continued her many activities despite the deepening political crisis. In 1950, she published two articles and coauthored a reading book series for fourth and fifth graders with her old friend Gretchen Wulfing and Wilhelmina Harper, a librarian in Redwood City.[24] In January 1950, she represented the California Department of Education at the Fourth Annual Conference of the Southwest Council on the Education of Spanish Speaking People, directed by George Sanchez. Perhaps inspired by that experience, in late June and early July Heffernan led a workshop on education for Spanish-speaking children in California. Some eighty people attended. In March, the

California School Supervisors' Association established a scholarship fund in her name "to recruit qualified persons into the field of supervision and to encourage supervisors to engage in graduate study."[25] But more and more of her time was dedicated to defending the schools.

In a speech to the Annual Conference on the Direction and Improvement of Instruction and on Child Welfare on October 10, 1951, she noted that despite the gains that had been made in increased attendance and the "decreased segregation of pupils on the basis of race," public schools had become the target of widespread attacks based upon unsupported accusations and claims. Why were the schools targeted? Heffernan answered that the real reason was a fear of schooling that would challenge students to think critically and creatively. In a December 1952 article in *California Schools*, Heffernan condemned the school critics, arguing that both teachers and students should recognize that "printed or spoken statements may be based on incomplete research, unauthentic sources, hearsay, or emotion, rather than fact; that not all the news in newspapers, magazines, and broadcasts is documented or verifiable."[26]

Heffernan's defense of democratic and critical education echoed the arguments of other progressive educators. In 1951, Theodore Brameld published *The Battle for Free Schools*, an edited collection of articles from *The Nation* documenting numerous examples of attempts at censorship and condemning the firing of "subversive" teachers.[27] In an article published in the *Harvard Educational Review* that year, David Berninghausen documented and condemned the attack on the schools. Berninghausen listed some of the publications from the Right, including those of Allen Zoll, pointing out that "even five years ago, such pamphlets might have been written off as the work of crackpots."[28] He concluded by calling up the image of Nazi Germany: "Educators have some choices to make. Will they sit quietly on the sidelines, hoping for the best, until too late? Germany's educators once made that choice."[29]

While educators like Heffernan, Brameld, and Berninghausen denounced the right-wing criticisms of the schools, at the same time Heffernan and other progressive educators supported ideas that gave credence to the criticisms that the schools were becoming nonacademic and weak. The most notorious of these was the life adjustment movement. Beginning in the late 1940s, the U.S. Office of Education had supported conferences, workshops, and two commissions on life adjustment education. Life adjustment classes were meant to address the educational needs of the majority of high school students who would not go on to college, but, as Lawrence Cremin pointed out in *The Transformation of the Schools*, this was a "terribly unfortunate choice of name."[30] The term "life adjustment" was indeed unfortunate, but underlying the movement were widely held beliefs about the need to improve "mental hygiene" and create healthy personalities that also left the schools open to criticism.[31] The 1950 Yearbook of the NEA's Association for Supervision and Curriculum Development was entitled *Fostering Mental Health in Our Schools*. The theme of the 1950 White

House Conference on Children and Youth was "For every child a healthy personality."[32]

Heffernan was one of a group of California educators who attended the White House Conference. Probably as a result of her attendance, she and several of her supporters organized a session on the healthy personality for the 1951 California Association of Elementary School Principals and District Superintendents of Schools conference. Heffernan's own understanding of mental health was more complex. She maintained her faith in psychology, but in a coauthored piece in the *California Journal of Elementary Education* entitled "The Organization of the Elementary School and the Development of a Healthy Personality," Heffernan and her coauthors presented a much more political discussion of mental health than was usual, arguing that mental health could only be achieved in an equitable society that provided basic resources to all members of the society. They pointed out that "demeaning poverty, inadequate school and health services, and racial or ethnic discrimination not only are in and of themselves handicapping to children but also constitute a denial of the democratic ideal that every person is precious and of equal worth."[33]

As Heffernan continued to defend and expand her conceptions of progressive and democratic schooling, Seeds increasingly retreated into the smaller world of UES. On May 18, 1950, the new UES building was finally dedicated.[34] Seeds's pleasure was marred by the absence of her friend and ally Provost Clarence Dykstra, who had died suddenly from a heart attack only a few days earlier. Although Heffernan was present at the dedication of the new building and she and Seeds continued to work together at the annual summer supervisors' conferences, their professional alliance as well as their personal relationship was changing. It is surely significant that at some point in 1950, Afton Nance began living with Heffernan in Heffernan's home at 3416 Land Park Drive in Sacramento.

Both Heffernan, who was then fifty-five, and Seeds, who was sixty-two, faced medical crises in 1951. In the summer, Seeds was successfully operated on for cancer. Heffernan came down from Sacramento to stay with her for a time, leaving Afton Nance back in Sacramento.[35] In December 1951, Heffernan experienced her own medical crisis. She was taken to a hospital in Berkeley with "cardiac difficulty" after an operation. She recuperated back home in Sacramento. Corinne and Sherman Seeds came to help out. There is little evidence of Heffernan's activities in the spring of 1952, probably because of her medical crisis. When the California Elementary School Administrators Association called upon California colleges and universities to undertake a cooperative study of elementary education, Heffernan was only listed as a consultant, and was not even mentioned in the article describing the project in *California Schools*.[36] Instead, a review board made up of "representatives of groups outside of education," including the National Association of Manufacturers, the state Chamber of Commerce, and the American Legion—hardly traditional allies of Heffernan or of progressive education—oversaw the work.

By the summer of 1952 Heffernan had recovered enough to teach a summer course at Harvard. She related her experiences in a series of letters to Afton Nance. Heffernan described her many trips to such scenic attractions as Cape Cod, Maine, and Salem, although there was no mention of Lawrence, where she was born and had lived until she was ten. She does not seem to have been impressed by her colleagues at Harvard, describing one talk by "another of the bright young men" as "an unparalleled illustration of inconclusive gobbledy-gook."[37] She also wrote to Nance of her ongoing tensions with Jay Conner. She wanted to stop in Albuquerque for a conference on her way back to California, but Conner wrote that he would allow her to be on salary but would not cover her expenses. Heffernan described her response to Nance: "I wrote to him airmail that I had other commitments which would prevent me from attending unless I had a definite assignment with travel and all expenses paid. The battle goes on and on."[38]

Uncovering Subversives in Postwar Los Angeles

Corinne Seeds was engaged in her own battles in 1952. Although there was now a beautiful new building for UES, the school was not complete. The original appropriation had been reduced by the university administration, and there was still a need for more buildings to house the full school. Parents from the Family School Alliance organized to put pressure on the legislature, the regents, and the university administration for an appropriation of another $600,000 to complete the project. In a conversation with President Sproul, Dean Lee reported that the parents were "once again getting up to the boiling point."[39]

Seeds faced other threats than the legislature's resistance to providing adequate financial support for her school. She must have been shaken by the sudden suspension of her good friend Martha Deane in the fall of 1952. Deane, the chair of the Women's Physical Education Department and one of only two tenured women full professors at UCLA, was accused by a neighbor of having sexual relations with another woman in her own home. This was enough to have her removed by the university administration. Although Deane fought her suspension and was quietly supported by her friends, after three years of suspension she accepted early retirement.[40] The persecution of a respected woman professor because of an intimate same-sex relationship was an indication of the growing homophobia of the Cold War years as homosexuality became conflated with subversion, and the witch hunt against covert Communists turned to hidden homosexuals. After the 1950 Senate report on "Sex Perverts in Government," the FBI investigated the sex lives of thousands of Americans and the federal government purged departments of suspected homosexuals.[41]

Seeds and Heffernan were well aware of the dangers of same-sex love. In 1944, Seeds had written to Heffernan about a mutual friend, Carleton Jenkins: "Did I tell you that *Bernard* told me all about Carleton Jenkins? He and the other person involved were caught by the M.P.s contributing to the delinquency of two young navy men! In the hands of the Federal Gov't. there was no escape. You probably know that. B. says C.J. is in Camarillo [Prison] now—for life. Such a mess."[42] No letters from either Seeds or Heffernan discussing Martha Deane's case have survived, but given their own relationships and those of their friends and colleagues, the case and the growing public panic about "sexual perversion" must have made them acutely aware of their own vulnerability.

They were vulnerable as well to the anti-Communist crusade. The Dilworth Committee continued to hold public hearings throughout the state.[43] In 1952, it conducted hearings in Los Angeles, in part in support of the actions of the Los Angeles School Board, which had just banned the UNESCO teachers' handbook from the Los Angeles public schools. Although UNESCO had been strongly supported by federal and state officials when it was founded in 1946, by the early 1950s right-wing groups across the country had mobilized against it.[44] Liberals condemned the banning of UNESCO materials in the Los Angeles schools, but the headline in Hearst's *Herald and Express* triumphed, "Outlaw UNESCO in schools! A Victory for Americanism."[45] A second purpose of the Dilworth Committee's Los Angeles hearings was to investigate the impact of the 1950 loyalty oath legislation on the Los Angeles public schools. Earlier that year, the Los Angeles School Board had used information from the Joint Fact-Finding Committee on Un-American Activities under state senator Hugh Burns to investigate possible subversives among Los Angeles teachers.[46] Not to be outdone by the Burns Committee, the Dilworth Committee decided to hold hearings to prove that loyalty oaths were vital to ferreting out subversives.[47] After hearing witnesses on the loyalty oath, the committee seems to have cast about for other traces of subversion in Los Angeles, calling a number of other, seemingly random witnesses. Among them was Corinne Seeds.

In her account of her testimony, Seeds described the committee as deeply hostile and presented herself as a courageous defender of freedom of thought.[48] In her account, when Dilworth asked her if she knew any Communists, she replied, "I don't investigate what the parents of all the children are, or what all of my students in my classes are. We live in America, and we're not supposed to ask people about their political affiliations. I'd never do that, nor would I ask about their church or anything else. That's a matter for their own conscience." Then, as she remembered it, "there was a little conference with Dilworth, and Dilworth said, 'Let's give her the works.'"[49] Seeds was deeply upset by the published account of her testimony in the committee's *Ninth Report*, which she called "that nasty book." The *Report*, she said, "wasn't even literate. It sounded as if I was a fool, and the comment was made in the first part that I was dangerous, because I was in the position to influence the school, the children, and the student teachers."[50]

The account published in the Dilworth Committee's *Ninth Report* is indeed different from Seeds's oral history. According to the *Report*, the committee had called her because it had noticed "from time to time the repeated mention of Miss Corinne Seeds in the public press and especially in the

Daily People's World in connection with organizations interested in Russia." The committee interrogator, Mr. Engelbright, began by asking Seeds if she objected to the loyalty oath. She said she had taken four such oaths and that she had no objection to signing an oath. She said that the safeguard against subversion should be "the behavior of people, and that those cases should be referred to committees for study and to the FBI." When asked if she knew of Communist activity in the schools, she replied: "Well, generally speaking, I believe that teachers come from all walks of life and so naturally we must have some Communists. But I do not know any Communists and I don't think I ever met one, at least that I knew was a Communist."[51] Despite Seeds's testimony that she had signed loyalty oaths and her claim that she did not know any Communists, the committee concluded that she was affiliated with "Communist-front activities."

The *Ninth Report* summarized the committee's case against her. She had been a member of the board of directors of the American Russian Institute between 1945 and 1948 and the 1946 chairman of the speaker program for the Citizens' Committee for Better Education, which the Tenney Committee had described as a Communist front organized to support "extreme leftists for election to the Los Angeles Board of Education." Moreover, Seeds was quoted in the Communist dominated *Daily People's World* as supporting students' "right to participate in off campus organizations." For the Dilworth Committee, being mentioned positively by the *Daily People's World* was evidence of Communist sympathy. In 1951, she had signed a letter seeking a new hearing for union members accused under the Smith Act. She was listed on the editorial board of the journal *Progressive Education* in 1950 along with such suspect figures as Alain Locke of Howard, Harold Rugg of Columbia, and Holland Roberts of the California Labor School. And, the committee claimed, summarizing the case against her, the honorary president of the PEA was John Dewey.[52]

Educational Wastelands

Anti-Communist hysteria and the political repression increased in 1953.[53] Schools and universities continued to be a major target for legislative investigating committees, at both the federal and state levels. In March 1953, HUAC, under the chairmanship of Congressman Velde, held hearings in Los Angeles to investigate subversion in the schools. That same year the California legislature passed the Dilworth Act, which not only required a new loyalty oath for school personnel, but also included a provision that refusal to answer questions of legislative committees or school boards would be grounds for dismissal. This meant that invoking the constitutional right guaranteed by the Fifth Amendment was now viewed as an admission of guilt. The Dilworth Act focused only on public elementary and secondary schools. The Luckel Act, passed at the same time, required a loyalty oath with the threat of similar penalties for all state employees, including those working at the University of California and all state colleges. Both the Dilworth and Luckel Acts were signed into law by Governor Warren on September 9, 1953, and remained in force until they were finally ruled unconstitutional in 1968.

One of the most striking developments in these years was the way right-wing claims were appropriated by mainstream groups and more "respectable" authors. The year 1953 saw the publication of Albert Lynd's *Quackery in the Public Schools,* Robert Hutchins's *The Conflict in Education,* Paul Woodring's *Let's Talk Sense about Our Schools,* and Arthur Bestor's *Educational Wastelands.* These books did not repeat the accusations of political conspiracy and subversion, but they did accept the claims that progressive methods were lax and anti-intellectual and that the schools were in crisis. The National Citizen's Commission for the Public Schools (NCCPS), a liberal group, found that articles on education in U.S. popular magazines increased from 124 to 319 between 1950 and 1953.[54] National magazines such as *The Atlantic Monthly, The Saturday Evening Post,* and *Colliers* all ran articles examining the public schools. The majority of these articles, along with popular books, echoed the right-wing accusations that the schools were failing to teach fundamentals and were thus betraying the nation in the Cold War struggle.

Bestor's *Educational Wastelands* was particularly influential in legitimating the claims of the Right. Bestor was himself an accomplished historian and his criticisms supported a general belief among liberal intellectuals that the country was dominated by a dangerous anti-intellectualism.[55] Bestor's major targets in *Educational Wastelands* were on the one hand the professional educators, whom he called "educationists," and on the other the life adjustment movement, which he claimed undermined democracy by failing to provide a rigorous education. He argued that schools needed to return to the "traditional" liberal arts disciplines, which would train students to be free thinkers suspicious of all ideologies. Although Bestor distanced himself from radical right-wing critics such as Allen Zoll, he employed a similar rhetoric. In one well-known passage, he argued: "Across the educational world today stretches an iron curtain which the professional educationists are busily fashioning. Behind it, in slave labor camps, are the classroom teachers, whose only hope of rescue is from without. On the hither side lies the free world of science and learning, menaced but not yet conquered."[56] While critics like Bestor did not themselves lead the witch hunts of supposed subversive teachers or the censorship of curriculum, their wholesale condemnation of the schools in the context of Cold War hysteria provided an intellectual justification for the rejection of progressive methods and bolstered and legitimated the attacks on the schools.

Race and the Schools

At the height of the anti-Communist crusade counter forces were at work that would transform U.S. society, particularly around race. The most dramatic example of this change of course was the 1954 *Brown v. Board of*

Education U.S. Supreme Court decision that school segregation based upon race was unconstitutional. Although historians have questioned the effectiveness of the Brown decision in actually leading to racial equity, there is no doubt about its symbolic importance.[57] In July 1953, while the Brown case was under consideration, the attorney general of Virginia wrote Heffernan asking for information about school segregation in California. Heffernan sent relevant materials along with a cover letter in which she wrote, "During the twenty-five years of my service as director for the elementary schools of California I have consistently opposed the establishment or the maintenance of separate schools for children on the basis of color, race, or creed."[58] Heffernan was one of eleven invited participants to a 1953 conference on "Inequalities of Educational Opportunity," sponsored by the Ford Foundation. Other attendees included African American historian Horace Mann Bond, Mexican American educator George Sanchez, and University of California sociologist Paul Taylor, who was well known for his studies of farm labor in California. Each of the participants made an initial statement. In hers, Heffernan argued that the public needed to be approached through "all the forms of mass communication—the press, radio, television." Typically, she argued that "when the people have the necessary facts and information concerning educational inequalities, they will find a way to deal intelligently with them."[59]

In California, the de facto segregation of African American children was not the immediate focus of attention after Brown; instead, it was discrimination against Mexican American and Spanish-speaking children. Despite the 1946 *Mendez v. Westminster* decision making the segregation of children on the basis of race illegal in California, little progress seems to have occurred in terms of the de facto segregation of Mexican American children. In March 1955, Heffernan published an article in *The Bulletin of the National Association of Secondary School Principals* on the question of the schooling of Mexican American children.[60] Heffernan saw the problems faced by Mexican children as grounded in the attitudes of the majority culture and in lack of economic opportunity. She cited poverty, language, poor housing, lack of health care.[61] Although the schools alone could not redress all forms of prejudice, she argued that respect for Mexican and Mexican American culture, bringing in role models from the Mexican American community and, in particular, supporting bilingualism were important steps the schools could take.[62] In terms of the vexing question of separate classes, she argued that Spanish-speaking children should have instruction in "unsegregated classes" but that they should also have tutors and classes in basic skills if needed. Concerns about how best to educate Spanish-speaking children merged with the problem of the schooling of migrant children, most of whom were Spanish speaking by the 1950s.[63] In 1954, Helen Heffernan proposed a state conference on the issue, in part in response to a planned White House Conference on Migrant Education to be held in 1955.[64]

In addition to her increasing involvement with the education of minority groups, Heffernan became more active on the national scene through her involvement with the Association of Supervisors and Curriculum Development (ASCD).[65] In 1954, she was elected member-at-large of the ASCD Board of Directors.[66] By the mid-1950s, Heffernan turned more and more to the ASCD for support and encouraged the California School Supervisors' Association, still her strongest ally, to participate in the ASCD. By 1954 California provided 1,200 members of the ASCD; the next largest state membership was New York, with 551. The California School Supervisors' Association changed its name to the California Association for Supervision and Curriculum Development in the late 1950s, thus making clear its connection to the national association.[67] Nonetheless, Heffernan could not escape the increasingly hostile political climate. Neither could Corinne Seeds.

Despite the successful fight to save UES, Seeds and her school continued to be cited as a source of dangerous and potentially subversive progressive ideas. In his 1954 *Colliers* article, "The Struggle for Our Children's Minds," for example, Howard Whitman used the example of UES to illustrate the familiar right-wing argument that progressive education was rooted in "collectivist ideas." He began the article with a description of his visit to the school, which he noted was led by Corinne Seeds, "a kindly elderly woman." Although he acknowledged that UES did provide direct instruction in spelling, arithmetic, and reading, most of his discussion focused on group project activities and dramatic play. The overall impression was that the school was frivolous and undemanding.[68] In this case, members of the UES community fought back. Mrs. Gladwin Hill, a UES parent, responded to the article with a letter to *Colliers,* noting that Whitman had only spent about four hours at the school, "during which he repeatedly warded off all attempts to interest him in the facts and figures and findings which support the success of its methods.... He preferred to hurry around glimpsing various groups of children in their dramatic play." Hill speculated that Whitman chose to focus on dramatic play because "it fitted in with his preconceived attitude that progressive education is all play with no work or learning attached."[69] A few months later, her husband Gladwin Hill, who was the chief of the *New York Times* Los Angeles bureau, published an article in the *Atlantic* defending the education his children received at UES. Hill argued that his children not only learned the fundamentals, but that they loved going to school.[70]

Grading Methods and Phonics

In 1955, the attacks on Heffernan's progressive program came closer. Heffernan continued to speak out against her critics and to advocate for the methods and ideas she believed in, but she now took a more cautious and defensive stance. In the summer of 1955, she was considering a research project on the topic "Developing International Understanding with Young Children," which she hoped to conduct with the teachers at UES. But, as she wrote to Helen Juneman, a consultant in elementary education for the Los Angeles County Schools: "Perhaps we had better seek a new name for this project since international understanding seems to have become emotionally charged for our die-hard isolationists."[71] She and her supporters were well aware of the dangers they could face personally. In 1954, she wrote to Afton Nance about a Ted Britton, a mutual friend. He had been "turned down by the FBI as a poor security risk. Apparently someone thinks he is too liberal... I know Ted Britton is no Communist but unfortunately the distinction is not too clearly drawn between liberals and Communists."[72] And the danger was even closer to her than she probably knew. The portions of her FBI file that are open to the public show close attention to her in 1954 and 1955. One memorandum noted that *The People's World* had described her as "the most progressive employee in the California Department of Education." Another investigator cited accusations that she was a Communist. This same memorandum also mentioned Corinne Seeds and claimed that Seeds's affiliations raised "serious questions of her loyalty."[73]

Heffernan's FBI file also referred to "a special agent" within the State Department of Education, who observed both her public and her private life. This agent, who also mentioned rumors that she was a lesbian, reported that "Miss HELEN HEFFERNAN had lent herself to the use of a front group during the war years, and pointed out that she has, in the past, submitted names of proposed speakers for several state sponsored educational meetings which the agent, in his position as screening officer, had felt it wise to reject, in view of their lack of judgment in some of their affiliations."[74] The Department of Education continued to employ a screening officer at least until 1959. A memo from that year refers to the internal process of investigating and clearing possible conference speakers. The memo lists eight possible speakers who had "clear records as far as our investigator can determine." This investigator or "screening officer" was doubtless the FBI informant referred to above.[75]

Despite the increasingly hostile and paranoid atmosphere, Heffernan did not shift from her own long-standing political beliefs. She continued to be sympathetic to organized labor, particularly to the Congress of Industrial Organizations (CIO), speaking at the 1955 California CIO school at California Hot Springs. Afterward, she wrote to George Guernsey, the CIO associate secretary in charge of education, "I always enjoy this group of enthusiastic people, and I am hoping that I really did stimulate them to think further about the whole problem of public education."[76] But Heffernan's public support for the CIO simply confirmed the suspicions of conservatives, who condemned what they saw as her support of lax and potentially subversive progressive practices. In March 1955, these suspicions came to a head around two related events: the controversy in the legislature's Ways and Means Committee over the proposed *Teachers Guides to Education in Early and Later Childhood*—one of Heffernan's pet projects that had been in preparation for several years—and the publication of the Dilworth Committee's *Twelfth Report*, attacking progressive grading methods.

The Ways and Means Committee was dominated by conservative assemblymen deeply antagonistic to Heffernan and suspicious of the Department of Education. Heffernan was away at a conference when the Ways and Means Committee hearings addressing the *Teachers Guides to Education in Early and Later Childhood* began. Jay Conner wrote to Heffernan describing the hearings: "I do not pretend to know what forces have operated behind the scenes to place the teachers' guides in the category of a lost cause, but I am sure that any who attended the Ways and Means Committee hearing will tell you the situation was utterly hopeless." The committee, Connor wrote, was primarily made up of "hatchet boys." When the legislative auditor recommended that the *Teachers Guides* be approved, Conner wrote, one of the assemblymen shouted, "for crying out loud, here's that turkey buzzard back in our laps again—those teachers' guides. How many times are we going to have to kill that thing before we can keep it from coming up here in this budget?" This comment led to an attack on the entire Department of Education, with several members of the committee recommending that whole sections be eliminated. Conner wrote to Heffernan that he had been "literally working around the clock to save our budget."[77]

By the time Heffernan returned to Sacramento, the Dilworth Committee's *Twelfth Report*, which included a "Report on Grading Methods," had been released. The *Twelfth Report* was a stinging denunciation of student evaluations based on parent conferences and individual progress reports, practices long supported by Helen Heffernan. Grading methods, the committee argued, should reflect "the sort of society the children will be launched into when they mature as adults. If this society is to be a free competitive one, as it has been in this country, certainly, then, competition must be acknowledged as a significant factor."[78] As was typical of conservative social analysis, the committee equated competition and freedom, while cooperation meant leveling and a loss of individuality.

The chief investigator for the Dilworth Committee's "Report on Grading Methods" was Mary Allen, who had previously been one of the editors of "FACTS in Education," a right-wing broadsheet published in Pasadena after the Goslin controversy, and who was at the time working on her book on the Pasadena school crisis, *Education and Indoctrination,* which would be published in 1956. For her investigation, Allen asked thirteen elementary school districts to submit the report cards they used and explain their reasons for using them. The State Department of Education had been contacted but its response was not included "because of lack of information." This was a reference to Allen's request to Afton Nance for data about report cards. Nance had told Allen that no files on report cards were kept, since this was the purview of local school districts.[79] Nance then called Nelson Dilworth to inquire about Allen's qualifications. According to Nance, when she asked Dilworth whether Allen had any experience as an educator, he replied, "Fortunately she has not, she has not been spoiled."[80]

The main body of the *Twelfth Report* on grading methods summarized the opinions of the administrators and laymen Mary Allen had contacted. Most of these defended the use of traditional report cards. The *Report* also included the earlier testimony of Eric Pridonoff, who had been attached to the American Embassy in Yugoslavia after the Second World War. Pridonoff testified that the first thing the Communists did in Yugoslavia was abolish the grading system and that Soviet officials had told him that the best way to prepare students for a socialized state was to "eliminate competition and prepare a group of loafers so the State can lead them later on."[81] Pridonoff's testimony was inserted into the 1955 *Twelfth Report* as evidence of the link between nonformal evaluation and Communism. In its "summarization" the Dilworth Committee presented its own conclusions. Educational methods, including grading practices, had to be understood in the light of the fact that "today, the free world is competing for survival against communist tyranny." Competition was the mark of democracy; without it, a society was vulnerable to socialism.[82]

Members of the Department of Education, including Jay Conner and Helen Heffernan, were already aware of the tenor of the *Report,* but they may not have been prepared for the publicity the *Report* received. All the major California newspapers covered its publication. The *Fresno Bee's* article, "Student Grading Method is Called Communistic," was typical in its sympathetic reporting of the Dilworth Committee's accusations. The *Los Angeles Times,* which ran two articles on the *Twelfth Report,* quoted the *Report* as though it were a scientific study: "Competition is an essential ingredient in our daily living as well as in world and national affairs...therefore children should learn about competition at an early age in their school work as well as in their outside activities. The grading method can contribute in this learning process."[83]

The controversy over the schools reached a wider audience in the spring of 1955 with the publication of Rudolph Flesch's *Why Johnny Can't Read,* an indictment of progressive reading methods that became a surprise national best seller. *Why Johnny Can't Read,* which claimed U.S. teachers, influenced by the progressive education movement, were only using the "word recognition" method instead of phonics, did not tie reading methods to Communist infiltration of the schools, but it did present a scathing attack on the schools, which Flesch claimed were producing a nation of illiterates. The book was serialized in a number of California papers, including the *Sacramento Bee,* the *San Diego Union,* and Hearst's *San Francisco Examiner.* Educators mobilized to counter Flesch's claims. Arthur Corey, the secretary of the California Teachers Association, asked Heffernan to wire him a fifty-word response to be printed in the *Examiner's* Sunday magazine on June 5, 1955.[84] Heffernan wrote that Flesch disregarded "more than half a century of reputable research in reading instruction," pointing out that both phonics and the sight recognition of words were used by California teachers. In terms of the supposed failure of U.S. schools, she wrote, "Official reports from other countries do not support Mr. Flesch's claims of superiority in reading ability or lack of reading difficulties."[85] Frank Hubbard, the director of the Research Division of the NEA, wrote to Heffernan promising to send her additional materials. He wrote: " 'The ounce of Flesch' is producing troubles all over the country. Fortunately, local committees of classroom teachers and administrators are doing an effective job of refutation thru PTA's and other means."[86]

The California Teachers Association ran a rebuttal, including Heffernan's statement, in all of the papers that had serialized *Why Johnny Can't Read*. It also published a brochure entitled "Be Proud California" defending the record of California public schools.[87] Heffernan herself defended the schools in a number of speeches and presentations. She denied the accusations that students were not learning by citing the achievements of California schools. In a 1955 speech entitled "Are the Schools Teaching the Three R's?" Heffernan argued that California schools were actually achieving remarkable results under very difficult conditions.[88] She noted the problems resulting from the rising birthrate and migration to California—teacher shortages, overcrowded classrooms, and half-day programs throughout the state. Despite these challenges, California ranked third, after Utah and Oregon, among the states in the percentage of students in high school. Although there were no uniform standardized measures of reading and arithmetic in the 1950s, Heffernan cited data from achievement tests from a variety of California districts to argue that children were actually doing quite well. In essence Heffernan argued that critics of the schools were making unfounded claims, basing their criticisms on anecdotal evidence rather than facts.

Jay Conner and Roy Simpson, in contrast, vacillated in their defense of the schools. In his speech before the Annual Conference of the California Association of School Administrators in December 1956, Simpson encouraged his audience to "get off the defensive attitude," to reach out to business and industrial leaders and the public at large in defense of the public schools.[89] On the other hand, in his forward to a report of a committee he had appointed in 1954 to examine the state social studies program, Simpson wrote that the goal of social studies was to have young people "understand and to appreciate our American way of life."[90] Gone was the concern for world peace and cooperation, let alone the "opposition to all forms of political, social, and economic injustice" of the 1948 frameworks. Although Heffernan was a member of the new social studies committee, Simpson had appointed Jay Conner as chair. A sense of Heffernan's response to all this can be seen in her comment in a 1957 letter to Afton Nance after a Los Angeles meeting of the committee: "The S.S. [Social Studies] meeting is too grim to write about."[91]

The Teachers Guides to Education in Early and Later Childhood

Despite the vocal opposition of members of the Ways and Means Committee, the first of the two contested *Teachers Guides,* the *Teachers Guide to Education in Early Childhood,* was finally published in 1956. The *Teachers Guide to Education in Later Childhood* followed the next year. The two volumes were significant revisions of the earlier *Teachers Guides* published in the 1930s and in many ways can be seen as the fullest expression of the educational philosophy of Heffernan, Seeds, and Nance. Although Heffernan was identified as responsible for the preparation of the *Guide to Education in Early Childhood,* Corinne Seeds contributed four chapters to the work. The titles of three of her four chapters included the phrase "A Child Becoming One with His World," a variant of the title Seeds had given to her proposed (and never completed) magnum opus, "A Child Becomes One with a Good World." The *Guide to Education in Later Childhood,* published in 1957, on the other hand, was jointly prepared by Helen Heffernan and Afton Nance. Of the *Guide to Education in Later Childhood*'s fifteen chapters, ten were written either by Heffernan alone or by Heffernan and Afton Nance together.

The *Teachers Guides* are striking in their respectful depiction of teachers, who are trusted for their professional judgment and intellectual abilities. The ideal curriculum should be flexible, include student input, and be led by "the best possible teacher."[92] Instead of a standardized curriculum that emphasized testing, both the *Teachers Guides* recommended a curriculum based on experiences inside and outside the classroom organized around activities and projects in which evaluation would be based on each child's individual progress. The *Teachers Guide to Education in Early Childhood* was firm in its stand against competition and formal grading, what it called "extrinsic motivation." The *Guide* warned that "material which is learned merely to escape disgrace and punishment or to enable the child to win a reward is frequently forgotten almost as soon as the purpose for which it was learned is satisfied."[93] Instead, teachers should motivate children to learn by making the curriculum meaningful to children's lives. A clearer rejection of the views of the Dilworth Committee in the *Twelfth Report* on grading methods cannot be imagined. For the rest of her career, Heffernan recommended the *Teachers Guide to Education in Early Childhood* and *Teachers Guide to Education in Later Childhood* to anyone who asked her about educational questions.

Leaving "Our School"

Corinne Seeds had little involvement with the educational battles now absorbing Helen Heffernan. In her final years, she was concerned with two issues at UES: the need for additional new buildings and the controversy over whether the school could serve as a research site for faculty members from the School of Education. The School of Education faculty wanted to open UES to their own scientific research, a move that reflected the shift of the School of Education from a teacher-training institution to a research-oriented graduate school. Seeds on the other hand was deeply opposed to having UES children and teachers become the subjects of other academics' research.[94] This question was not resolved in Seeds's remaining two years as principal. The other major issue was the need for additional school buildings for the preschool, kindergarten, and sixth grade. The Family School Alliance began a letter-writing campaign to pressure the regents to provide funding for the remaining buildings.[95] In a 1955 speech before the Family School

Alliance, Chancellor Raymond Allen proclaimed his support, noting that the school was "ranked high among the pioneering schools of its kind throughout the world."[96] Although university president Sproul was less enthusiastic, the combination of support from the UCLA administration and the vocal and well-connected Family School Alliance overcame his lukewarm support and the funding for more buildings was eventually secured.

In 1956, Corrine Seeds was finally promoted to full professor. She taught her final courses in spring and summer of 1957. This must have been a difficult time for her, made worse by the death of her father, Sherman. In an open letter to the parents in the Family School Alliance, she wrote, "The Spring of 1957 has brought to me two great separations which grip my very soul—the passing of my father, and leaving Our School—the teachers, the children, and you, the parents."[97] She concluded, "For all of your years of hard work, for your unbounded faith in Our School, for the support and understanding you will give our new principal as he moves along the pathway charted by Dr. Dewey and Dr. Kilpatrick, and for the strength and love you have given me along the way, I thank you!"[98]

Seeds never deviated from the ideas she first encountered at Teachers College. A typescript entitled "Let the Children Speak" from 1957, her last year at UES, repeated her by now familiar ideas. Addressing the demise of the journal *Progressive Education* that year, Seeds wrote that although the journal was now defunct, its spirit was still alive "in the minds and hearts of educators who would truly educate America's children to become understanding, participating, contributing members of their own democratic government, and also lend active, moral and economic support to other countries of the world in their struggles for freedom and democracy."[99] In the summer of 1957, Seeds for the last time taught ED 132, "Supervision of the Experience Program in the Elementary School," and EDS 131-B, "Units of Work Construction in the Social Studies."[100] Gone, however, were Helen Heffernan's course on supervision and the summer conference for school supervisors. Except for Heffernan's year in Japan, this was the first summer since 1942 that the two of them had not worked together at the UCLA summer session.

In 1957, Seeds retired, as did Dean Edwin Lee. President Sproul wrote to Seeds at her retirement, "It is not easy to put into words what I feel about the contributions you have made to the life of this institution and to the life of the community in the course of your years of University service."[101] A statement that could be taken in many different ways! According to Peggy Kiskadden of the Family School Alliance, administrators at the School of Education were committed to having a man take over as principal after Seeds retired. Kiskadden noted: "This was a requirement because they were through dealing with women. They were going to have a man there. This was, I think, the conviction of only a few of them, who happened not to like to deal with women. But, they were a powerful little few."[102] In the end, Philip Lambert was appointed principal, although he resigned after two years of controversy. It was only in 1960, with the appointment of John

Goodlad, that UES regained stability.[103] Seeds does not seem to have been involved in these struggles.

Heffernan and Seeds continued to have a close friendship after Seeds retired. Although she now lived with Afton Nance, Heffernan listed Seeds, not Nance, on her 1956 passport as the person to notify in case of death or accident. In 1958, Seeds, now traveling with Florence Itkins, visited Heffernan, who was teaching summer school in Colorado. Heffernan wrote to a mutual friend: "You will be interested to know that I am joining Corinne and Florence next Friday for a weekend at Aspen.... I am so glad that Corinne feels well enough to take this trip because it may mean that she will eventually undertake the long discussed "trip around the world."[104] That trip, however, never materialized, although Seeds and Florence Itkins did spend three months traveling in Europe in 1959. Instead, Seeds retreated to her home in Los Angeles, more and more isolated from the political battles that consumed Helen Heffernan.

CHAPTER 10

How to Teach the California Child

Despite continuing tension between the United States and the Soviet Union, the late 1950s saw a shift away from the repressive climate of the depths of the Cold War. As the Red Scare receded and the civil rights movement gained momentum, an alternative social narrative of what democracy could mean in the United States began to emerge. After the 1954 *Brown v. Board of Education* decision, both black freedom struggles and white southern racist resistance reached American living rooms through the new medium of television. Images such as those of angry white mobs blocking the entry of nine black teenagers into a previously all-white high school in Little Rock, Arkansas, shocked many white Americans. The more liberal climate began to affect electoral politics. In 1958, California Democrat Pat Brown defeated the conservative Republican William Knowland in the race for governor; in that election Democrats captured both houses of the legislature and all state executive offices except for secretary of state, marking the end of a century of Republican dominance. And in 1960, Democrat John F. Kennedy was elected president of the United States in a narrow victory over Richard Nixon.

Although the political climate was changing, the late 1950s and early 1960s saw a continued attack on California public schools from the Right. Both mainstream conservatives and right-wing fringe groups continued to publish polemics blaming the schools. Works such as Augustin Rudd's 1957 *Bending the Twig*, published by the Sons of the American Revolution, repeated the paranoid claims of earlier critics such as Allen Zoll and Frederick Rand Rogers that schools were not only academically weak, but politically subversive.[1] More mainstream critics continued to argue that the schools were failing to provide a strong academic foundation. The legislative critics of the schools in California mobilized for one last attack in 1958, when the Dilworth Committee issued its *Sixteenth Report*.

THE SIXTEENTH REPORT: CURRICULUM CHANGES

Instead of summarizing hearings as had been the case with previous reports, the *Sixteenth Report*, subtitled *Curriculum Changes*, presented an analysis of the teachers' guides and publications of the California Department of Education over a forty-year period. The impetus for the *Report* seems to have been the controversial publication of the *Teachers Guides to Education in Early and Later Childhood*. The *Sixteenth Report* began by briefly summarizing the state's early *Blue Bulletins,* published between 1915 and 1921. It contrasted the emphasis on patriotism, thrift, obedience, and good manners in the *Blue Bulletins* with the state's subsequent publications. These included the 1930 and 1936 editions of *The Teachers' Guide to Child Development,* the 1950 "Framework for Public Education in California," "The Elementary School Program in California," published in 1957, and most extensively, the controversial 1956 and 1957 *Teachers Guides to Education in Early and Later Childhood*. The Dilworth Committee made clear its suspicions about the source of the subversive ideas shaping these publications: "In checking the names of the people who had significant parts in preparing the *Guides,* the name of Helen Heffernan was the only one connected with the California State Department of Education that appeared in all of the *Guides* from 1930 to 1957."[2]

The committee did not examine the earlier *Guides* in any detail; instead it quickly moved to a more detailed analysis of the four publications from the 1950s, since these were the focus of the committee's current investigations. All four of these publications argued that schools should be organized around children's interests and experiences, stressed group work and cooperation, and encouraged a critical discussion of social issues. The *Sixteenth Report* was particularly concerned with the critical discussion of race and class in the 1956 and 1957 *Teachers Guides*. They were horrified at what they saw as an exaggerated emphasis on "inequalities between races and classes."[3] For the committee, this critical tone undermined patriotism and smacked of socialist subversion. The committee was equally concerned with what they saw as the abandonment of academic standards, echoing many of the claims of Rudolf Flesch's *Why Johnny Can't Read*.[4] The committee was also worried about the emphasis on the "wholesome development of the child's total personality" rather than traditional academic subjects and it showed deep unease with the emphasis in the *Teachers Guides* on creative expression and unstructured play. The *Report* warned: "Life is more than play and entertainment. The sooner children realize this, the better it is for them. Playtime is valuable and has its place, but schools are for work also, serious work to prepare to meet the challenging difficulties of reality."[5]

If the Dilworth Committee was dismayed by what they saw as a decline in academic standards, they were equally exercised by what they saw as the schools' failure to teach patriotism, a strong theme throughout all the committee's *Reports*. They pointed out that although the California State Education Code stated that schools must provide instruction in patriotism, the word "patriotism" was not found in the 1956 and 1957 *Teachers Guides*.[6] Instead, the committee saw the pernicious replacement of "patriotism" with a broad concept of "democracy." As evidence, the committee disapprovingly quoted the 1950 "Framework for Public Education in California," which stated that schools should seek to produce "citizens who are enthusiastic about the values of democracy for all peoples; who accept the responsibilities as well as the privileges of citizenship; and who are capable of grappling creatively with problems that arise."[7] For the committee, this embrace of "the values of democracy for all peoples," implied not patriotism, but the subversive idea of world citizenship. Although the committee acknowledged that the term "world citizenship" only occurred once in the four publications from the 1950s, they cited numerous passages from all four documents that encouraged children to understand global interrelationships and to seek to develop an ethical concern about the welfare of all peoples. For the committee, this suggested the "possibility that national loyalties may be disrupted. If a child is instructed in world-mindedness, he may be inclined to forget that his first loyalty is to his country. To offset this tendency, it seems desirable to emphasize instruction in patriotism, love of and duty to one's country."[8]

Another concern was the emphasis on cooperation in the *Teachers Guides*, which to the committee smacked of collective values. The *Sixteenth Report* noted disapprovingly that throughout the *Teachers Guides* there was a strong emphasis on "social consciousness and group performance, such as sharing and co-operation."[9] The committee acknowledged that the term collective was not used in any of the four documents, but argued that "in the *Guides*, the group appears to be a collective with collective planning experiences, enterprises, loyalty, welfare, and action." To the committee, this "group philosophy ... would have a tendency to weaken the American tradition of individual freedom, and to reconstruct society along collectivist lines in which you take from each according to his ability and give to each according to his needs."[10] In contrast to the emphasis on cooperation and loyalty to the group, there were "no favorable comments in the *Guides* relative to competition." Instead, the *Report* claimed, competition was "viewed as harmful to the healthy development of children."[11]

Echoing the Dilworth Committee's defense of ABCD report cards in its 1955 *Twelfth Report*, the *Sixteenth Report* not only defended ABCD report cards, but denounced forms of assessment based on the teacher's observations of children's social development and the keeping of written records on individual children. The committee particularly objected to the idea of monitoring children's mental health. While the committee acknowledged that the term "mental health" rarely appeared in the *Guides*, they considered the discussion of children's "attitudes, behaviors, and group adjustment" to be examples of the concept of mental health.[12] In its criticism of the concept of mental health and its objection to the surveillance of children's behavior and attitudes, the committee seemed to articulate a kind of Foucauldian critique of the social discipline and state surveillance implicit in the liberal state. For the committee, though, the underlying concern was not a broad critique of modernity, but worry that the school would introduce values they saw as antithetical to individualism and competition. Mental health implied participation in group activities, which, the committee argued, put "tremendous pressure on the child for group conformance"[13] The committee's main anxiety seems to have been not only that teachers would observe and record children's behavior, but that they would act politically and use education as a means to redress injustice and inequality. The *Teachers Guides,* the committee claimed, expected teachers "to study the social structure of the community, determine the social and economic backgrounds of her pupils, and use this knowledge to overcome race, class, and economic differences in the classroom as well as in the community."[14] For the committee, that kind of concern with broader issues of social justice implied a limitation on freedom, which they conceived of as a kind of free-floating power of choice by individuals unaffected by class or race.

The Dilworth Committee's *Sixteenth Report,* with its direct attack on the State Department of Education, provoked an immediate response. On July 8, 1958, state superintendent Roy Simpson called a meeting of officials from the State Department of Education and school administrators from across the state. Helen Heffernan, who had taken leave in the summer of 1958 to teach a summer course at the University of Colorado, was not present. Afton Nance summarized the meeting in a memo to Heffernan. At the meeting, state officials suggested various strategies to convince the public that public education in California was professional and successful. One official claimed that the basic problem was that there was "no really clear definition of what education is trying to accomplish. Basically, it appears to be a public relations problem."[15] Nance wrote, "My reaction to this report is somewhat violent." Nance was particularly incensed by the claim that there was "no really clear definition of what education is trying to accomplish." She suggested that the Department of Education should "indicate through all appropriate channels that we do not intend to join any retreat from the principles of universal, free, public education for all the children of all the people."[16] On her own copy of the minutes of the July 8 meeting, next to the passage "We find the question of 'who should be educated' and 'how much education' constantly brought up," Heffernan wrote, "All the children of all the people if we are to remain a democracy."[17]

How to Teach the California Child

The Dilworth Committee's attack on California public education and on Heffernan in particular found expression on the national stage in September 1958 in an *Atlantic Monthly* article by Mortimer Smith, "How to Teach the California Child." Smith, the author of two previous polemics against progressive education, *And Madly Teach* and *The Diminished Mind,* was, along with Arthur Bestor, a founding member of the Council for Basic Education, a group organized to combat what it claimed were the academic weaknesses of the public schools.[18] Building upon the argument put forward in his previous books and by Bestor in *Educational Wastelands,* and echoing the accusations of the Dilworth Committee's *Sixteenth Report,* Smith argued that California public schools were academically weak and anti-intellectual. He began by citing two studies, one comparing test results of small groups of soldiers from different states, and one comparing knowledge of arithmetic between British students and students from central California. In both of these cases, the California students scored low. Although Smith admitted that these two examples were "a straw in the wind" and were very fragmentary examples (it is not clear who exactly these students were, or what they had been taught, for example), he nonetheless presented them as conclusive evidence that California public schools were failing academically.

As further evidence of academic weakness, Smith cited the life-adjustment curriculum put into place in California high schools in the late 1940s and 1950s. He provided a number of anecdotes (without giving the name of the schools) describing courses in "bachelor living" and courses in which students conducted mock weddings. The cause of this disastrous decline in academic standards in California, Smith argued, was "the monopoly of what Arthur Bestor has called 'the interlocking directorate of professional educationists,'" who had "reached the conclusion that the primary task of the schools is not education but social conditioning."[19] Smith then turned to the 1950 *Framework for Public Education in California*. Instead of focusing on individual mastery of academic subject matter, Smith claimed, the *Framework* advocated a focus on "group problems, group living, group activities, and group action." Even more upsetting to Smith was a section of the *Framework* that asserted that some students required special attention. These included the mentally and physically handicapped as well as "those with superior capacity for intellectual achievement and leadership." Smith was outraged that these "superior" students would be grouped with such "deviates" as those with "impaired sight, hearing and speech." For him, this was yet another example of lowered academic standards.

Smith singled out Helen Heffernan as a key figure responsible for this state of affairs, describing Heffernan as "a devotee of Kilpatrickian progressivism who thinks schools exist for the purpose of social adjustment and the development of healthy personality and to whom all talk of academic standards and intellectual values is antediluvian." He was particularly incensed by Heffernan's rejection of ABCD report cards. He quoted the 1952 *California Journal of Elementary Education* article in which she had called report cards "nasty little status cards." For Smith this demonstrated her "contempt for intellectual standards."[20] Smith went on to attack high schools and junior colleges in California for their emphasis on life adjustment and weak academic curricula and to name Roy Simpson, the state superintendent of public instruction, professors of education in teachers colleges and universities, and the California Teachers Association as all complicit. The answer, for Smith, was to return to the study of academic disciplines, to diminish the power of teachers' associations and teachers' unions, professors of education, and the California State Department of Education.

Immediately after the publication of "How to Teach the California Child," Heffernan contacted her lawyer, Gardiner Johnson, to see if she had grounds for a suit. After consulting with his colleagues, Johnson replied, "Our unanimous opinion is that this is not the type of attack upon which to file a lawsuit."[21] Instead, Heffernan's allies mobilized to counter Smith's charges. Her old friend and colleague Faith Smitter wrote a letter denouncing Smith that was published in the next issue of the *Atlantic Monthly*. Arthur Corey, the head of the California Teachers Association (CTA), published a more extensive rebuttal in the December issue.[22] State superintendent Roy Simpson, on the other hand, remained quiet. In the October 3, 1958 issue of *U.S. News and World Report,* Simpson was quoted as saying that the schools should "emphasize the three R's as the foundation of everything."[23]

In October 1958, Heffernan tried to rally State Department of Education officials to respond to the attacks. She sent Jay Conner and Roy Simpson some of her speeches and a typescript entitled "How do you Answer the Questions?" In it, Heffernan set out three key questions: 1.) Who shall be educated? 2.) What are the ends education seeks? 3.) What shall we teach our children and youth to achieve these ends? The answer to the first question—Who shall be educated?—once was that everyone should be educated. But now, Heffernan argued, "we find creeping into the articles of the professional writers, the paid critics of American education—the 'have pen—will write' boys—the astonishing suggestion that we make education in this country aristocratic, the possession of the privileged few." To the second question, "What are the ends education seeks?" Heffernan replied: "We seek the highest development of the individual through which he can contribute most effectively to the quality of living in his community, state, nation, and world." To the third question, "What shall we teach our children and youth?" Heffernan argued that educators needed to prepare children for a rapidly changing society. She noted California's explosive rise in population and the growth of suburbs with their relatively isolated and anonymous social life. Educators needed to consider the implications of these shifts on children. But most importantly, Heffernan argued, educators needed to recognize the political nature of the attacks on the schools and to distinguish between well-intentioned concern and those seeking their own political gain.[24] There is no record of a response to Heffernan's memo from either Conner or Simpson.

THE NATIONAL DEFENSE EDUCATION ACT

The accusation that the schools were academically weak seemed validated by the Soviet launch of Sputnik, the first orbiting satellite, in 1957. The Soviet success caused widespread soul searching about how the Soviet Union could have achieved this breakthrough before the United States. The blame, of course, fell on the schools. As a result of these concerns, in September 1958, President Eisenhower signed legislation representing the most dramatic change in federal educational policy in decades, the National Defense Education Act, which provided direct federal funding to public schools for science, mathematics, and foreign language education.[25] Once the National Defense Education Act (NDEA) became law, Heffernan's attention turned to its possible impact on California schools.[26] Heffernan spoke of her conflicted response to the act in a 1959 address to the annual conference of the Association for Supervision and Curriculum Development in Cincinnati. She presented her own reservations about the act in the guise of speaking for "school people." There was the troublesome nature of the act's title—the National Defense Education Act—which "some people" saw as "the expression of a Sputnik-inspired fear psychosis which had gripped the nation."[27] For Heffernan, what was needed was not only an increase in funding for science and mathematics education, but an articulation of the state's obligation to provide a challenging and democratic education for all students and a defense of freedom of expression for teachers.

Despite her reservations about the NDEA, Heffernan soon became actively involved, presenting in-service workshops and organizing local conferences on mathematics, science, and foreign language teaching funded by the act.[28] She sought to allay the doubts of those who worried that federal funding meant centralized federal control. The act, she pointed out, specifically stated that "direction, supervision, or control over the curriculum" would remain in local hands.[29] She was more concerned about the possibility that "a nation-wide testing system may be fastened on the schools."[30] In an *NEA Journal* article, "Evaluation—More than Testing," she warned educators to make sure that schools did not become "unduly dominated by devices which, at best, measure only part of what we are attempting to do in our schools and which, if improperly used, may make the teaching of the more easily measurable segment of the educational program the major focus of the schools." She warned, "Educators must also take care that test-makers not be allowed to determine the curriculum."[31]

Worries over the state of the schools after Sputnik underlay the popularity of Admiral Hyman Rickover's widely read *Education and Freedom*, published in January 1959. Rickover, known as the architect of the nuclear navy, had written a number of articles in popular magazines in the late 1950s, denouncing what he claimed was the failure of public schools to prepare students in science and mathematics. *Education and Freedom*, based on these articles, repeated the familiar conservative claim that progressive methods explained the failure of U.S. schools to compete with the Soviets.[32] The first chapter, "Education is our First Line of Defense—Make it Strong," set the tone for the rest of the book. Repeating the accusations of Mortimer Smith, Arthur Bestor, and the Council for Basic Education that progressive education and life adjustment had undermined the academic standards of public education, Rickover compared the supposed academic strengths of the European, Japanese, and most ominously the Soviet educational systems to the weak, anti-intellectual approach that he said dominated American schools.[33] Rickover did argue for more funding for school buildings and equipment, but he was most concerned that these resources should support the education of "the gifted," those who would become the scientific elite.

State officials vacillated in their response to these criticisms. Some, like state superintendent Roy Simpson, tried to placate the critics by claiming the state was already committed to a strongly academic approach.[34] Helen

Heffernan, on the other hand, defended her long-standing progressive and democratic ideals. In a 1959 article, "The Young Adolescent," she attacked the demand for greater discipline and increased academic subjects advocated by Rickover and other critics of the schools. She condemned the "get-tough-with-the-kids" virus, which, she said, seemed "to have infected many adults who at the same time are exceedingly chary of any efforts that might lessen *their* comfort and require *their* increased effort."[35] Heffernan was particularly critical of the focus on the needs of "the gifted," one of Rickover's major themes. She noted the danger of creating a public school system based upon a narrow and standardized curriculum for most students and a more challenging and creative course of study for those deemed academically talented: "We must not be led into an educational program dominated by drill on irrelevant facts and skills. We must not be led into a program of special schools for the gifted and crumbs of education for everybody else." This approach, Heffernan said, was an example of the "teach the best and shoot the rest" philosophy of education.[36]

Civil Rights Stirrings

Although the attack on the public schools continued unabated in the late 1950s and early 1960s, these years also saw a new sensitivity to racial issues and the beginning of the fracturing of the Cold War consensus. California conservatives lost one of their most vocal spokesmen when Nelson Dilworth left his position as chairman of the Investigating Committee on Education in 1959; not coincidentally, that was the date of the committee's last published report. Although the committee continued to exist until the late-1960s, it was increasingly irrelevant to public policy and debate. These years also saw the growing visibility and impact of the civil rights movement. In 1958, Heffernan joined the Association for Childhood Education International, an organization dedicated to advocating for children and well known for its support of the civil rights movement. In October 1958, she pledged $1,000, a large sum for the time, to a fund to help build a children's center in Washington, D.C.[37] A sign of the growing awareness of race among California officials was the appointment in 1958 of Wilson Riles as "consultant in certified employment practices" in the State Department of Education. Riles, who had served as the regional secretary of the Fellowship of Reconciliation in Los Angeles between 1954 and 1958, was the first African American appointed to a position in the Department of Education.[38]

The reaction to the decision of the House Un-American Activities Committee to hold new hearings on subversion in California schools showed the new political mood. Whether by coincidence or not, in June 1959, only a few months after the publication of the Dilworth Committee's *Sixteenth Report* and Mortimer Smith's *Atlantic Monthly* article "How to Teach the California Child," HUAC issued subpoenas to over forty Northern California public school teachers demanding that they appear at hearings to be held in San Francisco to testify about their political beliefs.[39] But the response to

HUAC this time was much more defiant than had been the case with earlier investigations. A Bay Area group, San Franciscans for Academic Freedom and Education (SAFE), was formed to resist and denounce the hearings. The Northern California branch of the American Civil Liberties Union was also involved. In response to growing opposition from these groups and from labor unions, churches, politicians, and influential newspaper columnists like Herb Caen of the *San Francisco Chronicle*, HUAC cancelled the meetings; in the meantime, however, it turned over the names of the teachers to state superintendent Roy Simpson, who passed them on to local school boards. In the end, six of the teachers resigned or were fired.

These events called forth a much stronger reaction from the California Teachers Association than had been true earlier. On August 18, 1959 the CTA issued a press release describing a letter it had sent to Congressman Walter, the chair of HUAC, denouncing the release of the names of teachers and condemning HUAC. On September 16, 1959 the CTA wrote to all California district attorneys urging them to return the teachers' dossiers. When HUAC returned to San Francisco to hold hearings in May 1960, the committee was met with organized opposition, culminating in widely publicized confrontations in which numerous protestors—most of them college students—were arrested. The students condemned the committee's methods as fascistic and the committee itself as un-American. These student protests, inspired by the civil rights movement in the South, reflected a profound shift in public opinion and set the stage for the Berkeley free speech protests of 1964.

Heffernan must have been heartened by the protests against HUAC as a sign of political change. There was change as well inside the State Department of Education. At the end of 1960, her immediate supervisor and old adversary Jay Conner retired; he was replaced by Richard Clowes, who took office on December 1, 1960. Soon after his appointment, Clowes asked Heffernan for her opinion on a number of issues. She first sent Clowes a memorandum on the multiple reading methods used in California schools, emphasizing that this open approach should be contrasted to the strict phonics advocated by conservative critics such as Rudolph Flesch, the author of *Why Johnny Can't Read*.[40] Next, Clowes asked her to summarize and respond to the broader criticisms being directed against public education. Heffernan replied with another long memo. Heffernan summarized the critics' complaints, emphasizing that their claims were often contradictory and seldom were supported by objective evidence.[41] She concluded that she hoped the State Department of Education would present a defense of what Heffernan saw as California's "truly stupendous educational achievements."[42] There is no record of a response from Clowes.

Heffernan continued her usual active schedule in 1961, publishing articles, giving speeches, and organizing conferences and workshops.[43] But the summer conferences for supervisors she had co-led with Corinne Seeds, where she had both recruited and encouraged her supporters, were a thing of the past. A three-day conference on supervision held in Los Angeles in late October was a poor replacement. Nonetheless, Heffernan retained strong allies, not only in California, but at the U.S. Department of Health, Education, and Welfare as well. These supporters doubtless were responsible for her invitation to serve as the U.S. representative to a UNESCO conference in New Zealand in February 1960 on "The Use of Publications for Schools."[44] Heffernan, who had been a supporter of UNESCO since its inception, attended the New Zealand conference and later that year traveled to Hawaii, where she participated in the first educational conference for Asian countries held at the East-West center at the University of Hawaii. Heffernan's next international experience came in the spring of 1961, when she was one of seven U.S. women educators invited to participate in two United States State Department–sponsored conferences bringing together African and U.S. women educators held in Kenya and Nigeria.[45] Heffernan was the expert on elementary education and the only participant from the western United States.

The Coming of the Patriot

Although the early 1960s were marked by a move toward more liberal social policies nationwide and by the resurgence of the California Democratic Party, in 1961 a powerful new conservative spokesman emerged to continue the right-wing assault on California public education. This was Max Rafferty, a Southern California school superintendent. As a young man Rafferty had attended UCLA, where he had majored in history and received his teaching credential through the School of Education, which he later described as "rabid with Deweyism."[46] As an undergraduate, he was a member of the UCLA Americans, a conservative anti-Communist group.[47] Exempted from military service in the Second World War because of his flat feet, Rafferty taught in a number of small Southern California towns, eventually ending up as Superintendent of Schools in the desert community of Needles. Sometime in the early 1950s he began pursuing his doctorate in education from the University of Southern California, completing his degree in June 1956. That year he published the first of a series of articles that appeared in the *Phi Delta Kappan* and in the *CTA Journal* between 1956 and 1961 and which were collected in his first book, *Suffer, Little Children*, published in 1962. As a graduate of UCLA and a California school administrator, Rafferty was well acquainted with the progressive philosophies of both Corinne Seeds and Helen Heffernan. In a 1968 interview, he claimed that he had decided early in his career that "if God gives me the strength and the years, I'm going to bring this system down."[48]

In his early writings, Rafferty set out the themes that characterized his later political career. In the articles published in the *CTA Journal*, the official publication of the CTA, Rafferty took a moderate tone, defending public education from critics who claimed that the schools were responsible for the failure of American science in the aftermath of sputnik.[49] But from the beginning, there were other themes that help explain Rafferty's appeal to conservatives. His articles in the *Phi Delta Kappan* were much sharper in tone and more critical than those published in the *CTA Journal*.⁵⁰ In these, Rafferty echoed the claims of critics such as Arthur Bestor and Mortimer Smith that contemporary education was anti-intellectual and vapid, and argued for a return to basics. In the 1957 *Phi Delta Kappan* piece, "The Philistines," he argued that educators should not concern themselves with the movement for racial integration, which Rafferty called "an enormous spaghetti tangle of historical trends" and "a mighty headache," and instead should concern themselves solely with "intellectual standards."⁵¹ By 1958 the editors of the *Phi Delta Kappan* termed him "America's most volcanic School Superintendent-author."⁵²

In 1961 Rafferty was elected school superintendent in La Canada, a wealthy, conservative, and overwhelmingly white district that split off from Pasadena that year, in part so its students would not have to attend the integrated Pasadena High School. In June 1961, Rafferty, newly elected as school superintendent, delivered a speech, "The Passing of a Patriot," to a public meeting of the La Canada school board. This speech repeated many of the familiar right-wing accusations of the dangers of progressive education, but Rafferty presented his argument in unusually colorful and highly charged language. Like the Dilworth Committee's *Sixteenth Report* and Mortimer Smith's "How to Teach the California Child," Rafferty's articles targeted the California Department of Education, particularly the progressive ideas of Helen Heffernan.

Rafferty began by saying he was going to talk about a "vanishing species— the American patriot." Rafferty reminded his audience of the "sickening, staggering number of our young men just ten years ago who sold out their fellow American soldiers and licked the boots of the brutal Chinese and North Korean invaders, and made tape recordings praising Communism." Echoing the claims of other critics in the late 1950s who argued that the betrayal by American POWs was the result of their exposure to progressive education, Rafferty claimed that "these spineless, luxury-loving, spiritless creeps came right out of our classrooms."⁵³ As elementary school students, he continued, they went on field trips and "danced around ribboned poles at our May Festivals.... They were 'adjusted to their peer groups.' They were taught that competition was bad and cooperation was supremely good. They were told little about democratic capitalism, and that little was usually taught with a curled lip."

Rafferty then considered the stories in the "California state third grade reader" (a reference to Helen Heffernan's coauthored *All Aboard for Storyland*). He compared the drama and heroism of the McGuffey's *Readers* stories to "how Richard Lane and nice Miss Allen the Schoolteacher planted the flower bulbs in the window box for fifteen pages and 2600 words in *All Aboard for Storyland*," a reference to Helen Heffernan's story "Fun Gardening Indoors." According to Rafferty, the bland curriculum and failure to teach rousing patriotism had had disastrous effects: "The results are plain for all to see: the worst of our youngsters growing up to become booted, sideburned, ducktailed, unwashed, leatherjacketed Slobs, whose favorite sport is ravaging little girls and stomping polio victims to death." Young people had grown up in a world without moral standards. It is "no wonder so many of them welsh out and squeal and turn traitor when confronted with the brutal reality of Red military force and the crafty cunning of Red psychological warfare."[54] "The Passing of a Patriot" was a sensation. That October, it was reprinted in the *Reader's Digest* in slightly modified form under the title "What Happened to Patriotism?"[55] In 1962, the conservative organization America's Future published and distributed 150,000 copies of "The Passing of the Patriot."

YOUR SCHOOLS! YOUR CHILDREN!

The continuing concern with patriotism and the fear of Communism underlay the decision of the California legislature in October 1961 to add a section to the Education Code requiring that "patriotic exercises" begin every school day, a requirement that could be met by the reciting of "the pledge of allegiance to the Flag of the United States of America."[56] In November 1961, the *Los Angeles Herald-Express* repeated the call for greater patriotism in a series entitled "Your Schools! Your Children!" The theme of the series was the supposed failure of California schools to teach children love of their country. However histrionic the claims in the *Herald-Express*, Roy Simpson took them seriously enough to refute them in a Special Report to the State Board of Education, arguing that "this type of series is the best ally of communism, for it focuses unwarranted suspicion on our schools and the students in them."[57]

Helen Heffernan did not publicly respond to Rafferty's "Passing of the Patriot." The beginning of 1962 found her, as usual, at work on a number of different projects. Like other liberals, she was influenced by national events, particularly the social programs of the new Kennedy administration and the continuing civil rights struggles in the South. The field reports of the Bureau of Elementary Education in the early 1960s show increased focus on the needs of the children of migrant families and of Spanish-speaking children, although there was comparatively little attention paid to urban African American children, except for the work of Wilson Riles and Afton Nance.[58]

In late spring 1962, Heffernan received an honorary doctorate from the National College of Education. She was then sixty-six years old. Almost immediately after this honor, she experienced a personal blow and faced a new political challenge. In June, she fell from a ladder while harvesting apricots in her garden and fractured her back. She spent eighteen days in the hospital and then several months that summer going through what she described as a "slow and tedious convalescence."[59] She wrote to another friend that she was "encased in a most uncomfortable steel brace" and was forced to work at home as best she could.[60] One of her activities was a joint book project on creativity with Dr. William Burton, a well-known retired Harvard professor of child development. Burton, who had been a leader in defending progressive and public education against right-wing attacks in the 1950s, initially addressed his letters to "Miss Heffernan," but soon he became playful, addressing her as Helen Huff, H. Huff, and Helen the Huff. She continued to address him as "Dear Dr. Burton."[61] Heffernan wrote to Burton describing her accident: "When I tell you that on June 26 I fell off a ladder while picking my apricot crop and sustained a multiple fracture of the twelfth lumbar vertebra, I can just hear you say, 'Why won't those old gals act their age?'"[62] Burton replied: "No ma'am, when I got the news that you had fallen out of an apricot tree and are suffering from a fracture of the 12th lumbar vertebra, I did not say as you suspected, 'Why won't these old gals act their age.' What I did say to the family was, 'Well, never in my wildest imagination did I ever think of Helen, the Huff, as a Fallen Woman!"[63] Heffernan, the fallen woman, experienced more than physical pain and discomfort that summer. She was also faced with a new and powerful political enemy in Max Rafferty, who had decided to run for the position of state superintendent of public instruction.

In early 1962, Roy Simpson had announced that he was stepping down after seventeen years as state superintendent. After a crowded primary which included nine candidates, Dr. Ralph Richardson, the president of the Los Angeles Board of Education, and Max Rafferty emerged as the two finalists. The California superintendent of public instruction was traditionally an elected nonpartisan position, but the 1962 campaign split sharply along party lines. Republicans overwhelmingly favored Rafferty, who gained support from wealthy Southern California conservatives such as Walter Knox, business groups, and the American Legion, although Rafferty distanced himself from the extreme right-wing John Birch Society. Richardson was backed by Democrats, labor unions, the CTA, and the Democratic governor Pat Brown. Although Rafferty had some support among teachers, most teachers, understandably given Rafferty's scathing attacks on professional educators, favored Richardson. In 1962, national attention was focused on the California governor's race, where Democrat Pat Brown was faced by Republican former senator and vice president Richard Nixon, but the race for superintendent of public instruction was also hotly contested and was particularly acrimonious. Rafferty and Richardson conducted a series of debates during the fall. According to one account of the election, the debates "centered upon the dichotomous proposition of 'Dewey Progressivism versus the Three R's,'" with Rafferty charging his opponent with "sympathy for left-leaning liberalism" while Richardson accused Rafferty of having "the finest mind of the twelfth century."[64]

Rafferty played on the continuing fear of Communism. In September 1962, the California State Board of Education adopted a statement authorizing the schools to teach about Communism, since only by understanding "Communist ideology" would students be able to contrast it to free societies.[65] The new guidelines in the Social Studies Framework, that long-suffering document, stated that students should be taught about Communism "and its plan for world domination, the present strategy as revealed by Russia's declared aims, and regions vulnerable to communism" in the tenth grade. In the eleventh and twelfth grades the Framework recommended increasing "the student's understanding about communism in its various forms and its contrast with free societies."[66] The power of these continuing anti-Communist fears, along with the increasing Cold War tensions that culminated in the Cuban missile crisis that October, doubtless created a sympathetic audience for Rafferty's rhetoric.

While she was convalescing that summer and fall, Heffernan closely followed the campaign for state superintendent. In October, she wrote to a friend that she had just read Rafferty's *Suffer, Little Children,* which of course denounced everything Heffernan and Corinne Seeds had fought for during their entire careers. Heffernan wrote: "I have just finished reading *Suffer, Little Children* by Mr. Rafferty and am shocked by the sacrilegious nature of this title drawn from one of the greatest humanitarians of all time! This great religious leader never in all his brief but wonderful life expressed anything but love for mankind." Rafferty's book, on the other hand, was "a litany of hate."[67] There was also a gendered subtext in Rafferty's rhetoric expressed most directly in his essay "The Children of Uranus," first published in the *Phi Delta Kappan* and revised and reprinted in *Suffer, Little Children.* In "Children of Uranus," Rafferty speculated that education had become the target of such widespread criticism because it had put forward "an essentially feminine image—gentle, non-combative, benevolent, maternal, a little fussy." In reality, Rafferty claimed, "education is not feminine. Since the days of Socrates and Plato, and before, it has been masculine in its outlook and appeal...It seeks to change concepts, to conquer ignorance, to fight evil. It brings not peace, but a sword."[68] It is not hard to imagine Heffernan's reaction to these views.

Combating the Gospel of St. John Dewey

In the 1962 California election that November, Republicans lost almost all the races, including the governorship, in which Pat Brown defeated Richard Nixon. But despite the public opposition to his candidacy by virtually all state educational organizations, many professional educators, and nine of ten members of the State Board of Education, Max Rafferty was elected California state superintendent of public instruction, defeating Ralph Richardson by over 200,000 votes.[69] Rafferty's victory was greeted with dismay by liberals and the educational establishment and enthusiastically by conservatives, at least initially. Needless to say, Helen Heffernan was deeply distressed. She wrote to William Burton: "By now the outcome of the election has reached you. We think we have grave responsibility to stay on the job but the situation might become intolerable. However, the world is full of jobs for anyone who wants to work so I will not cross that bridge until I come to it."[70]

In December, after Rafferty's victory but before he formally took office, Heffernan sent a memo to her immediate superior Richard Clowes emphasizing the need to support the *California Journal of Elementary Education,* which she poignantly described as "our one continuing contact with the Elementary Schools of the State."[71] But Heffernan's fears were well founded. Immediately upon taking office Rafferty announced his decision to end the publication of the *California Journal of Elementary Education* with its May 1963 issue.[72] Its termination was noted in a brief statement announcing that a new journal, to be called *California Education*, would be created replacing both the *California Journal of Elementary Education* and another State Department publication, *California Schools*. There was no statement recognizing the accomplishments of the *California Journal of Elementary Education* or Heffernan's contributions.[73] Heffernan was not a member of the editorial board of *California Education*, but in the journal's second issue she published an article entitled "Let's Keep Our Perspective." In it, she repeated her commitment to the democratic function of education and said, pointedly: "It seems necessary to reiterate our commitment to the belief that in a democratic society all persons are precious."[74] This was the only article Heffernan ever contributed to Rafferty's *California Education*.

Once in office, Rafferty continued his rhetorical campaign against progressive education, but in practice he was constrained by the weight of the state bureaucracy and the hostility of both the legislature, which was controlled by the Democrats, and the State Board of Education. Although Rafferty acknowledged that he could not transform teaching practices in every classroom across the state, he proclaimed a new set of values, based on the teaching of basic skills, the classics, and traditional virtues of patriotism and good manners. Beginning with the first issue of *California Education* Rafferty contributed a column, "Education in Depth." In his column in the January 1964 issue of *California Education*, Rafferty claimed that "more changes occurred during [the last] 12 months than during the preceding 12 years." Among the accomplishments of 1964 Rafferty cited the "first opposition on a statewide level to the recent trend toward divorcing education and religion in the public schools." In addition, he wrote that evolution should be taught as only one theory among many.[75] Summarizing his first year's accomplishments, Rafferty wrote proudly: "No longer is our State Department of Education the citadel and stronghold of Progressive Education in this state. No longer do swarms of brochures, pamphlets, bulletins, and précis issue from its myriad bureaus as regularly as the swallows come back to Capistrano, and far more frequently, preaching the bliss of 'life adjustment' and the gospel according to St. John Dewey to every school and teacher from Yreka in the north to Calexico in the south." Rafferty's celebration of traditional education and his denunciation of progressive education and "St. John Dewey" heartened his right-wing base.

Other items on Rafferty's list of accomplishments, however, surprised his liberal critics and dismayed his conservative supporters. Despite his criticism of the "myriad bureaus" of the State Department of Education and his argument for a limited role of the school in terms of social services, once in office Rafferty argued for more funding for the education of mentally retarded children, programs to combat dropouts, and more state support for the schools. The California school finance bill of 1963 provided $25 million in school aid. Rafferty's more conservative supporters were uneasy with this expansion of state financial support for local public schools, but even more, they were upset by Rafferty's acknowledgement of de facto racial segregation and inclusion of educators of color in the State Department of Education. In his January 1964 message in *California Education,* he celebrated not only the expansion of opportunities to the "educationally handicapped" and the "mentally retarded," but also the "State Department of Education's Committee on Equal Employment for Teachers, now known as the Commission on Equal Opportunities in Education" and the "naming by the State Superintendent of distinguished Negro and Mexican-American educators to the highest state educational positions ever held in California by members of these racial groups."[76]

In part, Rafferty was following the actions of the courts and the State Board of Education, which in February 1963 for the first time required districts to act to address de facto segregation. The state legislature responded by passing legislation calling on the State Department of Education to give advice and assistance to school districts in their attempts to end segregation. Rafferty reported that his office had set up a bureau "to enable trained experts to go out into our state's 1600 school districts to give advice and counsel in the solving of this knotty puzzle."[77] In his summary of his first year in the State Department of Education, he proudly described his support of minority hirings: "Before 1963, did you have eminent Negro-American and Mexican-American educators occupying the highest appointive offices in California education? You do now."[78] And when a committee of American historians chaired by Kenneth Stamp and including Winthrop Jordan and Lawrence Levine wrote a critique of elementary school textbooks entitled "The Negro in American History Textbooks," Rafferty responded by calling for textbooks to be more balanced in their treatment of minorities. Right-wing grassroots groups were not pleased.

The most prominent African American educator in the Department of Education remained Wilson Riles, who had first been appointed to a position in the State Department of Education by state superintendent Roy Simpson in 1958. After joining the State Department of Education, Riles, who also spoke openly against the arms race and nuclear weapons, became the public voice of the department on racial issues. Between 1958 and 1962 Riles delivered literally hundreds of presentations to community groups, educational organizations, and churches, consulted with school boards and administrators, and conducted numerous workshops.[79] Although Riles employed the language of moderation (he used the term "discrimination" rather than "racism" in his speeches, for example), he was consistent in his support of teachers of color and his demand for racial equity. In a typical 1962 speech, Riles referred to the 1946 *Mendez v. Westminster* decision and subsequent legislation repealing all California laws permitting racial segregation, cautioning that "de facto segregation separates races and ethnic groups in schools in certain areas of the state almost as effectively as do the massive resistance techniques practiced in some of the schools of the Deep South."[80]

Rafferty not only asked Riles to advise the department on problems of school segregation, but he also invited him to contribute articles on the continued de facto segregation of California schools in the first and third issues of *California Education*.[81] When the Bureau of Intergroup Relations was established in 1963, Rafferty appointed Riles as its secretary. In 1965, Riles was promoted to a new position as director of compensatory education; subsequently his position was changed to chief, Bureau of Intergroup Relations. Doubtless as a result of Riles's leadership, the State Department of Education continued to support efforts to combat racial discrimination. In March 1965, for example, the California Commission on Equal Opportunities in Education sponsored a conference on "Equal Educational Opportunities in a Changing Society" with the distinguished African American historian John Hope Franklin as keynote speaker.[82]

While Rafferty supported initiatives to address racial issues within the Department of Education, in his public statements he appealed to a more conservative audience. His support of equal employment opportunities or the inclusion of minority history in textbooks for example—stances that might alienate conservative voters—were not mentioned in his newspaper columns. Rafferty refused to support California's fair housing act, which sought to counter ongoing practices that led to de facto segregation.[83] And although he acknowledged that as a result "California has schools which are almost completely segregated," he rejected compulsory busing as a solution. "A man," he wrote, "should have the right to send his kids to school in his own neighborhood." Instead, he supported voluntary busing programs, which meant in practice that small numbers of children of color rode the bus to white-dominated schools, but not the reverse.[84]

Keeping Ahead of the Hounds

Heffernan was deeply distressed by Rafferty's election, but despite her isolation and loss of power within the California State Department of Education (or perhaps in response to it) Heffernan was professionally very active in the mid-1960s. Her textbook for middle-school children, *Man Improves His World: The Water Story*, which she coauthored with George Shaftel, was published in 1963.[85] In 1964, the coauthored book she had been working on for several years with William H. Burton, *The Step Beyond: Creativity*, was published by the NEA. That year also saw the publication of another coauthored work, *The Years Before School*, an extensive study of early childhood she wrote with Vivian Edmiston. This volume of over 600 pages was reprinted in several subsequent editions, the last in 1977.[86] Although she was professionally very productive, there is no doubt that she was sensitive to the hostile political environment in which she now worked. She began one 1964 speech: "This talk is entitled 'The Importance of Teaching' but in education today I sometimes think my real speech should be entitled 'Keeping Ahead of the Hounds.' "[87]

When the *California Journal of Elementary Education* ceased publication in May 1963, Heffernan lost her last forum to speak directly to the teachers of California. Perhaps in response to the loss of the *California Journal of Elementary Education,* a few months after it ceased publication she began a monthly column in the *Grade Teacher,* a national journal directed at elementary school teachers. Between September 1963 and April 1965, Heffernan contributed both columns and articles to the *Grade Teacher,* touching on familiar themes, among them the debates over the social studies, phonics, and homework.[88] Rafferty himself began a weekly column (later syndicated) in the *Los Angeles Times* at almost exactly the same time. In contrast to the relatively measured prose of his pieces in State Department of Education publications, in his syndicated columns Rafferty returned to the colorful rhetoric of earlier speeches such as "The Passing of a Patriot" to attack his favorite targets of progressive education and John Dewey.

Although Heffernan and Rafferty did not refer directly to one another, their columns and speeches continued their debate about what exactly public schooling should be. In her first column in the *Grade Teacher,* Heffernan defended the concept of social studies instead of separate academic disciplines as the organizing principle of the school curriculum. She described disciplines such as geography, history, and sociology as human inventions, not necessarily universal truths.[89] Rafferty, of course, was adamantly opposed to the idea of the social studies, which he saw as emblematic of the politically suspect and academically weak approach of progressive education. In November 1964, he issued a memo stating that "in the future, the term 'Social Studies' will not be used in any Department publications, correspondence, bulletins, or official documents. Either 'History and Geography' or 'Social Sciences' will be used instead."[90] He confirmed the decision in a brief notice in *California Education,* which began "Term, Social Studies—No More."[91]

Heffernan and Rafferty also clashed over the use of phonics, a continuing issue since the popular success of Flesch's *Why Johnny Can't Read.* For Rafferty, as for many of his conservative supporters, the question of reading instruction was highly charged and phonics was the only appropriate method of teaching reading. Heffernan argued for an inclusive approach. In her second article in the *Grade Teacher,* she pointed out that the "recognized reading series by reputable publishers" all employed a phonetic approach along with others; what was important was mastering the art of reading itself, not the specific method used. Reading, Heffernan argued, should be the result of first experiencing and then reflecting upon the world. In general, Heffernan argued that the struggle over "phonics or no phonics" was fabricated, since "every reading expert" understood the usefulness of phonics. She asked readers to consider the political nature of the reading wars: "Could it be that we are using such differences of opinion, where no really significant difference exists, to escape coming to grips with the truly gigantic problems confronting the contemporary world?...It really won't matter if 'Johnny Can't Read' if Johnny and all his contemporaries are vaporized by H-bombs."[92]

In another article, Heffernan argued against the idea that elementary school students be given homework. She wrote that children should be introduced to rich experiences at school, but at home "children need time to explore, to talk to other children and adults, to experiment, to adventure, perhaps just time to cogitate to become the unique personalities they are capable of becoming."[93] She argued that it was fine if children pursued their school interests at home and involved their families, but overall she was suspicious of routine homework. Drill, she wrote, "actually dulls interest and may make all learning distasteful to the creative child." Sentiments like these were anathema to Rafferty, who continued to rail against progressive education and defend the need for homework in his *Los Angeles Times* articles. In a May 1964 column, he argued that even now, when "progressive education under its many masks and aliases" was on the defensive, many educators still clung "stubbornly and blindly to the Dewey-eyed dogmas of the 1930s and 1940s." These educators challenged the idea of homework, refused to teach the alphabet to first graders, and rejected the ABCDF graded report card.[94]

In her final *Grade Teacher* column of 1963, Heffernan addressed the impact of the widespread criticism the schools had received in the past fifteen years. She noted that the United States was the wealthiest country in the world and that public education was crucial to the country's success. She then analyzed those who criticized the schools: the "fearful ones" who are afraid that "some ideological enemy" may "surpass us in the conquest of space"; the "ignorant ones" who long for the little red schoolhouse and the three R's; "the disgruntled ones," who blame teachers for their children's shortcomings. Then there were the more dangerous critics, those who "advocate breaking with our commitment to education for all the children of all the people." And last, there were "the camp followers, who see a golden opportunity to profit by any lessening of the public faith in the ability of trained professional educators. They move in with their cure-alls guaranteed to solve the problem if the school districts buy their system of teaching phonics, drilling in mathematics, or whatever get-rich-quick materials they can devise."[95]

In many ways, Heffernan and Rafferty were reenacting old battles, but by the mid-1960s they encountered a new political landscape. In the 1960s, social protest moved from the civil rights movement in the South to the rest of the nation. In California, the 1964 Free Speech Movement led to massive student protests at the University of California Berkeley, while the Watts riots of August 1965 demonstrated the depth of both white racism and black anger. Both of these events shook the social conformity of the 1950s and were striking challenges, both to conservatives like Max Rafferty but also to New Deal liberals like Heffernan. Rafferty was scornful of the Free Speech Movement. In a typically colorful 1965 speech, Rafferty condemned college students who, he claimed, did not petition peacefully, but instead, preferred "to bellow obscenities over commandeered campus public address systems, and to kidnap campus cops and bite them on the legs in a veritable orgy of childish malevolence which would have been shocking in a reform school and would have raised eyebrows in an institution for the emotionally disturbed."[96] Rafferty saw these university students, like the "turncoat" GIs of the Korean War, as the products of lax and indulgent schools. Within progressive education, Rafferty wrote, lay "the seeds of the rumbles and the riots, the frantic search for 'kicks,' the newsstand filth and the cinematic garbage which mark the last descent into the cloying, clinging sickness of ultimate decay by every civilization which has even permitted this infection to overcome its resistance."[97]

While Rafferty reacted histrionically to the Free Speech Movement, what captured Heffernan's imagination were the social critiques of U.S. society that began to emerge in the early 1960s and the social legislation of the Kennedy and Johnson administrations, which recalled the vision and promise of the New Deal. In a presentation to the 1964 Fourth Annual Conference on Families Who Follow the Crops, Heffernan cited both John Kenneth Galbraith's *The Affluent Society* (1958) and Michael Harrington's *The Other America* (1962) to support her argument that economic inequality was a structural problem in U.S. society. She pointed out that "school people have learned long ago that you cannot teach hungry children, and hungry children come from families whose income is insufficient to provide proper nutrition." Schools needed to provide summer programs, child care centers, and free lunches, but schools could not themselves eliminate poverty and inequality. In response to the passage of the Economic Opportunity Act, which established Head Start and VISTA, Heffernan wrote: "Before all of us, who respect and love young children, lies the opportunity about which we have woven our hopes and dreams."[98]

A Teacher Affects Eternity

On September 1, 1965, Heffernan officially retired.[99] There was no public announcement from the State Department of Education. The *Sacramento Bee* reported: "Helen Heffernan, who exerted more influence on instruction in California elementary schools than any other educator in modern times, has retired without fanfare or ceremony from the State Department of Education. There was not even a press release to announce the end of 39 years of service as chief of the Bureau of Elementary Education." The *Bee* concluded that there were no plans to replace her: "Under an upcoming consolidation of the elementary and secondary bureaus, her job will be abolished."[100] The October issue of the department's official publication *California Education* included a brief article on her retirement. The article mentioned her year in Japan and her involvement with the African women educators project and listed the summer courses she had taught. It also mentioned that the National College of Education in Evanston, Illinois, had awarded her an honorary Doctor of Humane Letters in 1962. There was no mention of her contribution to California education.[101]

Although her retirement was ignored by the State Department of Education, Heffernan's supporters celebrated her accomplishments. On September 27, 1965, Assemblyman Alfred Alquist presented a resolution in the state legislature congratulating her on her "many valuable contributions in the field of elementary education." In the fall of 1965, immediately after her retirement, Heffernan undertook an extensive tour of the East, speaking at a number of conferences and meetings. Back in California, her friends and admirers discussed what sort of memorial should be created to mark her achievements. They decided that raising money to purchase a redwood grove in Northern California as part of the ongoing campaign to establish Redwoods National Park would be a fitting tribute and would reflect Heffernan's love of nature, gardening, and the California landscape. The event was widely publicized among her supporters. The Helen Heffernan Honor Grove was dedicated on October 1, 1966.

There were a number of speeches at the dedication of the redwood grove. Mary Lane, professor of education at San Francisco State and one of the organizers of the event, spoke about Heffernan's career and influence, quoting from the many admiring letters about Heffernan that she had received in the previous weeks.[102] Heffernan responded with a brief speech thanking the organizers. She was moved by the symbolism of the redwood grove: "I feel greatly honored to stand here with you among the giants. No greater honor could come to any man or woman than to have his friends and colleagues wish to associate his name with the enduring strength and timeless beauty of the redwoods." She saw the choice of the redwoods as particularly appropriate to honor an educator, since both were concerned with growth. She did not refer to the battles of the past two decades, but typically looked at the work that needed to be done in the future: "As a people we have enlisted in the war on poverty, for even in these prosperous times, about a quarter of our people are living at a substandard level and about a fifth of them have fallen into the abyss of abject, dismal, hopeless poverty." She spoke again of her belief in social democracy and the positive role of the state. "With the greatest zeal, we need to pursue the ways we are now trying—job corps, nursery schools, literacy programs, enrichment programs for disadvantaged children, youth and adults, programs for children of migrant workers." And at the end of her brief speech she tied together the beauty of the redwoods and the human spirit: "Now is the time for us to leave this lovely place where we have thought together of the mystery of growth in life on our planet. Incomprehensible eons have bought us here together—these magnificent trees and these aspiring human beings—both the manifestations of the secret of life."[103]

EPILOGUE

The Long Retreat from Democratic Education

Helen Heffernan and Corinne Seeds took different pathways in retirement. Seeds removed herself from public life; her long-promised book summarizing her educational philosophy never appeared. The University Elementary School underwent a series of changes after she retired, eventually becoming a highly desirable private school, still located on the UCLA campus. Seeds, who had had cancer in the early 1950s, seems to have become ill again in the mid-1960s. Heffernan remained supportive but was preoccupied with her own struggles. In Los Angeles, Seeds relied on old friends from UES such as Diana Anderson, who had taught physical education at the school for many years. In 1965, Anderson convinced Seeds to move to a rest home. Describing the move in a letter to Afton Nance, Heffernan wrote: "I am glad Diana was able to get Corinne out of her apartment. She is a better man than I am."[1] Seeds died in March 1969 and was buried next to her parents in a West Los Angeles cemetery.

Heffernan, on the other hand, remained professionally active for many years after her retirement. She traveled widely, accompanied by Afton Nance. Her passports show visits not only to European countries, but also to Australia, New Zealand, and Japan, where she was greeted by old friends from her year on MacArthur's staff. In 1969, she published a coauthored book, *Elementary Teacher's Guide to Working with Parents*, with Vivian Edmiston Todd, with whom she had earlier written *The Years Before School*.[2] She and Todd prepared two further editions of *The Years Before School*, which appeared in 1970 and 1977.[3] Heffernan was also active as a speaker in the years immediately after her retirement, appearing frequently at conferences and meetings.

In her later speeches, Heffernan returned again and again to the importance of education for democracy, echoing the words of John Dewey. She also addressed what she saw as key issues of the present. In a 1966 speech, she reflected on the accomplishments of the Johnson administration, particularly the war on poverty, the establishment of Head Start, and the Elementary and Secondary School Act of 1965. Placing these achievements in historical perspective, she recalled George Counts's call from the 1930s for the schools to "build a new social order." Counts, she said, "suffered as have other good men who lived ahead of their time and for many years the role of the school in challenging the social conscience of the people was in eclipse." But, she continued, "the question is no longer: Dare the school build a new social order? Now, we have a mandate to the schools to *build a new social order,* a mandate to mobilize all the resources of education in the war on poverty." She argued that educators needed to recognize that their work was deeply political: "You ask: Are you suggesting that school people get into politics? The answer is 'Yes.' In a democracy, politics should be our highest social art. An insolent public official recently reiterated the statement about 'education being too important to leave to the educators.' Let us paraphrase that—'politics is too important in a democracy to be left to the politicians.'"[4]

Heffernan's political adversary, Max Rafferty, was reelected California state superintendent of education in 1966, but when he ran for reelection in 1970, he was opposed by Wilson Riles, the African American educator who had served in the California State Department of Education since 1958. On May 1, 1970, Heffernan sent a mimeographed letter to educators across California urging support for Riles's campaign. She wrote that she had known Wilson Riles for seventeen years and that he was "a man of superior professional competency, unimpeachable personal integrity, unusual ability in working cooperatively with people, and complete dedication to the ideals and principles of democratic government."[5] She called for Riles's election as a way of repairing the damage done during Max Rafferty's administration. In the November election, Riles soundly defeated Rafferty and became the state's first African American superintendent of public instruction.[6] He was reelected to two subsequent terms, serving for twelve years.

With Wilson Riles's election, the conservative back-to-basics message of Max Rafferty was replaced by a new concern with issues of multicultural curriculum and racial integration. The free and open school movements, the radical social critiques of the New Left, the explosive growth of the Women's, Chicano/a, and Asian American Movements built upon the civil rights movement of the 1950s and 1960s to demand a more just and democratic society. In education, this meant calls for greater community participation in public schools, more equitable educational opportunities, and the revision of the curriculum to express the histories and realities of all the people. In 1976, six years after Riles's victory over Rafferty, Helen Heffernan celebrated her eightieth birthday. For her birthday, her friends organized a luncheon in her honor they called "Festival HH." There were speeches and Japanese dances performed by young Japanese American schoolchildren. At the conclusion of the luncheon, Heffernan gave a short speech of thanks, reflecting that eighty felt not very different from sixty or forty, although "in all honesty, it is not as spry and energetic as twenty or thirty!" As a summation of her life she quoted Robert Browning's own reflection on his life as he approached eighty:

> One who never turned his back but marched breast forward,
> Never doubted clouds would break.

> Never dreamed, though right were worsted, wrong would triumph,
> Held we fall to rise, are baffled to fight better.
> Sleep to wake.[7]

Browning's poem certainly captures Heffernan's indomitable spirit, just as the social movements of the 1970s represented the renewal of a vision of a more inclusive and representative democracy.

The promise of a renewed commitment to democratic schooling for all children, however, did not long survive in California. Two years after Heffernan's eightieth birthday party, the goal of making the schools more responsive to the needs of all Californians and of creating a genuinely equitable education was damaged if not destroyed with the passage of Proposition 13, which sharply restricted the ability of communities to raise property taxes, the major source of local funding for public schools. The result was an unending series of fiscal crises and the abandonment of attempts to redress the gap between rich and poor school districts. California's support of public education plunged from being among the highest to close to the bottom of all states. Class sizes increased, achievement on standardized tests declined, and classrooms in the crowded schools of the urban centers, filled almost exclusively by poor children of color, deteriorated to shocking conditions.[8] By this time, Heffernan was only an observer. In her later years, she moved into a Sacramento rest home, where she lived until her death on August 26, 1987, at the age of ninety-one.

How can we understand the legacy of Helen Heffernan and Corinne Seeds? They were charismatic and influential educators whose careers and achievements have been overlooked and should be incorporated into our understanding of the history of education in the United States. But it is also important to view them through a gendered lens, to consider the ways in which their lives were shaped by gender and sexuality, or, more accurately, sexism and homophobia. From the perspective of feminist history, their stories illuminate the connection between the personal and the political, one of the earliest feminist concerns. As talented and ambitious young women, they took advantage of the historical world into which they were born, a time when conceptions of woman's nature were deeply contested. They used the possibility of waged work as teachers to construct lives outside the patriarchal family. As women who loved other women, they lived in parallel worlds, one public, one kept very private. And as they became more successful and influential, they met resistance and hostility, particularly in the era of the feminine mystique and the Cold War, with its rigid gender roles, aggressive homophobia, and political paranoia. Making gender the focus of historical analysis reveals the richness of their experience, but it also illuminates the techniques of power in a society marked by male privilege and what Adrienne Rich has called "compulsory heterosexuality."

Politically, their conception of education, grounded in the belief in human potentiality and the possibility of strong state institutions, is a powerful vision that needs to be recovered. There is a widely accepted belief that public schools in the United States have failed and, in the apocalyptic vision of the 1983 federal report "A Nation at Risk," are the cause of the nation's ills, particularly its loss of global economic dominance. This claim and subsequent panics about the culpability of the schools have become disassociated from their origins and are now taken as common sense truths. The genealogy of these claims can be traced to the attacks on the schools during the Cold War, when anti-Communist cries of subversion and lack of patriotism merged with assertions of the supposed educational weaknesses that led to Soviet ascendancy in science and technology. In California, the attacks of the legislative investigating committees gave legitimacy to right-wing accusations that the schools were subversive and to subsequent and highly publicized claims that the schools were lax and failed to teach fundamentals. The history of public education in these years demonstrates clearly the deeply political nature of debates over the schools.

The retreat from the idea of well-supported public schools for all children must be seen in the light of the long-standing conservative hostility to the idea of a strong redistributive state and the abandonment of any concerted and systematic attempt to address the impact of poverty and racism. In California, the demographic and social changes of the last half century, in particular the sharp increase in the number of people of color, who moved to California seeking new opportunities, changed the composition of the schools. The new Californians brought greater ethnic and cultural diversity to the cities, but even sharper racial demarcations between cities and suburbs. Critics of the schools who now argue that public education has failed and that the schools need to be "reformed" by private initiatives do not consider that the failure to provide high-quality education to all children is the result of historical choices—a resistance to funding the schools adequately or to address profound and ongoing racial and class divisions. The vision of Helen Heffernan and Corinne Seeds that democracy rests on well-supported public schools, offering opportunities for intellectual and creative growth to all children, led by well-prepared and committed teachers, has largely vanished, replaced by an obsession with accountability as shown by the results of standardized tests, a rigid curriculum dominated by packaged materials and teacher scripts, punitive measures to punish "failing" teachers and schools, and the view that education matters only as a means of increasing economic growth.

Heffernan and Seeds argued that learning should be joyous and creative and that schools should offer all children the opportunity to learn and grow. Their ideas may have been constrained by the limitations of the liberal discourse through which they saw the world, with its failure to see racism and its unquestioning confidence in the knowledge of experts and the beneficence of the state, but despite these limitations, I believe that Heffernan and Seeds were utopian in the best sense of deeply desiring a more just and equitable society. The goal they sought—a critical and challenging education made available to all children equally as the basis for a strong democracy—is one that continues to be worth fighting for.

Abbreviations

BL	The Bancroft Library, University of California, Berkeley
CSA	California State Archives, Sacramento
CJEE	*California Journal of Elementary Education*
COUCLA	UCLA Chancellor's Office, Administrative Files of the Chancellor's Office, 1936–1959, Series 359, University Archives, Charles Young Research Library, UCLA
CSDP	Corinne A. Seeds Documentation Project 1925–1958, Series 1419, Special Collections, Charles Young Research Library, UCLA
CSPUCLA	Corinne Seeds Papers 1945–1956, Series 838, Special Collections, Charles Young Research Library, UCLA
CSPR	Corinne Seeds Papers, Collection 118, Special Collections and Archives, Tomas Rivera Library, University of California Riverside
HH/CSR	Helen Heffernan Correspondence with Corinne Seeds, Collection 117, Special Collections and Archives, Tomas Rivera Library, University of California Riverside
HHPR	Helen Heffernan Papers, Collection 116, Special Collections and Archives, Tomas Rivera Library, University of California Riverside
JTP	Joseph Trainor Papers, 1933-1980, Hoover Institution Archives, Stanford University
RSPBL	Robert Gordon Sproul Personal Papers, CU-301, University of California Archives, The Bancroft Library, University of California, Berkeley
SCUCLA	Department of Special Collections, Charles Young Research Library, UCLA
UAUCLA	University Archives, Charles Young Research Library, UCLA
WJE	*Western Journal of Education*

Notes

Introduction

1. C. Wright Mills, *The Sociological Imagination* (Oxford University Press, 1959).
2. Jacqueline Dowd Hall, "To Widen the Reach of Our Love: Autobiography, History, and Desire," *Feminist Studies* 26, no. 1 (Spring 2000): 231.
3. Robin Muncy, *Creating a Female Dominion in American Reform* (Oxford University Press, 1991).
4. See, for example, Ellen Lewin, ed., *Inventing Lesbian Cultures in America* (Beacon Press, 1996); Lillian Faderman, *Odd Girls and Twilight Lovers: A History of Lesbian Life in Twentieth Century America* (Penguin Books, 1992); John D'Emilio, *Sexual Politics, Sexual Communities* (University of Chicago Press, 1998); Martin Duberman, Martha Vicinus, and George Chauncy, eds., *Hidden from History: Reclaiming the Gay and Lesbian Past* (Penguin Books, 1991).
5. John Dewey, Introduction to Elsie Ridley Clapp, *Use of Resources* (Harper and Brothers, 1952), 3.
6. Lawrence Cremin, *The Transformation of the School* (Vintage Books, 1964).
7. Cremin, *The Transformation of the School*, 349.
8. Arthur Zilversmit, *Changing Schools: Progressive Education Theory and Practice 1930–1960* (University of Chicago Press, 1993), 170.
9. Helen Heffernan, "Inventory of the Gains," *CJEE* 20(August 1951): 122.

1 Working Girls of the Golden West

1. Patricia Limerick, *The Legacy of Conquest* (W. W. Norton, 1987); Valerie Matsumoto and Blake Allmendiger, eds., *Over the Edge: Remapping the American West* (University of California Press, 1999); Patricia Limerick, Clyde Milner, and Charles Rankin, eds., *Trails: Toward a New Western History* (University Press of Kansas, 1991); William Cronon, George Miles, and Jay Gitlin, eds., *Under An Open Sky: Rethinking America's Western Past* (W. W. Norton, 1992).
2. Susan Armitage and Elizabeth Jameson, eds., *The Women's West* (University of Oklahoma Press, 1987); Elizabeth Jameson and Susan Armitage, eds., *Writing the Range* (University of Oklahoma Press, 1997); Virginia Scharff, *Twenty Thousand Roads* (University of California Press, 2002); Mary Irwin and James Brooks, eds., *Women and Gender in the American West* (University of New Mexico Press, 2004).

3. Ardis Cameron, *Radicals of the Worst Sort: Laboring Women in Lawrence, Massachusetts, 1860–1912* (University of Illinois Press, 1995), 26. See also Donald Cole, *Immigrant City* (University of North Carolina Press, 1963).
4. Anne Ellis, *Life of an Ordinary Woman* (University of Nebraska Press, 1980), 109.
5. Sally Zanjani and Guy Louis Rocha, *The Ignoble Conspiracy: Radicalism on Trial in Nevada* (University of Nevada Press, 1986), 54–55.
6. Sally Zanjani, *Goldfield* (Ohio University Press, 1992), 104; also, Mrs. Hugh Brown, *Lady in Boomtown* (University of Nevada Press, 1968), 43.
7. See Mary Murphy, "The Private Lives of Public Women: Prostitution in Butte, Montana, 1878–1917," *Frontiers* 7, no. 3 (1984): 194.
8. Edward Krug, *The Shaping of the American High School* (Harper and Row, 1964), 169.
9. *The Joshua Palm* [Senior Annual of Goldfield High School] (Goldfield, Nevada, 1912), n. p., HHPR.
10. Kate Rousmaniere, *Citizen Teacher: The Life and Leadership of Margaret Haley* (Teachers College Press, 2005); Joan Smith, *Ella Flagg Young: Portrait of a Leader* (Northern Illinois Press, 1979).
11. Nineteenth- and twentieth-century teacher training schools were called normal schools after the French *ecole normale*.
12. Christine Ogren, *The American State Normal School* (Palgrave Macmillan, 2005); Kathleen Underwood, "The Pace of Their Own Lives: Teacher Training and the Life Course of Western Women," *Pacific Historical Review* 55 (Nov. 1986); see also Merle Borrowman, *The Liberal and Technical in Teacher Education* (Teachers College Press, 1956); Paul Mattingly, *The Classless Profession* (New York University Press, 1975); Willard Elsbree, *The American Teacher* (American Book Company, 1939); Richard Altenbaugh and Kathleen Underwood, "The Evolution of Normal Schools," in *Places Where Teachers are Taught,* ed. John Goodlad, Roger Soder, Kenneth Sirotnik (Jossey-Bass Publishers, 1990), 136–86; Jurgen Herbst, *And Sadly Teach: Teacher Education and Professionalization in American Culture* (University of Wisconsin Press, 1989).
13. Romanzo Adams, "University Notes," *Nevada School Journal* 3, no. 1 (1912): 10.
14. Anne Howard, *The Long Campaign: A Biography of Anne Martin* (University of Nevada Press, 1985).
15. *Goldfield News and Weekly Tribune* (July 31, 1915): 8.
16. "Times of Challenge—Years of Building," in *A Teacher Affects Eternity*, 6, HHPR.
17. "Times of Challenge—Years of Building," 5.
18. Lynn Gordon, *Gender and Higher Education in the Progressive Era* (Yale University Press, 1990).
19. Cited in Maresi Nerad, *The Academic Kitchen: A Social History of Gender Stratification at the University of California, Berkeley* (SUNY Press, 1999), 29.
20. Cited in Gordon, *Gender and Higher Education*, 64.
21. Gordon, *Gender and Higher Education*, 84.
22. Nancy Loe, *Life in the Altitudes: An Illustrated History of Colorado Springs* (Windsor Publications, 1983), 39.
23. Elizabeth Jameson, *Building Colorado* (Denver: Colorado State Council of Carpenters, 1984), 16–17.

24. See Elizabeth Jameson, *All That Glitters: Class, Conflict, and Community in Cripple Creek* (University of Illinois Press, 1998).
25. Corinne Seeds, "U.E.S.: The History of the Creative Elementary School" (Oral History Project, University of California Los Angeles, 1963), 6.
26. Jameson, *Building Colorado*, 17.
27. Henry Markham Page, *Pasadena: Its Early Years* (Lorrin Morrison, Printing and Publishing, 1964), 74.
28. Mike Davis, *City of Quartz* (Verso Books, 1990), 25.
29. Robert Fogelson, *The Fragmented Metropolis: Los Angeles 1950-1830* (University of California Press, 1993), 145.
30. Pasadena Board of Education, *Annual Report, 1908*, 37.
31. Seeds, "U.E.S.: The History of the Creative Elementary School," 1.
32. *Bulletin of the State Normal School, Los Angeles 1908-09* (Los Angeles Normal School, 1908), 11.
33. David Florell, "Origin and History of the School of Education, University of California, Los Angeles" (EdD diss., UCLA, 1946), 135.
34. The Los Angeles State Normal School, *A Quarter Centennial History 1882-1907*. n.d., 13. UAUCLA.
35. The close supervision of students can be seen in the minutes of LA Normal School faculty meetings. "Faculty Meeting Minutes 1907-1913," California State Normal School Minutes of Faculty and Administrative Committees, 1883-1918, Series 252, UAUCLA.
36. *The Exponent 1910*, n. p., Series 252, UAUCLA.
37. George Monroy, *Rebirth: Mexican Los Angeles from the Great Migration to the Great Depression* (University of California Press, 1999).
38. Fogelson, *The Fragmented Metropolis 1850-1930*, 123.
39. Lawrence DeGraff, "The City of Black Angels: Emergence of the Los Angeles Ghetto, 1890-1930," *Pacific Historical Review* 39 (1970): 343.
40. Monroy, *Rebirth*, 139.
41. For a more extensive discussion of Seeds's narrative, see Kathleen Weiler, "Corinne Seeds and the Avenue 21 School," *Historical Studies in Education* 14, no. 2 (2002): 191-218.
42. John Mahoney, *Training Teachers for Americanization*, United States Bureau of Education Bulletin No. 12 (United States Bureau of Education, 1920), 14.
43. John McClymer, "Gender and the American Way of Life," *Journal of American Ethnic History* 10, no. 3 (Spring 1991): 8
44. George Sanchez, "Go After the Women: Americanization and the Mexican Immigrant Woman, 1915-1929," in *Unequal Sisters: A Multicultural Reader in U.S. Women's History*, ed. Vicki Ruiz and Ellen DuBois (Routledge, 1994), 289. See also Maxine Seller, "The Education of the Immigrant Woman: 1900-1935," *Journal of Urban History* 4, no. 3 (May 1978): 307-30; Katrina Irving, *Immigrant Mothers: Narratives of Race and Maternity 1890-1925* (University of Illinois Press, 2000).
45. Seeds, "U.E.S.: The History of the Creative Elementary School," 31.
46. Seeds, "U.E.S.: The History of the Creative Elementary School," 27.
47. Seeds, "U.E.S.: The History of the Creative Elementary School," 31.
48. Hortense Spillers, "Mama's Baby, Papa's Maybe: An American Grammar Book," *Diacritics* 17, 2 (Summer 1987): 65.
49. Seeds, "U.E.S.: The History of the Creative Elementary School," 29.
50. Seeds, "U.E.S.: The History of the Creative Elementary School," 35.

51. Gullet, "Women Progressives," 73.
52. McClymer, "Gender and the American Way of Life."
53. Seeds, "U.E.S.: The History of the Creative Elementary School," 37.
54. Ellen Lagemann, *An Elusive Science: The Troubling History of Education Research* (University of Chicago Press, 2000), 65–66.
55. Seeds, "U.E.S.: The History of the Creative Elementary School," 37.
56. Seeds, "U.E.S.: The History of the Creative Elementary School," 38.
57. John Beineke, *And There Were Giants in the Land* (Peter Lang, 1998), 94–96.
58. William Kilpatrick, "The Project Method," *Teachers College Record* 19, no. 4 (September 1918): 319–35.
59. Lawrence Cremin, *The Transformation of the School* (Vintage Books, 1964), 217.
60. Kilpatrick, "The Project Method," 319.
61. Cited in Beineke, *And There Were Giants in the Land*, 192.
62. Geraldine Clifford, "'Lady Teachers' and the Politics of Teaching in the United States, 1850–1930," in *Teachers: The Culture and Politics of Work*, ed. Martin Lawn and Gerald Grace (Falmer Press, 1987); John Rury, *Education and Women's Work* (SUNY Press, 1991); Courtney Vaughn-Roberson, "Having a Purpose in Life: Western Women in the Twentieth Century," in *The Teacher's Voice*, ed. Richard Altenbaugh (Falmer Press, 1992); Jackie Blount, *Destined to Rule the Schools* (SUNY Press, 1998); Margaret Gribskov, "Feminization and the Women School Administrator," in *Women and Educational Leadership*, ed. Sari Biklen and Marilyn Brannigan (Lexington Books, 1980).

2 The Child and the Curriculum

1. George Mowry, *The California Progressives* (University of California Press, 1951); Jackson Putnam, *Age-Old Politics in California: From Richardson to Reagan* (Stanford University Press, 1970); William Deverell and Tom Sitton, eds., *California Progressivism Revisited* (University of California Press, 1994).
2. William Reese, "The Origins of Progressive Education," *History of Education Quarterly* 41, no. 1 (Spring, 2001): 23.
3. See James Wallace, *Liberal Journalism and American Education 1914–1941* (Rutgers University Press, 1991).
4. John Dewey, "Education as Politics," *New Republic* 32 (1922). Reprinted in *John Dewey: The Middle Works, 1899–1924*, 13, ed. Jo Ann Boydston (Southern Illinois University Press, 1983), 333.
5. Dewey, "Education as Politics," 334.
6. Harold Rugg and Ann Shumaker, *The Child Centered School* (World Book Company, 1928); Agnes De Lima, *Our Enemy the Child* (New Republic Inc., 1926); Stanwood Cobb, *The New Leaven* (Day Publishers, 1928).
7. De Lima, *Our Enemy the Child*, 35.
8. Corinne Seeds, "U.E.S.: The History of the Creative Elementary School" (Oral History Project, University of California Los Angeles, 1963), 47.
9. Seeds, "U.E.S.: The History of the Creative Elementary School," 47.
10. Seeds, "U.E.S.: The History of the Creative Elementary School," 52.

11. Arthur Phelan, "The Administration of the University Elementary School of the University of California, Los Angeles, 1882-1957 (EdD diss., University of California, Los Angeles), 36.
12. Charles Waddell, "History of the University Elementary School," Typescript, 1938, 1, Series 193, Box 2, SCUCLA.
13. Seeds, "U.E.S.: History of the Creative Elementary School," 63.
14. Seeds, "U.E.S.: History of the Creative Elementary School," 66.
15. "Test Program." n.p., n.d., Series 193, Box 2, SCUCLA.
16. Charles Waddell, "A Visit of One Month Among Progressive Schools Across the U.S. February, 1923," Series 193, Box 2, SCUCLA.
17. Seeds, "U.E.S.: A History of the Creative Elementary School," 70.
18. Howard Whitman, "Progressive Education, Which Way is Forward?" *Collier's* (May 14, 1954): 32.
19. Charles Waddell, Personal Interview, February 5, 1960, cited in Phelan, "The Administration of the University Elementary School," 361.
20. Phelan, "The Administration of the University Elementary School," 303.
21. Phelan, "The Administration of the University Elementary School," 38.
22. Charles Waddell, "Steps in the Decline of University Control over the Laboratory School," n.d., Series 193, Box 2, SCUCLA.
23. Waddell, "History of the University Elementary School," 2.
24. Robert Fogelson, *The Fragmented Metropolis: Los Angeles 1950-1830* (University of California Press, 1993), 78
25. Fogelson, *The Fragmented Metropolis*, 127.
26. Edwin Layton, "The Better America Federation: A Case Study of Superpatriotism," *Pacific Historical Review* 30 (May 1961): 137-47; William Deverell, "My America or Yours?" in *Metropolis in the Making: Los Angeles in the 1920s*, ed. Tom Sitton and William Deverell (University of California Press, 2001), 277-301. Mike Davis, "Sunshine and the Open Shop: Ford and Darwin in 1920s Los Angeles," in *Metropolis in the Making*, 116.
27. "The Elementary School of the University of California at Los Angeles," Typescript, n.d., 1. CSPR.
28. "The Elementary School of the University of California at Los Angeles," 2.
29. "The Elementary School of the University of California at Los Angeles," 4.
30. Charles Waddell to Ernest Moore, May 18, 1926, Series 193, Box 2, Folder: Some Reports on the Work of UES During the First Few Years Under the University Regime, SCUCLA.
31. Ellen Lagemann, *An Elusive Science: The Troubling History of Education Research* (University of Chicago Press, 2000), 65-66.
32. Helen Heffernan, "Objective Measurement of Educational Progress in Country Schools," (MA thesis, University of California, December, 1924).
33. Heffernan, "Objective measurement," 2.
34. Heffernan, "Objective measurement," 62-63.
35. David Tyack, *The One Best System* (Harvard University Press, 1971).
36. Kathleen Weiler, "Women and Rural School Reform: California 1900-1940," *History of Education Quarterly* 34, no. 1 (Spring 1994): 25-47, and Kathleen Weiler, *Country Schoolwomen: Teaching in Rural California, 1850-1950* (Stanford University Press, 1998).
37. Virginia Scharff, *Taking the Wheel* (University of New Mexico Press, 1991).
38. Lee Richmond to Helen Heffernan, n. d., HHPR.

39. Ruth Morpeth, "Dynamic Leadership: Helen Heffernan and Progressive Education in California" (PhD diss. University of California Riverside, 1989), 37.
40. Heffernan, "Objective Measurement," 18.
41. "Praises Schools of Kings County," *Hanford Morning Journal* (June 30, 1926): 7.
42. Helen Heffernan, "Division of Rural Education," *California Biennial Report of the State Department of Education,* 1927–28 (Sacramento, 1928): 56; Richard Boone, *A History of Educational Organization in California* (San Jose, CA, 1926), 99.
43. "Rural Club at San Francisco State College," *WJE* 34, 7 (July 1929): 8.
44. Morpeth, "Dynamic Leadership," 96.
45. H. Wennerberg interview with Ruth Morpeth, 1988, cited in Morpeth, "Dynamic Leadership," 62.
46. Beulah Hartman, "California Rural Supervisors Hold Significant Convention at Lake Tahoe, October 4th to 8th," *California Exchange Bulletin in Rural Education* 1, no. 1 (November 1926): 33.
47. Mrs. O. Mae Willet, "Vitalizing the Teaching in Rural Schools by the Introduction of Projects," *California Exchange Bulletin in Rural Education* 1, no. 3 (March 1927): 33–40; Edna McRae, "The Possibilities of the One-Teacher School," *California Exchange Bulletin in Rural Education* 1, no. 4 (May 1927): 13–18; Ada York, "The Course of Study in Rural Schools," *California Exchange Bulletin in Rural Education* 1, no. 1 (November 1926): 45–46; Ada York, "Specific Points of Teacher Training for Rural Service," *California Exchange Bulletin in Rural Education* 2, no. 1 (October 1927): 8–9.
48. Helen Heffernan, "High Lights of Rural School Supervision," *WJE* 35, no. 10 (December 1929): 9.
49. Helen Heffernan, "Graduation—Chico—1919," Typescript, HHPR.
50. *Biennial report of the California State Department of Education 1931–32* (California State Printing Office, 1932), 85.
51. Heffernan, "High Lights in Rural School Supervision," 5.
52. Clara Coldwell, "Teaching the Children of Seasonal Workers," *California Exchange Bulletin in Rural Education* 1, no. 2 (January 1927): 59–62.
53. Lillian Hill, Report of the Bureau of Attendance and Migratory Schools. *Biennial Report of the California State Department of Education 1929–1930* (California State Printing Office, 1930), 159.
54. Iva Elleson, "Being a Teacher in a Migratory School," *WJE* 36, no. 3 (March 1930): 9.
55. Helen Heffernan. Editor's Note to "The Education of Migrant Children in Ventura County," *WJE* 35, no. 10 (December 1929): 8.
56. Alexandra Stern, *Eugenic Nation* (University of California Press, 2005), 92–99. Also, Ruben Donato, *The Other Struggle for Civil Rights* (SUNY Press, 1997); Martha Menchaca and Richard Valencia, "Anglo-Saxon Ideologies in the 1920s and 1930s: Their Impact on the Segregation of Mexican Students in California." *Anthropology and Education Quarterly* 21, (1990): 222–49; Gilbert Gonzalez, "Segregation of Mexican Children in a Southern California City: The Legacy of Expansionism and the American Southwest," *Western Historical Quarterly* 16, no. 1 (January 1985): 55–76; Carlos Blanton, "From Intellectual Deficiency to Cultural Deficiency: Mexican Americans, Testing,

and Public School Policy in the American Southwest, 1920–1940," *Pacific Historical Review* 72, no. 1 (2003): 39–62; Charles Wollenberg, *All Deliberate Speed*. (University of California Press, 1978).
57. Helen Heffernan, "Progressive Education and Mental Hygiene," *WJE* 36, no. 4 (April 1930): 3.
58. In 1928, Heffernan, along with well-known rural educators Fannie Dunn and Katherine Cook, was asked to prepare a volume on rural schools by the National Society for the Study of Education. This work was published in 1931 with the title *The Status of Rural Education*.
59. For a discussion of Carney's career, see Kathleen Weiler, "Mabel Carney at Teachers College: From Home Missionary to White Ally," *Teachers College Record* 107, no. 12 (2005): 2599–633.
60. National Education Association, *Addresses and Proceedings* (National Education Association, 1930), 10.
61. "Report of the Committee on Resolutions, Department of Rural Education," National Education Association, *Addresses and Proceedings* (National Education Association, 1931), 539–40.
62. Seeds, "U.E.S.: The History of the Creative Elementary School," 230.
63. California State Department of Education, *Teachers' Guide to Child Development* (California State Printing Office, 1930).
64. See the discussion of various progressive state bulletins from the 1930s in Hollis Caswell, "Administrative Considerations in Curriculum Development" in *Democracy and the Curriculum: Third Yearbook of the John Dewey Society*, ed. Harold Rugg (D. Appleton-Century Company, 1939).
65. *The Teachers' Guide to Child Development* [1930], xv, xvi.
66. *The Teachers' Guide to Child Development* [1930], 488.
67. *The Teachers' Guide to Child Development* [1930], 488–89.
68. Corinne Seeds, "Fellow Teachers." November 3, 1930, 3, CSPR.
69. Seeds, "Fellow Teachers," 1–2.
70. Seeds, "U.E.S.: The History of the Creative Elementary School," 230.
71. "News and Comments," *WJE* 36, no. 9 (November 1930): 10.
72. Mabel Carney, *Country Life and The Country School* (Row, Peterson and Company, 1912); Elsie Ridley Clapp, "A Rural Community School in Kentucky," *Progressive Education* 10, 3 (March, 1933). For a discussion of Clapp's career, see Sam Stack, *Elsie Ripley Clapp (1879–1965): Her Life and the Community School* (Peter Lang: 2004).

3 DARE THE SCHOOL BUILD A NEW SOCIAL ORDER?

1. David Tyack, Robert Lowe, and Elisabth Hansot, *Public Schools in Hard Times* (Harvard University Press, 1984).
2. George Counts, *Dare the School Build a New Social Order?* (John Day Co., 1932), 9.
3. Cited by Daniel Perlstein, "'Indoctrination': George Counts and the Civic Dilemmas of Democratic Educators," in *Reconstructing the Common Good in Education*, ed. Larry Cuban and Dorothy Shipps (Stanford University Press, 2000,), 57.
4. Helen Heffernan to Vierling Kersey, August 1, 1933, F3752:511, CSA.

5. Helen Heffernan, "Interpreting the School Program to the Public," *Proceedings of the 1932 Superintendents' Convention* (California State Printing Office, 1932), 123.
6. Helen Heffernan, "The Problem of Youth and Unemployment," 6, F3752:511, 1933–34, CSA.
7. "The State Department of Education: Its Organization and Functions," 19–20.
8. W. M. Culp, "Jottings of a Traveling Bookman," *WJE* 38, no. 9 (November 1932): 9. See also Irving Hendrick, "California's Response to the 'New Education' in the 1930s," *California Historical Quarterly* 53 (Spring 1974): 25–40.
9. Irving Hendrick, "The Impact of the Great Depression on Public School Support in California," *Southern California Quarterly* 54 (1972): 177–95.
10. "The Annual Convention, Mission Inn, Riverside, California," *WJE* 37, no. 8 (October 1931): 13–14.
11. Lillian Hill to Helen Heffernan, n.d., HHPR.
12. Hill to Heffernan.
13. Unsigned letters to Helen Heffernan, October 1933, HHPR.
14. Helen Heffernan, "A Statement of the Philosophy and the Purposes of the Elementary School," *CJEE* 1, no. 3 (February 1933): 109.
15. Corinne Seeds, "An Interpretation of the Integrated Program in the Elementary School," *CJEE* 3, no. 2 (November 1934): 89–98.
16. Laverna Lossing, "Creative Music," *CJEE* 3, no. 4 (May 1935): 207–12.
17. Elizabeth Bruene, "The Activity Procedure and the Fundamentals," *CJEE* 4, no. 2 (November 1935): 104–8. .
18. Corinne Seeds, "The School and Its Tasks," *CJEE* 5, no. 4 (May 1937): 198–210; Corinne Seeds, "Next Steps in the Preparation of Teachers," *CJEE* 7, no. 2 (November 1938): 119–28.
19. Corinne Seeds to Charles Waddell, May 31, 1933, Series 193, Box 2, SCUCLA.
20. Charles Waddell, "History of the University Elementary School," *Typescript, 1938, 1, Series 193, Box 2, SCUCLA.*
21. "Training Department, University of California at Los Angeles, 1933–1934," Series 193, Box 2, SCUCLA.
22. Charles Waddell, Corinne Seeds, and Natalie White, *Major Units in the Social Studies* (John Day Company, 1932).
23. Corinne Seeds, "Our Present Educational Point of View," in Waddell, Seeds, and White, *Major Units in the Social Studies*, 34–35.
24. Seeds, "Our Present Educational Point of View," 10–11.
25. Seeds, "Our Present Educational Point of View," 9.
26. Diana Anderson, "Teaching Physical Education at the University Elementary School" (Oral History Program, University of California Los Angeles, 1988), 4.
27. Corinne Seeds to Charles Waddell, May 31, 1933, Series 193, Box 2, SCUCLA.
28. Kevin Starr, *Endangered Dreams: The Great Depression in California* (Oxford University Press, 1996), 194
29. Carey McWilliams, *The Education of Carey McWilliams* (Simon and Schuster, 1978), 75.
30. Kevin Starr, *Endangered Dreams*, 199.

31. Michael Rogin and John Shover, *Political Change in California: Critical Elections and Social Movements* (Greenwood Publishing Co., 1970), 126.
32. John Dewey to Ernest Moore, November 2, 1943, Series 124, Box 7, SCUCLA.
33. Murray Lee and Dorris May Lee, "Keeping Informed," *CJEE* 3, no. 3 (February 1935): 242.
34. Paula Fass, "Without Design: Education Policy in the New Deal," *American Journal of Education* 91, no. 1 (November 1982): 42.
35. Helen Heffernan, "Health Problems in Rural Schools," *CJEE* 3, no. 3 (February 1935): 152.
36. Helen Heffernan, "The Problem of Youth and Unemployment: Report on Youth and Unemployment Conference, Washington, D.C. June 1–2, 1934," F3752:511, 1933–34, CSA.
37. Helen Heffernan, "The Problem of Youth and Unemployment," 2.
38. Helen Heffernan, "The Problem of Youth and Unemployment," 8.
39. Vierling Kersey to Helen Heffernan, June 29, 1934, F3752:511, 1933–34, CSA.
40. Vierling Kersey to County Superintendents of Schools, July 9, 1934, F3752:511, 1933–34, CSA.
41. Vierling Kersey to Helen Heffernan, August 24, 1934, F3752:511, 1933–34, CSA.
42. Vierling Kersey to Helen Heffernan, October 17, 1934, F3752:511, 1933–34, CSA.
43. "Conference on Curriculum and Guidance," *WJE* 42, no. 6 (July 1936): 7.
44. "Conference on Curriculum and Guidance," 7.
45. Paul Hanna, "Master Teachers and Modern Education," *CJEE* 4, no. 2 (November 1935): 97–103.
46. Hanna, "Master Teachers and Modern Education," 99.
47. Jared Stallones, *Paul Robert Hanna* (Hoover Institution Press, 2002), 35.
48. Seeds to Heffernan, n.d., from internal evidence late September or October, 1941, HH/CSR.
49. Paul Hanna, "The Problem of Social Education," in *Social Education*, ed. Stanford Education Conference (Macmillan, 1939), 14.
50. Helen Heffernan, "The Leadership of the Kindergarten Primary Group in the Field of American Education," n.d., n.p., HHPR.
51. "Suggested Course of Study in Reading and Literature for Elementary Schools," (California State Printing Office, 1935), v–vi.
52. Helen Heffernan to Ruth Edmands, October 13, 1938, F3752:1826, 1938–39, CSA.
53. Ruth Edmands, "The New Educational Order," *CJEE* 3, no. 3 (February 1935): 153–57.
54. Ruth Edmands to Helen Heffernan, May 13, 1939, F3752:1826, 1938–39, CSA.
55. See, for example, Corinne Seeds, "Democratic Thinking and Living in the Classroom," *Educational Method* 14, no. 2 (November 1934): 57.
56. Helen Heffernan to Vierling Kersey, July 24, 1933, F3752:511, 1933–34, CSA.
57. Helen Heffernan to Vierling Kersey, May 26, 1934. F3752:511, 1933–34, CSA.

58. Clayton Burrow, "Community Life in the Harbor," California Dept of Education Bulletin, No. 16 (California State Printing Office, 1935).
59. Christine K. Erikson, "'I Have Not Had One Fact Disproven': Elizabeth Dilling's Crusade against Communism in the 1930s," *Journal of American Studies* 36, no. 3 (2002): 473–89. Christine K. Erikson, "'We Want No Teachers Who Say There are Two Sides to Every Question: Conservative Women and Education in the 1930s," *History of Education Quarterly* 46, no. 4 (Winter 2006): 487–502.
60. Mrs. Arthur Heineman to Vierling Kersey, April 10, 1935, F3752:498, 1934–37, CSA.
61. Florence Irish to Grace Hudson, April 10, 1935, F3752:498, 1934–37, CSA.
62. Mrs. Arthur Heineman to Vierling Kersey, April 18, 1935. F3752:498, 1934–37. CSA.
63. Mrs. Heineman to Mr. Vierling Kersey. April 29, 1935, F3752:498, 1934–37. CSA.
64. M. L. Darsie to Charles Waddell, October 23, 1936, Series 193, Box 2, SCUCLA.
65. Corinne Seeds to Charles Waddell, October 28, 1936, Series 193, Box 2, SCUCLA.
66. Seeds to Heffernan, n.d., from internal evidence March 1942, HH/CSR.
67. Charles Waddell to Dean Darsie, October 29, 1936, Series 193, Box 2, SCUCLA.
68. Charles Waddell to Robert Sproul, July 24, 1937, Series 193, Box 2, SCUCLA.
69. Robert Sproul, "Memoranda," 1937, 253, RSPBL.
70. Robert Sproul, "Memoranda," 1937, 253, RSPBL.
71. Robert Sproul, "Memoranda," 1936, 208, RSPBL.
72. Robert Sproul, "Memoranda," 1936, 280, RSPBL.
73. "The Report of the Survey of the University Elementary School, University of Los Angeles" (UCLA, 1945), 6, Series 193, Box 2, SCUCLA.
74. "The Report of the Survey of the University Elementary School," 2.
75. Robert Sproul, "Memoranda," 1938, 246, RSPBL.
76. Robert Sproul, "Memoranda," 1938, 134–35, RSPBL.
77. Mrs. Heineman, Report on the Southern California Regional Conference Progressive Education Association Biltmore Hotel, April 25, 26, 27, 1937, F3752:545, CSA.
78. Lawrence Cremin, *The Transformation of the School* (Vintage Books, 1964), 201.
79. Helen Heffernan and Gladys Potter, "Chapter One: Point of View," in California State Curriculum Commission, *Teachers' Guide to Child Development in the Intermediate Grades* (California State Department of Education, 1936), 1.
80. Heffernan and Potter, "Point of View," 2.
81. "California School Supervisors Association," *CJEE* 5, no. 1 (August 1936): 4.
82. Helen Heffernan to Vierling Kersey, August 14, 1936, F3752:505, 1936–37, CSA.
83. James G. Force to Vierling Kersey, September 24, 1936, F3752:505, 1936–37. CSA.

84. Vierling Kersey to James G. Force, November 4, 1936, F3752:505. 1936–37. CSA.
85. Robert Sproul, "Memoranda," 1937, 174. RSPBL.
86. Helen Heffernan to Walter Dexter, February 9, 1937, F3752:557, CSA.
87. Helen Heffernan to Dr. Dexter. March 15, 1937, F3752: 470. CSA.
88. John Hockett, "Facing Realities in Elementary School Social Studies," *CJEE* 4, no. 3 (February 1937): 136–47; John Hockett "The Evaluation of the Elementary School Program," *CJEE* 6, no. 4 (May 1938): 210–17.
89. Beginning in 1934, the state began publishing a ten-volume *Science Guide for Elementary Schools*, written in cooperation with various state colleges. Helen Heffernan, "Science in the Professional Education of Teachers for the Elementary School," *CJEE* 6, no. 2 (November 1937): 100–104.
90. A state conference on the problem of "transients" was held in August 1933 with a meeting of the Federal Relief Commission the following day. Gladys Potter to Vierling Kersey, August 31, 1933, F3752:511, 1933–34, CSA.
91. Cited in Heffernan, "Report on Conference on Education of Children of Seasonal Workers, Fresno State College, December 9–10, 1938," *CJEE* 7, no. 3 (February 1939): 188.
92. Heffernan, "Report on the Conference on Education of Children of Seasonal Workers," 189.

4 Was Progressive Education Progressive?

1. Corinne Seeds. "An Interpretation of the Integrated Program in the Elementary School," *CJEE* 3, no. 2 (November 1934): 89.
2. Dolores Litsinger, "The Theory and Method of Social Studies Instruction at the University Elementary School U.C.L.A.," (EdD Diss., University of California Los Angeles, 1962), 56.
3. Benjamin Barber, *Strong Democracy: Participatory Politics for a New Age* (University of California Press,1984).
4. Corinne Seeds, "Democratic Thinking and Living in the Classroom," *Educational Method*, 14, no. 2 (November, 1934): 59.
5. Seeds, "An Interpretation of the Integrated Program," 96.
6. As cited in Ruth Cahan, "The Implementation of the John Dewey Philosophy in the University Elementary School, University of California at Los Angeles" (MA thesis, University of California, Los Angeles, June, 1958), 124–25.
7. John Dewey, "Progressive Education and the Science of Education," Address presented to the Progressive Education Association, March 8, 1928. Reprinted in *John Dewey: The Later Works, 1925–1953*, vol. 4: 1928, ed. Jo Ann Boydston (Southern Illinois University Press, 1981), 262.
8. John Dewey, "Progressive Education and the Science of Education," 266.
9. John Dewey, "How Much Freedom in New Schools?" in *John Dewey: The Later Works 1925–1953*, vol. 5: 1929–1930, ed. Jo Ann Boydston (Southern Illinois University Press, 1984), 319–25.
10. Dewey, "How Much Freedom in the New Schools?" 322.
11. Dewey, "How Much Freedom in the New Schools?" 324–25.
12. Robert Treacy, "Progressivism and Corinne Seeds" (PhD diss., University of California Los Angeles, 1971), 131.

13. Helen Heffernan, "The Leadership of the Kindergarten Primary Group in the Field of American Education," n.d., n.p., HHPR.
14. Helen Heffernan, "The Guiding Philosophy of the Unitary Type of Curriculum Organization," *WJE* 43, no. 1 (January 1937): 6.
15. Helen Heffernan, "The Guiding Philosophy," 6–7.
16. Helen Heffernan, "Creativity—The Step Beyond." Typescript, n.p., n.d., HHPR.
17. Corinne Seeds, *Childhood Expressions* (Stewart Publishing, 1937), 8.
18. Corinne Seeds, *Childhood Expressions*, 6.
19. Corinne Seeds, "Our Present Educational Point of View," in Waddell, Seeds, and White, *Major Units in the Social Studies*, 15–16.
20. Seeds, "An Interpretation of the Integrated Program," 98.
21. All subsequent references are from Corinne Seeds's notes to Education S131a and Education S131b, 1938, n.p., CSPR.
22. Dolores Litsinger, "The Theory and Method of Social Studies Instruction at the University Elementary School U.C.L.A. (EdD diss., University of California, Los Angeles, 1962), 18.
23. *Sequences of Activities, Fourth to Seventh Grades, inc. University Elementary School.* Series 208, Box 1, UAUCLA.
24. Seeds, "Our Present Educational Point of View," 18–20.
25. *Sequences of Activities.*
26. Corinne Seeds, "The Language Arts and Elementary School Activities," *Progressive Education*, 10, no.4 (April 1933): 204–9.
27. Seeds, "The Language Arts and Elementary School Activities," 204.
28. Corinne Seeds, "Democratic Thinking and Living in the Classroom," *Educational Method*, 14, no. 2 (November 1934): 57–63.
29. Treacy, "Progressivism and Corinne Seeds," 163.
30. See Valerie Walkerdine, *Schoolgirl Fictions* (Verso, 1990); Kevin Brehony, "From the Particular to the General, the Continuous to the Discontinuous: Progressive Education Revisited," *History of Education*, 30, no. 5 (2001): 429.
31. Michel Foucault, "The Means of Correct Training," in *The Foucault Reader*, ed. Paul Rabinow (Pantheon Books, 1988), 188.
32. Nikolas Rose, "Identity, Genealogy, History," in *Questions of Cultural Identity*, ed. Stuart Hall and Paul DuGay (Sage Publications, 1996), 134.
33. Thomas Popkewitz, "A Changing Terrain of Knowledge and Power: A Social Epistemology of Educational Research," *Educational Researcher* 26, no. 9 (December 1997): 27.
34. Walkerdine, *Schoolgirl Fictions*, 19.
35. Walkerdine, *Schoolgirl Fictions*, 20.
36. Marianne Bloch, Kertin Holmlund, Ingeborg Moquist, and Tom Popkewitz, "Global and Local Patterns of Governing the Child, Family, Their Care, and Education," in *Governing Children, Families and Education: Restructuring the Welfare State,* ed. M. Bloch, K. Holmlund, I. Moquist, and T. Popkewitz (Palgrave Macmillan, 2003), 6.
37. Arthur Zilversmit, *Changing Schools: Progressive Education Theory and Practice 1930–1960* (University of Chicago Press, 1993).
38. Corinne Seeds's notes to Education S131a and Education S131b, 1938, n.p., CSPR.

39. Heffernan and Potter, "Point of View," in California State Curriculum Commission, *Teachers' Guide to Child Development for the Intermediate Grades* (California State Department of Education, 1936),18.
40. Corinne Seeds, "The School and Its Task," *CJEE*, 5, no. 4 (May 1937): 202–3.
41. Corinne Seeds, "Guide to Recording Attitude Development," Unpublished typescript, n.d. [internal evidence suggests late 1930s], CSPR.
42. Seeds, "The School and Its Task," *CJEE*, 5, no. 4 (May 1937): 204.
43. Seeds, "The School and Its Task," *CJEE*, 5, no. 4 (May 1937): 206.
44. Seeds, "The School and its Task," *CJEE*, 5, no. 4 (May 1937): 207.
45. Gary Gerstle, "The Protean Character of American Liberalism," *American Historical Review*, 99, no. 4 (October 1994): 1046.
46. Thomas Popkewitz, "Inventing the Modern Self and John Dewey: Modernities and the Traveling of Pragmatism in Education—An Introduction," in *Inventing the Modern Self and John Dewey*, ed. Thomas Popkewitz (Palgrave Macmillan, 2005), 4.
47. See Charles Waddell, "The Pragmatic Value of the Army Alpha Scores for Success in Practice Teaching," *Educational Administration and Supervision* (December 1927): 577–92.
48. "Division of Rural and Elementary Education," State of California, *Biennial Report of the Department of Education 1931–32* (Sacramento: State Printing Office, 1932), 84.
49. Helen Heffernan, "The Guiding Philosophy of the Unitary Type of Curriculum Organization," *WJE* 43, no. 1 (January 1937): 6.
50. Heffernan, "The Reconstruction of the Elementary School Program," Unpublished manuscript, 18, HHPR.
51. Heffernan, "The Reconstruction of the Elementary School Program," 122.
52. Heffernan and Potter, "Point of View,"11–12.
53. Helen Heffernan, "The Principal's Responsibility in Guidance," in *Guidance in the Elementary School* [California Elementary School Principals Association Tenth Yearbook)] (California State Printing Office, 1938), 3.
54. Helen Heffernan, "What California Parents Think of the Report Card," *CJEE* 1, no. 1 (November 1932): 82.
55. Helen Heffernan, "Supervision Appropriate for Progressive Schools," *CJEE* 6, no. 1 (August 1937): 233.
56. Helen Heffernan, "Classification and Promotion Policies in Some City School Systems," *CJEE* 5, no. 4 (May 1936): 228.
57. Lawrence Chenoweth, Helen Heffernan, and William Paden, "Interpreting the School to the People," *CJEE* 2, no. 3 (February 1934): 113–14.
58. Kathleen Weiler, "The Genealogy of Gender in the History of Progressive Education in the United States," *Paedagogica Historica* 42, nos. 1&2 (February 2006): 161–76.
59. Corinne Seeds, "Follow Teachers," Unpublished manuscript, 15. CSPR.
60. Corinne Seeds, "What Learning Experiences Are Likely to Prove Developmental During Later Childhood," *CJEE* 10, no. 5 (August 1941): 43.
61. Corinne Seeds, "Rhythmic Expression: An Outgrowth of Learning," *Progressive Education* 11, no. 11 (November 1934): 405.
62. May V. Seagoe, "Follow-Up of University Elementary School Graduates Pilot Project," October 1957, Case 949692143-16, Unpublished manuscript, Box 2, CSDP.

63. Seeds, "What Learning Experiences Are Likely to Prove Developmental During Later Childhood," 51.
64. Helen Heffernan, "Supervision Appropriate for Progressive Schools," *CJEE* 6, no. 1 (August 1937): 21.
65. For a perceptive analysis of the middle class bias of progressive educators, particularly Dewey, see Aaron Schultz, *Social Class, Social Action, and Education* (Palgrave MacMillan, 2010).
66. "Judging from the "Write-Up" What Grade Did Each of These Students Make?" Series 192, Box 2, SCUCLA.
67. See Lisa Delpit, *Other People's Children* (The New Press, 2006).
68. Heffernan and Potter, "Point of View," 4.
69. Heffernan and Potter, "Point of View," 5.
70. Helen Heffernan, Irmagarde Richards, and Alice Salisbury, *Desert Treasure* (Hart Wagner Publishing Company, 1939).
71. Corinne Seeds, *Childhood Expressions*, 63.
72. Helen Heffernan, "Review of Corinne A. Seeds, *Childhood Expressions*," *California Schools* 8, no. 2 (February 1937): 68.
73. *Sequences of Activities.*
74. Corinne Seeds, "Children's Interest in Rhythm in the Elementary School," Typescript, 1, CSPR.
75. Seeds, "Children's Interest in Rhythm in the Elementary School," 7. Henry's story is also presented in Corinne Seeds, "Children's Interests in Rhythmic Bodily Expression," in *Children's Interests Elementary School Level* [California Elementary School Principals' Association Twelfth Yearbook] (California State Printing Office, 1940), 122–27.
76. Corinne Seeds and Lorraine Sherer, "Some Philosophical Considerations Which Are Basic to Curriculum Building," Typescript, 2, CSPR.
77. Seeds and Sherer, "Some Philosophical Considerations," 7.
78. Seeds and Sherer, "Some Philosophical Considerations," 8.
79. Corinne Seeds and Sherer, "Some Philosophical Considerations," 9.

5 Love and War

1. By the late 1930s, political power in California had shifted dramatically. In 1930, 78 percent of registered voters in the state were Republicans. By 1938, registered Democrats outnumbered Republicans. Michael Rogin and John Shover, *Political Change in California: Critical Elections and Social Movements* (Greenwood Publishing Co., 1970), 119.
2. See Carey McWilliams, *The Education of Carey McWilliams* (Simon and Schuster, 1978).
3. Elizabeth Eudey cited in Dorothy Healey and Maurice Isserman, *California Red: A Life in the American Communist Party* (University of Illinois Press, 1993), 69.
4. "Joint Institute, Humboldt and Mendocino Counties," *WJE* 44, no. 7 (October 1938): 7.
5. Corinne Seeds and Lorraine Sherer, "Some Philosophical Considerations Which Are Basic to Curriculum Building," Typescript, 2, CSPR.
6. Corinne Seeds's notes to Education S131a and Education S131b, 1938, n.p., CSPR.

7. "The Little Red School House is Gone," KMPC, May 10, 1939, Typescript, 7, CSPR.
8. "The Little Red School House is Gone," 2, 4.
9. "Meeting of Bay Section Elementary Principals," *WJE* 45, no. 8 (November 1939): 8–9.
10. "An Outstanding Yearbook Presented," *WJE* 46, no. 3 (March 1940): 5.
11. "California State Department Represented at Oregon Conference," *WJE* 45, no. 5 (May 1939): 5.
12. Helen Heffernan, Irmagarde Richards, and Alice Salisbury, *Desert Treasure* (Hart Wagner Publishing Company, 1939).
13. School Notes, *WJE*, 45, no. 4 (April 1939): 5.
14. Aubrey Douglass, "Preliminary Report of Committee on Scope and Sequence of Major Learnings in the Curriculum," *CJEE*, 4, no. 4 (May 1937): 199.
15. "Annual Conference California School Supervisors," *WJE* 44, no. 7 (October 1938): 6.
16. "Air-Minded California Educators Attend Idaho Institutes," *WJE* 45, no. 8 (August 1939): 7.
17. "Gladys L. Potter Appointed Primary Supervisor at Long Beach," *WJE* 45, no. 9 (September 1939): 4.
18. "California's Rural Schools," *WJE* 44, no. 2 (February 1938): 1.
19. Seeds's personal papers passed to Heffernan at Seeds's death and are held along with the Heffernan papers at the University of California, Riverside. But Heffernan's letters to Seeds are not in the collection. There is no way to know whether Seeds destroyed Heffernan's letters to her or whether someone else removed them.
20. Trisha Franzen, *Spinsters and Lesbians: Independent Womanhood in the United States* (NewYork University Press, 1996), 129–30.
21. Estelle Freedman, "'The Burning of Letters Continues': Elusive Identities and the Historical Construction of Sexuality," *Journal of Women's History* 9, no. 4 (Winter 1998): 181–206.
22. Amanda Gilroy and W. M. Verhoeven, "Introduction," in *Epistolary Histories: Letters, Fiction, Culture*, ed. Amanda Gilroy and W. M. Verhoeven (University of Virginia Press, 2000), 1.
23. Rosemarie Bodenheimer, *The Real Life of Mary Ann Evans* (Cornell University Press, 1994), 17.
24. Seeds to Heffernan, October 12, 1939, HH/CSR.
25. Seeds to Heffernan, January 5, 1941, HH/CSR.
26. Seeds to Heffernan, n.d. [From internal evidence early winter, 1942], HH/CSR.
27. Seeds to Heffernan, n.d. [From internal evidence November, 1942], HH/CSR.
28. Seeds to Heffernan. n.d. [From internal evidence April 1941], HH/CSR.
29. Biographical Sketch of Lydia Sicher, Alfred Adler Institute of San Francisco, http://ourworld.compuserve.com/homepages/hstein/sic-bio.htm (accessed March 20, 2009).
30. Lillian Faderman, *Odd Girls and Twilight Lovers: A History of Lesbian Life in Twentieth Century America* (Penguin, 1992), 57; see also Donna Penn, "The Sexualized Woman: The Lesbian, the Prostitute, and the Containment of Female Sexuality in Postwar America," in *Not June Cleaver: Women and*

Gender in Postwar America, 1945–1960, ed. Joanne Meyerowitz (Temple University Press, 1994), 358–81.
31. Nancy Sahli, "Smashing: Women's Relationships before the Fall," *Chrysalis* 8 (1979): 17–27.
32. Franzen, *Spinsters and Lesbians,* 123.
33. John D'Emilio, *Sexual Politics, Sexual Communities* (University of Chicago Press, 1998), 95. See also Leila Rupp, "Imagine My Surprise," in *Hidden from History: Reclaiming the Gay and Lesbian Past,* ed. Martin Duberman, Martha Vicinus, and George Chauncy (Penguin Books, 1991); Elizabeth Lapovsky Kennedy, "'But We Would Never Talk About It': The Structures of Lesbian Discretion in South Dakota, 1928–1933," in *Inventing Lesbian Cultures in America,* ed. Ellen Lewin (Beacon Press, 1996), 15–39.
34. Rupp, "Imagine My Surprise," 407.
35. Seeds to Heffernan, July 4, 1942, HH/CSR.
36. Kennedy, "'But We Would Never Talk About It,'" 17.
37. United States Civil Service Commission, "Record Search Information: Helen Heffernan." 1.23.61.3437.
38. Seeds to Heffernan, n.d. [from internal evidence Spring, 1943], HH/CSR.
39. Seeds to Heffernan, n.d. [from internal evidence 1942], HH/CSR.
40. Franzen, *Spinsters and Lesbians,* 129–130.
41. Seeds to Heffernan, April 14, 1941, HH/CSR.
42. Gretchen Wulfing to Helen Heffernan, December 31, 1940, HHPR.
43. Faderman, *Odd Girls and Twilight Lovers,* 1991, 181.
44. Seeds to Heffernan, n.d. [from internal evidence November, 1942], HH/CSR.
45. Seeds to Heffernan, n.d. [from internal evidence 1944], HH/CSR.
46. Seeds to Heffernan, n.d. [from internal evidence 1942], HH/CSR.
47. Corinne Seeds, "Guiding Teachers in the Construction of Curriculum Units," Typescript, speech presented before the California Elementary School Principals' Association, March, 1940, n.d., 1, CSP.
48. Helen Heffernan, "How Can We Make a Rural School Democratic for Children, Teachers, and Parents?" *CJEE* 8, no. 4 (May 1940): 211–16. Helen Heffernan, "New Emphases in Primary Curriculum," *CJEE* 7, no. 5 (August 1939): 15–20.
49. Edwin Lee, "Woman's Education as a Man Sees It," Typescript, speech before the Emanu-El Sisterhood, Page and Laguna Streets, May 25, 1934, Series 918, Box 12, SCUCLA.
50. Seeds to Heffernan, n.d. [from internal evidence January, 1943], HH/CSR.
51. Seeds to Heffernan, July 11, 1943, HH/CSR.
52. Vierling Kersey, superintendent, to Mr. Fred M. Good, Board of Education City of Los Angeles June 1, 1939, CU-5.1, Box 41, Folder 25: University Elementary School, BL.
53. Seeds to Heffernan, n.d. [from internal evidence April 1942], HH/CSR.
54. Seeds to Heffernan, n.d. [from internal evidence, 1942], HH/CSR.
55. Seeds to Heffernan, n.d. [from internal evidence Spring, 1943], HH/CSR.
56. Report of the Dean of the School of Education to President Sproul, June 26, 1940. Reports for the president of the University of California from Academic Departments of Los Angeles 1930–1942, CU-5.1, Box 5, Folder 30, BL.
57. Constance Helene Torre to Board of Regents, University of California, May 31, 1940, Series 596, Box 1, SCUCLA.

58. Robert Sproul to Helen Heffernan, June 6, 1940, 1940, CU5.2, Box 480, Education and Training School Documents, BL.
59. Jessie Bond to Deming Malaise, Business Manager, UCLA, June 30, 1941, CU-5.1, Box 41 Folder 25, BL.
60. Ernest Horn to Edwin Lee, July 12, 1940, Series 617, Box 1, File, Dean—School of Education, UAUCLA.
61. Ruth Hockett to Helen Heffernan. January 29, 1941, HHPR.
62. Corinne Seeds to Helen Heffernan, January 5, 1941, HH/CSR.
63. Dean Lee to President Sproul. August 16, 1941. Series 359, Box 109, Teacher Training (1941), UAUCLA.
64. LEE, DEAN EDWIN A., Los Angeles Sept 15, 1941, Robert Sproul "Memoranda," 1941, 265, RSPBL.
65. J. H. Corley to Robert Sproul, March 24, 1942; Vierling Kersey to James Corley, April 1, 1942; Edwin Lee to Robert Sproul, April 20, 1942, CU-5.2, Box 480, Education and Training School Documents, 1942, BL.
66. Madeleine Veverka to Helen Heffernan, October 18, 1941, HHPR.
67. Helen Heffernan to Madeleine Veverka, October 23, 1941, HHPR.
68. April 8, 1942, School of Education. "Report of the Committee on the University Elementary School, University of California at Los Angeles," Typescript, Series 596, Box 1, Folder 3, UAUCLA.
69. "School Supervisors' State Conference," *WJE* 47, no. 11 (November 1941): 8.
70. Joint letter to Sproul, Lee, Bond, Seeds, Dexter, and Heffernan, August 5, 1941, Series 359, Box 109, Teacher Training (1941), UAUCLA.
71. Seeds to Heffernan, n.d. [from internal evidence Summer 1943], HH/CSR.
72. California Board of Education, *Biennial Report*, 1943–44, 8. F3752:580, CSA.
73. Seeds to Heffernan, n.d. [from internal evidence May 1942], HH/CSR.
74. See letters from Louise Fairman and Eloise Mays to Helen Heffernan from 1941, and from Hester Roberts South to Helen Heffernan, apparently from 1944, HHPR.
75. Seeds to Heffernan, December 7, 1940, HH/CSR.
76. Seeds to Heffernan, n.d. [from internal evidence 1942], HH/CSR.
77. Seeds to Heffernan, n.d. [from internal evidence April 1942], HH/CSR.
78. Seeds to Heffernan, n.d. [from internal evidence Spring 1942], HH/CSR.
79. Gretchen Wulfing, "Enriching the Rural School Curriculum," *CJEE* 3, no.1 (August 1934): 34–40. Gretchen Wulfing, "Maturation as a Factor in Learning," *CJEE* 4, no. 2 (November 1935): 72–84. Gretchen Wulfing, "The Implications of the Major Educational Principles for Supervision and the Direction of Instruction," *CJEE* 8, no. 2 (February,1940): 151–58.
80. Helen Heffernan, Wilhelmina Harper, and Gretchen Wulfing, *All Aboard for Storyland* (Benj. H. Sanbord and Co, 1941).
81. See the series of letters from Gretchen Wulfing to Helen Heffernan from the early 1940s, HHPR.
82. Gretchen Wulfing to Miss Helen Heffernan c/o Miss Corinne Seeds, 1416 Holmby Avenue, Los Angeles, December 31, 1940, HHPR.
83. Seeds to Heffernan, August 4, 1941, HH/CSR.
84. Seeds to Heffernan, n.d. [from internal evidence 1944], HH/CSR.
85. "State School Supervisors' Conference at Pasadena October 2–5," *WJE* 46, no. 10 (October 1940): 8.

86. Vierling Kersey to Miss Heffernan, November 27, 1933, F3752: 511, Folder: 1933-34, CSA.
87. Cited in Jared Stallones, *Paul Robert Hanna* (Hoover Institution Press, 2002), 43.
88. "Comments on the Treatment of Government and Its Administration in the Rugg Social Science Series," 2, F3752: 511, Folder: 1933-34, CSA.
89. For a narrative of the Rugg controversy, see Jonathan Zimmerman, *Whose America? Culture Wars in the Public Schools* (Harvard University Press, 2002).
90. "Charges against Current Events Magazines Retracted," *California Schools* 10, no. 9 (November 1940): 315.
91. For a detailed discussion of the committee's work, see Stuart Foster, *Red Alert!* (Peter Lang, 2000).
92. As cited by Stuart Foster, *Red Alert!* (Peter Lang, 2000), 32.
93. Helen Heffernan, "Poll on Youth and Education," *CJEE* 9, no. 4 (May 1941): 197.
94. Edward Barrett, *The Tenney Committee* (Cornell University Press, 1951). See also Jack B. Tenney, "California Legislator," UCLA Oral History Project, 1969.
95. M. J. Heale, "Red Scare Politics: California's Campaign against Un-American Activities, 1940-1970," *Journal of American Studies* 20, no. 1 (1986): 5-32.
96. October 14, 1941. "Resolution," Read at the October 14, 1941, Meeting of the California School Supervisors' Association, Typescript, HHPR.
97. "Resolution," HHPR.
98. Helen Heffernan, "Shall the Modern Educator Recant? The Darkness beyond Tomorrow." Typescript, n.d., n.p., HHPR.
99. Corinne Seeds, "Are We Meeting the Challenge of the Times?" in *Guiding Children in Democratic Living* [California Elementary School Principals' Association Fourteenth Yearbook] (California State Printing Office, 1942), 18.
100. Marilyn Johnson, *The Second Gold Rush: Oakland and the East Bay in World War II* (University of California Press, 1993); "Fortress California at War: San Francisco, Los Angeles, Oakland, and San Diego." Special issue of *Pacific Historical Review*, ed. Roger Lotchin, 63, no. 3 (August, 1994); Arthur Verge, *Paradise Transformed: Los Angeles during the Second World War* (University of Iowa Press, 1993); Roger Lotchin, ed., *The Way We Really Were: The Golden State in the Second World War* (University of Illinois Press, 2000).
101. Seeds to Heffernan, n.d., [from internal evidence November, 1942], HH/CSR.
102. "Education and the War," *Sierra Educational News* 42, no. 1 (January 1943): 11.
103. Corinne Seeds, "Are We Meeting the Challenge of the Times?" Typescript, n.d., 1, CSPR.
104. Seeds, "Are We Meeting the Challenge of the Times?" 13.
105. Heffernan, "Shall the Modern Educator Recant? The Darkness beyond Tomorrow."

6 Prejudice

1. Gary Gerstle, "The Protean Character of American Liberalism," *American Historical Review* 99, no. 4 (October 1994): 1070.
2. O. L. Davis, "Rachel Davis DuBois: Intercultural Education Pioneer," in *Bending the Future to Their Will*, ed. Margaret Crocco and O. L. Davis

(Rowman and Littlefield, 1999); Nicholas Montalto, *A History of the Intercultural Educational Movement 1924–1941* (Garland Press, 1982); Abraham Citron, Collin Reynolds, and Sarah Taylor, "Ten Years of Intercultural Education in Educational Magazines," *Harvard Educational Review*, 15, no. 2 (March 1945): 129–33; Shafali Lal, "Securing the Children: Social Science, Children, and the Meaning of Race 1939–1968" (PhD diss., Yale University, 2002).

3. Cited in Ronald Goodenough, "Racial and Ethnic Tolerance in John Dewey's Educational and Social Thought: The Depression Years," *Educational Theory* 27, no. 1 (Winter 1977): 53.
4. As cited in Mary Dudziak, *Cold War Civil Rights* (Princeton University Press, 2000), 8–9.
5. Cited in David Kennedy, *Freedom from Fear* (Oxford University Press, 1999), 760.
6. There is of course an extensive literature on the Japanese internment. For the education of Japanese American children in the camps, see Thomas James, *Exile Within* (Harvard University Press, 1987).
7. Arthur Verge, "The Impact of the Second World War on Los Angeles," *Pacific Historical Review* 63, no. 3 (August 1994): 295.
8. Lothrop Stoddard, *The Rising Tide of Color against White World-Supremacy* (Scribners and Son, 1927); V. S. McClatchy, ed., *Four Anti-Japanese Pamphlets* (Arno Press, 1978).
9. Corinne Seeds. "Are We Meeting the Challenge of the Times?" in *Guiding Children in Democratic Living* [California Elementary School Principals' Association, Fourteenth Yearbook] (California State Printing Office, 1942), 18.
10. Corinne Seeds to Helen Heffernan, April 1, 1942. F3752:1841, General Correspondence, J-L. CSA.
11. Corinne Seeds, "U.E.S.: The History of the Creative Elementary School"(Oral History Project, University of California Los Angeles, 1963), 131.
12. "Santa Anita Center Officials Defended," *Los Angeles Times*, May 31, 1942, p. 16.
13. Seeds, "U.E.S.: The History of the Creative Elementary School," 134.
14. Sproul, "Memoranda," 1942, 225, RSPBL.
15. Walter K. Mitchell to the Board of Regents, University of California, June 4, 1942, Box 136, File: Teacher Training, COUCLA.
16. Robert Sproul to Walter K. Mitchell, June 22, 1942, Box 136, File: Teacher Training, COUCLA.
17. Sproul, "Memoranda," 1942, 251, RSPBL.
18. Richard Valencia, "The Mexican American Struggle for Equal Educational Opportunity in Mendez v. Westminster," *Teachers College Record* 107, no. 3 (March 2005): 402.
19. Sproul, "Memoranda," 1942, 266, RSPBL.
20. March 22, 1940. "Committee [not identified] to President Sproul," CU5-Series 2, 480, Training School, BL.
21. Sproul, "Memoranda," 1942, 266, RSPBL.
22. Seeds, "U.E.S.: The History of the Creative Elementary School," 138.
23. Seeds to Heffernan, n.d. [From internal evidence June, 1942], HH/CSR.
24. "InterAmerican Demonstration Project," *California Schools* 13, no. 2 (February 1942): 29–30.

25. Bureau of Elementary Education, "Our American Neighbors," F3752:1831, CSA.
26. "Conference on Inter-American Education," *WJE* 48, no. 4 (April 1942): 11–13.
27. Seeds to Heffernan, October 31, 1941, HH/CSR.
28. Helen Heffernan, "Education for Inter-American Friendship," in *Guiding Children in Democratic Living* [California Elementary School Principals' Association Fourteenth Yearbook] (California State Printing Office, 1942), 112–16; Helen Heffernan, "Inter-American Education in the War Effort," *CJEE*, 11, no. 6 (August 1942): 13–21.
29. "Teacher Reveals Need for Training in 3 R's," *Los Angeles Examiner*, n.d., clipping in HHPR.
30. Seeds to Heffernan, October 13, 1942, HH/CSR.
31. Seeds to Heffernan, n.d. [From internal evidence, Fall, 1942], HH/CSR.
32. Seeds to Heffernan, n.d. [From internal evidence Spring, 1943], HH/CSR.
33. Seeds to Heffernan, n.d. [From internal evidence January, 1943], HH/CRR.
34. Arthur Verge, "The Impact of the Second World War on Los Angeles," *Pacific Historical Review* 63, 3 (August 1994): 302.
35. "Tentative Report of the Committee Appointed November 11, 1942 to Sub-Committee on Children in Wartime of Committee on Health, Welfare and Consumer Interests of Office of Civilian Defense," F3752:580, 1943–44, CSA.
36. "California's Program for the Care of Children of Working Mothers," Mimeograph, n.d., F3752: 551, Child Care Centers, CSA.
37. "Standards for Child Care Centers," March 20, 1943, F3752: 551, Child Care Centers, CSA.
38. Helen Heffernan, "The Children of Women Workers in Wartime," *WJE* 49, no. 1 (January 1943): 9.
39. "California's Program for the Care of Children of Working Mothers," Mimeograph, n.d., F3752: 551, Child Care Centers, CSA.
40. W. Norton Grubb and Marvin Lazerson, "Child Care, Government Financing, and the Public Schools: Lessons for the California Children's Centers," *School Review* 86, no. 1 (November, 1977): 12–13; Charles Dorn, *American Education, Democracy, and the Second World War* (Palgrave Macmillan, 2007). For the broader debate about child care policy in the United States, see Sonya Michel, *Children's Interests/Mother's Rights: The Shaping of America's Child Care Policy* (Yale University Press, 1999); Barbara Beatty, *Preschool Education in America: the Culture of Young Children from the Colonial Era to the Present* (Yale University Press, 1995); Elizabeth Rose, *A Mother's Job: The History of Day Care, 1890–1960* (Oxford University Press, 1999).
41. Helen Heffernan, "Foreword," *The Elementary School Faces the Problems of Migration* [California Elementary School Principals' Association Fifteenth Yearbook] (California State Printing Office, 1943), iv. In her chapter in the 1943 yearbook, Heffernan argued for increased federal aid to education. Helen Heffernan, "Population Migrations and Federal Aid for Education," in *The Elementary School Faces the Problems of Migration*, 26–28.
42. Corinne Seeds to Helen Heffernan, n.d., HH/CSR.

43. Helen Heffernan to Walter Dexter, May 21, 1943, F3752:580, 1943–44, CSA.
44. "Elementary Education—Wartime Child Care Program," 1944 Report from the Division of Elementary Education, F3752:580, 1943–44, CSA.
45. Seeds to Heffernan, December 25, 1942, HH/CSR.
46. "Statement of John Harold Swan," *Senate Daily Journal*, March 17, 1943, 581, California Legislature, Fifty-fifth Session.
47. "Senator Criticizes Education System," *Los Angeles Times*, March 18, 1941, 8.
48. "Statement of John Harold Swan," 581.
49. Helen Heffernan, "What Practices Are Defensible in Education in Time of Crisis?" *The National Elementary Principal* (April 1941), 152–53.
50. Heffernan, "What Practices Are Defensible in Education in Time of Crisis?" 155.
51. In a February letter to Heffernan, Corinne Seeds mentioned her own efforts to mobilize support against Swan's bill. Seeds to Heffernan, n.d. [From internal evidence February, 1943], HH/CSR.
52. Harry Lintz to John Harold Swan, with copies to Helen Heffernan and Walter Dexter, March 25, 1943, F3752:567, CSA.
53. Helen Heffernan to Dr. A. R. Lang, September 29, 1943, F3752:26, State Curriculum Commission 1942–43, CSA.
54. "Report of the Senate Committee to Investigate the Establishment of Nursery Schools and Child Care Centers," *Senate Daily Journal* (April 20, 1943), 2001; California Legislature, Fifty-fifth Session; California State Department of Education, "Report of Child Care Centers Administered and Operated by California School Districts. A Three Year Report March 1946 to March 1949," F3640:1140, Education-Child Care and Day Nurseries, CSA.
55. Helen Heffernan, "Pioneering in Child-Care Services," *CJEE* 12, no. 1 (1944): 169.
56. By 1950, California was one of only three states along with the District of Columbia that continued to support child care centers. See Ellen Reese, "Maternalism and Political Mobilization: How California's Postwar Child Care Campaign Was Won," *Gender and Society* 10, no. 5 (October 1996): 566–89; Emily Stolzfus, *Citizen, Mother, Worker: Debating Public Responsibility for Child Care after the Second World War* (University of North Carolina Press, 2003).
57. Helen Heffernan, "A Heritage of Freedom," *WJE* 48, no. 9 (October 1942): 6–7.
58. "Series of Teachers Manuals and Resource Units on Race and Culture Problems in American Education," *California Schools* 13, no. 12 (December 1942): 274.
59. Helen Heffernan, "Education for Inter-American Friendship," in *Guiding Children in Democratic Living* [California Elementary School Principals' Association Fourteenth Yearbook] (California State Printing Office, 1942), 114.
60. Heffernan, "Education for Inter-American Friendship," 114.
61. Carey McWilliams, *Brothers under the Skin* (Little, Brown and Co., 1943), 5.
62. Eduardo Obregon Pagon, *Murder at the Sleepy Lagoon: Zoot Suits, Race, and Riot in Wartime L.A* (University of North Carolina Press, 2003).

63. Cited in Rob Wagner, *Red Ink White Lies: The Rise and Fall of Los Angeles Newspapers 1920–1967* (Dragonfly Press, 2000), 177.
64. Kevin Leonard, " 'Brothers under the Skin?' African Americans, Mexican Americans, and World War II in California," in *The Way We Really Were: The Golden State in the Second World War*, ed. Roger Lotchin (University of Illinois Press, 2000), 200.
65. Lucy Wilcox Adams, "Education in the Relocation Centers," *CJEE* 17, no. 8 (December 1942): 477–79. See also Wanda Robertson, "Developing World Citizens in a Japanese Relocation Center," *Childhood Education* (October 1943): 66–71.
66. James, *Exile Within*, 71.
67. Helen Heffernan, "What Practices Are Defensible in Education in Time of Crisis?" *The National Elementary Principal* (April, 1941), 152.
68. Seeds to Heffernan, n.d. [From internal evidence summer, 1943], HH/CSR. For a fascinating discussion of the informal education at Manzanar, see Eileen Tamura, "Value Messages Collide with Reality: Joseph Kurihara and the Power of Informal Education," *History of Education Quarterly* 50, no.1 (January 2010): 1–33.
69. Helen Heffernan to Genevieve Carter, October 11, 1943, F3752:1847, Japanese Children, CSA.
70. Genevieve Carter to Helen Heffernan, October 19, 1943, F3752:1847, Japanese Children, CSA.
71. Fred Trott, "Education in the Postwar World—Supervisors Conference," *WJE* 49, no. 9 (November 1943): 9.
72. Helen Heffernan to Genevieve Carter, November 23, 1943, F3752:1847, Japanese Children, CSA.
73. Helen Heffernan to Genevieve Carter, November 23, 1943, F3752:1847, Japanese Children, CSA.
74. Cited in Carey McWilliams, *The Education of Carey McWilliams* (Simon and Schuster, 1978), 114.
75. Carey McWillliams, *Prejudice: Japanese Americans: Symbol of Racial Intolerance* (Little Brown, 1945), 11.
76. "Elementary Education," 1944, F3752:580, 1943–44. CSA.
77. Helen Heffernan, "Progress in Elementary Education during the Next Decade," *WJE* 50, no. 4 (April 1944): 7–9.
78. Seeds to Heffernan, n.d. [From internal evidence 1944], HH/CSR.
79. Seeds to Heffernan, August 13, 1942, HH/CSR.
80. Seeds to Heffernan, n.d. [From internal evidence January, 1943], HH/CSR.
81. Seeds to Heffernan, n.d. [From internal evidence May, 1942], HH/CSR.
82. Seeds to Heffernan, April 22, 1945, HH/CSR.
83. Seeds to Heffernan, n.d. [From internal evidence Spring, 1942], HH/CSR.
84. *Education for Cultural Unity* [California Elementary School Principals' Association, Seventeenth Yearbook] (California State Printing Office, 1945).
85. Afton Dill Nance, "Remarks at CASCD Scholarship Luncheon," San Diego, November 18, 1969, HHPR. See also the collection of over 200 letters written to Nance from incarcerated Japanese American children during the internment. Afton Dill Nance papers, 1942–1981. Japanese American National Museum, Los Angeles.
86. Afton Nance, "Return of the Nisei," in *Education for Cultural Unity*, 65.

87. Nance, "Return of the Nisei," 66.
88. Helen Heffernan and Corinne Seeds, "Intercultural Education in the Elementary School," in *Education for Intercultural Unity*, 76–85.
89. Heffernan and Seeds, "Intercultural Education in the Elementary School," 76.
90. Heffernan and Seeds, "Intercultural Education in the Elementary School," 77.
91. Heffernan and Seeds, "Intercultural Education in the Elementary School," 78.
92. For a discussion of liberal children's books of this period, see Julia Mickenberg, *Learning from the Left* (Oxford University Press, 2006).
93. Heffernan and Seeds, "Intercultural Education in the Elementary School," 79.
94. Heffernan and Seeds, "Intercultural Education in the Elementary School," 84.
95. Heffernan and Seeds, "Intercultural Education in the Elementary School," 85.
96. McWilliams, *The Education of Carey McWilliams*, 115.

7 The Battle of Westwood Hills

1. A summary of the conflict over the UES appears in Geraldine Clifford and James W. Guthrie, eds., *School: A Brief for Professional Education* (University of Chicago Press, 1988). Their account is heavily influenced by Robert Treacy's 1972 dissertation, "Progressivism and Corinne Seeds" (PhD. diss., University of California Los Angeles, 1972).
2. Seeds to Heffernan, n. d. [from internal evidence 1945], HH/CSR.
3. Corinne Seeds, "What is the task which lies before us, the members of the California School Supervisors' Association?" Typescript, 2, CSPR.
4. Seeds to Heffernan, n.d. [from internal evidence February, 1943], HH/CSR.
5. Seeds to Heffernan, April 9, 1942, HH/CSR.
6. Seeds to Heffernan, December 8, 1943, HH/CSR.
7. Corinne Seeds, "U.E.S.: The History of the Creative Elementary School" (Oral History Project, University of California Los Angeles, 1963), 126–27.
8. Seeds, "U.E.S.: The History of the Creative Elementary School," 123.
9. Los Angeles, March 20, 1943, Mr. George Bagnall and Dean Lee, Robert Sproul, "Memoranda," 1943, 152, RSPBL.
10. Jesse Bond to Frank Cowgill, June 4, 1943, Box 157, Teacher Training (1943), COUCLA.
11. Jessie Bond to Frank Cowgill, October 14, 1943, Box 157, Teacher Training (1943), COUCLA.
12. Corrine Seeds to Jessie Bond, October 11, 1943, Box 1, Folder 2, CSPUCLA.
13. Seeds to Heffernan, October 11, 1943, HH/CSR.
14. Jessie Bond to Frank Cowgill, October 14, 1943, Box 157, Teacher Training (1943), COUCLA.
15. The Staff of the University Elementary School of U.C.L.A. to Dr. Edwin Lee, Dean of the School of Education, November 8, 1943, Box 157, Teacher Training (1943), COUCLA.

16. Seeds to Heffernan, n.d. [from internal evidence 1943], HH/CSR.
17. The Staff of the University Elementary School of U.C.L.A. to Dr. Edwin Lee, November 8, 1943.
18. Seeds to Heffernan, December 4, 1943, HH/CSR.
19. June 28, 1944, Robert Sproul, "Memoranda," 1944, 326, Box 1, RSPBL.
20. James Corley to Vierling Kersey, July 5, 1944. Box 195, Teacher Training (1944), COUCLA.
21. Vierling Kersey to James Corley, July 18, 1944, Box 195, Teacher Training (1944), COUCLA.
22. Seeds to Heffernan, n.d. [from internal evidence May, 1944], HH/CSR.
23. Lee to Sproul, June 9, 1944, Box 175, Teacher Training (1944), COUCLA.
24. Robert Sproul, "Memoranda, 1944," 460, September 19, 1944, RSPBL.
25. Marcus McClure to Dr. Robert Gordon Sproul, October 18, 1944, Box 175, Teacher Training (1944), COUCLA.
26. Edwin Lee to Marcus McClure, October 25, 1944; Lee to Sproul, October 24, 1944, Box 175, Teacher Training (1944), COUCLA.
27. Seeds to Heffernan, n. d., 1945, HH/CSR.
28. Seeds to Heffernan, n.d. [from internal evidence 1945], HH/CSR.
29. "3 R's Demanded in Westwood Grade School," *Los Angeles Examiner,* July 6, 1945: 1. See also "UCLA School Project Scored," *Los Angeles Times,* July 8, 1945: 1.
30. *Los Angeles Times,* July 6, 1945: 1.
31. "Progressive Teaching Upheld by 50 Parents," *Los Angeles Times,* July 10, 1945: 10.
32. Los Angeles School Board minutes, July 2, 1945; July 5, 1945; July 9, 1945, Warner Avenue School Records, Los Angeles School Board, Los Angeles, California.
33. Dean Edwin Lee to Superintendent Vierling Kersey, July 14, 1945, Box 195, Teacher Training (1945), COUCLA.
34. Vierling Kersey to James Corley, July18, 1945, Box 195, Teacher Training (1945), COUCLA.
35. Treacy, "Progressivism and Corinne Seeds," 26.
36. Helen Heffernan, "Dear Co-Worker," August 9, 1945. Box 195, Teacher Training 2, COUCLA.
37. Box 195, COUCLA.
38. Helen Heffernan to Clarence Dykstra, August 10, 1945, Box 195, UES, 1, COUCLA.
39. Lee to Dykstra, August 10, 1945, Box 195, UES 1, COUCLA.
40. Nelda Salisger, Executive Secretary of the Executive Board of the Beverly-Westwood Citizens Committee, to Dr. Clarence Dykstra, September 17, 1945, HHPR.
41. "Subject of Teaching Methods Gets Too Hot; Debate Halted," *Westwood Hills Press,* September 14, 1945: 1.
42. Treacy, "Progressivism and Corinne Seeds," 124.
43. "The Report of the Survey of the University Elementary School, University of Los Angeles," UCLA, 1945, 4, Box 195, Teacher Training (1945), COUCLA.
44. "The Report of the Survey of the University Elementary School, University of Los Angeles," 54–55.

45. "The Report of the Survey of the University Elementary School, University of Los Angeles," 60.
46. C. A. Dykstra to President Sproul, "Memorandum on Elementary School," October 10, 1945, Box 195, Teacher Training (1945), UCOUCLA.
47. C. A. Dykstra, September 17, 1945, Robert Sproul, "Memoranda," 244, RSPBL.
48. Heffernan to Lu Wright, October 11, 1945, F3752:1843, Bureau of Elementary Education, General Correspondence N-Z, CSA.
49. "Debate Fate of School on Warner Ave," *Westwood Hills Press*, October 26, 1945: 1.
50. Training School (UCLA) 1945: 480A. Education and Training School Documents, CU5-Series 2, BL.
51. Peggy Kiskadden, "A Parent's View of UES" (Oral History Program, UCLA, 1965), 10
52. "40 Million for UCLA," *Westwood Hills Press*, December 21, 1945: 1.
53. Edward Barrett, *The Tenney Committee* (Cornell University Press, 1951), 158–67. See also Martha Kransdorf, *A Matter of Loyalty* (Caddo Gap Press, 1994).
54. Barrett, *The Tenney Committee*, 105–121.
55. California Senate Fact-Finding Committee on Un-American Activities, Un-American Activities in California Reports 1942–1947 (California State Printing Office, 1947), 169–78.
56. "Russian-American Friendship Inspires Successful Concert," *Westwood Hills Press*, June 1, 1945: 8.
57. American Russian Institute San Francisco, *Annual Report for Year 1945*, San Francisco, February 1946, F3752:1809, American-Russian Institute, 1944–45, CSA.
58. United States Civil Service Commission, "Record Search Information: Helen Heffernan,"1.23.61.3437. Information about Seeds is included in Heffernan's file.
59. California Legislature, Senate, *Fourth Report of the Joint Fact-Finding Committee on Un-American Activities in California* (California State Printing Office, 1948), F3752:1809, Department of Education Subject Files: American-Russian Institute, 1944–45, CSA.
60. "Dykstra Defends Academic Freedom," *Westwood Hills Press*, December 14, 1945: 1.
61. Minutes, Meeting of the American Russian Institute, November 9, 1944, F3752:1809, American-Russian Institute, 1944–45, CSA.
62. Heffernan to Walter Dexter, December 7, 1944, Memo: Conference on Education for American-Soviet Understanding, F3752:1809, American-Russian Institute, 1944–45, CSA.
63. Heffernan to Dr. Holland Roberts, President, American Russian Institute, January 9, 1945, F3752:1809, American-Russian Institute, 1944–45, CSA.
64. Heffernan to Holland Roberts, March 9, 1945, F3752:1809, American Russian Institute, 1944–45. CSA.
65. Heffernan to Holland Roberts, April 3, 1945, F3752:1809 Department of Education Subject Files: American Russian Institute, 1944–45. CSA.
66. Seeds to Heffernan, May 1, 1944, HH/CSR.
67. American Russian Institute San Francisco, *Annual Report for Year 1945*, 12.
68. Seeds to Heffernan, n.d. [from internal evidence 1944], HH/CSR.

69. Seeds to Heffernan, n.d. [from internal evidence Fall, 1943], HH/CSR.
70. Heffernan and Seeds, "Intercultural Education in the Elementary School," 81; Corinne Seeds, "Playing Ukrainian Farmer," *Progressive Education* 22, 7 (May 1945): 30–31.
71. There are many boxes of curricular materials from UES in the Helen Heffernan Papers at the University of California Riverside and the Corinne Seeds Documentation Project and Corinne Seeds Papers at UCLA, but I have not been able to find any materials from the unit-of-work on Ukrainian farmers.
72. Seeds, "U.E.S.: The History of the Creative Elementary School," 139.
73. "Santa Monica Educator Says Examiner Misquoted Him," *Westwood Hills Press*, January 11, 1946: 8.
74. "Elementary School Principal Tells How Pupils Study Russia," *Westwood Hills Press*, January 11, 1946: 8.
75. "Elementary School Principal Tells How Pupils Study Russia," *Westwood Hills Press*, January 11, 1946: 8.
76. Seeds, "U.E.S.: The History of the Creative Elementary School," 143–48.
77. "Results of Questionnaire Given to 47 Children who Studied the Ukraine Last Year," Box 1, Folder 3, CSPUCLA
78. Seeds, "U.E.S.: The History of the Creative Elementary School," 166.
79. Mrs. Eliscu, January 14, 1946, Robert Sproul, "Memoranda," 1946, 18, RSPBL.
80. Robert Sproul to Lawrence Larrabee, President of the Board of Education, March 12, 1946. Box 224, Teacher Training (1946), COUCLA.
81. "UCLA School on Warner to Move on July 1," *Westwood Hills Press*, June 21, 1945: 1.
82. "U.C.L.A. Summer Session," *WJE* 52, 7 (September 1946): 5.
83. Los Angeles City Board of Education, "Directive on the Teaching of Moral and Spiritual Values in Education," Eleanor Allen File, Los Angeles School Board, Los Angeles, California.
84. Eleanor Allen, "The Fundamental Issue in Education," *Los Angeles Times*, June 6, 1945.
85. Walter Allen to Clarence Dykstra, July 17, 1946, Box 224, Teacher Training, COUCLA.
86. Corinne Seeds to Edwin Lee, July 30, 1946, Box 224, Teacher Training (1946), COUCLA.
87. Clarence Dykstra to Walter Allen, July 31, 1946, Box 224, Teacher Training (1946), COUCLA.
88. Walter Allen to Clarence Dykstra, August 5, 1946, Box 224, Teacher Training (1946), COUCLA.
89. Jean Trapnell to Robert Sproul, July 27, 1946, Box 224, Teacher Training (1946), COUCLA.
90. Edwin Lee to Provost Clarence Dykstra, June 11, 1946, Box 224, Teacher Training (1946), COUCLA.
91. "To the Editor of the Evening Outlook," *Santa Monica Evening Outlook*, July 18, 1946, Box 224, Teacher Training 2, COUCLA.
92. Jean Trapnell to Clarence Dykstra, August 19, 1946, Box 224, Teacher Training 2, COUCLA.
93. "Cut Program of Elementary School in Fall," *Westwood Hills Press*, September 10, 1946: 1.

94. Attorney Calkins, Berkeley, October 10, 1946, Robert Sproul, "Memoranda," 1946, 391, RSPBL.
95. Family School Alliance Notebook, n.d., Box 1, CSPUCLA
96. Family School Alliance "Bulletin," October, 1946, Box 224, Teacher Training (1946), COUCLA.
97. "UC Elementary Training School Opens Monday," *Westwood Hills Press,* June 19, 1947: 1.
98. Robert Kirsch, "Pupil Aptitude Studied in Fundamental Skills," *Westwood Hills Press,* June 26, 1947: 1.
99. "The Battle of Westwood Hills," *Time,* July 14, 1947, http://www.time.com/time/magazine/article/0,9171,779176,00.html, accessed March 15, 2011.

8 Exporting Democracy / Defending Democracy

1. "Report of Senate Interim Committee on the Study of Public Education," (California State Printing Office, 1945), 3729.
2. "Report of Senate Interim Committee on the Study of Public Education," 3732.
3. Even after he was no longer a member of the State Senate, Swan continued his attack. See "Progressive Education Given Full Share of Blame for High Degree of Illiteracy in California Schools," *Westwood Hills Press* (September 14, 1945): 1.
4. Helen Heffernan, "Methods in the Social Studies," *CJEE* 13, no. 4 (May 1945): 244–52; Helen Heffernan, "Discussion, a Technique of Democratic Education," *CJEE* 14, no. 1, (August 1945): 146–52.
5. Heffernan, "Methods in the Social Studies," 244.
6. Helen Heffernan, "Discussion, a Technique of Democratic Education," 146.
7. Heffernan, "Discussion, a Technique of Democratic Education," 150.
8. Heffernan, "Discussion, a Technique of Democratic Education," 152.
9. "In Memoriam: Walter Friar Dexter," *California Schools* 16, no. 11 (November 1945): 204.
10. Seeds to Heffernan, n.d. [from internal evidence October, 1945], HH/CSR.
11. Seeds to Heffernan, October 31, 1945, HH/CSR.
12. "Appointment of Superintendent of Public Instruction," *California Schools* 16, no. 12 (December 1945): 241.
13. "Annual Conference of School Supervisors Association," *WJE* 53, no. 4 (April 1946): 4.
14. Minutes, March 27, 28, 29, 1939, Meeting of the State Curriculum Commission, 3, F3752:25, State Curriculum Commission, 1939–41, CSA.
15. Seeds to Heffernan, April 22, 1945; Seeds to Heffernan, n.d., [From internal evidence 1944], HH/CSR.
16. Minutes, May 6, 7 1946, State Curriculum Commission, F3752:23-28, Curriculum Commission,1946–47, CSA.
17. Helen Heffernan, "Implementation of the Framework of the Social Studies in the Elementary School," Mimeograph, June 8, 1946, F3752:28, State Curriculum Commission, 1946–47, 4, CSA.
18. Heffernan, "Implementation of the Framework," 5.
19. Aara Sargent to Roy Simpson and Jay Conner, June 27, 1946, F3752:1788, Helen Heffernan-Personal, CSA.

20. "To the California State Board of Education," July 12, 1946, F3752:1788, Helen Heffernan-Personal, CSA.
21. "Study Units Meet Demands of New Curriculum," *California Schools* 10, no. 6 (June 1939): 153.
22. Department of Education, State Board of Education, F3752:28, State Curriculum Commission 1946–47, CSA.
23. Curtis Warren, Secretary to the Board of Education to Roy Simpson, Chairman, State Curriculum Commission, August 14, 1946, F3752:649, 1946–48, CSA.
24. Minutes, California State Curriculum Commission, August 24, 1946, Los Angeles, F3752:28, State Curriculum Commission 1946–47, CSA.
25. Heffernan to Roy Simpson, July 27, 1946, F3752:1799, CSA.
26. Heffernan to Elsie Bowman, June 24, 1946, HHPR.
27. "Leave of Absence," *California Schools* 17, no. 11 (November 1946): 287.
28. Seeds to Heffernan, May 5, 1943, F3752:1828, CSA.
29. John Saito, Jr., "Letters of Conscience," *Japanese American National Museum Magazine* 2 (August 2007), http://www.discovernikkei.org/en/journal/2007/8/2/janm-magazine/, accessed August 9, 2010.
30. Afton Dill Nance, "The Role of a Coordinator in a Program of Intergroup Education," Paper for Education 218, "Practicum in School Administration," University of Southern California, Summer Session, 1946, HHPR.
31. Heffernan to Afton Nance, August 19, 1946, F3752:1828, CSA.
32. Afton Nance to Heffernan, October 8, 1946, F3752:1828, CSA.
33. Heffernan to Afton Nance, October 31, 1946, F3752:1828, CSA.
34. Family School Alliance, "Bulletin," October, 1946, Box 224, Teacher Training, 1946, COUCLA.
35. Seeds to Heffernan, n.d. [From internal evidence October, 1946], HH/CSR.
36. "'Hello' From Helen Heffernan," *WJE* 52, no. 12 (December 1946): 9.
37. "'Hello' From Helen Heffernan," 8–9.
38. Marlene Mayo, "Planning for the Education and Re-education of Defeated Japan, 1943–45," in *The Occupation of Japan: Educational and Social Reform*, ed. Thomas Bunkman (MacArthur Memorial, 1982), 25–32.
39. Ronald Anderson, "Japan: Three Epochs of Modern Education," *Bulletin* 1959, No. 11 (US. Department of Health, Education, and Welfare, 1959).
40. Pearl Wanamaker, "Education Mission to Japan," *WJE* 52, no. 10 (October 1946): 8.
41. Donald Roden, "From 'Old Miss' to New Professional: A Portrait of Women Educators under the American Occupation of Japan 1945–52," *History of Education Quarterly* 23, no. 4 (Winter 1983): 472.
42. Supreme Commander for the Allied Powers, *Report of the U.S. Educational Mission to Japan* (United States Government Printing Office, 1946), 4.
43. John Dower, *Embracing Defeat: Japan in the Wake of World War II* (New Press, 1999), 208.
44. Helen Heffernan to Afton Nance, March 2, 1947, HHPR.
45. Christopher Shannon, "A World Made Safe for Differences: Ruth Benedict's 'The Chrysanthemum and the Sword,'" *American Quarterly* 47, no. 4 (Dec. 1995): 664.
46. "Letter from Helen Heffernan," *WJE* 53, no. 2 (February 1947): 6–7.
47. Mire Koikari, "Exporting Democracy? American Women, 'Feminist Reforms,' and the Politics of Imperialism in the U.S. Occupation of Japan, 1945–1952," *Frontiers* 23, no. 1 (2002): 25. See also Mire Koikari, "Rethinking Gender

and Power in the UC Occupation of Japan, 1945–1952," *Gender and History* 11, no. 2 (July 1999): 313–38.
48. Ruth Morpeth, "Dynamic Leadership: Helen Heffernan and Progressive Education in California" (PhD diss., University of California Riverside, 1989), 251.
49. See Mark Orr, "Educational Reform Policy in Occupied Japan" (PhD diss., University of North Carolina, 1954).
50. Eiji Takemae, *Inside GHO* (Continuum, 2002), 187.
51. " 'Hello' From Helen Heffernan," 8.
52. Helen Heffernan, "Elementary Education—Comments," manuscript, n.d., Box 24, SCAP GHQ CIE Education Division Elementary Education, JTP.
53. Minoru Miyoishi, "The Trends of Educational Psychology in Japan," *Education in Japan: Journal for Overseas* 1 (1966), 99; Civil Information and Education Section, Supreme Commander for the Allied Powers, *Education in the New Japan* 1 (1948), 297.
54. Helen Heffernan to Afton Nance, March 2, 1947, HHPR.
55. Franziska Seraphim, *War Memory and Social Politics in Japan 1945–2005* (Harvard University Press, 2006), 87.
56. Edward Beauchamp and Richard Rubinger, *Education in Japan: A Source Book* (Garland Books, 1989), 304–5.
57. Anderson, *Japan: The Three Epochs of Modern Education*, 105.
58. "A Proposed Program of Activities for the Elementary Schools, June 23, 1947," Box 24, SCAP GHQ CIE Education Division, JTP.
59. Helen Heffernan to Afton Nance, March 2, 1947, HHPR.
60. Helen Heffernan to Afton Nance, March 2, 1947, HHPR.
61. "Letter from Helen Heffernan," *WJE* 53, no. 2 (February 1947): 6.
62. Helen Heffernan, "Building a New Democracy in Japan," *WJE* 54, no. 2 (February 1948): 7.
63. Victor Kobayashi, *John Dewey in Japanese Educational Thought* (University of Michigan Comparative Education Dissertation Series Number 2, 1964): 97.
64. Alice Miel, "Education's Part in Democratizing Japan," *Teachers College Record* 55, 4 (October 1953): 11.
65. Kobayashi, *John Dewey in Japanese Educational Thought*, 112.
66. Helen Heffernan to Mr. Orr, December 10, 1947, "Evaluation of Present Status of Elementary Education in Japan in Terms of the Recommendations of the United States Education Mission to Japan of 30 March 1946," 12, Box 24, SCAP GHQ CIE Education Division, JTP.
67. Helen Heffernan to Afton Nance, November 25, 1947, HHPR.
68. H. Heffernan, Elementary Schools Officer, "Report on Conference on the Organization, Administration, and Supervision of Elementary Schools—Beppu, Oita Prefecture, 16-18 November, 1947," Monthly Report, October 1947, Box 6, SCAP GHQ CIE Education Division, JTP.
69. Helen Heffernan to Mr. Orr, December 10, 1947, "Evaluation of Present Status of Elementary Education in Japan in Terms of the Recommendations of the United States Education Mission to Japan of 30 March 1946," 12, Box 24, SCAP GHQ CIE Education Division, JTP.
70. Heffernan to Mr. Orr, December 10, 1947, "Evaluation of Present Status of Elementary Education in Japan," 2.
71. Heffernan to Mr. Orr, December 10, 1947, "Evaluation of Present Status of Elementary Education in Japan," 15.

72. Kobayashi, *John Dewey in Japanese Educational Thought*, 129.
73. Kobayashi, *John Dewey in Japanese Educational Thought*, 130.
74. Helen Heffernan to Afton Nance, November 25, 1947, HHPR.
75. Herbert Passin, "The Occupation—Some Reflections," *Daedalus* 119, no. 3 (Summer 1990): 2.
76. Dower, *Embracing Defeat*, 250.
77. From Chief of Section (JRM) to Chief, Education Division, June 8, 1949, Box 24, SCAP GHQ CIE Education Division Elementary Education, JTP.
78. Takemae, *Inside GHQ*, 182.
79. Helen Heffernan, "Building a New Democracy in Japan," 7.
80. Helen Heffernan to Afton Nance, November 25, 1947, HHPR.
81. Maxine Lonsdale, "The Impact on City School Systems, Teacher Education and the Nation," n.p., in "Festival HH" (privately printed, 1976), HHPR.
82. Roger Lotchin, *Fortress California 1910–1961* (Oxford University Press, 1992).
83. Lisa McGirr, *Suburban Warriors: The Origin of the New American Right* (Princeton University Press, 2001), 51.
84. Roy Simpson, "Postwar Progress in the Public School System," *California Schools* 17, no. 11 (November 1947): 241–50.
85. Gilbert Gonzalez, "Segregation of Mexican Children in a Southern California City: The Legacy of Expansionism and the American Southwest," *Western Historical Quarterly* 16, no. 1 (January 1985): 55–76; Richard Valencia, "The Mexican American Struggle for Equal Opportunity in Mendez v. Westminster: Helping to Pave the Way for Brown v. Board of Education," *Teachers College Record* 107, no. 3 (March 2005): 389–423.
86. To the California State Board of Education from the California Curriculum Commission, January 4, 1947, F3752:649, 1946–48, CSA.
87. Senate Investigating Committee on Education, *Third Report: Textbooks* (California State Printing Office, 1948), 7.
88. "Report of the Senate Committee on Education," *California Schools* 17, no. 8 (August 1947): 169–71.
89. *Journal of the Senate 1947* (California State Printing Office), 1208.
90. Roy Simpson to George W. Fisher, chairman, Un-American Activities Committee American Legion, Department of California. n. d. [From internal evidence 1947], F3752:612, CSA.
91. The department had been reorganized in response to the 1945 Strayer Report.
92. Helen Heffernan to Roy Simpson, February 24, 1948, F3752:1799, CSA.
93. "State Conference Highlights," *California Schools* 19, no. 2 (February 1948): 35.
94. Helen Heffernan, "The World Community," typescript, n.d., 2, HHPR.
95. Helen Heffernan, "The World Community," 4.
96. Corinne Seeds, "Application for Sabbatical or Semi Sabbatical Leave," July 30, 1948, CSPR.
97. Kersey's file in the Los Angeles School District records includes a 1940 complaint from the Municipal League of Los Angeles about his reappointment that year, calling him "mediocre" but also referring to "documentary evidence of a character that should, in our judgment, have kept you from repeating the wrong to young life and to democracy perpetrated by a former Board in electing Vierling Kersey in the face of unanswered condemnatory

evidence against him." Municipal League of Los Angeles to Los Angeles School Board, July 15, 1940, Vierling Kersey File, Board Secretariat Records Management, Los Angeles Unified School District.
98. Helen Heffernan to Afton Nance, November 25, 1947, HHPR.
99. Afton Nance to Helen Heffernan, June 23, 1948, F3752:1828, CSA.
100. Helen Heffernan to Afton Nance, June 22, 1948, F3752:1828, CSA.
101. Minutes of Divisional Staff Meeting, March 30, 1949, F3752:626, CSA.
102. Heffernan to Afton Nance, n.d., HHPR.
103. Roy Simpson, "Helen Heffernan Annual Evaluation, 1949," HHPR.
104. Helen Heffernan, "The Elementary School of 1975," typescript, 1949, HHPR.
105. Helen Heffernan, "What is a Good Community?" typescript, n.d., (late 1940s by internal evidence), 2, HHPR.

9 "PROGRESSIVE" EDUCATION IS SUBVERTING AMERICA

1. Frederick Redefer, "What Has Happened to Progressive Education?" *School and Society* 67, no. 1741 (May 8, 1948): 349.
2. David Marden, "The Cold War and American Education" (PhD diss. University of Kansas, 1975), 170.
3. Stuart Foster, *Red Alert!* (Peter Lang, 2000). See also Ronald Lora, "Education: Schools as Crucible in Cold War America," in *Reshaping America: Society and Institutions 1945–1960,* eds. Robert Bremner and Gary Reichard (Ohio State University Press, 1982); Andrew Hartman, *Education and the Cold War* (Palgrave Macmillan, 2008).
4. Association for Supervision and Curriculum Development, Forces Affecting American Education (Washington, D.C., 1953).
5. For the Cold War impact on higher education, see Ellen Schrecker, *No Ivory Tower* (Oxford University Press, 1986).
6. House Un-American Activities Committee, "100 Things You Should Know About Communism and Education," (1949), 68–69, http://www.archive.org/details/100thingsyoushou1949unit (accessed, December 10, 2008).
7. Cited by Marden, "The Cold War and American Education," 104.
8. Robert Iverson, *The Communists and the Schools* (Harcourt, Brace and Co., 1959), 246.
9. Allen Zoll, "'Progressive' Education is Subverting America" (National Council for American Education, n.d.); Frederick Rand Rogers, "Progressive Education: Irresponsible and Immoral Pedagogy" (National Council for American Education, 1952); Milo McDonald, "'Progressive' Poison in Public Education" (American Education Association, 1951); Milo McDonald, "American Education: The Old, the Modern, and the 'New'" (American Education Association, 1952). All can be found in the Radical Right Collection, Box 47, Hoover Institution Archives, Stanford University.
10. Rogers, "Progressive Education: Irresponsible and Immoral Pedagogy," 6.
11. Rogers, "Progressive Education: Irresponsible and Immoral Pedagogy," 20.
12. Foster, *Red Alert!* 62.
13. Zoll, "'Progressive' Education is Subverting America," 3–4.
14. Zoll, "'Progressive' Education is Subverting America," 5.

15. Zoll, "'Progressive' Education is Subverting America," 6–8.
16. Burton Brazil, "The 1950 Election in California," *Western Political Quarterly* 4, no. 1 (March 1951): 67–71.
17. In 1950 Tenney unsuccessfully ran for Congress; in 1952 he ran as the vice-presidential candidate with General MacArthur for the Christian Nationalist Party, an anti-Semitic party associated with Gerald L. K. Smith.
18. Helen Heffernan, "Symposium on School-Community Relationships," *CJEE*, 19 (August 1950): 129–35.
19. Helen Heffernan, "Symposium on School-Community Relationships," 135.
20. Roy Simpson, "Dividends from Public Education," *California Schools* 21, no. 8 (August 1950): 294.
21. David Hulburd, *This Happened in Pasadena* (Macmillan, 1951). Other observers pointed to the importance of race in the controversy. See Carey McWilliams, "The Enemy in Pasadena," *Christian Century* (January 3, 1951); "Pasadena Revisited," *Time* (May 7, 1951).
22. David Gardner, "By Oath and Association: The California Folly," *Journal of Higher Education*, 40, no. 2 (February 1969): 125.
23. Cited in Stuart Graybill, "Bending the Twig: Conservative Educational Criticism and the Revival of the Right, 1900–1960" (PhD diss., University of California Davis, 1999), 395.
24. Helen Heffernan, "Readiness for Oral and Written Language," in *Readiness for Reading and Related Language Arts* (National Conference on Research in English, 1950), 34–39; Helen Heffernan, "From Prunes to Nuts to Cotton," *NEA Journal* 39 (October 1950): 500–501.
25. "The Helen Heffernan Scholarship," *California Schools* 21, no. 3 (March 1950), 79.
26. Helen Heffernan, "Obsolescence of Instructional Materials," *California Schools* 23, no.12 (December 1952): 525.
27. Theodore Brameld, ed., *The Battle for Free Schools* (Beacon Press, 1951); William Brickman, "Attack and Counterattack in American Education," *School and Society* 74 (October 1951): 262–69; National Education Association, "A List of Articles and Books Concerned with Recent Wave of Attacks on Public Education." (National Commission for the Defense of Democracy Through Education, NEA, 1951).
28. David Berninghausen, "A Policy to Preserve Free Public Education," *Harvard Educational Review* (Summer 1951): 140.
29. Berninghausen, "A Policy to Preserve Free Public Education," 152.
30. Lawrence Cremin, *The Transformation of the Schools* (Vintage Books, 1964), 336.
31. Mona Gleason, *Normalizing the Ideal* (University of Toronto Press, 1999); Sol Cohen, "The Mental Hygiene Movement, the Development of Personality and the School: The Medicalization of American Education," *History of Education Quarterly* 23, no. 2 (Summer 1983): 123–49.
32. Helen Heffernan and Faith Smitter, "Highlights of the Mid-Century White House Conference on Children and Youth, Dec. 3–7, 1950," *California Schools* 22, no. 4 (April 1951): 101–15.
33. Helen Heffernan, Lloyd Bevans, Ruth Edmands, Bernard Lonsdale, Afton Dill Nance, and Faith Smitter, "The Organization of the Elementary School and the Development of a Healthy Personality," *California Journal of Elementary Education* 29 (August 1951): 130.

34. University Elementary School, Los Angeles, May 18, 1950, Robert Sproul, "Memoranda," 1950, 257, RSPBL.
35. Heffernan to Afton Nance, August 23, 1951, HHPR.
36. "Co-operative Study in Elementary Education," *California Schools* 25, no. 3 (March 1954): 108–9.
37. Heffernan to Afton Nance, July 6, 1952, cited in Ruth Morpeth, "Dynamic Leadership: Helen Heffernan and Progressive Education in California" (PhD diss., University of California Riverside, 1989), 267.
38. Heffernan to Afton Nance, August 6, 1952, F3752:1828, CSA.
39. Dean Edwin Lee, Los Angeles, October 30, 1950, Robert Sproul, "Memoranda," 1950, 550–51, RSPBL.
40. Kathleen Weiler, "The Case of Martha Deane," *History of Education Quarterly* 107, no. 12 (Fall 2007): 470–96.
41. In Florida, the infamous Johns committee first sought to tie civil rights organizations such as the NAACP with "subversives." It then turned to homosexuals. James Schnur, "Closet Crusaders: The Johns Committee and Homophobia, 1956–1965" in *Carryin' On in the Gay and Lesbian South*, ed. John Howard (New York University Press, 1997), 132–63; Karen Graves, *And They Were Wonderful Teachers: Florida's Purge of Gay and Lesbian Teachers* (University of Illinois Press, 2009).
42. Seeds to Heffernan, November 8, 1944, HH/CSR.
43. M. J. Heale, "Red Scare Politics: California's Campaign against Un-American Activities, 1940–1970," *Journal of American Studies* 20, no. 1 (April 1986): 25.
44. "UNESCO month, October 28 to November 30, 1946," *California Schools* 17, 9 (October, 1946), 271.
45. Martha Kransdorf, *A Matter of Loyalty: The Los Angeles School Board vs. Frances Eisenberg* (Caddo Gap Press, 1994), 39–41.
46. California Senate, Fact-Finding Committee on Un-American Activities, *Ninth Report, Un-American Activities in California* (California Printing Office, Sacramento, 1953), 211.
47. Senate Investigating Committee on Education, *Ninth Report: Are Loyalty Oaths Effective?* (California State Printing Office, 1952), 8.
48. Seeds's description of her testimony before the Dilworth Committee in her oral history is somewhat confused. She stated that she testified before the committee in 1947, for example, when in fact it was 1952. Corinne Seeds, "U.E.S.: The History of the Creative Elementary School" (Oral History Project, University of California Los Angeles, 1963), 155.
49. Seeds, "U.E.S.: The History of the Creative Elementary School," 159–61.
50. Seeds, "U.E.S.: The History of the Creative Elementary School," 162.
51. Senate Investigating Committee on Education, *Ninth Report*, p. 93.
52. Senate Investigating Committee on Education, *Ninth Report*, p. 95.
53. Heale, "Red Scare Politics: California's Campaign against Un-American Activities," 29.
54. Marden, "The Cold War and American Education," 49.
55. John Rudolph points to Adlai Stevenson's defeat in the 1952 presidential election as exacerbating this view among liberal academics. John Rudolph, *Scientists in the Classroom* (Palgrave Macmillan, 2002), 24.
56. Cited in Rudolph, *Scientists in the Classroom*, 30.

57. Michael Klarman, "How Brown Changed Race Relations," *Journal of American History* 81, no. 1 (June 1994): 81–118; Clayborne Carson, "Two Cheers for Brown v. Board of Education," *Journal of American History* 91, no. 1 (June 2004): 26–31.
58. Helen Heffernan to Richard Mayers, July 22, 1953, HHPR.
59. Helen Heffernan, "Report of a Conference on Inequalities of Educational Opportunity," *California Schools* 24, no. 5 (May 1953): 171.
60. Helen Heffernan, "Some Solutions to Problems of Students of Mexican Descent," *The Bulletin of the National Association of Secondary School Principals* 39, no. 209 (March 1955): 43–53.
61. Heffernan, "Some Solutions to Problems of Students of Mexican Descent," 43.
62. Heffernan, "Some Solutions to Problems of Students of Mexican Descent," 49.
63. "The Education of Children of Seasonal Agricultural Workers in the San Joaquin Valley," Report to the Governor's Committee, July 1, 1950, CU-893, Box 10, BL.
64. Heffernan to Helen Wood, October 25, 1954, F3752:1850, CSA.
65. In these years, Heffernan also continued to publish curricular materials and articles, primarily in the *California Journal of Elementary Education*. Helen Heffernan, "The Education of Gifted Children," *CJEE*, 22 (August 1953): 135–39; Helen Heffernan, "In-Service Education of Teachers in the Modern School," *CJEE* 25, no. 5 (August 1956): 3–11; Helen Heffernan, "Strengths and Resources in the Democratic School," *CJEE* 22 (August 1953): 184–92. In 1954, she oversaw the production of a film strip called "A Good Day in the Kindergarten," one of a series of filmstrips on "good days" in various grades. The Kindergarten filmstrip focused on the kindergarten classroom of Esther Swain at UES. "A Good Day in the Kindergarten," mimeographed filmstrip script, F3752:1832, CSA.
66. Bureau of Elementary Education Subject Files: Nance, Afton D, F3752:1852, CSA.
67. In 1955 Heffernan was named editor of a social studies series, *Living in Our World*, published by Harr Wagner, and coordinated a series of four articles in the *NEA Journal* on space and school buildings. She wrote two of the articles herself: Helen Heffernan, "Space for Living," *NEA Journal* 44 (April 1955): 142–44; Helen Heffernan, "Freedom for Development of Individuality," *NEA Journal* 44 (May 1955): 282–84.
68. Howard Whitman, "Progressive Education—Which Way Forward?" *Colliers* (May 14, 1954): 32–36.
69. Mrs. Gladwin Hill to the Editor, *Colliers* (May 14, 1954): 2.
70. Gladwin Hill, "A Father Looks at Progressive Education," *The Atlantic* (December 1954): 55–57.
71. Helen Heffernan to Helen Juneman, June 8, 1955, F3752:1827, CSA.
72. Helen Heffernan to Afton Nance, August 13, 1954, HHPR.
73. United States Civil Service Commission, "Record Search Information: Helen Heffernan," 1.23.61.3437.
74. "Record Search Information: Helen Heffernan," 1.23.61.3437.
75. Donald Kitch to Dan Dawson, July 16, 1959, F3752:1818, CSA.
76. Helen Heffernan to George Guernsey, November 2, 1955, F3752: 1839, CSA.
77. Jay Conner to Helen Heffernan, March 15, 1955, F3752:1804, CSA.

78. Senate Investigating Committee on Education, *Twelfth Report: Current Problems in Education* (California State Printing Office, 1955), 75–77.
79. Afton Nance to Helen Heffernan, "Telephone Conversation with Senator Nelson Dilworth," May 12, 1955, F3752:1797, CSA.
80. Afton Nance to Helen Heffernan, "Telephone Conversation with Senator Nelson Dilworth.
81. Senate Investigating Committee on Education, *Eighth Report: Education in Pasadena* (California State Printing Office, 1951), 27.
82. Senate Investigating Committee on Education, *Twelfth Report*, 77–79.
83. "Old-Style Report Card Called Best," *Los Angeles Times* (March 17, 1955): 1; "Red Methods in Schools Grading Seen," *Los Angeles Times* (March 17, 1955): 8; "Student Grading Method is Called Communistic," *Fresno Bee* (March 17, 1955), 1.
84. Arthur Corey to Helen Heffernan, May 18, 1955, F3752:1821. CSA.
85. Helen Heffernan to Arthur Corey, Western Union Telegram, May 23, 1955, F3752:1821, CSA.
86. Frank Hubbard, Director, Research Division, National Education Association to Helen Heffernan, May 25, 1955, F3752:1854, CSA.
87. California Teachers Association, 1954-55, F3752:1821, CSA.
88. Helen Heffernan, "Are the Schools Teaching the Three R's?" Typescript, 1955, HHPR.
89. Roy Simpson, "California's Investment in Educational Leadership," *California Schools* 28, no. 2 (February 1957): 4–5.
90. Central Committee on Social Studies, "Building Curriculum in Social Studies for the Public Schools of California: A Progress Report" (California State Printing Office, 1957), 5.
91. Helen Heffernan to Afton Nance, Jan.17, 1957, HHPR.
92. Bureau of Elementary Education, *Teachers Guide to Education in Early Childhood*, 11.
93. Bureau of Elementary Education, *Teachers Guide to Education in Early Childhood*, 11.
94. Robert Treacy, "Progressivism and Corinne Seeds" (PhD diss. University of California Los Angeles, 1971), 284.
95. Deans Edwin Lee and Paul Dodd, Los Angeles, June 25, 1952, Robert Sproul, "Memoranda,"1952, 422. RSPBL.
96. Raymond Allen, "Our University Elementary School," Address to the Family School Alliance, June 1, 1955, Box 3, CSDP.
97. Corinne Seeds to Members of the Executive Board of the F.S.A. and the Parents whom they represent, n. d., Box 1, CSDP.
98. Corinne Seeds to Members of the Executive Board of the F.S.A. and the Parents whom they represent.
99. Corinne Seeds, "Let the Children Speak,"1957, typescript, 1, CSPR.
100. "Education S131-B Unit of Work Construction in the Social Studies, Summer Session 1957, Corinne A. Seeds Instructor," CSPR.
101. Robert Sproul to Corinne Seeds, March 5, 1957, Corinne Seeds Biographical File, CSPUCLA.
102. Jean Trapnell and Margaret Kiskadden, "The Parents View of UES" (Oral History Program, University of California, Los Angeles), 1965, 15.
103. Robert Wenkert and Merilee Finley, "The University Elementary School at UCLA: A Historical Overview, Chronology, and Annotated Bibliography"

(unpublished manuscript, Graduate School of Education, University of California Los Angeles, April, 1983), 6–7.
104. Helen Heffernan to Diana Anderson, July 8, 1958, HHPR.

10   How to Teach the California Child

1. Augustin Rudd, *Bending the Twig* (Sons of the American Revolution, 1957).
2. Senate Investigating Committee on Education, *Sixteenth Report: Curriculum Changes* (Sacramento: State Printing Office, 1958): 37.
3. Senate Investigating Committee on Education, *Sixteenth Report*, 74.
4. Senate Investigating Committee on Education, *Sixteenth Report*, 110.
5. Senate Investigating Committee on Education, *Sixteenth Report*, 48.
6. Senate Investigating Committee on Education, *Sixteenth Report*, 55.
7. Cited in Senate Investigating Committee on Education, *Sixteenth Report*, 55.
8. Senate Investigating Committee on Education, *Sixteenth Report*, 57.
9. Senate Investigating Committee on Education, *Sixteenth Report*, 62.
10. Senate Investigating Committee on Education, *Sixteenth Report*, 67.
11. Senate Investigating Committee on Education, *Sixteenth Report*, 99.
12. Senate Investigating Committee on Education, *Sixteenth Report*, 81.
13. Senate Investigating Committee on Education, *Sixteenth Report*, 96.
14. Senate Investigating Committee on Education, *Sixteenth Report*, 36–37.
15. Minutes of Administrators' Meeting, San Francisco, July 8, 1958, 2, F3752: 1794, CSA.
16. Afton Nance to Helen Heffernan, October 16, 1958, F3752:1794, CSA.
17. State of California Department of Education Minutes of Administrators' Meeting San Francisco, July 8, 1958, 2, F3752:1794, CSA.
18. Mortimer Smith, *And Madly Teach* (H. Regnery Co., 1949); Mortimer Smith, *The Diminished Mind* (H. Regnery Co., 1954).
19. Mortimer Smith, "How to Teach the California Child: Notes from Never Never Land," *Atlantic Monthly* 202 (September 1958): 33.
20. Smith, "How to Teach the California Child," 34.
21. Gardiner Johnson to Helen Heffernan, October 28, 1958. F3752: 1794. CSA.
22. Arthur Corey, "California Schools Do Educate: A Reaffirmation," *Atlantic Monthly* 202 (December, 1958): 63–66.
23. "New Era in Classrooms: It Will Take More Work Now to Get a Diploma," *U.S. News and World Report* (October 3, 1958): 48–50.
24. Helen Heffernan, "How do you Answer the Questions?" n.d., n.p., mimeograph, F3752:1803, CSA.
25. Wayne Urban, *More Than Science and Sputnik: The National Defense Education Act of 1958* (University of Alabama Press, 2010).
26. Helen Heffernan, "How Do You Answer the Questions?" n.d., n.p., mimeograph, F3752:1803. CSA.
27. Helen Heffernan, "A Curriculum Worker Looks at the Federal Commitment to Schools," Address given to the Fourteenth Annual Conference, Association for Supervision and Curriculum Development, Cincinnati, March 4, 1959, 4, F3752:626, CSA.
28. "Editorial comment and News Notes," *CJEE* 28, no. 4 (May 1960): 193.
29. Heffernan, "A Curriculum Worker Looks at the Federal Commitment," p. 8.

30. Heffernan, "A Curriculum Worker Looks at the Federal Commitment," p. 8.
31. Helen Heffernan, "Evaluation—More than Testing," *NEA Journal* 47 (1958): 227–29.
32. Hyman Rickover, *Education and Freedom* (Dutton, 1959); see also Hyman Rickover, "Let's Stop Wasting Our Greatest Resource," *Saturday Evening Post* 129 (March 2, 1957): 9, 108–11.
33. Rickover, *Education and Freedom*, 52.
34. Roy Simpson, "Maintaining a Balanced Educational Program," *California Schools* 31, no. 2 (February, 1960): 61. The public criticisms of the schools by Rickover and others led to the appointment of the Citizens Advisory Commission, made up of twenty-seven "distinguished citizens of the state," by the California legislature. The commission's final report on October 22, 1960 recommended that California create a system of statewide examinations and require that two-thirds of all instruction in elementary school be in "the three R's." See Mortimer Smith, "California's Latest Educational Committee," *Tax Digest* 37 (May 1959): 106, 115; Don Robinson, "The Conservative Revolution in California Education," *Phi Delta Kappan* 2, no. 3 (December 1960): 95.
35. Helen Heffernan, "The Young Adolescent," *CJEE* 28, no. 4 (November 1959): 71. See also Helen Heffernan, "Where Do You Stand on the Issues?" *California Journal for Instructional Improvement* 3, no. 4 (December 1960): 7; Helen Heffernan, "Pressures to Start Formal Instruction Early?" in *Don't Push Me!*, ed. Margaret Rasmussen, 14–18 (Association for Childhood International, 1960).
36. Helen Heffernan, "The Teacher's Role in Developing Quality Education," speech to staff at Santa Monica City Schools, September 14, 1959, F3752:1802, CSA. See also Helen Heffernan, "Evaluation—More than Testing," *NEA Journal* 47 (April 1958): 227–29; Helen Heffernan, "Where Do You Stand on the Issues?" *California Journal for Instructional Improvement* 3, no. 4 (December 1960): 7–12; Helen Heffernan, "Let's Give Them Time to Be Children," *California Journal for Instructional Improvement* 4, no. 2 (May 1961): 12–15. An example of Heffernan's own proposals can be seen in *The California Journal of Elementary Education* special issue on individualized reading programs, "Special Issue," *CJEE* 27, no. 1 (February 1959).
37. Helen Heffernan to Dr. Winifred Bain, October 8, 1958, F3752: 1810, CSA. Heffernan also served as a member of the advisory board of the *Instructor*, a leading journal in elementary education, and was a member of the board of editors of the respected national journal *Childhood Education*.
38. Riles was born in New Orleans but moved to Arizona as a youth; he attended Arizona State and taught in segregated schools in Arizona before moving to California. In the State Department of Education he served as executive secretary of the newly founded Commission on Discrimination in Teacher Employment.
39. Joshua Paddison, "Summer of Worry, Summer of Defiance," *California History* (Fall 1999): 188.
40. Helen Heffernan to Richard Clowes, "Memo." March 14, 1961, 3, F3752:1801, CSA.
41. Helen Heffernan to Richard Clowes, March 16, 1961, F3752:1801, CSA.
42. Helen Heffernan to Richard Clowes, March 16, 1961, F3752:1801, CSA.

43. Among other activities, she worked closely with the California Association for Childhood Education, and was actively involved in organizing a research conference on the young adolescent. With Vivian Todd she coauthored *The Kindergarten Teacher* (D.C. Heath and Co., 1960). In February 1961 she published an article on creativity in which she repeated the familiar argument for a curriculum based on contact with the natural world, even reprising examples from the UES unit on the harbor. Helen Heffernan, "You Can Release Creativity in Children," *CJEE* 29, 1 (February 1961): 184–88. In the early 1960s, when she was in Rhode Island delivering a number of presentations, the governor pronounced Helen Heffernan Day in the State of Rhode Island.
44. Mrs. Fredericka Tandler to Helen Heffernan, Dec. 2, 1959, F3752: 1840, CSA.
45. Oliver Sause to Helen Heffernan, December 14, 1960, F3752:1811, CSA.
46. Cited in Stuart Greybill, "Bending the Twig," 422.
47. Franklin Parker, "School Critic Max Rafferty (1917–1982) and the New Right," *Review Journal of Philosophy & Social Science* 10, 2 (1985): 130.
48. Robert Treacy, "Progressivism and Corinne Seeds (PhD diss., University of California Los Angeles, 1971), 353.
49. Max Rafferty, "The Scapegoat," in Max Rafferty, *Suffer, Little Children* (Devin-Adair Company, 1962), 136–37.
50. Max Rafferty, "Suffer the Little Children," *Phi Delta Kappan* 36 (December 1956): 89–92; Max Rafferty, "A Chronicle of Masks," *Phi Delta Kappan* 37 (May 1957): 298–301; Max Rafferty, "The Philistines," *Phi Delta Kappan* 38 (November 1957): 42–46; Max Rafferty, "The Cult of the Slob," *Phi Delta Kappan* 40 (November 1958): 56–59; Max Rafferty, "Open Season," *Phi Delta Kappan* 41 (November 1959): 49–52; Max Rafferty, "Children of Uranus," *Phi Delta Kappan* 42 (October 1960): 20–23; Max Rafferty, "The Seven Grim Fairy Tales," *Phi Delta Kappan* 42 (December 1960): 114–20.
51. Rafferty, "The Philistines," 42.
52. Editor's Introduction to Rafferty, "The Cult of the Slob," 56.
53. H. H. Wubben, "American Prisoners of War in Korea: A Second Look at the 'Something New in History' Theme," *American Quarterly* 22, no. 1 (Spring 1970): 3–19. See also E. Merrill Root, *Brainwashing in the High School* (Devin-Adair, 1958).
54. Max Rafferty, "The Passing of a Patriot," reprinted from *The Ledger* (July 6, 1961), Series 50, Box 66, Folder: Committee of Teachers to Elect Max Rafferty, SCUCLA.
55. Max Rafferty, "What Happened to Patriotism?" *Reader's Digest* (October, 1961): 107–10. As Stuart Graybill notes, "What Happened to Patriotism" "bears a striking resemblance to the fourteenth report of the Dilworth Committee. It seems likely that he was familiar with it or borrowed it as a basic resource." Stuart Graybill, "Bending the Twig: Conservative Educational Criticism and the Revival of the Right, 1900–1960" (PhD diss., University of California Davis, 1999), 431.
56. Herbert Gwinn, "The Flag, the Pledge, and You," *California Schools* 32, no. 9 (October 1961): 7.
57. Roy Simpson, "Special Report to the State Board of Education," *California Schools* 32, no. 1 (January 1962): 1.

58. Field Reports, 1961, 1962, F3752:1789-1792; Afton Nance to Helen Heffernan, April 26, 1962, F3752:1789, CSA.
59. Heffernan to John Bryant, October 3, 1962, F3752:1824, CSA.
60. Helen Heffernan to Alfred Artuso, October 9, 1962, F3752:1824, CSA.
61. Bureau of Elementary Education, F3752:1838, Subject Files: General Correspondence B-D, CSA.
62. Heffernan to Dr. William Burton, July 23, 1962, F3752:1838, General Correspondence B-D, CSA.
63. William Burton to Helen Heffernan, October 6, 1962, F3752:1838, General Correspondence B-D, CSA.
64. Torron J. Anderson and Eugene Lee, "The 1962 Election in California," *Western Political Quarterly* 16, no. 2 (June 1963): 411.
65. California State Department of Education, "Statement Concerning Teaching About Communism," May, 1962, 6, F3752:1800, CSA.
66. California State Department of Education, "Statement Concerning Teaching About Communism," 2.
67. Helen Heffernan to Alfred Arturo, October 9, 1962, F352:1824, 1946-62, CSA. This is one Heffernan's few references to religion. That she saw Jesus as a humanitarian and not as divine is suggested by her comment in a letter to Afton Nance: "I always wish I weren't a heathen—in time of trouble. Some folks seem to get some relief in prayer but you know prayers are not in my pattern." Heffernan to Afton Nance, March 24, 1957, HHPR.
68. Rafferty, "Children of Uranus," in Rafferty, *Suffer, Little Children*, 129.
69. Graybill, *Bending the Twig*, 42.
70. Helen Heffernan to Dr. William Burton, November 26, 1962, F3752:1838, General Correspondence B-D, CSA.
71. Helen Heffernan to Richard Clowes, December 23, 1962. F3752:1800, 1962, CSA. See also Helen Heffernan, "Notes for Richard Clowes," November 9, 1962, F3752:1800; Helen Heffernan to Richard Clowes, December 12, 1962, F3752:1800, 1962, CSA.
72. Heffernan's last article in the *California Journal of Elementary Education* was Helen Heffernan, "Promising Practices in Summer Schools Serving the Children of Seasonal Agricultural Workers," *CJEE* 31, no. 1 (February 1963): 137-43.
73. "Special Announcement: California Education to be New Professional Journal," *CJEE* 31, 4 (May 1963): 193-94.
74. Helen Heffernan, "Let's Keep Our Perspective," *California Education* 1, no. 2 (October 1963): 25-26.
75. Max Rafferty, "Education in Depth," *California Education* 1, no. 6 (February 1964): 1.
76. Rafferty, "Education in Depth," *California Education* 1, no. 5 (January 1964): 1.
77. Max Rafferty, "Three Wonderful Years—1963," F3752: 855, CSA.
78. Max Rafferty, "Education and the Big Lie," typescript, 1965, n.p., F3752: 855. CSA.
79. Wilson Riles Collection, Box F1:5, 7, California State University at Sacramento.
80. Wilson Riles, "A Brief History of Education and Integration in California's Public Schools," 4, transcript of speech delivered to the Human Relations Committee of the Whittier Coordinating Council. March 1, 1962, Whittier,

CA, Wilson Riles Collection Box F1:7, California State University at Sacramento.
81. Wilson Riles, "School Boards and 'de facto' Segregation," *California Education* 1, no. 3 (November 1963): 7; See also Wilson Riles, "Problems of *de facto* Segregation," *California Education* 1, no. 1 (September 1963): 39.
82. California Commission on Equal Opportunities in Education, "Equal Educational Opportunities in a Changing Society," report of a conference March 16–18, 1965. West Sacramento, CA, Wilson Riles Collection Box F2: 49. California State University at Sacramento.
83. William O'Neill, *Readin, Ritin, and Rafferty* (Glendessary Press, 1969), 27.
84. Max Rafferty, "The Puzzle of De Facto Segregation," in Max Rafferty, *On Education* (Devin-Adair Company, 1968), 37, 38.
85. Helen Heffernan and George Shaftel, *The Water Story: Man Improves His World* (L. W. Singer Co., 1963).
86. Helen Heffernan and Vivien Edmiston Todd, *The Years before School* (Macmillan, 1964) Helen Heffernan, "What is Good Education in Nursery School and Kindergarten? *Childhood Education* 41, no. 1 (September 1964): 2–28.
87. Helen Heffernan, "The Importance of Teaching." Handwritten manuscript, n.d. (1964 by internal evidence), 1, HHPR.
88. Heffernan's was not the only voice attacking the school critics. See Mary Anne Raywid, *The Ax-Grinders* (Macmillan, 1963).
89. Helen Heffernan, "Questions Parents Ask," *Grade Teacher* 81, no. 2 (September 1963): 23.
90. Memo from Max Rafferty, November 24, 1964, F3752: 839, Campaign correspondence 1962, 1966, 1967, CSA.
91. Max Rafferty, "Education in Depth," *California Education* 2, no. 4 (January 1965): 1.
92. Helen Heffernan, "Are the Schools Teaching Phonics?" *Grade Teacher* 81, no. 3 (October 1963): 60, 124.
93. Helen Heffernan, "Questions Parents Ask: Should Elementary School Children Have Homework?" *Grade Teacher* 81, no. 3 (October 1963): 149.
94. Max Rafferty, "Teacher-Training Change Needed," *Los Angeles Times* (May 26, 1964): Section 2, 5.
95. Helen Heffernan, "Questions Parents Ask: What is the Effect of Criticism on Teachers?" *Grade Teacher* 81, 4 (December 1963): 82.
96. Max Rafferty, "Education and the Big Lie," typescript of speech, 1965, n.p., F3752: 855. CSA.
97. Max Rafferty, "The Trouble with Life Adjustment," *Los Angeles Times* (October 26, 1964): Section 2, 7.
98. Helen Heffernan, "Will the Anti-Poverty Bill Affect Me?" *Grade Teacher* 82, no. 6 (February 1965): 59.
99. In 1964 and 1965 Heffernan continued to publish widely. Helen Heffernan, "Fostering the Child's Potential," *Childhood Education* (October 1965): 98–107; Helen Heffernan, Miriam Crenshaw, and Aline Merritt, *The Mysterious Swamp Rider : Life in the Young Republic* (Hans Wagner Publishing Co., 1965); Helen Heffernan and Leslee Bishop, "The Supervisor and Curriculum Director at Work," in Association for Supervision and Curriculum Development, *Role of Supervisor and Curriculum Director in a Climate of Change* (Association for Supervision and Curriculum

Development, 1965), 143; Helen Heffernan, "Why Nursery School for My Child?" *Grade Teacher* 82, no. 1 (September 1964): 23–24, 133, 135; Helen Heffernan, "Is Our School a Good School?" *Grade Teacher* 82, no. 3 (November 1964): 13-14, 130–31; Helen Heffernan, "Do Our Elementary Schools Really Teach Science?" *Grade Teacher* 82, no. 5 (January 1965): 32, 130–34; Helen Heffernan, "What is Individualized Reading?" *Grade Teacher* 82, no. 7 (March 1965): 28, 141–43;

100. "Helen Heffernan Retires from Education Bureau," *The Sacramento Bee* (September 2, 1965): 1.
101. "Helen Heffernan Retires," *California Education* 3, no. 2 (October 1965): 1.
102. Mary B. Lane, "Decades of Progress," typescript of speech at the dedication of the Helen Heffernan Honor Grove, October 1, 1966, F3752: 1788, CSA.
103. Helen Heffernan, "Response to Presentation," October 1, 1966, F3752:1788, CSA.

Epilogue

1. Helen Heffernan to Afton Nance, November 17, 1965, HHPR.
2. Helen Heffernan and Vivian Edmiston Todd, *Elementary Teacher's Guide to Working with Parents* (Parker Publishing Company, 1969).
3. Helen Heffernan and Vivian Edmiston Todd, *The Years Before School*, Second Edition (Macmillan, 1970); Helen Heffernan and Vivian Edmiston Todd, *The Years Before School*, Third Edition (Macmillan, 1977). She also published three articles: Helen Heffernan, "Fostering the Child's Potential," *Childhood Education* 44, 2 (October 1965): 98–107; Helen Heffernan, "Needed: New Compacts in Education," *Childhood Education* 43, 7 (March 1967): 382–84; and Helen Heffernan, "Early Childhood Education: Influence on the Elementary School," Today's Education 59 (April 1970): 41–42.
4. Helen Heffernan, "As We Move Ahead," EKNE Workshop Luncheon Session, June, 25, 1966, 3, 4, 7, typescript, HHPR.
5. Helen Heffernan, "Dear Friend," May 1, 1970, HHPR.
6. After his defeat by Riles, Rafferty took a position as dean of education at Troy University in Alabama. He died in a one-person automobile accident in 1982.
7. Helen Heffernan, "How it Feels to be Eighty," in "Festival HH," February 7, 1976, HHPR.
8. For a discussion of the impact of Proposition 13, see Peter Schrag, *Paradise Lost: California's Experience, America's Future* (University of California Press, 1999).

Bibliography

Works by Helen Heffernan in Chronological Order

Heffernan, Helen. "Objective Measurement of Educational Progress in Country Schools." MA thesis, University of California, 1924.

———. "Rural Education—A Challenge, a Responsibility." *California Exchange Bulletin in Rural Education* 1, no. 1 (November 1926): 8.

———."How Big Is Your Opportunity?" *California Exchange Bulletin in Rural Education* 1, no. 3 (March 1927): 10.

———. "The Problem of Differentiating Rural Education Supervision." *Addresses and Proceedings*, 65th Annual Meeting of the National Education Association. Minneapolis, Minnesota (July 1-6, 1928): 460-461.

———. "Division of Rural Education." *California Biennial Report of the State Department of Education*, 1927-28 (Sacramento, 1928): 50-58.

———. "Experimental Attempts to Improve Instruction in Rural Schools." *Western Journal of Education* 35, no. 1 (January 1929): 9.

———. "Articulation of Rural Elementary and Secondary Education." *Western Journal of Education* 35, no. 3 (March 1929): 5-6.

———. "High Lights of Rural School Supervision." *Western Journal of Education* 35, no. 10 (December 1929): 9.

———. "Group Versus Grade Class Organization." *Addresses and Proceedings*, 66th Annual Meeting of the National Education Association, 1929, 494.

———. "Progressive Education and Mental Hygiene." *Western Journal of Education* 36, no. 4 (April 1930): 3-4.

———. "Interpreting the School Program to the Public." *Proceedings of the 1932 Superintendents' Convention*. California State Printing Office, 1932, 123-124.

———. "What California Parents Think of the Report Card." *California Journal of Elementary Education* 1, no. 1 (November 1932): 82-85.

———. "A Statement of the Philosophy and the Purposes of the Elementary School." *California Journal of Elementary Education* 1, no. 3 (February 1933):109-113

———. Lawrence Chenoweth, and William Paden. "Interpreting the School to the People." *California Journal of Elementary Education* 2, 3 (February 1934): 108-114.

———. "The Case for Kindergarten in Public Education." *California Journal of Elementary Education* 3, no. 1 (August 1934): 30-33.

———. "The Panel Technique of Group Discussions." *California Journal of Elementary Education* 3, no. 2 (November 1934): 74-82.

———. "Health Problems in Rural Schools." *California Journal of Elementary Education* 3, no. 3 (February 1935): 147-152.

———. and Gladys Potter. "Point of View." California State Department of Education, *Teachers' Guide to Child Development for the Intermediate Grades*. California State Department of Education, 1936, 18.

Heffernan, Helen. "Classification and Promotion Policies in Some City School Systems." *California Journal of Elementary Education* 5, no. 4 (May 1936): 228–234.

———. "The Guiding Philosophy of the Unitary Type of Curriculum Organization." *Western Journal of Education* 43, no. 1 (January 1937): 6–7.

———. "Review of Corinne A. Seeds, *Childhood Expressions*." *California Schools* 8, no. 2 (February 1937): 6.

———. "Supervision Appropriate for Progressive Schools." *California Journal of Elementary Education* 6, no. 1 (August 1937): 21–25.

———. "Science in the Professional Education of Teachers for the Elementary School." *California Journal of Elementary Education* 6, no. 2 (November 1937): 100–104.

———. "The Principal's Responsibility in Guidance." California Elementary School Principals' Association. *Guidance in the Elementary School*. Tenth Yearbook. Parker School: Oakland, California, 1938.

———, Irmagarde Richards, and Alice Salisbury. *Desert Treasure*. Hart Wagner Publishing Company, 1939.

———. "Report of Conference on Education of Children of Seasonal Workers—Fresno State College, December 9–10, 1938." *California Journal of Elementary Education* 7, no. 3 (February 1939): 181–191.

———. "New Emphases in Primary Curriculum." *California Journal of Elementary Education* 7, no. 6 (August 1939): 15–20.

———. "Selection and Education of Elementary School Principals." California Elementary School Principals' Association. *The Elementary Principal as Supervisor in the Modern School*. Eleventh Yearbook, 1939: 29–33.

———. "Education through Interest." California Elementary School Principals' Association. *Children's Interests Elementary School Level*. Twelfth Yearbook, 1940: ii.

———. "How Can We Make a Rural School Democratic for Children, Teachers, and Parents?" *California Journal of Elementary Education* 8, no. 4 (May 1940): 211–216.

———, Wilhelmina Harper, and Gretchen Wulfing, *All Aboard for Storyland*. Benj. H. Sanbord and Co., 1941.

———. "What Practices Are Defensible in Education in Time of Crisis?" *The National Elementary Principal* (April 1941): 152–156.

———. "Poll on Youth and Education." *California Journal of Elementary Education* 9, no. 4 (May 1941): 196–197.

———. "The Health Program in Rural Schools." *California Journal of Elementary Education* 9, no. 4 (May 1941): 235–240.

———. "The Significance of Environment in the Learning Process." California Elementary School Principals' Association. *Elementary School Environment and the Modern Curriculum*. Thirteenth Yearbook, 1941: 11–14.

———. "Education for Inter-American Friendship." California Elementary School Principals' Association. *Guiding Children in Democratic Living*. Fourteenth Yearbook, 1942: 112–116.

———. "Inter-American Education in the War Effort." *California Journal of Elementary Education* 11, no. 7 (August 1942): 13–21.

———. "A Heritage of Freedom." *Western Journal of Education* 48, 9 (October 1942): 6–7.

———. "The Children of Women Workers in Wartime." *Western Journal of Education* 49, no. 1 (January 1943): 9–10.

———. "Foreword." California Elementary School Principals' Association. *The Elementary School Faces the Problems of Migration*. Fifteenth Yearbook, 1943: iii–v.
———. "Population Migrations and Federal Aid for Education." In California Elementary School Principals' Association. *The Elementary School Faces the Problems of Migration*. Fifteenth Yearbook, 1943: 26–28.
———. "Correspondence with British Children." *California Journal of Elementary Education* 12 (1943–1944): 46–65.
———. "Pioneering in Child-Care Services." *California Journal of Elementary Education* 12 (1943–1944): 161–171.
———. "School Teachers Carry on in Wartime England." *California Journal of Elementary Education* 12 (1943–1944): 112–116.
———. "Progress in Elementary Education During the Next Decade." *California Journal of Elementary Education* 13, no. 1 (August 1944): 44–55.
———. "Report on the White House Conference on Rural Education, October 3–5, 1944." *California Journal of Elementary Education* 13, no. 2 (November 1944): 69–81.
———, and Corinne Seeds. "Intercultural Education in the Elementary School." California Elementary School Principals' Association. *Education for Intercultural Unity*. Seventeenth Yearbook, 1945.
———. "Methods in the Social Studies." *California Journal of Elementary Education* 13, no. 4 (May 1945): 244–252.
———. "Discussion, a Technique of Democratic Education." *California Journal of Elementary Education* 14, no. 1 (August 1945): 146–152.
———. "Evaluation and the Continuous Professional Education of Teachers." *California Journal of Elementary Education* 15, no. 1 (August 1946): 51–56.
———. "'Hello' from Helen Heffernan." *Western Journal of Education* 52, no. 10 (December 1946): 8–9.
———. "Letter from Helen Heffernan." *Western Journal of Education* 53, no. 2 (February 1947): 7–8.
———. "Building a New Democracy in Japan." *Western Journal of Education* 54, no. 2 (February 1948): 8–9.
———. "The New Education in Japan." *Educational Leadership* 6, no. 1(October 1948): 40–44.
———. "The Role of the Principal in Curriculum Development." California Elementary School Principals' Association. *The Principal and Curriculum Building*. Twentieth Yearbook. Sacramento, 1948: 9–17.
———. "Conferences on Rural Life and Education Point the Way." *California Journal of Elementary Education* 18, no. 3 (August 1949): 193–206.
———. "Symposium on School-Community Relationships." *California Journal of Elementary Education* 19, no. 3 (August 1950): 129–135.
———. "Readiness for Oral and Written Language." *Readiness for Reading and Related Language Arts*. National Conference on Research in English, 1950: 34–39.
———. "From Prunes to Nuts to Cotton." *NEA Journal* 39, 10 (October 1950): 500–501.
———, and Faith Smitter. "Highlights of the Midcentury White House Conference on Children and Youth, Dec. 3–7, 1950." *California Schools* 22, no. 4 (April 1951):101–115.
———. "Inventory of the Gains." *California Journal of Elementary Education* 20, no. 3 (August 1951): 120–128.

Heffernan, Helen, Lloyd Bevans, Ruth Edmands, Bernard Lonsdale, Afton Dill Nance, and Faith Smitter. "The Organization of the Elementary School and the Development of a Healthy Personality." *California Journal of Elementary Education* 20, no. 3 (August 1951): 129–153.

———, Ruth Edmands, and Faith Smitter. "Promising Practices for Implementation of the 'Framework' in the Elementary Schools." *California Schools* 22, no. 9 (September 1951): 309–317.

———. "Obsolescence of Instructional Materials." *California Schools* 23, no.12 (December 1952): 524–525.

———. "Teaching is More than Flying Blind." *Childhood Education* (October 1952): 61–64.

———. "The Educational Setting in 1952." Handwritten manuscript. Helen Heffernan Collection, University of California Riverside.

———. "Report of a Conference on Inequalities of Educational Opportunity." *California Schools* 24, no. 5 (May 1953): 168–173.

———. "The Education of Gifted Children." *California Journal of Elementary Education* 22, no. 3 (August 1953): 135–139.

———. "Strengths and Resources in the Democratic School." *California Journal of Elementary Education* 22, no. 3 (August 1953): 184–192.

———. "Some Solutions to Problems of Students of Mexican Descent." *The Bulletin of the National Association of Secondary School Principals* 39, no. 209 (March 1955): 43–53.

———. "Space for Living." *NEA Journal* 44, no. 4 (April 1955): 142–144.

———. "Freedom for Development of Individuality." *NEA Journal* 44, no. 5 (May 1955): 282–284.

———. "In-Service Education of Teachers in the Modern School." *California Journal of Elementary Education* 25, no. 3 (August 1956): 3–11.

———. "A Philosophy for the Education of Young Adolescents." *California Journal of Elementary Education* 25, no. 3 (August 1956): 82–88.

———. "Successful Teaching in the Social Studies." Typescript, July 11, 1957. Helen Heffernan Collection, University of California Riverside.

———. "Induction of New Teachers." *California Journal of Elementary Education* 26, no. 3 (August 1957): 54–64.

———. "Evaluation—More than Testing." *NEA Journal* 47 (April 1958): 227–229.

———. "The Young Adolescent." *California Journal of Elementary Education* 28, no. 4 (November 1959): 69–79.

———. "Pressures to Start Formal Instruction Early?" In *Don't Push Me!* edited by Margaret Rasmussen, 14–18. Association for Childhood International, 1960.

———, and Vivian Todd. *The Kindergarten Teacher.* D. C. Heath and Co., 1960.

———. "Where Do You Stand on the Issues?" *California Journal for Instructional Improvement* 3, no. 4 (December 1960): 7–12.

———. "You Can Release Creativity in Children." *California Journal of Elementary Education* 29, no. 1 (February 1961): 184–188.

———. "Let's Give Them Time to Be Children." *California Journal for Instructional Improvement* 4, no. 2 (May 1961): 12–15.

———. "Migrant Children in California Schools." *California Journal of Elementary Education* 25, no. 3 (May 1962): 228–236.

———. "Today's Challenge: The Full Development of Human Potential." *California Journal for Instructional Improvement* 5, no. 4 (December 1962): 3–10.

———. "Promising Practices in Summer Schools Serving the Children of Seasonal Agricultural Workers." *California Journal of Elementary Education* 31, no. 1 (February 1963): 137–143.

———. "Questions Parents Ask." *Grade Teacher* 81 (September 1963): 23, 92.

———. "Let's Keep Our Perspective." *California Education* 1, no. 2 (October 1963): 25–26.

———. "Are the Schools Teaching Phonics?" *Grade Teacher* 81 (October1963): 60, 124.

———. "Questions Parents Ask: Should Elementary School Children Have Homework?" *Grade Teacher* 81, no. 3 (November 1963): 55, 149.

———. "Questions Parents Ask: What is the Effect of Criticism on Teachers?" *Grade Teacher* 81, no. 4 (December 1963): 42, 82, 84.

———, and George Shaftel. *The Water Story: Man Improves His World*. L.W. Singer Co., 1963.

———. "Questions Parents Ask." *Grade Teacher* 81, no. 6 (February 1964): 45, 111, 114.

———. "Questions Parents Ask." *Grade Teacher* 81, no. 7 (March 1964): 106.

———. "Questions Parents Ask: Homogeneous Grouping! Yes? No?" *Grade Teacher* 81, no. 8 (April 1964): 8, 122.

———. "Questions Parents Ask: Report Cards or Parent Conferences." *Grade Teacher* 81, no. 9 (May 1964): 22, 105, 106, 107.

———. "Questions Parents Ask: Beginning Reading! When? How?" *Grade Teacher* 81, no. 9 (June 1964): 8, 90, 91.

———. "Reality, Responsibility and Respect in the Education of Children from Families who Follow the Crops." *Fourth Annual Conference on Families Who Follow the Crops Bakersfield, CA, February 27–28, 1964, Report and Recommendations*. Governor's Advisory Committee on Children and Youth, Sacramento, California, 1964.

———, and Vivian Edmiston Todd. *The Years before School*. Macmillan, 1964.

———, and William Burton. *Creativity*. National Education Association, 1964.

———. "Why Nursery School for my Child?" *Grade Teacher* 82, no. 1 (September 1964): 23–24, 133, 135.

———. "What is Good Education in Nursery School and Kindergarten?"*Childhood Education* 41, no. 1 (September 1964): 25–28.

———. "Is Our School a Good School?" *Grade Teacher* 82, no. 3 (November 1964): 13–14, 130–131.

———. "Do Our Elementary Schools Really Teach Science?" *Grade Teacher* 82, no. 5 (January 1965): 32, 130–134.

———. "Will the Anti-Poverty Bill Affect Me?" *Grade Teacher* 82, no. 6 (February 1965): 58–59, 109.

———. "What is Individualized Reading?" *Grade Teacher* 82, no. 7 (March 1965): 28, 141–143.

———. "Fostering the Child's Potential." *Childhood Education* 83, no. 2 (October 1965): 98–107.

———, and Leslee Bishop, "The Supervisor and Curriculum Director at Work." In Association for Supervision and Curriculum Development, *Role of Supervisor and Curriculum Director in a Climate of Change*, 1965: 87–143.

———, Miriam Crenshaw, and Aline Merritt. *The Mysterious Swamp Rider: Life in the Young Republic*. Hans Wagner Pub. Co., 1965.

———. "Needed: New Compacts in Education." *Childhood Education* 85 (March 1967): 382–384.

Heffernan, Helen. and Vivian Edmiston Todd. *Elementary Teacher's Guide to Working with Parents*. Parker Publishing Company, 1969.

———. "Early Childhood Education: Influence on the Elementary School." *Today's Education* 59 (April 1970): 41–42.

Works by Corinne Seeds in Chronological Order

Seeds, Corinne. "Classroom Control." In *The Classroom Teacher*, edited by Milo Hillegas. The Classroom Teacher, Inc., 1927.

———. "Our Present Educational Point of View." In *Major Units in the Social Studies*, edited by Charles Waddell, Corinne Seeds, and Natalie White. John Day, 1932.

———, Charles Waddell, and Natalie White. *Major Units in the Social Studies*. John Day, 1932.

———. "The Language Arts and Elementary School Activities." *Progressive Education* 10, no. 4 (April 1933): 204–209.

———. "Does the New Education Demand a New Type of Supervision?" In California Elementary School Principals' Association, *Supervision: Fifth Yearbook*, 1933: 25–30.

———. "Democratic Thinking and Living in the Classroom." *Educational Method* 14, no. 2 (November 1934): 57–63.

———. "An Interpretation of the Integrated Program in the Elementary School." *California Journal of Elementary Education* 3, no. 2 (November 1934): 89–98.

———. "Rhythmic Expression: An Outgrowth of Learning." *Progressive Education* 11, no. 7 (November 1934): 398–406.

———. *Childhood Expressions*. Stewart Publishing, 1937.

———. "The School and Its Tasks." *California Journal of Elementary Education* 5 (May 1937) 198–210.

———. "Next Steps in the Preparation of Teachers for Later Childhood Education." *California Journal of Elementary Education* 7, no. 2 (November 1938): 119–128.

———. "Newer Practices Involving Dramatic Play." *Newer Instructional Practices of Promise*. Twelfth Yearbook. Department of Supervisors and Directors of Instruction, National Education Association. National Education Association, 1940.

———. "Children's Interests in Rhythmic Bodily Expression." California Elementary School Principals' Association. *Children's Interests Elementary School Level*. Twelfth Yearbook, 1940: 122–127.

———. "What Learning Experiences are Likely to Prove Developmental During Later Childhood. *California Journal of Elementary Education* 10, no. 1 (August 1941): 41–55.

———. "The Elementary Schools of California Meet the Challenge of the Time." *Western Journal of Education* 48, no. 2 (February 1942): 7–8.

———. "Are We Meeting the Challenge of the Times?" California Elementary School Principals' Association. *Guiding Children in Democratic Living*. Fourteenth Yearbook, 1942: 18–27.

———. "Are We Meeting the Challenge of the Times?" Unpublished typescript, n. d. Helen Heffernan Papers, University of California, Riverside.

———. "Dramatic Play as a Means to Democratic Social Living." *California Journal of Elementary Education* 13, 1 (January 1943): 218–222.

———. "The Need of a State Wide Curricular Pattern in the Social Studies for the Elementary School." California School Principals' Association. *The Elementary School Faces Migration*. Fifteenth Yearbook, 1943: 118–122.

———. "Playing Ukrainian Farmer." *Progressive Education* 22, no. 7 (May 1945): 30–31.

———. "The Social Studies." *The Elementary School at the Mid-Century*. Twenty-third Yearbook. California Elementary School Administrators' Association, 1951.

———. "How a Child Becomes One With His World," "Guidance Through Major Areas of Experience," "Helping a Child Become One with his World," and "Evaluation of the Child's Success in Becoming One with his World." In *Teachers Guide to Education in Early Childhood*. California State Department of Education, 1956.

———. "U.E.S.: The History of the Creative Elementary School." Oral History Project, University of California Los Angeles, 1963.

———, and Helen Heffernan. "Postwar Planning for the Social Studies: Curriculum in the Elementary School." Unpublished manuscript, n.d. Helen Heffernan Papers, University of California Riverside,

Works Consulted

Adams, Lucy Wilcox. "Education in the Relocation Centers." *California Journal of Secondary Education* 17, no. 8 (December 1942): 477–479.

Adams, Romanzo. "Nevada Men and the Schools." *Nevada School Journal* 3, no. 1 (1912): 17–18.

Adams, Romanzo. "University Notes." *Nevada School Journal* 3, no. 1 (1912): 10.

Almack, John. "The Supervisory Program." *California Exchange Bulletin in Rural Education* 1, no. 3 (March 1927): 2–24.

Altenbaugh, Richard, and Kathleen Underwood. "The Evolution of Normal Schools." In *Places Where Teachers are Taught*, edited by John Goodlad, Roger Soder, and Kenneth Sirotnik, 136–186. Jossey-Bass Publishers, 1990.

Anderson, Diana. "Teaching Physical Education at the University Elementary School." Oral History Program, University of California Los Angeles, 1988.

Anderson, Ronald. *Japan: Three Epochs of Modern Education*. Bulletin No. 11. U.S. Department of Health, Education, and Welfare, 1959.

Anderson, Torron J., and Eugene Lee, "The 1962 Election in California." *The Western Political Quarterly* 16, no. 2 (June 1963): 396–420.

"Are We Better or Less Educated Than 50 Years Ago? A Symposium on U.S. Schools Today." *U.S. News and World Report* 42 (June 7, 1957): 120–130.

Armitage, Susan, and Elizabeth Jameson, eds. *The Women's West*. University of Oklahoma Press, 1987.

Association for Supervision and Curriculum Development. *Forces Affecting American Education*. National Education Association, 1953.

———. *Fostering Mental Health in Our Schools*. National Education Association, 1950.

Barber, Benjamin. *Strong Democracy: Participatory Politics for a New Age*. University of California Press, 1984.

Barrett, Edward. *The Tenney Committee*. Cornell University Press, 1951.

Beatty, Barbara. *Preschool Education in America: The Culture of Young Children from the Colonial Era to the Present*. Yale University Press, 1995.

Beauchamp, Edward. "The Development of Japanese Educational Policy, 1945–1985." *History of Education Quarterly* 27, no. 3 (Autumn 1987): 299–324.
Beauchamp, Edward, and Richard Rubinger. *Education in Japan: A Source Book.* Garland Books, 1989.
Beineke, John. *And There Were Giants in the Land.* Peter Lang, 1998.
Benedict, Ruth. *The Chrysanthemum and the Sword.* Houghton Mifflin, 1946.
Berninghausen, David. "A Policy to Preserve Free Public Education." *Harvard Educational Review* (Summer 1951): 138–154.
Biklen, Sari. "The Progressive Education Movement and the Question of Women." *Teachers College Record* 80, no. 2 (December 1978): 316–335.
Blair, Karen. *Clubwoman as Feminist: True Womanhood Redefined.* Holmes and Meier Press, 1980.
Blanton, Carlos. "From Intellectual Deficiency to Cultural Deficiency: Mexican Americans, Testing, and Public School Policy in the American Southwest, 1920–1940." *Pacific Historical Review* 72, no. 1 (Winter 2003): 39–62.
Bloch, Marianne, Kertin Holmlund, Ingeborg Moquist, and Tom Popkewitz. "Global and Local Patterns of Governing the Child, Family, Their Care, and Education." In *Governing Children, Families and Education: Restructuring the Welfare State*, edited by Marainne Bloch, M. K. Holmlund, I. Moquist, and T. Popkewitz. Palgrave Macmillan, 2003.
Blount, Jackie. *Destined to Rule the Schools.* SUNY Press, 1998.
———. *Fit to Teach.* SUNY Press, 2006.
Bodenheimer, Rosemarie. *The Real Life of Mary Ann Evans.* Cornell University Press, 1994.
Bone, Hugh. "New Party Associations in the West." *The American Political Science Review* 45, no. 4 (December 1951): 1115–1125.
———. "The 1956 Election in Washington." *Western Political Quarterly* 10, no. 1 (March 1957): 161–165.
Bonser, Frederick. *The Elementary School Curriculum.* The Macmillan Company, 1922.
Boone, Richard. *A History of Educational Organization in California.* San Jose, CA, 1926.
Borrowman, Merle. *The Liberal and Technical in Teacher Education.* Teachers College Press, 1956.
Boulton, Helen, and Natalie White. *How the Pioneers Moved Westward.* California Department of Education Bulletin 1, no. 2 (April 1938), State Printing Office.
Brameld, Theodore, ed. *The Battle for Free Schools.* Beacon Press, 1951.
Branigan, John. "Education of Over-age Mexican Children." *Sierra Educational News* 29, no. 10 (December 1933): 37–39.
Brazil, Burton. "The 1950 Election in California." *Western Political Quarterly* 4, no. 1 (March 1951): 67–71.
Brehony, Kevin. "From the Particular to the General, the Continuous to the Discontinuous: Progressive Education Revisited." *History of Education* 30, no. 5 (2001): 413–432.
Brickman, William. "Attack and Counterattack in American Education." *School and Society* (October 27, 1951): 262–269.
Brown, Mrs. Hugh. *Lady in Boomtown.* University of Nevada Press, 1968.
Bruene, Elizabeth. "The Activity Procedure and the Fundamentals." *California Journal of Elementary Education* 4, no. 2 (November 1935): 104–108.

Cahan, Ruth. "The Implementation of the John Dewey Philosophy in the University Elementary School University of California at Los Angeles." MA dissertation, UCLA, 1958.
———. "Rationale for the Selection of Dramatic Play as a Teaching Strategy in the Elementary School." EdD dissertation, UCLA, 1971.
California Bureau of Elementary Education. *Teachers Guide to Education in Early Childhood*. California State Department of Education, 1956.
———. *Teachers Guide to Education in Later Childhood*. California State Department of Education, 1957.
California Framework Committee. "A Framework for Public Education in California." California State Printing Office, 1950.
California Senate Fact-Finding Committee on Un-American Activities. *Ninth Report: Un-American Activities in California*. California State Printing Office, 1953.
California Senate Investigating Committee on Education. *Eighth Report: Education in Pasadena*. California State Printing Office, 1951.
———. *Ninth Report: Are Loyalty Oaths Effective?* California State Printing Office, 1952.
———. *Twelfth Report: Current Problems in Education*. California State Printing Office, 1955.
———. *Sixteenth Report: Curriculum Changes*. California State Printing Office, 1958.
California State Department of Education. *Teachers' Guide to Child Development*. California State Department of Education, 1930.
———. *Teachers' Guide to Child Development for the Intermediate Grades*. California State Department of Education, 1936.
———. *The Social Studies Program for the Public Schools of California*. Bulletin 17, no. 4. Prepared under the direction of the State Curriculum Commission. California State Department of Education, 1948.
Cameron, Ardis. *Radicals of the Worst Sort: Laboring Women in Lawrence, Massachusetts, 1860–1912*. University of Illinois Press, 1995.
Carney, Mabel. *Country Life and the Country School*. Row, Peterson and Company, 1912.
Carson, Clayborn. "Two Cheers for Brown v. Board of Education" *Journal of American History* 91, no. 1 (June 2004): 26–31.
Caswell, Hollis. "Administrative Considerations in Curriculum Development." In *Democracy and the Curriculum: Third Yearbook of the John Dewey Society*, edited by Harold Rugg. D. Appleton-Century Company, 1939.
Central Committee on Social Studies. "Building Curriculum in Social Studies for the Public Schools of California: A Progress Report." California State Printing Office, 1957.
Chapman, Paul. *Schools as Sorters: Lewis Terman, Applied Psychology and the Intelligence Testing Movement, 1890–1939*. New York University Press, 1988.
———. "Schools as Sorters: Testing and Tracking in California, 1910–1925." *Journal of Social History* 14, no. 4 (Summer 1981): 701–717.
Citron, Abraham, Collin Reynolds, and Sarah Taylor, "Ten Years of Intercultural Education in Educational Magazines." *Harvard Educational Review*, 15 (March 1945): 129–133.
Civil Information and Education Section, Supreme Commander for the Allied Powers. *Education in the New Japan*. 2 vols. Supreme Commander for the Allied Powers, 1948.

Clifford, Geraldine. "'Lady Teachers' and the Politics of Teaching in the United States, 1850–1930." In *Teachers: The Culture and Politics of Work*, edited by Martin Lawn and Gerald Grace. Falmer Press, 1987.

Clifford, Geraldine, and James W. Guthrie. *Ed School: A Brief for Professional Education*. University of Chicago Press, 1988.

Cobb, Stanwood. *The New Leaven*. Day Publishers, 1928.

———. "A New Movement in Education." *Atlantic Monthly* (May 1922): 227–234.

Cohen, Sol. "The Mental Hygiene Movement, the Development of Personality and the School: The Medicalization of American Education." *History of Education Quarterly* 23, no. 2 (Summer 1983): 123–149.

Cohen, Theodore, ed. *Remaking Japan: The American Occupation as New Deal*. Free Press, 1987.

Coldwell, Clara. "Teaching the Children of Seasonal Workers." *California Exchange Bulletin in Rural Education* 1, no. 2 (January 1927): 59–62.

Cole, Donald. *Immigrant City: Lawrence, Massachusetts 1845–1921*. University of North Carolina Press, 1963.

"Conference on Organization and Supervision of the Elementary School." *California Schools* 24, no. 9 (September 1953): 399.

———. *California Schools* 24, no. 10 (October 1953): 465–66.

"Co-operative Study in Elementary Education." *California Schools* 25, no. 3 (March 1954): 108–109.

Corey, Arthur. "California Schools Do Educate: A Reaffirmation." *Atlantic* 102 (December 1958): 63–66.

Counts, George. *Dare the School Build a New Social Order?* John Day Co., 1932.

Crabtree, Charlotte. "The Development and Evaluation of a Fifth Grade Unit of Work: How the Pioneers Moved Westward." MA thesis, UCLA, 1954.

Cremin, Lawrence, David Shannon, and Mary Townsend. *A History of Teachers College Columbia University*. Columbia University Press, 1954.

———. *The Transformation of the School*. Vintage Books, 1964.

Crocco, Margaret, Petra Munro, and Kathleen Weiler. *Pedagogies of Resistance*. Teachers College Press, 1999.

Cronon, William, George Miles, and Jay Gitlin, eds. *Under An Open Sky: Rethinking America's Western Past*. W.W. Norton, 1992.

Culp, W. M. "Jottings of a Traveling Bookman." *Western Journal of Education* 38, no. 9 (November 1932): 9.

Cummings, William. "The Egalitarian Transformation of Postwar Japanese Education." *Comparative Educational Review* 26, no. 1 (February 1982): 16–35.

Davis, Mike. *City of Quartz*. Verso Books, 1990.

Davis, Mike. "Sunshine and the Open Shop: Ford and Darwin in 1920s Los Angeles." In *Metropolis in the Making*, edited by Tom Sitton and William Deverell. University of California Press, 2001.

Davis, O. L. "Rachel Davis DuBois: Intercultural Education Pioneer." In *Bending the Future to Their Will*, edited by Margaret Crocco and O. L. Davis. Rowman and Littlefield, 1999.

DeGraff, Lawrence. "The City of Black Angels: Emergence of the Los Angeles Ghetto, 1890–1930." *Pacific Historical Review* 39, no. 3 (August 1970): 323–352.

D'Emilio, John. *Sexual Politics, Sexual Communities*. University of Chicago Press, 1998.

De Lima, Agnes. *Our Enemy the Child*. New Republic Inc., 1926.
Delpit, Lisa. *Other People's Children*. The New Press, 2006.
Deverell, William. "My America or Yours?" In *Metropolis in the Making: Los Angeles in the 1920s*, edited by William Deverell and Tom Sitton, 277–301. University of California Press, 2001.
———, and Tom Sitton, eds. *California Progressivism Revisited*. University of California Press, 1994.
Dewey, John. "Education as Politics." *New Republic* 32 (1922), 139–141. Reprinted in *John Dewey: The Middle Works, 1899–1924*, Vol. 13: *1921–1922*, edited by Jo Ann Boydston. Southern Illinois University Press, 1983.
———. "How Much Freedom in New Schools?" *The New Republic*, July 1930. Reprinted in *John Dewey: The Later Works, 1925–1953*, Vol. 5: *1929–1930*, edited by Jo Ann Boydston. Southern Illinois University Press, 1984.
———. "Introduction." In Elsie Ridley Clapp, *Use of Resources*. Harper and Brothers, 1952.
———. "Progressive Education and the Science of Education." Address presented to the Progressive Education Association, March 8, 1928. Reprinted in *John Dewey: The Later Works, 1925–1953*, Vol. 4: *1928*, edited by Jo Ann Boydston. Southern Illinois University Press, 1981.
———, and Evelyn Dewey. *Schools of To-morrow*. E. P. Dutton and Company, 1915.
Donato, Ruben. *The Other Struggle for Civil Rights*. SUNY Press, 1997.
Dorn, Charles. *American Education, Democracy, and the Second World War*. Palgrave Macmillan, 2007.
———. "'Treason in the Textbook': Reinterpreting the Harold Rugg Textbook Controversy in the Context of Schooling During World War II." *Paedagogica Historica* 44, no. 4 (2008) 457–479.
Doten, Samuel. *An Illustrated History of the University of Nevada*. University of Nevada Press, 1924.
Douglass, Aubrey. "Preliminary Report of Committee on Scope and Sequence of Major Learnings in the Curriculum." *California Journal of Elementary Education* 4, no. 4 (May 1937): 198–199.
Dower, John. *Embracing Defeat: Japan in the Wake of World War II*. The New Press, 1999.
Duberman, Martin, Martha Vicinus, and George Chauncy, eds. *Hidden from History: Reclaiming the Gay and Lesbian Past*. Penguin Books, 1991.
Dudziak, Mary. *Cold War Civil Rights*. Princeton University Press, 2000.
Duke, Ben. "American Educational Reforms in Japan: Twelve Years Later." *Harvard Educational Review* 34, no. 4 (Fall 1964): 525–536.
———. "The Irony of Japanese Postwar Education." *Comparative Education Review* 6, no. 3 (February 1963): 212–217.
Eastman, George. "The Ideologizing of Theories: John Dewey's Educational Theory, a Case in Point." *Educational Theory* 17, no. 2 (1967): 103–119.
Edmands, Ruth. "The New Educational Order." *California Journal of Elementary Education* 3, no. 3 (February 1935): 153–157.
Eells, Walter Crosby. *The Literature of Japanese Education 1945–1954*. The Shoe String Press, 1955.
Elleson, Iva. "Being a Teacher in a Migratory School." *Western Journal of Education* 36, no. 3 (March 1930): 9–10.
Ellis, Anne. *The Life of an Ordinary Woman*. 1929. Reprint, University of Nebraska Press, 1980

Elsbree, Willard. *The American Teacher*. American Book Company, 1939.
Erickson, Christine. "'We Want No Teachers who Say There are Two Sides to Every Question': Conservative Women and Education in the 1930s." *History of Education Quarterly* 46, no. 4 (Winter 2006): 487–502.
Erickson, Christine. "'I Have Not Had One Fact Disproven': Elizabeth Dilling's Crusade Against Communism in the 1930s." *Journal of American Studies* 36, no. 3 (2002): 473–489.
Faderman, Lillian. *Odd Girls and Twilight Lovers: A History of Lesbian Life in Twentieth Century America*. Penguin, 1992.
Fass, Paula. "Without Design: Education Policy in the New Deal." *American Journal of Education* 91, no. 1 (November 1982): 36–64.
Florell, David. "Origin and History of the School of Education, University of California, Los Angeles." EdD dissertation, UCLA, 1946.
Fogelson, Robert. *The Fragmented Metropolis: Los Angeles 1850–1930*. Harvard University Press, 1967.
Foster, Stuart. *Red Alert!* Peter Lang, 2000.
Foucault, Michel. "Nietzsche, Genealogy, History." In *The Foucault Reader*, edited by Paul Rabinow. Pantheon Books, 1984.
———. "The Means of Correct Training." In *The Foucault Reader*, edited by Paul Rabinow, Pantheon Books, 1984.
Franzen, Trisha. *Spinsters and Lesbians: Independent Womanhood in the United States*. New York University Press, 1996.
Freedman, Estelle. "'The Burning of Letters Continues': Elusive Identities and the Historical Construction of Sexuality." *Journal of Women's History* 9, no. 4 (Winter 1998): 181–206.
Gardner, David. "By Oath and Association: The California Folly." *Journal of Higher Education* 40, no. 2 (February 1969): 122–134.
Gerstle, Gary. "The Protean Character of American Liberalism." *American Historical Review* 99, no. 4 (October 1994): 1043–1073.
Gilroy, Amanda, and W. M. Verhoeven, "Introduction." In *Epistolary Histories: Letters, Fiction, Culture*, edited by Amanda Gilroy and W. M. Verhoeven. University of Virginia Press, 2000.
Gleason, Mona. *Normalizing the Ideal*. University of Toronto Press, 1999.
Gluck, Carol. "Foreword." Tsuchimochi, Gary. *Education Reform in Postwar Japan: The 1946 U.S. Education Mission*. University of Tokyo Press, 1993.
Gonzalez, Gilbert. "Segregation of Mexican Children in a Southern California City: The Legacy of Expansionism and the American Southwest." *Western Historical Quarterly* 16, no. 1 (January 1985): 55–76.
Goodenough, Ronald. "Racial and Ethnic Tolerance in John Dewey's Educational and Social Thought: The Depression Years." *Educational Theory* 27, no. 1 (Winter 1977): 48–64.
Goodman, Roger and David Phillips, eds. *Can the Japanese Change their Educational System?* Continuum Books, 2003.
Goodsell, Willystine. "Mary Adelaide Nutting: Educator and Builder." *Teachers College Record* 27, no. 5 (January 1926): 382–393.
Gordon, Linda. "Family, Violence, Feminism, and Social Control." In *Women, the State, and Welfare*, edited by Linda Gordon. University of Wisconsin Press, 1990.
Gordon, Lynn. *Gender and Higher Education in the Progressive Era*. Yale University Press, 1990.

Gordon, Rosalie M. "What's Happened to Our Schools?" America's Future, Inc. 1956.
Gould, Stephen J. *The Mismeasure of Man.* W. W. Norton, 1996.
Graham, Patricia. *Progressive Education: From Arcady to Academe.* Teachers College Press, 1967.
Graves, Karen. *And They Were Wonderful Teachers: Florida's Purge of Gay and Lesbian Teachers.* University of Illinois Press, 2009.
Graybill, Stuart. "Bending the Twig: Conservative Educational Criticism and the Revival of the Right, 1900–1960." PhD dissertation, University of California Davis, 1999.
Gribskov, Margaret. "Feminization and the Women School Administrator." In *Women and Educational Leadership,* edited by Sari Biklen and Marilyn Brannigan. Lexington Books, 1980.
Grubb, W. Norton, and Marvin Lazerson. "Child Care, Government Financing, and the Public Schools: Lessons for the California Children's Centers." *School Review* 86, no. 1 (November 1977): 5–37.
Gullet, Gayle. "Women Progressives and the Politics of Americanization in California, 1915–1920." *Pacific Historical Review* 64, no. 1 (February 1995): 71–94.
———. *Becoming Citizens.* University of Illinois Press, 2000.
Gwinn, Herbert. "The Flag, the Pledge, and You." *California Schools* 32, no. 9 (October 1961): 15–16.
Haiducek, Nicholas. *Japanese Education: Made in the USA.* Praeger, 1991.
Hall, Jacqueline Dowd. "To Widen the Reach of Our Love: Autobiography, History, and Desire." *Feminist Studies* 26, no. 1 (Spring 2000): 231–247.
Hall, Robert. *Education for a New Japan.* Yale University Press, 1949.
Hanna, Paul. "Master Teachers and Modern Education." *California Journal of Elementary Education* 4, no. 2 (November 1935): 97–103.
———. "The Problem of Social Education." In *Social Education,* ed. Stanford Education Conference. Macmillan, 1939.
Hartman, Andrew. *Education and the Cold War.* Palgrave Macmillan, 2008.
Hartman, Beulah. "California Rural Supervisors Hold Significant Convention at Lake Tahoe, October 4th to 8th." *California Exchange Bulletin in Rural Education* 1, no. 1 (November 1926): 33
Heale, M. J. "Red Scare Politics: California's Campaign Against Un-American Activities, 1940–1970." *Journal of American Studies* 20, no. 1 (April 1986): 5–32.
Healey, Dorothy, and Maurice Isserman. *California Red: A Life in the American Communist Party.* University of Illinois Press, 1993.
Helbling, M. (1941). "The Guidance Program in the Elementary School." *California Journal of Elementary Education* 10, no. 2 (November 1941): 77–86.
"Helen Heffernan Retires from Education Bureau." *The Sacramento Bee.* September 2, 1965.
"Helen Heffernan Retires." *California Education* 3, no. 2 (October 1965): 1.
Hendrick, Irving. "California's Response to the 'New Education' in the 1930s." *California Historical Quarterly,* 53 (Spring 1974): 25–40.
———. "The Impact of the Great Depression on Public School Support in California." *Southern California Quarterly,* 54 (1972): 177–195.
Herbst, Jurgen. *And Sadly Teach: Teacher Education and Professionalization in American Culture.* University of Wisconsin Press, 1989.
Hill, Gladwin. "A Father Looks at Progressive Education." *The Atlantic* (December 1954): 55–57.

Hockett, John. "Facing Realities in Elementary School Social Studies." *California Journal of Elementary Education* 4, no. 3 (February 1937): 136–147.

———. "The Evaluation of the Elementary School Program." *California Journal of Elementary Education* 6, no. 4 (May 1938): 210–217.

Horowitz, Helen. *Alma Mater*. University of Massachusetts Press, 1984.

———. *Campus Life: Undergraduate Cultures from the End of the Eighteenth Century to the Present*. Alfred A. Knopf, 1987.

———. *The Passion of M. Carrie Thomas*. Alfred A. Knopf, 1994.

House Un-American Activities Committee. "100 Things You Should Know About Communism and Education." Washington, D. C., 1949, 68–69. http://www.archive.org/details/100thingsyoushou1949unit (accessed December 10, 2008).

Howard, Anne. *The Long Campaign: A Biography of Anne Martin*. University of Nevada Press, 1985.

Huchel, Frederick. *A History of Box Elder County*. Utah Historical Society, 1999.

Hulburd, David. *This Happened in Pasadena*. The Macmillan Company, 1951.

Irving, Katrina. *Immigrant Mothers: Narratives of Race and Maternity 1890–1925*. University of Illinois Press, 2000.

Irwin, Mary, and James Brooks, eds. *Women and Gender in the American West*. University of New Mexico Press, 2004.

Iverson, Robert. *The Communists and the Schools*. Harcourt Brace, 1959.

James, Thomas. *Exile Within*. Harvard University Press, 1987.

Jameson, Elizabeth. *Building Colorado: The United Brotherhood of Carpenters and Joiners of America in the Centennial State*. Colorado State Council of Carpenters, 1984.

Jameson, Elizabeth. *All That Glitters: Class, Conflict, and Community in Cripple Creek*. University of Illinois Press, 1998.

———, and Susan Armitage, eds. *Writing the Range*. University of Oklahoma Press, 1997.

Jeffreys, Sheila. *The Spinster and Her Enemies*. Pandora Press, 1986.

Johnson, Marilyn. *The Second Gold Rush: Oakland and the East Bay in World War II*. University of California Press, 1993.

Jones, Kitty, and Robert Oliver. *Progressive Education is Red-ucation*. Meador Publishing Co., 1956.

Kennedy, David. *Freedom from Fear*. Oxford University Press, 1999.

Kennedy, Elizabeth. "'But We Would Never Talk About It': The Structures of Lesbian Discretion in South Dakota, 1928–1933." In *Inventing Lesbian Cultures in America*, edited by Ellen Lewin. Beacon Press, 1999.

Kennedy, Elizabeth, and Madeleine Davis. *Boots of Leather, Slippers of Gold*. Routledge, 1993.

Kilpatrick, William. "The Project Method." *Teachers College Record* 19, no. 4 (September 1918): 319–335.

Kilpatrick, William. *Foundations of Method: Informal Talks on Teaching*. Macmillan, 1925.

Klarman, Michael. "How Brown Changed Race Relations." *Journal of American History* 81, no. 1 (June 1994): 81–118.

Kliebard, Herbert. *The Struggle for the American Curriculum*. Routledge, 1987.

Knight, Harold. *Working in Colorado: A Brief History of the Colorado Labor Movement*. Center for Labor Education and Research, 1971.

Kobayashi, Victor. *John Dewey in Japanese Educational Thought.* University of Michigan Comparative Education dissertation Series, No. 2, 1964.
Koikari, Mire. "Rethinking Gender and Power in the U.S. Occupation of Japan 1945–1952." *Gender and History* 11, no. 2 (July 1999): 313–335.
———. "Exporting Democracy? American Women, 'Feminist Reforms,' and the Politics of Imperialism in the U.S. Occupation of Japan, 1945–1952." *Frontiers* 11, no. 2 (January 2002): 313–338.
Kransdorf, Martha. *A Matter of Loyalty: The Los Angeles School Board Vs. Frances Eisenberg.* Caddo Gap Press, 1994.
Krug, Edward. *The Shaping of the American High School.* Harper and Row, 1964.
Lagemann, Ellen. *An Elusive Science: The Troubling History of Education Research.* University of Chicago Press, 2000.
Laird, Susan. "Women and Gender in John Dewey's Philosophy of Education." *Educational Theory* 38, no. 1 (Winter 1988): 111–129.
Lal, Shafali. "Securing the Children: Social Science, Children, and the Meaning of Race 1939–1968," PhD dissertation, Yale University, 2002.
Layton, Edwin. "The Better America Federation: A Case Study of Superpatriotism." *Pacific Historical Review* 30, no. 2 (May 1961): 137–147.
Lee, Murray, and Dorris May Lee. "Keeping Informed." *California Journal of Elementary Education* 3, no. 3 (February 1935): 242.
Leonard, Kevin. "'Brothers Under the Skin?' African Americans, Mexican Americans, and World War II in California." In *The Way We Really Were: The Golden State in the Second World War,* edited by Roger Lotchin, 187–214. University of Illinois Press, 2000.
Lewin, Ellen, ed. *Inventing Lesbian Cultures in America.* Beacon Press, 1996.
Limerick, Patricia. *The Legacy of Conquest.* W. W. Norton, 1987.
Limerick, Patricia, Clyde Milner, and Charles Rankin, eds. *Trails: Toward a New Western History.* The University Press of Kansas, 1991.
Litsinger, Dolores. "The Theory and Method of Social Studies Instruction at the University Elementary School U.C.L.A." EdD dissertation, University of California, Los Angeles, 1962.
———. *Social Studies Instruction at the University Elementary School, UCLA.* University of California Publications in Education, 16. University of California Press, 1965.
Loe, Nancy. *Life in the Altitudes: An Illustrated History of Colorado Springs.* Windsor Publications, 1983.
Lora, Ronald. "Education: Schools as Crucible in Cold War America." In *Reshaping America: Society and Institutions 1945–1960,* edited by Robert Bremner and Gary Reichard. Ohio State University Press, 1982.
Lossing, Laverna. "Creative Music." *California Journal of Elementary Education* 3, no. 4 (May 1935): 207–212.
Lotchin, Roger. *Fortress California 1910–1961.* Oxford University Press, 1992.
———, ed. "Fortress California at War: San Francisco, Los Angeles, Oakland, and San Diego." *Pacific Historical Review* 63, no. 3 (August 1994): 277–468.
———, *The Way We Really Were: The Golden State in the Second World War.* University of Illinois Press, 2000.
Marden, David. "The Cold War and American Education." PhD dissertation, University of Kansas, 1975.
Martin, Edwin. *The Allied Occupation of Japan.* Stanford University Press, 1948.

Martin, Jane Roland. "Excluding Women from the Educational Realm." In *The Education Feminism Reader*, edited by Lynda Stone. Routledge, 1994.
Matsumoto, Valerie, and Blake Allmendiger, eds. *Over the Edge: Remapping the American West*. University of California Press, 1999.
Mattingly, Paul. *The Classless Profession*. New York University Press, 1975.
May, Elaine. *Homeward Bound American Families in the Cold War Era*. Basic Books, 1988.
Mayo, Marlene. "Planning for the Education and Re-education of Defeated Japan, 1943–45." In *The Occupation of Japan: Educational and Social Reform*, edited by Thomas Bunkman. MacArthur Memorial, 1982.
McClatchy, V. S., ed. *Four Anti-Japanese Pamphlets*. Arno Press, 1978.
McClymer, John. "Gender and the American Way of Life: Women in the Americanization Movement." *Journal of American Ethnic History* 10, no. 3 (Spring 1991): 3–20.
McDonald, Milo. "American Education: The Old, the Modern, and the 'New.'" American Education Association, 1952.
———. "'Progressive' Poison in Public Education." American Education Association, 1951.
McGirr, Lisa. *Suburban Warriors: The Origin of the New American Right*. Princeton University Press, 2001.
McRae, Edna. "The Possibilities of the One-Teacher School." *California Exchange Bulletin in Rural Education* 1, no. 4 (May 1927): 13–18.
McWilliams, Carey. *Brothers Under the Skin*. Little, Brown and Co., 1943.
———. *The Education of Carey McWilliams*, Simon and Schuster, 1978.
———. "The Enemy in Pasadena." *Christian Century* 68, no. 1 (January 3, 1951): 9–12.
———. *Prejudice: Japanese Americans: Symbol of Racial Intolerance*. Little Brown, 1945.
Menchaca, Martha and Richard Valencia, "Anglo-Saxon Ideologies in the 1920s and 1930s: Their Impact on the Segregation of Mexican Students in California." *Anthropology and Education Quarterly* 21, 3 (1990): 222–249.
Michel, Sonya. *Children's Interests/Mother's Rights: The Shaping of America's Child Care Policy*. Yale University Press, 1999.
Mickenberg, Julia. *Learning from the Left*. Oxford University Press, 2006.
Miel, Alice. "Education's Part in Democratizing Japan." *Teachers College Record* 55 (October 1953): 10–19.
Mills, C. Wright. *The Sociological Imagination*. Oxford University Press, 1959.
Miyoishi, Minoru. "The Trends of Educational Psychology in Japan." *Education in Japan: Journal for Overseas* 1, 1 (1966): 94–108.
Molasky, Michael. *The American Occupation of Japan and Okinawa*. Routledge, 1999.
Monroy, George. *Rebirth: Mexican Los Angeles from the Great Migration to the Great Depression*. University of California Press, 1999.
Montalto, Nicholas. *A History of the Intercultural Educational Movement 1924–1941*. Garland Press, 1982.
Moore, Ernest. *I Helped Make a University*. Dawson's Book Shop, 1952.
Morpeth, Ruth. "Dynamic Leadership: Helen Heffernan and Progressive Education in California." PhD dissertation, University of California Riverside, 1989.
Morrisett, Lloyd, Frank Freeman, John Sexson, and Frank Thomas. "The Report of the Survey of the University Elementary School, University of California at Los Angeles." Unpublished manuscript, September 1945.

Mowry, George. *The California Progressives*. University of California Press, 1951.
Muncy, Robyn. *Creating a Female Dominion in American Reform*. Oxford University Press, 1991.
Murphy, Mary. "The Private Lives of Public Women: Prostitution in Butte, Montana, 1878–1917." *Frontiers* 7, 3 (1984): 30–35.
Nance, Afton. "The Return of the Nisei." California Elementary School Principals Association. *Education for Cultural Unity*. Seventeenth Yearbook. Sacramento, 1945.
National Education Association. "A List of Articles and Books Concerned with Recent Wave of Attacks on Public Education." National Commission for the Defense of Democracy through Education, NEA, 1951.
Nerad, Marei. *The Academic Kitchen*. SUNY Press, 1999.
"New Era in Classrooms: It Will Take More Work Now to Get a Diploma." *U.S. News and World Report* (October 3, 1958): 48–50.
Nishi, Toshio. *Unconditional Democracy: Education and Politics in Occupied Japan 1945–52*. Hoover Institution Press, 1982.
Ogawa, Taro. "Reflections on Postwar Education." [Originally published as "Nihon kyoiku no kozo," 1955] *Journal of Social and Political Ideas in Japan* 1, 3 (December 1963): 24–30.
Ogren, Christine. *The American State Normal School*. Palgrave Macmillan, 2005.
"Old-Style Report Card Called Best." *Los Angeles Times* (March 17, 1955): 1.
O'Neill, William. *Readin, Ritin, and Rafferty*. Glendessary Press, 1969.
Orr, Mark. "Education Reform in Occupied Japan." PhD dissertation, University of North Carolina, 1955.
Paddison, Joshua. "Summers of Worry, Summers of Defiance: San Franciscans for Academic Freedom and the Bay Area Opposition to HUAC, 1959–1960." *California History* 78, no. 3 (Fall 1999): 188–201.
Page, Henry Markham. *Pasadena: Its Early Years*. Lorrin Morrison, Printing and Publishing, 1964.
Pagon, Eduardo Obregon, *Murder at the Sleepy Lagoon: Zoot Suits, Race, and Riot in Wartime L.A.* University of North Carolina Press, 2003.
Palmieri, Patricia. *In Adamless Eden*. Yale University Press, 1995.
Parker, Franklin. "School Critic Max Rafferty (1917–1982) and the New Right." *Review Journal of Philosophy & Social Science* 10, no. 2 (1985): 129–140.
"Pasadena Revisited." *Time* (May 7, 1951): 46.
Pascoe, Peggy. *Relations of Rescue*. Oxford, 1990.
Passin, Herbert. "The Occupation—Some Reflections." *Daedalus* 119, no. 3 (Summer 1990): 107–129.
Penn, Donna. "The Sexualized Woman: The Lesbian, the Prostitute, and the Containment of Female Sexuality in Postwar America." In *Not June Cleaver: Women and Gender in Postwar America, 1945–1960*, edited by Joanne Meyerowitz. Temple University Press, 1994.
Perlstein, Daniel. "Minds Stayed on Freedom: Politics and Pedagogy in the African-American Freedom Struggle." *American Educational Research Journal* 39, no. 2 (Summer 2002): 249–277.
———. "'Indoctrination': George Counts and the Civic Dilemmas of Democratic Educators." In *Reconstructing the Common Good in Education*, edited by Larry Cuban and Dorothy Shipps. Stanford University Press, 2000.
Phelan, Arthur. "The Administration of the University Elementary School of the University of California, Los Angeles, 1882–1957." EdD dissertation, University of California, Los Angeles.

Popkewitz, Thomas. "A Changing Terrain of Knowledge and Power: A Social Epistemology of Educational Research." *Educational Researcher* 26, no. 9 (December 1997): 18–29.

Popkewitz, Thomas. "Inventing the Modern Self and John Dewey: Modernities and the Traveling of Pragmatism in Education—An Introduction." In *Inventing the Modern Self and John Dewey*, edited by Thomas Popkewitz. Palgrave Macmillan, 2005.

Putnam, Jackson. *Age-Old Politics in California: From Richardson to Reagan.* Stanford University Press, 1970.

Rafferty, Max. "Children of Uranus." *Phi Delta Kappan* 42 (October 1960): 20–23.

———. "A Chronicle of Masks." *Phi Delta Kappan* 38 (May 1957): 298–301.

———. "The Cult of the Slob." *Phi Delta Kappan* 40 (November 1958): 56–59.

———. "Education in Depth." *California Education* 1, no. 1 (September 1963): 7–8.

———. "Education in Depth." *California Education* 1, no. 5 (January 1964): 1–3.

———. "The Elements of Patriotism." *California Education* 2, no. 1 (September 1964): 2–4.

———. *On Education*. The Devin-Adair Company, 1968.

———. "Open Season." *Phi Delta Kappan* 41 (November 1959): 49–52.

———. "The Philistines." *Phi Delta Kappan* 39 (November 1957): 42–46.

———. "The Seven Grim Fairy Tales." *Phi Delta Kappan* 42 (December 1960): 114–120.

———. *Suffer, Little Children*. Devin-Adair Company, 1962.

———. "Suffer the Little Children." *Phi Delta Kappan* 36 (December 1956): 89–92.

———. "Teacher-Training Change Needed." *Los Angeles Times* (May 26, 1964): 2, 5.

———. "The Trouble with Life Adjustment." *Los Angeles Times* (October 26, 1964): 2, 7.

———. "What Happened to Patriotism?" *The Reader's Digest* (October 1961): 107–110.

Ravitch, Diane. *Left Back: A Century of Failed School Reforms*. Simon and Schuster, 2000.

Raywid, Mary Anne. *The Ax-Grinders*. Macmillan, 1963.

Read, H. S. "Trends in the Social Studies – Science Program in the Kindergarten and Primary Grades." *California Journal of Elementary Education* 10, no. 4 (May 1942): 243–253.

"Red Methods in Schools Grading Seen." *Los Angeles Times* (March 17, 1955): 1.

Redefer, Frederick. "What Has Happened to Progressive Education?" *School and Society* 67, 1741 (May 8, 1948).

Reese, Ellen. "Maternalism and Political Mobilization: How California's Postwar Child Care Campaign Was Won." *Gender and Society* 10, no. 5 (October 1996): 566–589.

Reese, William. "The Origins of Progressive Education." *History of Education Quarterly* 41, no. 1 (Spring 2001): 1–24

"Report of the California Central Committee on Social Studies." *California Schools* 27, no. 12 (December 1956): 431–436.

Rickover, Hyman. *Education and Freedom*. E. P. Dutton, 1959.

———. "Let's Stop Wasting Our Greatest Resource." *Saturday Evening Post* 229 (March 2, 1957): 19, 108–111.

Riles, Wilson. "Problems of *de facto* Segregation." *California Education* 1, no. 1 (September 1963): 39.

———. "School Boards and 'de facto' Segregation." *California Education* 1, no. 3 (November 1963): 7–8.

Robertson, Wanda. "Developing World Citizens in a Japanese Relocation Center." *Childhood Education* (October 1943): 66–71.

Robinson, Don. "The Conservative Revolution in California Education." *Phi Delta Kappan* (December 1960): 90–100.

Roden, D. "From 'old miss' to new professional: A portrait of women educators under the American Occupation of Japan 1945–1952." *History of Education Quarterly* 23, no. 4 (Winter 1983): 469–489.

Rogers, Frederick Rand. "Progressive Education Irresponsible and Immoral Pedagogy." National Council for American Education, 1952.

Rogin, Michael, and John Shover, *Political Change in California: Critical Elections and Social Movements*. Greenwood Publishing Co., 1970.

Root, E. Merrill. *Brainwashing in the High School*. Devin-Adair, 1958.

Rose, Elizabeth. *A Mother's Job: The History of Day Care, 1890–1960*. Oxford University Press, 1999.

Rose, Nikolas. "Identity, Genealogy, History." In *Questions of Cultural Identity*, edited by Stuart Hall and Paul DuGay, 128–150. Sage Publications, 1996.

Rousmaniere, Kate. *Citizen Teacher: The Life and Leadership of Margaret Haley*. Teachers College Press, 2005.

Rudd, Augustin. *Bending the Twig*. Sons of the American Revolution, 1957.

Rugg, Harold, and Ann Shumaker. *The Child Centered School*. World Book Company, 1928.

Rupp, Leila. "Imagine My Surprise." In *Hidden from History: Reclaiming the Gay and Lesbian Past*, edited by Martin Duberman, Martha Vicinus, and George Chauncy. Penguin Books, 1991.

Rury, John. *Education and Women's Work*. SUNY Press, 1991.

Rudolph, John. *Scientists in the Classroom*. Palgrave, 2002.

Sadovnik, Alan, and Susan Semel, eds. *Founding Mothers and Others: Women Educational Leaders during the Progressive Era*. Palgrave Publishers, 2002.

Sahli, Nancy. "Smashing: Women's Relationships Before the Fall." *Chrysalis* 8 (1979): 17–27.

Saito, John Jr., "Letters of Conscience." *Japanese American National Museum Magazine*, August 2, 2007. http://www.discovernikkei.org/en/journal/2007/8/2/janm-magazine/ (accessed August 9, 2010).

San Bernadino County Schools. *Social Studies for Democracy's Children*. Office of the Superintendent of Schools, 1955.

Sanchez, George. "Go After the Women: Americanization and the Mexican Immigrant Woman, 1915–1929." In *Unequal Sisters: A Multicultural Reader in U.S. Women's History*, edited by Vicki Ruiz and Ellen DuBois. Routledge, 1994.

Satow, Hideo, Eiichi Suzuki, and Gary Tsuchimochi, eds. *Educational Reform in Japan 1945–52: Part I*. University Publications of America. Microfiche.

Scharff, Virginia. *Taking the Wheel*. University of New Mexico Press, 1991.

———. *Twenty Thousand Roads*. University of California Press, 2002.

Schnur, James. "Closet Crusaders: The Johns Committee and Homophobia, 1956–1965." In *Carryin' On in the Gay and Lesbian South*, edited by John Howard, 132–163. New York University Press, 1997.

Schrag, Peter. *Paradise Lost: California's Experience, America's Future*. University of California Press, 1999.

Schrecker, Ellen. *No Ivory Tower.* Oxford University Press, 1986.
Schultz, Aaron. *Social Class, Social Action, and Education.* Palgrave Macmillan, 2010.
Seller, Maxine. "The Education of the Immigrant Woman: 1900–1935." *Journal of Urban History* 4, no. 3 (May 1978): 307–330.
———. "G. Stanley Hall and Edward Thorndike on the Education of Women: Theory and Policy in the Progressive Era." *Educational Studies* 11 (1981): 365–374.
Seraphim, Franziska. *War, Memory, and Social Politics in Japan 1945–2005.* Harvard University Press, 2006.
Shannon, Christopher. "A World Made Safe for Differences: Ruth Benedict's "The Chrysanthemum and the Sword." *American Quarterly* 47, no. 4 (December 1995): 659–680.
Simpson, Roy. "California's Investment in Educational Leadership." *California Schools* 28, no. 2 (February 1957): 4–5.
———. "Dividends from Public Education." *California Schools* 21, no. 8 (August 1950): 294.
———. "Education in an Age of Uncertainty." *California Schools* 33, no. 1 (January 1962): 8–18.
———. "Maintaining a Balanced Educational Program." *California Schools* 31, no. 2 (February 1960): 61.
———. "Postwar Progress in the Public School System." *California Schools* 17, no. 11 (November 1947): 241–250.
———. "Special Report to the State Board of Education." *California Schools* 33, no. 1 (January 1962): 1–7.
———. "The Study of History, Geography, and Related Subjects in the California Schools. A Statement by the Superintendent of Public Instruction, Roy E. Simpson, to the State Board of Education and Curriculum Commission, August 24, 1946, Los Angeles, California." Department of Education files F3752:649 1946–48. California State Archives, Sacramento.
——— and H. M. McPherson. "A Summary of Actions of the State Board of Education and the State Curriculum Commission in Adopting 'Building America'." *California Schools* 18, no. 4 (April 1947): 59–69.
Skocpol, Theda. *Protecting Soldiers and Mothers.* Harvard University Press, 1992.
Smith, Joan. *Ella Flagg Young: Portrait of a Leader.* Northern Illinois Press, 1979.
Smith, Mortimer. *And Madly Teach: A Layman Looks at Public School Education.* H. Regnery Co., 1949.
———. "California's Latest Educational Committee." *Tax Digest* 37 (May 1959): 106, 115.
———. *The Diminished Mind: A Study of Planned Mediocrity in Our Public Schools.* H. Regnery Co., 1954.
———. "How to Teach the California Child: Notes from Never Never Land." *Atlantic Monthly* 202, no. 3 (September 1958): 32–36.
Solomon, Barbara. *In the Company of Educated Women.* Harvard University Press, 1985.
Spillers, Hortense. "Mama's Baby, Papa's Maybe: An American Grammar Book." *Diacritics* 17, no. 2 (Summer 1987): 64–81.
Sprague, Marshall. *Newport in the Rockies.* Ohio University Press, 1987.
Stack, Sam. *Elsie Ripley Clapp (1879–1965): Her Life and the Community School.* Peter Lang, 2004.
Stallones, Jared. *Paul Robert Hanna.* Hoover Institution Press, 2002.

Starr, Kevin. *Endangered Dreams: The Great Depression in California*. Oxford University Press, 1996.

Stern, Alexandra. *Eugenic Nation*. University of California Press, 2005.

Stoddard, Lothrop. *The Rising Tide of Color Against White World-Supremacy*. Scribner, 1927.

Stolzfus, Emily. *Citizen, Mother, Worker: Debating Public Responsibility for Child Care after the Second World War*. University of North Carolina Press, 2003.

"Student Grading Method is Called Communistic." *Fresno Bee* (March 17, 1955): 1.

Takemae, Eiji. *Inside GHO*. New York: Continuum, 2002.

Tamura, Eileen. "Value Messages Collide with Reality: Joseph Kurihara and the Power of Informal Education." *History of Education Quarterly* 50, no. 1 (January 2010): 1–33.

Tenenbaum, Samuel. *William Heard Kilpatrick: Trail Blazer in Education*. Harper, 1951.

Tenney, Jack. *California Legislator*. Oral History Program, UCLA, Vol. 3, 1969.

Thakur, Yoko. "History Textbook Reform in Allied Occupied Japan, 1945–52." *History of Education Quarterly* 35, no. 3 (Autumn 1995): 261–278.

Trapnell, Jean, and Margaret Kiskadden, "The Parents View of UES." Oral History Program, University of California, Los Angeles, 1965.

Treacy, Robert. "Progressivism and Corinne Seeds." PhD dissertation, University of California Los Angeles, 1971.

Trott, Fred. "Education in the Postwar World—Supervisors Conference." *Western Journal of Education* 49, no. 9 (November 1943): 9–10.

Tsuchimochi, Gary. *Education Reform in Postwar Japan: The 1946 U.S. Education Mission*. University of Tokyo Press, 1993.

Tyack, David. *The One Best System*. Harvard University Press, 1971.

Tyack, David, Robert Lowe, and Elisabth Hansot. *Public Schools in Hard Times*. Harvard University Press, 1984.

Valencia, Richard. "The Mexican-American Struggle for Equal Educational Opportunity in Mendez v. Westminster." *Teachers College Record* 107, no. 3 (March 2005): 389–423.

Vaughn-Roberson, Courtney. "Having a Purpose in Life: Western Women in the Twentieth Century." In *The Teacher's Voice*, edited by Richard Altenbaugh. Falmer Press, 1992.

Underwood, Kathleen. "The Pace of Their Own Lives: Teacher Training and the Life Course of Western Women." *Pacific Historical Review* 55, no. 4 (November 1986): 513–530.

"UNESCO month, October 28 to November 30, 1946." *California Schools* 17, 10 (October 1946): 271.

United States, Education Mission to Japan. *Report of the Second United States Education Mission to Japan*. U.S. Government Printing Office, 1950.

———. *Report of the United States Education Mission to Japan*. U.S. Government Printing Office, 1946.

Urban, Wayne. *More Than Science and Sputnik: The National Defense Education Act of 1958*. University of Alabama Press, 2010.

Valencia, Richard. "The Mexican-American Struggle for Equal Educational Opportunity in Mendez v. Westminster." *Teachers College Record* 107, no. 3 (March 2005): 389–423.

Verge, Arthur. "The Impact of the Second World War on Los Angeles." *Pacific Historical Review* 63, no. 3 (August 1994): 289–314.

Verge, Arthur. "Daily Life in Wartime California." In *The Way We Really Were: The Golden State in the Second World War*, edited by Roger Lotchin, 13–29. University of Illinois Press, 2000.

———. *Paradise Transformed: Los Angeles during the Second World War*. University of Iowa Press, 1993.

Waddell, Charles. "The Pragmatic Value of the Army Alpha Scores for Success in Practice Teaching." *Educational Administration and Supervision* (December 1927): 577–592.

Wagner, Rob. *Red Ink White Lies: The Rise and Fall of Los Angeles Newspapers 1920–1962*. Dragonfly Press, 2000.

Walkerdine, Valerie. *Schoolgirl Fictions*. Verso, 1990.

Wallace, James. *Liberal Journalism and American Education 1914–1941*. Rutgers University Press, 1991.

Wanamaker, Pearl. "Education Mission to Japan." *Western Journal of Education* 52, 10 (October 1946): 8–9.

Weiler, Kathleen. "The Case of Martha Deane." *History of Education Quarterly* 47, no. 4 (Fall 2007): 470–496.

———. "Corinne Seeds and the Avenue 21 School." *Historical Studies in Education* 14, no. 2 (2002): 191–218.

———. *Country Schoolwomen: Teaching in Rural California, 1850–1950*. Stanford University Press, 1998.

———. "The Genealogy of Gender in the History of Progressive Education in the United States." *Paedagogica Historica* 42, nos. 1&2 (February 2006): 161–176.

———. "Mabel Carney: From Home Missionary to White Ally." *Teachers College Record* 107, no. 12 (2005): 2599–2633.

———. "Women and Rural School Reform: California 1900–1940." *History of Education Quarterly* 34, no. 1 (Spring 1994): 25–47.

Wenkert, Robert, and Merilee Finley. "The University Elementary School at UCLA: A Historical Overview, Chronology, and Annotated Bibliography." Unpublished manuscript. Graduate School of Education, University of California Los Angeles, April, 1983.

Whitman, Howard. "Progressive Education—Which Way Forward?" *Colliers* (May 14, 1954): 32–36.

Willet, Mrs. O. Mae. "Vitalizing the Teaching in Rural Schools by the Introduction of Projects." *California Exchange Bulletin in Rural Education* 1, no. 3 (March 1927): 33–40.

Wollenberg, Charles. *All Deliberate Speed*. University of California Press, 1978.

Wubben, H. H. "American Prisoners of War in Korea: A Second Look at the 'Something New in History' Theme." *American Quarterly* 22, no. 1 (Spring 1970): 3–19.

Wulfing, Gretchen. "Enriching the Rural School Curriculum." *California Journal of Elementary Education* 3, no. 1 (August 1934): 34–40.

———. "The Implications of the Major Educational Principles for Supervision and the Direction of Instruction." *California Journal of Elementary Education* 8, no. 2 (February 1940): 151–158.

———. "Maturation as a Factor in Learning." *California Journal of Elementary Education* Part I 4, 2 (November 1935): 72–84; Part II 4, 3 (February 1936): 68–79.

Wunderlich, Herbert. "The Japanese Textbook Problems and Solution, 1945–46." PhD dissertation, Stanford University, 1952.

York, Ada. "The Course of Study in Rural Schools." *California Exchange Bulletin in Rural Education* 1, no. 1 (November 1926): 45–46.

———. "Specific Points of Teacher Training for Rural Service." *California Exchange Bulletin in Rural Education* 2, no. 1 (October 1927): 8–9.

Zanjani, Sally. *Goldfield*. Ohio University Press, 1992.

——— and Guy Louis Rocha, *The Ignoble Conspiracy: Radicalism on Trial in Nevada*. University of Nevada Press, 1986.

Zilversmit, Arthur. *Changing Schools: Progressive Education Theory and Practice 1930–1960*. University of Chicago Press, 1993.

Zimmerman, Jonathan. *Whose America?* Harvard University Press, 2002.

Zoll, Allen. "'Progressive' Education is Subverting America." National Council for American Education, n.d.

Index

"Activity Procedure and the Fundamentals, The" (Bruene), 41
activity program, 34, 60, 61, 64
Adams, Jane, 49
Adams, Lucy, 111
Adler, Alfred, 84
administrative progressives, xv, 27
adult education, 12–13, 46
Advisory Committee of Fifteen, 155
Affluent Society, The (Galbraith), 198
African Americans, 12–14, 19, 25, 35, 53, 75–76, 97, 100, 109–10, 113–15, 117, 157, 169–70, 186, 190, 194
Alexander, Miss, 130
Alexander, Robert, 135
All Aboard for Storyland (Heffernan), 93, 189–90
Allen, Eleanor, 53, 120, 123–24, 126, 134, 136
Allen, Mary, 172–73
Allen, Raymond, 176
Allen, Walter, 53, 134
Alquist, Alfred, 199
American Civil Liberties Union, 187
American Dilemma, An (Myrdal), 113
American Education and International Tensions, 158
"American Education" (McDonald), 159
Americanization programs, 13–15
American Legion, xvi, 51, 94, 95, 159, 164, 191
American Observer, 95
American Russian Institute, 129–32, 167
American Society for Russian Relief, 133
American Unity and Asia (Buck), 100
America's Future, 190

Anderson, Diana, 43, 62, 93, 201
And Madly Teach (Smith), 182
anti-Communism, xiii, xvi, 50–51, 94–97, 118, 128, 142, 149–52, 157–62, 165–77, 179, 188, 190–92, 204
anti-Semitism, 100, 109, 114–15
"Are the Schools Teaching the Three R's?" (Heffernan), 174
art and music curriculum, 41–42
Association for Childhood Education International, 186
Association for Supervision and Curriculum Development (ASCD), 159, 163, 170, 185
Atlantic Monthly, 23, 170, 182–84, 186
attitude chart, 67, 77
Avenue 21 School, 12–15, 22, 74

Bagnall, George, 120–24, 126
Barber, Benjamin, 59
Battle for Free Schools, The (Brameld), 163
Beam, Lura, 84
Beineke, John, 17
Bending the Twig (Rudd), 179
Benedict, Ruth, 143–44, 146
Berninghausen, David, 163
Bestor, Arthur, 168, 182–83, 185, 189
Better America Foundation, 25
Bettington, Blanche, 128
Beverly-Westwood Citizens Committee, 126
bilingualism, 169
Blue Bulletins, 180
Bode, Boyd, 54
Bond, Horace Mann, 169
Bond, Jesse, 87, 89, 91–92, 102–3, 120–22, 127
Boston marriages, 84

Bowron, Fletcher, 100–1
"Boy of Leningrad" curriculum,
  129–30
Brameld, Theodore, 54, 163
Bridges, Harry, 157
Britton, Ted, 171
Brothers Under the Skin (McWilliams),
  109–10
Brown, Pat, 179, 191, 192
Browning, Robert, 202–3
Brown v. Board of Education, 151,
  168–69, 179
Bruene, Elizabeth, 41
Buck, Pearl, 100
Building America, 140, 151–52
Burns, Hugh, 161, 166
Burrow, Clayton, 50
Burton, William, 190–92, 195

Caen, Herb, 187
California Association for Supervision
  and Curriculum Development, 170
California Association of Elementary
  School Principals and District
  Superintendents of Schools, 164
California Association of School
  Administrators, 174
California Commission on Equal
  Opportunities in Education, 195
California Education, 193–96, 198
California Elementary School
  Administrators Association, 161
California Elementary School
  Principals' Association, 87,
  106, 116
*California Exchange Bulletin in Rural
  Education*, 31, 41
*California Journal of Elementary
  Education*, 41, 45, 48–50, 56,
  72, 93, 95, 108, 111, 155,
  164, 183, 192–93, 196
California Office of Elementary
  Education, 161
California Rural Supervisors
  Association (*later* California
  School Supervisors Association),
  29–32, 40, 55, 138
California Schools, 38, 163, 193
California School Supervisors
  Association (*later* California
Association for Supervision and
  Curriculum Development), 29,
  55, 87, 92, 96, 119, 163, 170
California State Assembly, 96
  Ways and Means Committee,
  171–72, 174
California State Board of Education,
  140, 151
California State Chamber of
  Commerce, 164
California State Curriculum
  Commission, 138, 139, 140, 151
California State Department of
  Education, 34–35, 38–40, 46,
  50, 54–55, 62, 71, 105–7, 111,
  138, 152–56, 161–62, 171–73,
  180–84, 186–87, 189–92, 194
California State legislature, 126, 133,
  160–61, 165, 190
California State Postwar Building
  Fund, 128
California State Senate, 108, 151
  Journal, 137
California Supreme Court, 151, 162
California Taxpayers Association, 39
California Teachers Association (CTA),
  29–30, 39, 56, 161, 173–74,
  183–84, 187–89, 191
California Youth Authority, 161
"Call to the Teachers of the Nation, A"
  (Counts), 38, 41
Cameron, Ardis, 2
Carley, Verna, 144
Carney, Mabel, 27, 33, 36
Carter, Genevieve, 112–13
Caswell, Hollis, 47, 148
child
  autonomy and growth of, 60–61,
  67, 70, 77
  "natural," 19–21
Child and the Curriculum, The
  (Dewey), 16, 34
child care centers, 105–8, 152–53
child-centered education, xv, 16,
  20, 23, 25, 34–35, 64
Child Centered School, The (Rugg and
  Shumaker), 21, 34
Childhood Expressions (Seeds), 75
"Children of Uranus, The"
  (Rafferty), 192

Chinese Americans, 53, 74
Chrysanthemum and the Sword, The (Benedict), 143
Citizens' Committee for Better Education, 167
Civic Leader, 95
Civil Information and Education Section (CI&E), 142–49
Civil Rights Act (1964), xviii
civil rights movement, xii, 157, 179, 186–88, 197, 202
Clapp, Elsie Ridley, 36, 54
"Classification and Promotion Policies" (Heffernan), 70
Cloud, Roy, 29
Clowes, Richard, 187, 192–93
Cobb, Stanwood, 21, 23, 34
Cold War, xvi, 149–50, 157, 165, 168, 179, 192, 203–4
College Equal Suffrage League, 8
Colliers, 170
Collings, Ellsworth, 31
Columbia University
  Lincoln School, 34, 47
  Teachers College, xvii, 15–18, 20–21, 23, 26–27, 33, 36–37, 43, 45, 47–48, 51, 87, 89, 139, 176
Committee for the Defense of Democracy Through Education, 95
Committee on Equal Employment for Teachers, 194
Committee on Scope and Sequence, 47, 81
common good, 76–77
Communism, 191–92
Communist Party, Japan, 145, 149
Communist Party USA, 45, 96, 158
Communists and the Schools, The (Iverson), 159
"Community Life in the Harbor," 50, 62–63
competition, xv, 70, 172–73, 181
Conference of Supervisors and Directors of Instruction and Supervisors of Child Welfare and Attendance, 49
Conference on Curriculum and Guidance, 47
Conference on Direction and Improvement of Instruction and Child Welfare Conference, 163
Conference on Education of Children of Seasonal Workers, 56
Conference on Families Who Follow the Crops, 198
Conference on Inter-American Education, 104
Conference on Youth and Unemployment, 46
Conflict in Education, The (Hutchins), 168
Congress of Industrial Organizations (CIO), 171
Conner, Jay, 139, 154–55, 165, 172–74, 184, 187
conservatives, xii-xiv, xvi-xviii, 20, 25, 44–46, 50, 69–70, 94–97, 104, 112, 138–42, 150–51, 156–61, 163, 168, 170–77, 179, 188–90, 193–94, 204
cooperation, 70, 138, 139, 172, 181
Corey, Arthur, 173, 184
Corley, James, 122, 124
Council for Basic Education, 182, 185
Country Life and the Country School (Carney), 27
Counts, George, 37–39, 41, 47, 140, 201–2
Cowgill, Frank, 120–24, 126
Cowgill, Mrs. Frank, 53
Crain, Lucille Cardin, 159
Creative Expressions (Seeds), 62
Cremin, Lawrence, xv, xvi, 20, 163
Cripple Creek strike, 1, 9, 10
Cunningham, Mr., 53

Daily People's World, 167, 171
"Dare Progressive Education Be Progressive?" (Counts), 37
"Dare the School Build a New Social Order" (Counts), 38, 140
Darsie, Marvin, 51–52, 87
Daughters of the American Revolution, 94
Davis, Katherine Bement, 84
Davis, Mrs. Phillip, 53
Davis, Percy, 132
Deane, Martha, 43, 62, 92, 112, 165–66

Debs, Eugene, 13
Delpit, Lisa, 73
D'Emilio, John, 85
democracy
  control of children and, xvii, 65–67, 76–78
  education and, xiv, xvii, 16, 20, 25, 59–61, 76–78, 98, 201–2, 204
  patriotism and, 180–81
  postwar Japan and, 142, 146–47
  WW II and, 80, 98, 99, 109–10
Democracy and Education (Dewey), 16–17, 21
Democratic Party, 44, 79, 96, 179, 188, 191
Depression, xvii, 37–40, 44–47, 57
Desert Treasure (Heffernan), 74, 81
Detroit riots (1943), 110, 114
Deutsch, Helene, 150
DeVore, Emily, 48
Dewey, Alice, 16
Dewey, Evelyn, 31
Dewey, John, xiv–xv, 15–17, 21–27, 34, 39, 41–43, 45, 54, 57, 59–64, 80, 99–100, 126, 147–48, 160, 167, 176, 191, 193, 196, 201–2
Dewey, Thomas, 153
DeWitt, General, 102
Dexter, Walter, 56, 92, 106–8, 129, 138
Dictionary of the New Education (Japan), 148
Dies, Martin, 96
Dilling, Elizabeth, 50, 94
Dilworth, Nelson, 151–52, 172, 186
Dilworth Act (1953), 167–68
Dilworth Committee, xvi, 151–52, 162
  Ninth Report, 166–67
  Sixteenth Report, 179–83, 186, 189
  Twelfth Report, 171–73, 175
Diminished Mind, The (Smith), 182
"Directive on the Teaching of Moral and Spiritual Values," 134
Discipline and Punish (Foucault), 65
disciplining power, xvii, 64–67, 77–78
"Discussion, A Technique of Democratic Education" (Heffernan), 137–39
Division of Elementary Education, 106–8, 113, 137, 140, 154–56
Division of Instruction, 152, 155
Division of Rural and Elementary Education, 38–41
Dixon, Mr., 53
Donovan, Eileen, 144
Donzelot, Jacques, 65
Dorsey, Susan, 22, 49
Douglas, Helen Gahegan, 160
Dower, John, 149
DuBois, Rachel Davis, 54, 116
Dunbar, Paul Lawrence, 75
Dunn, Fanny, 31, 36
Dykstra, Clarence, 119, 125–29, 132–34, 164

Economic Opportunity Act (1962), 198
Edmands, Ruth, 49
Educational Mission to Japan, 142–43
Educational Policies Commission, 158
educational psychology, 15, 27, 144
Educational Psychology (Thorndike), 17
Educational Reviewer, The (newsletter), 159
Educational Wastelands (Beston), 168, 182
Education and Freedom (Rickover), 185
Education and Indoctrination (Allen), 172
Education for All American Children, 158
Education for Cultural Unity, 116, 141
"Education for Inter-American Friendship" (Heffernan), 109
Education of Children Two to Six, The (Heffernan), 148
"Effective Learning in Rural Schools" (Heffernan and Potter), 56
Eisenberg, Francis, 128
Eisenhower, Dwight D., 184
Elementary and Secondary School Act (1965), 201
"Elementary School Faces the Problems of Migration, The" (Heffernan), 106
"Elementary School of 1975, The" (Heffernan), 155–56
"Elementary School Program in California," 180
Elementary Teacher's Guide to Working with Parents (Heffernan and Todd), 201
Eliscu, Mrs., 133

Ellis, Havelock, 84
Engelbright, Mr., 167
EPIC (End Poverty in California), 44
eugenics, 25, 32
"Evaluation—More than Testing" (Heffernan), 185
Everett, Marcia, 31, 36
"Experiment with the Project Curriculum" (Collings), 31

Factories in the Fields (McWilliams), 79
"FACTS in Education," 172
Faderman, Lillian, 84–86
Fair Employment Practices Commission, 100
Fair Housing Act, 195
Family School Alliance, 121, 124, 126–28, 133–36, 141, 165, 175–76
Farm Security Administration, 114
Farnham, Marynia, 150
fascism, 78–80, 91, 97, 100
Federal Bureau of Investigation (FBI), 85, 102, 129, 165, 167, 171
Federal Works Agency, 106, 108
feminism, xii-xiv, xvii, 8, 203
Fifth Amendment, 167
Flesch, Rudolph, 173–74, 180, 187
Fogelson, Robert, 10
Forbes, 95
Force, James, 55
Forces Affecting American Education, 159
Fort, Mrs. William A., 124
Fostering Mental Health in Our Schools, 163
Foucault, Michel, 65–66, 70, 77–78, 181
Foundations of Method (Kilpatrick), 42, 60
Four Years in a Country School (Everett), 31
"Framework for Public Education in California," 180–81, 183
Frankfurter, Felix, 160
Franklin, John Hope, 195
Franzen, Tricia, 82, 85–86
Freedman, Estelle, 82
Freeman, Frank, 123
Fresno Bee, 173
Fresno State Teachers College, 29

Freud, Sigmund, 84
Friends of the American Way, 141
Fundamental Law of Education (Japan, 1947), 145
fundamentals (Three R's), 63–64, 69–70, 104, 107, 126, 138, 168, 170, 173–74, 183–84, 191, 204
"Fun Gardening Indoors" (Heffernan), 93

Galbraith, John Kenneth, 198
gender issues, xii-xiv, xvii, 6–7, 11–14, 26–29, 34, 47–49, 71–72, 78, 87–88, 192, 203
Generation of Vipers (Wylie), 150
Gerstle, Gary, 68, 99
Gessell, Arnold, 128
Giddings, Francis, 34
"gifted" programs, 185–86
Golden Gate International Exposition, 79
Goodlad, John, 177
Goodykroonz, Bess, 56
Goslin, Willard, 161–62, 172
Grade Teacher, 196–97
Graham, Malbone, 130
Grapes of Wrath (film), 37
Grapes of Wrath (Steinbeck), 79
"Growth Pattern, The," 60
Guernsey, George, 171
Guidance and Evaluation of Learning in the Elementary Schools, The (Heffernan), 148
guidance counselors, 69
"Guide to Recording Attitude Development" (Seeds), 66
"Guiding Philosophy of the Unitary Type of Curriculum Organization, The" (Heffernan), 61
Gullett, Gayle, 15

Haley, Margaret, 5
Hall, G. Stanley, xv, 22
Hall, Jacqueline, xii
Handbook on the Administration and Supervision of Elementary Schools (Heffernan), 147–48
Hanna, Paul, 47–49, 93, 111
Harding, Warren, 19
Harlem riots (1943), 110, 114
Harper, Wilhemina, 93, 162

278 ❖ INDEX

Harrington, Michael, 198
Harris, Joel Chandler, 75
Hartman, Beulah, 30–31
Harvard Educational Review, 163
Harvard University, 165
Hawagawa, Miss, 15
Head Start, 198, 201
"Health Problems in Rural Schools" (Heffernan), 45–46
Hearst newspapers, 45, 95, 104, 110–12, 126, 166, 173
Hedrick, Provost, 102
Heffernan, Arthur (brother), 2
Heffernan, Edward (brother), 2, 7
Heffernan, Helen
  achievements of, xi, 36, 190–91, 195–96, 203–4
  activity curriculum and, 61
  attacks on, xviii, xvi, 55–56, 94–97, 99, 107–8, 137–42, 157, 161–65, 170–75, 180–84, 187, 189–98
  background and education of, xiii–xiv, xvii–xviii, 1–8, 17–18, 26–27, 48, 55
  columns by, 31–32, 41, 196–97
  death of, 203
  democracy and education and, xvi, 21, 64–78, 80
  Depression and, 37
  Dewey and, 59–61
  as Division for Elementary Education, assistant chief, 152–56
  as Division of Rural and Elementary Education, chief, 39–41
  as elementary education commissioner, 30–32, 38–39
  gender issues and, 47–49, 71
  health problems and, 164–65, 190–91
  honors, 165, 190, 199, 202–3
  Inter-American Demonstration Centers and, 103–5, 109
  Japan and, 140–50, 153–54
  Japanese internment and, 101, 111–13
  Mexico and, 39
  migrant workers and, 32, 56–57
  Nance and, xiv, 141–42, 153–54
  NDEA and, 184–85
  NEA and, 33, 95
  networks created by, 30–32, 49
  New Deal and, 45–47
  personal relationships of, xiv, 40–41
  race and, xviii, 32, 57, 74, 75, 99, 108–9, 112–18, 137, 141, 155, 169–70, 180, 186–88
  retirement of, xviii, 198–99, 201–2
  rural schools and, 26–30, 40
  same-sex persecutions and, 165–66, 171
  Seeds relationship and, xi, 33–36, 43–44, 49–50, 81–87, 92–94, 153–54, 164, 177
  Seeds UES conflicts and, 87–92, 119–21, 125–28, 133–36
  social studies and, 129–30, 137–42
  summer conferences and, 30, 92
  Teachers Guides and, 35–36, 54–55, 174–75
  WW II and, 80–81, 97–99, 103–9
Heffernan, James (brother), 2
Heffernan, Margaret (mother), 1, 2
Heffernan, Margaret (sister), 2, 3
Heffernan, Michael (father), 1
Heinemann, Mrs. Arthur, 50–51
Helen Heffernan Honor Grove, 199
"Heritage of Freedom, A" (Heffernan), 109
Hill, Gladwin, 170
Hill, Lillian, 32, 40, 81
Hill, Mrs. Gladwin, 170
Hill, Patty, 49
Hiss, Alger, 157
Hitler, Adolf, 99–100, 123
Hockett, John, 56, 89–90, 102, 120–22, 127
Hockett, Ruth, 89
Hollywood Ten, 150
Hollywood Writers' Mobilization, 128, 133
Holmes, Lulu, 144
homework, 196–97
homophobia, 165, 203
Hook, Sidney, 159
Horn, Ernest, 89
House Un-American Activities Committee (HUAC), 96, 112, 150, 152, 159, 167, 186–87
"How Can We Make a Rural School Democratic?" (Heffernan), 87

How to Develop a Unit of Work, 146
"How to Teach the California Child" (Smith), 182–84, 186, 189
Hubbard, Frank, 173–74
Hughes, Langston, 75
Hughes, Marie, 103
Hurlburd, David, 162
Hutchens, Robert, 168
Huxley, Aldous, 128

immigrants, 12–14, 28, 35
"Implementation of the Frameworks of the Social Studies" (Heffernan), 137, 139–40
individualism, xv, xvi, 10, 20, 74, 76–77, 138, 172
Inequalities of Educational Opportunity Conference, 169
Institute for Education Leadership in Occupied Japan, 147
integrated curriculum, 55, 64
intelligence testing, 21, 23, 32, 68, 70
Inter-American Demonstration Project, 103–5, 109
"Intercultural Education in the Elementary School" (Seeds and Heffernan), 116–17, 130, 141
intercultural movement, 99, 109
Internal Security Act (1950), 158
"Interpretation of the Integrated Program, An" (Seeds), 41, 50
"Interpreting the School Program to the Public" (Heffernan), 38–39
Isaka, Mr., 147
Itkins Florence, 177
Iverson, Robert, 159

Japan, xviii, 100, 109, 141–50, 153–54, 201
Japanese Americans, 15, 32, 53, 128
  internment of, xviii, 15, 74, 100–3, 109–14, 116, 118, 141
Japanese Educational Workers Union, 145
Japanese Education Reform Council, 143
Japanese Equal Rights Amendment, 144
Japan Teachers' Union, 145
Jenkins, Carleton, 165

Johnson, Gardiner, 183–84
Johnson, Hiram, 19, 100
Johnson, Lyndon B., 198, 201
Jordan, Winthrop, 194
Juneman, Helen, 170

"Karl Marx and the American Teacher" (Brameld), 54
Kefauver, Grayson, 47
"Keeping Informed" (Lee and Lee), 45
Kennan, George, 149
Kennedy, John F., 179, 190, 198
Kennedy, Liz, 85
Kersey, Vierling, 12, 38–39, 46–47, 50, 55–56, 88, 90–91, 94–95, 120, 122–26, 153
Kilpatrick, William Heard, xv, xvii, 15–17, 20–21, 23, 26, 33, 42, 54–55, 57, 59–61, 183
kindergarten movement, 49
Kiskadden, Peggy, 128, 176
Klemperer, Otto, 129
Knowland, Wiliam, 179
Knox, Walter, 191
Kobayashi, Victor, 147
Korean War, 157, 189, 198
Krafft-Ebing, Richard von, 84
Kuhn, Irene Corball, 159
Ku Klux Klan, 25
Kumai, Kaoru, 101
Kunugi, Yoshiko, 144
Kyoiku Shinri (Educational Psychology), 144

labor movement, xvii, 3, 14, 17, 22, 43–45, 71–73, 171
Lafayette, Mattie, 14
Lambert, Philip, 176
Lane, Mary, 199
Lang, Mamie, 29
Lange, Dorothea, 37
Lanham Act, 105–6, 108
Lantz, Harry, 107–8
League of Women Voters, 50, 124
Lee, Dorris May, 45
Lee, Edwin, 87–92, 102–3, 120–26, 134–35, 165, 176
Lee, Murray, 45
Lenin, V. I., 130, 131

"Let's Keep Our Perspective" (Heffernan), 193
Let's Talk Sense about Our Schools (Woodring), 168
"Letter from Japan" (Heffernan), 142, 144, 149
Levering, Harold, 162
Levering Act (1950), 161–62
Levine, Lawrence, 194
liberals, 20, 25, 44, 68, 99–100, 110, 126, 171
life adjustment, xv, 163–64, 168, 183, 185
Lima, Agnes de, 21
Lippman, Walter, 20–21
literacy classes, 13–15
Little Rock High School, 179
Locke, Alaine, 116, 167
Lonsdale, Bernard, 106, 140
Loomis, Alfred, 149
Los Angeles Board of Education, 22, 24, 89–90, 123–28, 133–34, 153, 166
Los Angeles City Council, 53
Los Angeles City Schools, UES conflict and, 55, 90–91, 122, 136
Los Angeles Council for Civil Unity, 110
Los Angeles County Advisory Council, 50
Los Angeles County Committee for Interracial Progress, 110
Los Angeles County Committee on Americanism, 51
Los Angeles Evening Herald, 110
Los Angeles Examiner, 104, 110, 120, 124
Los Angeles Herald-Express, 166, 190
Los Angeles Normal School (*later* University of California Southern Branch, Training School), 11–12, 18, 22
Los Angeles Times, 101–2, 120, 124, 134, 138, 173, 196, 197
Lossing, Laverna, 50
loyalty oaths, 150, 158, 160–62, 166–68
Luckel Act (1953), 167–68
Lundberg, Ferdinand, 150
Lynd, Albert, 168

MacArthur, Douglas, xviii, 140, 142–43, 145, 149, 201
Major Units in the Social Studies (Seeds, Waddell, and White), 42–43, 63
male privilege, 8, 12, 18, 48–49, 71, 85, 90–91, 120–21, 203
"Man and His Changing Society" (Rugg), 95
Man Improves His World: The Water Story (Heffernan and Shaftel), 195
Mann, Thomas, 129
Manzanar camp, 111–13
Martin, Anne, 6
"Master Teachers and Modern Education" (Hanna), 48
McCarthy, Joseph, 142, 157–58
McClure, Marcus, 120–24, 126, 135
McClymer, John, 13
McDonald, Milo, 159
McGirr, Lisa, 151
McGuffey *Readers*, 189
McIntyre, Myrtle, 12
McWilliams, Carey, 37, 44–45, 79, 109–10, 112–13, 118, 127
Meek, Lois, 54
Mendez v. Westminster, 103, 151, 194
mental health, 68–70, 163–64, 181
Merriam, Frank, 44
"Methods in the Social Studies" (Heffernan), 137–39
Mexican Americans, 12, 14, 19, 25, 32, 35, 53, 103, 109–10, 114–15, 117, 151, 169, 194
Miel, Alice, 147
migrant farm workers, 32, 56–57, 79, 169, 190
Mill, C. Wright, xi
Mitchell, Lucy Sprague, 8
Mitchell, Walter K., 102
Modern Woman (Lundberg and Farnham), 150
Mooney, Tom, 79
Moore, Ernest, 22, 42, 45, 51
Moral Rearmament, 123
Morrisett Committee, 123, 126–27
Muncy, Robyn, xiii
"My Pedagogic Creed" (Dewey), 43, 59, 63
Myrdal, Gunner, 113

Nance, Afton, xiv, 116, 141–43, 145–46, 148, 153–55, 164–65, 171–72, 174–75, 177, 182, 190, 201
Nation, 20, 21, 25, 163
National Association of Manufacturers, 95, 164
National Association of Secondary School Principals, 169
National Citizens Commission for the Public Schools, 158, 168
National College of Education, 190, 198–99
National Commission for the Defense of Democracy Through Education, 158–59
National Congress of Parents and Teachers Conference, 33
National Council of Education, 37–38
National Defense Education Act (1958), 184–86
National Education Association (NEA), 30, 33, 37, 54, 95, 157–59, 173
    Defense Committee, 162
    Journal, 185
National Education Policies Commission, 138
National Student League, 45
"Nation at Risk, A," 204
Native Americans, 74, 100, 109
Nazis, xviii, 76, 84, 99–100, 109, 163
Nazi-Soviet Pact, 79, 96
"Negro in American History Textbooks, The" (Stamp), 194
Neideffer, R. T., 56
New Deal, 37, 45–47, 72, 79, 142, 198
new education, 20–21, 31, 36, 39, 60–61
"New Educational Program, The" (Edmands), 49
New Education Movement (Japan), 147
"New Education Ten Years After" (symposium), 42, 61
New Leaven, The (Cobb), 21, 34
"New Movement in Education, A" (Cobb), 23
New Republic, 20, 21, 25, 42, 45, 61
New Schools for Old (Dewey), 31
New York Society for Ethical Culture, 100

"Next Steps in the Preparation of Teachers" (Seeds), 41
Nixon, Richard, 150, 160, 179, 191, 192
normal schools, 4–5, 11–12, 18
Nugent, Donald, 149

"Objective Measurement of Educational Progress" (Heffernan), 27
observation, xvii, 77, 181
Olson, Culbert, 79, 100
"100 Things You Should Know About Communism and Education" (HUAC), 159
"Organization of the Elementary School, The" (Heffernan), 164
Orr, Mark, 144
Other America, The (Harrington), 198
Our Enemy the Child (de Lima), 21

Pasadena school crisis, 161–62, 172
Passin, Herbert, 149
"Passing of a Patriot, The" (Rafferty), 189–90, 196
pastoral relations, 65–66, 77
patriotism, 180–81, 190
Peixotto, Jessica, 8
People's Education Center, 129, 132
People's World, 130, 132–33
Phi Delta Kappan, 188–89
"Philistines, The" (Rafferty), 189
phonics, 173, 187, 196–97
"Plan for the Care of Children of Working Mothers," 106
"Playing Ukrainian Farmer" (Seeds), 130–31
"Point of View" (Heffernan and Potter), 74
Popkewitz, Tom, 65, 66
Potter, Gladys, 39, 54–56, 66, 74, 81, 83
poverty, 34–35, 202, 204
pragmatism, 160
Prejudice (McWilliams), 113
Preston, Morrie, 3
Pridonoff, Eric, 172–73
Pro-America, 123
"Problem of Social Education, The" (Hanna), 48

progressive education
    attacks on (*See specific individuals and groups*)
    defined, xv, 20–21
    Dewey and democracy and, 59–61 (*See also* democracy)
    Foucauldian critique of, 77–78
    Japan and, 143, 145–47
    spread of, 53–57
    See also child-centered education; democracy; new education; *and specific individuals and institutions*
Progressive Education, 20, 62, 64, 75, 130, 167, 176
"Progressive Education" (Rogers), 159
"Progressive Education and the Science of Education" (Dewey), 42, 60
Progressive Education Association (PEA), xv, 20, 24, 30, 37–38, 53–54, 60, 104
"Progressive Education Increases Delinquency" (Zoll), 162
"'Progressive' Education is Subverting America" (Zoll), 159–60
"'Progressive' Poison in Public Education" (McDonald), 159
project method, 26, 36
"Project Method, The" (Kilpatrick), 17, 26
Proposition 13, 203
Proposition One, 40
psychology, 68, 70, 84, 94. *See also* mental health
Psychology of Women (Deutsch), 150
"purposeful act," 17, 60

Quackery in the Public Schools (Lynd), 168

race and racism, xii, xvii-xviii, 13–15, 17, 34, 35, 70–76, 78, 155, 161, 163, 168–70, 180, 186–88, 193–95, 204
    Heffernan and, xviii, 32, 57, 74, 75, 99, 108–9, 112–18, 137, 141, 155, 169–70, 180, 186–88
    Seeds and, xviii, 74–76, 99, 114–18
    WW II and, 99–101, 108–15
Rafferty, Max, xviii, 188–89, 191–98, 202

Randolph, a. Philip, 100
rationality, 68, 77
Read, Helen, 43
Readers' Digest, 190
record keeping, xvii, 27, 67, 77, 181
Redefer, Frederick, 158
Red Network, The (Dilling), 50, 94
report cards, 69–70, 172–73, 175, 181, 183, 197
Republican Party, 44, 48, 96, 160–61, 179, 191
"Return of the Nisei, The" (Nance), 116, 141
rhythmic expression, 42, 62, 72
"Rhythmic Expression" (Seeds), 62, 75
Rice, Tom, 50
Rich, Adrienne, 203
Richards, Irmagarde, 81
Richardson, Ralph, 191–92
Richmond, Lee, 28–29
Rickover, Hyman, 185–86
Riles, Wilson, 186, 190, 194–95, 202
Ringer, Miss, 53
Roberts, Holland, 116, 129–30, 167
Robeson, Paul, 129
Rogers, Frederick Rand, 159–60, 179
"Role of Education in the Defense of Democratic Principles, The" (Sexson), 94
Roosevelt, Franklin D., 100–101, 113, 123
Rose, Nikolas, 65
Rosenberg Foundation, 161
Rousseau, Jean-Jacques, 76
Rudd, Augustin, 179
Rugg, Harold, 21, 33–34, 37, 54, 95, 107, 167
rural schools, 28, 30, 35, 46, 68, 27
Russell, Bertrand, 128

Sacramento Bee, 173, 198
Salisbury, Alice, 81
Salisbury, Ethel, 34, 120
Salisger, Nelda, 126
same-sex relationships, xiv, 82, 84–85, 165–66, 171, 203
Sanchez, George, 162, 169
San Diego Union, 173
San Franciscans for Academic Freedom and Education (SAFE), 187

San Francisco Chronicle, 187
San Francisco Examiner, 173
Santa Monica Evening Outlook, 135
Sargent, Aara, 139–40
Schoenberg, Arnold, 127
Scholastic, 95
"School and its Task, The" (Seeds), 41
School and Society (Dewey), 16, 34
School and Society (journal), 158
school desegregation, 179, 189, 193–95
School Development Council (Pasadena), 161–62
School Education Law (Japan, 1947), 145
scientific progressivism, 23
Seeds, Corinne, 144, 187
  achievements of, xi, 36, 119, 203–4
  attacks on UES and, xviii, 49–53, 87–92, 96–97, 99, 119–36, 166–67, 170–71
  as Avenue 21 principal, 12–15
  background and education of, xiii-xiv, xvii, 1–2, 4, 9–13, 17–18, 22
  begins career at UCLA Training School (UES), 22–26
  Columbia Teachers College and, 15–17, 23
  death of, 201
  death of mother, 104–5
  democracy and education and, xv, 21, 59–61, 64–68, 70–78, 80
  Depression and, 37
  gender issues and, 71
  Heffernan relationship and, xii, xiv, 33–36, 49–50, 81–87, 92–94, 141–42, 153–54, 164, 177
  illness and death of, 164, 201
  inter-American project and, 104
  Japanese internment and, 101–3, 112
  psychology and, 68
  race and, xviii, 74–76, 99, 114–18
  retirement of, 176–77, 201
  retreat of, in 1950s, 157, 164
  same-sex persecutions and, 165–66
  social studies and, 129–32, 138
  summer sessions and, 42, 67, 72, 92, 176
  Teachers Guides and, 35–36, 175
  as UCLA assistant professor, 26
  as UCLA full professor, 176
  UES and UCLA in later years, 175–76
  UES methods and, 23–26, 33, 36, 41–44, 56, 61–64
  UES move to Westwood and, 24–25
  WW II and, 80–81, 97, 99, 106–7
Seeds, Mary (mother), 1, 9, 10
Seeds, Sherman (father), 1, 9, 10, 87, 176
"Seeds boxes," 62–63
segregation, 32, 103, 109, 112–14, 117–18, 151, 155, 161, 163, 169–70, 194–95
  See also school desegregation
Senate Daily Journal, 107
sensory experience, 61–62
Sequences of Activities, University Elementary School, 62–63, 75
Service Bureau for Intercultural Education, 99
sex education, 128
"Sex Perverts in Government," 165
Sexson, John, 94, 123
Shackled Youth (Yeoman), 21
Shaftel, George, 195
Sherer, Lorraine, 80
Shumaker, Ann, 21, 34
Sicher, Dr. Lydia, 84, 94, 114
Silva, John, 3
Simpson, Roy, 138–39, 151–52, 154–55, 174, 182–85, 187, 190–91, 194
Sinclair, Upton, 44
Single Women, The (Beam), 84
Sleepy Lagoon murder case, 110
Smith, Joseph, 3
Smith, Lillian, 114
Smith, Mortimer, 182–86, 189
Smith Act (1940), 96, 167
Smitter, Faith, 184
social adjustment, 70–76
social class, xiii, 17, 34–35, 71–73, 78
Social Education Conference (Stanford), 48
social engineering, 138
Social Frontier, 45, 54
socialism, 3, 13, 44, 79, 145

social reconstructionists, xv, xvii, 37, 41, 45, 47, 48
social studies, 94–95, 137–42, 174, 191–92, 196
"Some Philosophical Considerations" (Seeds and Sherer), 80
Somervell, General, 97
Sons of the American Revolution, xvi, 39, 139–42, 151, 179
Southwest Council of the Education of Spanish Speaking People, 162
Soviet Union, 80, 129–32, 138, 157–58, 184, 185
Spanish Civil War, 79
Spanish-speaking children, 162, 169, 190. *See also* Mexican Americans
Sparks, John, 3
Spillers, Hortense, 14
Sproul, Robert, 45, 52–53, 88–92, 102–3, 120–23, 126–27, 133–35, 165, 176
Sputnik, 184, 185
Stamp, Kenneth, 194
standardized tests, 68, 77, 126–27
Stanford Achievement Test, 41
Stanford-Binet intelligence test, 23
Stanford University, 30, 47–48, 55, 93
Starr, Kevin, 44
"Statement of the Philosophy and the Purposes of the Elementary School, A" (Heffernan), 41
Steinbeck, John, 37, 79
Step Beyond, The (Burton and Heffernan), 195
Stern, Alexandra, 32
Strange Fruit (Smith), 114
Stravinsky, Igor, 128
Strayer, George, 48
"Struggle for Our Children's Minds, The" (Whitman), 170
Studebaker, John, 47
Suffer, Little Children (Rafferty), 188, 192
"Suggested Course of Study in Reading and Literature for Elementary Schools," 49
Summer Conference on Supervision, 92–93
Superintendents and Rural Supervisors, Annual Convention, 39

"Supervision Appropriate for Progressive Schools" (Heffernan), 72–73
Supreme Command of the Allied Powers (SCAP), 142, 144–47, 149
surveillance, 70, 77–78
Swan, John Harold, 107–8, 137
Swope, Caroline, 30

Takemae, Eiji, 149
taxes, 40, 161–62
Taylor, Paul, 116, 169
Teacher and the New Elementary School, The (Isaka), 147
teachers, attacks on, 159, 161–63, 168, 173–74, 183, 186–87
Teachers Guides to Education in Early and Later Childhood, 171–72, 174–75, 180–82
Teachers' Guide to Child Development for Intermediate Grades, The, 34–35, 54, 66, 69, 74, 180
teachers unions, 145, 183
Tenney, Jack, 96, 151, 161
Tenney Committee, xvi, 96, 112, 128, 131–33, 136, 152, 157, 161, 167
testing, xvii, 16, 20, 23, 27, 31, 68, 174, 182–83, 185
textbooks, 94–95, 107, 140–41, 151–52, 159, 194, 195
This Happened in Pasadena (Hurlburd), 162
Thomas, Frank, 123
Thorndike, Edward, xv, 15–16, 23, 26–27
Time, 119, 136, 162
Todd, Vivian Edmiston, 195, 201
"Too Much Freedom in the New Schools?" (Dewey), 60–61
traditionalists, xiii, xvi, 21, 25, 168, 193. *See also* fundamentals
Transformation of the School, The (Cremin), xv, xvi, 20, 163
Trapnell, Jean, 134–35
"Treason in the Texbooks," 95
Tremonten, Utah, 7
Trott, Fred, 106
Truman, Harry S., 150, 153, 158
Trumbo, Dalton, 110
Turner, Grade, 22

Twelve Million Black Voices, 114
Tyack, David, 27

UCLA Americans, 188
Ukrainian Farmers curriculum, 130–33
UNESCO, 143, 153, 166, 188
United Nations, 116, 137–38, 143, 153
U.S. Congress, 96, 158, 160. *See also* House Un-American Activities Committee (HUAC)
U.S. Constitution, 116
U.S. Department of Education, 157
U.S. Office of Education, 46, 54, 104, 155, 163
U.S. Senate, 160, 165
U.S. State Department, 157–58, 188
U.S. Supreme Court, 3, 160, 169
units-of-work method, 36, 42, 51, 55, 61–64, 74, 139
University Elementary School (UES), 23, 33–34, 36, 41–43, 49–53, 55, 59, 61–64, 80–81, 97, 157, 164
   attacks on, 51–53, 56, 87–91, 118–36, 141, 170
   class, gender, and race and, 71–76
   Heffernan and, 141
   Japanese internment and, 101, 103
   moves to Westwood, 24–26
   Seeds retires, 176–77, 201
   standardized tests and, 68
   summer school and conferences, 42, 63, 92, 134, 135
   UCLA buildings and, 164–65, 175–76
   Warner Avenue lease ended, 123–28, 133–36
University of California
   Board of Regents, 22, 91, 102, 126–28, 162, 175
   loyalty oaths, 161, 162, 167
   Southern Branch, Training School (*later* University Elementary School), 22–26
University of California, Berkeley, 7–8, 18, 129
   Free Speech movement, xviii, 187, 197–98
   School of Education, 26, 30
   summer school, 56, 89

University of California, Los Angeles (UCLA), 22, 24, 29, 45, 50, 135, 165–66
   School of Education, 51–53, 62, 71, 87–91, 103, 119–22, 127, 129, 135–36, 157, 175–76
   summer courses and conferences at, 30, 33–34, 42, 52, 63, 92, 125–26, 134
   Teachers College, 52, 56, 68, 87
University of Chicago, 22
   Laboratory School, 16, 62
University of Nevada, 5–6, 11, 18
U.S. News and World Report, 184

Valeska, (photographer), 131
Velde, Congressman, 167
Veverka, Madeleine, 90–91
Virginia curriculum, 148
VISTA, 198
vocational education, 32, 46
Voorhis, Jerry, 150
Voting Rights Act (1965), xviii

Waddell, Charles, 22–24, 29, 36, 42–43, 51–53, 63, 68, 87, 91
Walkerdine, Valerie, 65–66
Wallace, Henry, 153
Walter, Congressman, 187
Ward, Ethel, 29
War Relocation Authority (WRA), 111
Warren, Earl, 79, 100, 133, 138, 150–51, 168
Weekly News Review, 95
Welles, Orson, 110
Well of Loneliness, The (Hall), 84
Western Journal of Education, 31–32, 36, 40–41, 47–48, 109, 113
Westwood Hills Press, 132, 135–36
"What Practices are Defensible in Time of Crisis" (Heffernan), 107, 111–12
"What Society Has a Right to Expect of the Modern School" (Heffernan), 81
Wheeler, Benjamin, 8
White, Helen, 43
White, Natalie, 41–43, 50, 92
White House Conferences, 164, 169
Whitman, Howard, 170

Why Johnny Can't Read (Flesch), 173–74, 180, 187
"Why You Buy Books that Sell Communism" (Kuhn), 159
Willkie, Wendell, 113
"Woman's Education as a Man Sees It" (Lee), 88
woman suffrage, xiii, xvii, 1–2, 5–6, 8, 14, 17
women
 roles of, xiii, xvii, 1–2, 4–5, 8, 11, 13–14, 17, 29, 90–91, 105–7, 144, 150, 176–77
 single, in teaching, xiv, 43, 84–86
 See also gender issues
Women's Army Corps (WACs), 144
Women's Associated Student Government, 8
Woodring, Paul, 168
"World Community, A" (Heffernan speech), 153
World War II, xviii, 79–80, 97–100, 105–6, 109, 113–15, 119, 125
Wulfin, Gretchen, 92–94, 162
Wylie, Philip, 150

Years Before School, The (Heffernan and Todd), 195, 201
Yeoman, Edward, 21
Yorty, Sam, 96
Young, Clement, 19
Young, Ella Flagg, 5, 49
"Young Adolescent, The" (Heffernan), 186
"Your Child is Their Target" (Kuhn), 159

Zilversmit, Arthur, xv
Zirbes, Laura, 54
Zoll, Allen, 159–60, 162–63, 168, 179
Zoot Suit Riots, xviii, 110, 114, 128

GPSR Compliance
The European Union's (EU) General Product Safety Regulation (GPSR) is a set of rules that requires consumer products to be safe and our obligations to ensure this.

If you have any concerns about our products, you can contact us on

ProductSafety@springernature.com

In case Publisher is established outside the EU, the EU authorized representative is:

Springer Nature Customer Service Center GmbH
Europaplatz 3
69115 Heidelberg, Germany

www.ingramcontent.com/pod-product-compliance
Lightning Source LLC
LaVergne TN
LVHW021947060526
838200LV00043B/1944